Empire Families

Empire Families

Britons and Late
Imperial India

ELIZABETH BUETTNER

OXFORD
UNIVERSITY PRESS

OXFORD
UNIVERSITY PRESS

Great Clarendon Street, Oxford OX2 6DP

Oxford University Press is a department of the University of Oxford.
It furthers the University's objective of excellence in research, scholarship,
and education by publishing worldwide in

Oxford New York

Auckland Bangkok Buenos Aires Cape Town Chennai
Dar es Salaam Delhi Hong Kong Istanbul Karachi Kolkata
Kuala Lumpur Madrid Melbourne Mexico City Mumbai Nairobi
São Paulo Shanghai Taipei Tokyo Toronto

Oxford is a registered trade mark of Oxford University Press
in the UK and in certain other countries

Published in the United States
by Oxford University Press Inc., New York

British Library Cataloguing in Publication Data
Data available

Library of Congress Cataloging in Publication Data
Data available

ISBN 0-19-924907-5

1 3 5 7 9 10 8 6 4 2

Typeset by SNP Best-set Typesetter Ltd., Hong Kong
Printed in Great Britain
on acid-free paper by
Biddles Ltd,
King's Lynn, Norfolk

For Bernhard

and

in memory of my grandmothers,
Helen Taylor (1912–2002) and
Ethel Buettner (1896–1994)

ACKNOWLEDGEMENTS

This study began as a doctoral dissertation at the University of Michigan, Ann Arbor, and could never have been completed without the help of countless individuals and institutions. My dissertation supervisor, Sonya Rose, made it possible in every sense of the word, providing intellectual guidance, moral support, and friendship every step of the way. No one could ask for a better mentor. Nick Dirks, Martha Vicinus, and Simon Gikandi contributed invaluable input at many stages and, as members of my dissertation committee, went far beyond the call of duty. During my first years at Michigan Geoff Eley and Dror Wahrman helped me to develop my understandings of the issues I deal with here, while the scholarship of Carolyn Steedman and Ann Stoler sparked my initial interest in this topic. I am indebted to them all for their inspiration.

Since coming to Britain I have benefited immeasurably from the academic encouragement and friendship of Peter Marshall, who gives a whole new meaning to the concept of generosity. David Cannadine's support and advice have been greatly appreciated, as have suggestions over the years from Angela Woollacott, Antoinette Burton, Jim Epstein, Dennis Dworkin, Martin Daunton, Judith Brown, and Louise Jackson. Erika Rappaport and Dane Kennedy both painstakingly read my entire manuscript and provided brilliant feedback. Thank you.

The many archivists who guided me through their collections are too numerous to mention all by name, but include Tim Thomas at the Oriental and India Office Collections of the British Library, Kevin Greenbank of the Cambridge South Asian Archive, and Kevin Haleywell of the National Library of Scotland. My analysis of Bedford's British-Indian community relies in part upon documents previously gathered and catalogued by Patricia Bell, the retired County Archivist of Bedfordshire. Her guidance, hospitality, and camaraderie made my time in Bedford a pleasure. Faculty members of the schools in Britain and India I visited while compiling case studies for Chapters 2 and 4 spent a great deal of time locating institutional records on my behalf and making me feel a welcome guest even during their busiest times of year. I wish to express my gratitude to the principals and staff of the following Indian schools: St George's College, Mussoorie; Wynberg Allen School, Mussoorie; the Bishop Cotton School, Shimla; and Mount Hermon School, Darjeeling. In Britain, thanks go to the principals, teachers, and librarians who assisted me at

Haileybury, Bedford School, Bedford High School, Cheltenham College, Cheltenham Ladies' College, Walthamstow Hall, and Eltham College. A number of men and women shared their memories of growing up in British India with me in interviews conducted in 1994 and 1995. They gave me an endless range of new perspectives on my project, and our discussions count among my most enriching research experiences. Many other individuals provided detailed responses to my questionnaire. I was able to contact many through the generous assistance of Theon Wilkinson and the British Association for Cemeteries in South Asia.

Constructive scholarly advice coupled with comic relief at the workplace has kindly been provided by many of my colleagues past and present: Tony Stockwell, Paul Ward, Martin Francis, and Ruth Geuter at Royal Holloway, University of London; Chris Wickham, Matthew Hilton, Corey Ross, Francesca Carnevali, and Graeme Murdock at the University of Birmingham; and Mark Ormrod, Doug Hamilton, Joanna de Groot, John Howard, Trev Broughton, Mark Jenner, Alan Forrest, Shane O'Rourke, Richard Bessel, Jim Walvin, and Stuart and Debbie Carroll at the University of York. Sincerest thanks go to Mary Garrison, Simon Ditchfield, and Matt Roberts for carefully reading drafts of selected chapters. At Oxford University Press, meanwhile, Ruth Parr tirelessly has seen this book through to publication from the earliest stages. I thank her for her patience as much as for her enthusiasm.

Since I entered graduate school friends and family have pulled me through good times and not-so-good times alike. Amy Schlenker, Jon Williams, Konstanze Scharring, Miriam Garber, Mary Coomes, Alex Protopapas, Eric Rath, Kelly Pemberton, Ray Honeycutt, Tim Wilson, Andrew Chang, and Noelle Plack—you're the best. Thanks to my dad, Don Buettner, who always heard more than he bargained for after asking 'So how's the book going?' but put on a good show of listening patiently none the less. I have gained as many insights on the theme of family culture from relatives as from books, especially from Joan and Russ Ward, Bill Taylor, and Tom and Gail Taylor. This book is dedicated to the memory of my grandmothers, Helen Taylor and Ethel Buettner, who never enjoyed the academic opportunities I've had. My husband, Bernhard Rieger, shares the honor. His love, support, good advice, impishness, and sense of fun have never failed to keep me going.

Financial assistance to complete my research and writing has come from many sources. At the University of Michigan these include the Department of History, the Horace H. Rackham School of Graduate Studies, the International Institute, and the Center of South and Southeast Asian Studies. Without support from a Mellon Dissertation Fellowship and Foreign

Language Area Studies Fellowships for Hindi-Urdu, I could not have completed my language studies nor my research in Britain and India. I also wish to thank the Institute of Historical Research in London for awarding me the 1996–7 Royal Historical Society Centenary Research Fellowship. The final stages of revising this manuscript were funded by the Arts and Humanities Research Board's Research Leave Scheme (project no. 042R00433).

PERMISSIONS

Portions of this book have appeared in earlier versions. I would like to thank Manchester University Press for permission to reproduce, in a revised form, parts of my essay 'Parent-Child Separations and Colonial Careers: The Talbot Family Correspondence in the 1880s and 1890s', in *Childhood in Question: Children, Parents, and the State*, ed. by Anthony Fletcher and Stephen Hussey (Manchester University Press, 1999), 115–32. I thank *Women's History Review* for permission to draw upon my article 'Problematic Spaces, Problematic Races: Defining "Europeans" in Late Colonial India', *Women's History Review* 9/2, Special Issue: 'Borders and Frontiers in Women's History' (2000), 277–97. Berg Publishers has allowed me to revise my essay 'From Somebodies to Nobodies: Britons Coming Home from India', in *Meanings of Modernity: Britain from the Late-Victorian Era to the Second World War*, ed. by Martin Daunton and Bernhard Rieger (Berg, 2001), 221–40.

In the course of my research I consulted many collections of family papers throughout Britain. I am grateful to Mr J. P. C. Bannerman for permission to cite from Helen and William Bannerman's letters housed at the National Library of Scotland. Excerpts from the Martin family papers are reproduced here by permission of Perth and Kinross Council Archive. The Bedfordshire and Luton Archives and Records Service has kindly allowed me to draw upon a number of their documents, including the letters of Evelyn Chaldecott. Quotes from Rudyard Kipling's work appear with permission of A. P. Watt Ltd on behalf of the National Trust for Places of Historical Interest or Natural Beauty. Special thanks to the Centre of South Asian Studies at the University of Cambridge (Cambridge South Asian Archive) for permission to use photographs from their collections as well as to quote from a wide range of written material. Other photographs appear here by permission of the British Library's Oriental and India Office Collections, as do quotes from many of their European Manuscript collections. Brief passages from William Beveridge's papers are cited with permission by the British Library of Political and Economic Science, London School of Economics.

CONTENTS

LIST OF ILLUSTRATIONS

(between pp. 178–179)

1 Home leave, March 1912, on 'S. S. Macedonia'. Bourne Collection, Cambridge South Asian Archive.
2 Frances with Ayah, 1922. Hunter Collection, Cambridge South Asian Archive.
3 Child in a dandy with five servants, c.1908. Hudson Collection, Cambridge South Asian Archive.
4 Christmas 1925. D'Arcy Croften (Waters) Collection, Cambridge South Asian Archive.
5 Mum, Dad, Me and Three Office Staff, probably in a NWFP Station, c.1920. Scott Papers, Oriental and India Office Collections, British Library.
6 Wedding of Iris Butler and Gervas Portal, Central Provinces, January 1927. Sir Montagu Butler Papers, Oriental and India Office Collections, British Library.
7 Family of Benjamin L. Rice and Mary Sophia Rice, Naini Tal (?), 1901. Rice Collection, Cambridge South Asian Archive.
8 Granny Rice [Mary Sophia Rice], 1869. Bevan Collection, Cambridge South Asian Archive.
9 Children's Picnic at Fairy Falls, Kodai, May 1911. Bourne Collection, Cambridge South Asian Archive.
10 Laetitia, Herman, William, and Jeannette Beveridge with two of the family's servants, c.1888. Beveridge Collection, Oriental and India Office Collections, British Library.
11 Gravestones of Laetitia Beveridge and Herman Beveridge, Eastbourne Cemetery. Beveridge Collection, Oriental and India Office Collections, British Library.
12 Port Said, April 1938. Scott Papers, Oriental and India Office Collections, British Library.

LIST OF ABBREVIATIONS

BLARS	Bedfordshire and Luton Archives and Records Service, Bedford (UK)
BCSS	Bishop Cotton School, Shimla (India)
BHSA	Bedford High School Archives, Bedford
BSA	Bedford School Archives, Bedford
CCA	Cheltenham College Archives, Cheltenham (UK)
CPLRD	Cheltenham Public Library Reference Department, Cheltenham
CSAA	Cambridge South Asian Archive, Cambridge
ECA	Eltham College Archives, Eltham (UK)
HCA	Haileybury College Archives, Hertford (UK)
LSE	London School of Economics, Archives Division of the British Library of Political and Economic Science, London
MHSA	Mount Hermon School Archives, Darjeeling (India)
NLS	National Library of Scotland, Edinburgh
OIOC	Oriental and India Office Collections, British Library
PKCA	Perth and Kinross Council Archive, A. K. Bell Library, Perth
SGCM	St George's College, Mussoorie (India)
WASM	Wynberg Allen School, Mussoorie (India)
WHSA	Walthamstow Hall School Archives, Sevenoaks (UK)

Introduction

Making 'British-Indians':
Children, Family Traditions of Indian
Service, and Cycles of Migration

Linked to the chain of Empire one by one,
Flushed with long leave, or tanned with many a sun,
    .   .   .   .
And how so many score of times ye flit
With wife and babe and caravan of kit,
    .   .   .   .
Bound in the wheel of Empire, one by one,
The chain-gangs of the East from sire to son,
The Exiles' Line takes out the exiles' line
And ships them homeward when their work is done.[1]

When Rudyard Kipling wrote 'The Exiles' Line' in 1890, he shed light on many of the defining features of the British community in late imperial India. To begin with, 'The Exiles' Line' literally referred to the steamships run by the P. & O. and other companies that not only took Britons to India but also allowed those participating in the work of empire periodically to go home. Between visits to the metropole Britons living in India became 'exiles', separated from their national homeland, friends, and many family members. Many, but certainly not all: as Kipling's poem insists, British men making their careers in India were often accompanied by their wives and children (Illustration 1). Over time, India became a family concern as children followed in their parents' imperial footsteps. 'Exile', then, formed part of family lineage 'from sire to son' and involved permanent impermanence—repeated comings and goings—between metropole and colony, between 'home' and 'away'. This

---

[1] Rudyard Kipling, 'The Exiles' Line', in *Rudyard Kipling: Complete Verse: Definitive Edition* (New York, 1989), 162–3.

book explores these links between transience and the creation of imperial identities, and frequently their perpetuation, among Britons in the subcontinent. It takes as its particular focus the transmission of a British-Indian status from parents to children between the late nineteenth century and the end of the raj in 1947.

Empire Families examines the integral role of family practices in the reproduction of imperial rule and its personnel, accounting for the substantial degree of family continuity among the middle classes engaged with the raj. Statements such as 'the same families served in India for generation after generation; my father's for three and my mother's for five' recur innumerable times throughout post-colonial accounts of growing up among the colonial community.[2] Such families both made, and were made by, the raj. What is more, since India was not among the parts of Britain's empire meant for permanent white settlement, those maintaining a presence there over several generations did so without formally emigrating. They became defined by long-term patterns of work and residence overseas that alternated with time spent in Britain for schooling, on periodic furloughs, and ultimately in retirement. This created specific forms of racial, class, and geographical identity that enabled them to remain separate not only from Indians but also from members of European-descended communities domiciled in India who failed to participate in ongoing cycles of migration. Furthermore, although British-Indians shared some features in common with members of their class in the metropole who lacked overseas backgrounds, they were also set apart upon their return from 'exile'—self-imposed though it was—by distinct imperial experiences and understandings. They indeed personify the differences, yet simultaneously the inseparability and blurring of boundaries, between Britain's domestic and imperial histories that academics now chart with increasing regularity.[3] More

---

[2] Maurice Willoughby, *Echo of a Distant Drum: The Last Generation of Empire* (Sussex, 2001), vii. Other suggestions of this tendency are found in Rudyard Kipling, 'The Tomb of His Ancestors', in *The Day's Work* (1898; repr. London, 1988), 102; Aroon Tikekar, *The Kincaids: Two Generations of a British Family in the Indian Civil Service* (New Delhi, 1992), 1.

[3] This analytical move is explored in Ann Laura Stoler and Frederick Cooper, 'Between Metropole and Colony: Rethinking a Research Agenda' and other essays in Ann Laura Stoler and Frederick Cooper (eds.), *Tensions of Empire: Colonial Cultures in a Bourgeois World* (Berkeley, CA, 1997), 1–56; Edward W. Said, *Culture and Imperialism* (New York, 1993); Nicholas B. Dirks, 'Introduction: Colonialism and Culture', in Nicholas B. Dirks (ed.), *Colonialism and Culture* (Ann Arbor, MI, 1992), 1–25; Catherine Hall, 'Introduction: Thinking the Post-Colonial, Thinking the Empire', and Antoinette Burton, 'Who Needs the Nation?: Interrogating "British" History', in Catherine Hall (ed.), *Cultures of Empire: A Reader: Colonizers in Britain and the Empire in the Nineteenth and Twentieth Centuries* (Manchester, 2000), 1–33, 137–53. Other key studies among this burgeoning field of scholarship include Anne McClintock, *Imperial Leather: Race, Gender and Sexuality in the Colonial Contest* (New York, 1995); Simon Gikandi, *Maps of Englishness: Writing Identity in the Culture of Colonialism* (New York, 1996); Catherine Hall, *Civilising Subjects: Metropole*

importantly, they constitute what Mrinalini Sinha has termed 'an imperial social formation', whose contours are reducible neither to metropolitan nor indigenous colonized society but rather characterize the transnational intermediate zone bridging them.[4]

Scholars and other critics now routinely assert the centrality of travel and migration to identity formation. As writers like Paul Gilroy and Caryl Phillips argue, ships and sea voyages creating multiple African diasporas in America and Europe from the era of slavery to the present day exemplify a hybridity that refutes conceptualizations of exclusionary national boundaries predicated upon notions of 'insiders', 'outsiders', and 'authentic' ethnic and cultural identities.[5] The impact of travel upon both individual and community identities, however, varied drastically according to historical circumstances and the background of the traveller. Within the British empire, for instance, some undertook journeys by force as slaves, indentured workers, or convicts, while others—encompassing colonizers, colonials, and colonized alike—willingly left their place of birth in search of greater opportunities overseas.[6] In her study of white Australian women who embarked for London between the late nineteenth century and the interwar years, Angela Woollacott explores how voyages to and time in the metropole brought their concurrent standing as both colonials and colonizers to the fore. As 'insiders in the empire because of their whiteness while simultaneously outsiders in England due to their colonial origins and subordinated because of their sex', the steamships on which these women travelled allowed them to position themselves in racial terms in opposition to the indigenous peoples they

and Colony in the English Imagination, 1830–1867 (Cambridge, 2002); Antoinette Burton, *Burdens of History: British Feminists, Indian Women and Imperial Culture, 1865–1915* (Chapel Hill, NC, 1994); Robert Bickers, *Britain in China: Community, Culture, and Colonialism, 1900–49* (Manchester, 1999); Susan Thorne, *Congregational Missions and the Making of an Imperial Culture in Nineteenth Century England* (Stanford, CA, 1999); Mrinalini Sinha, *Colonial Masculinity: The 'Manly Englishman' and the 'Effeminate Bengali' in the Late Nineteenth Century* (Manchester, 1995); C. A. Bayly, *Imperial Meridian: The British Empire and the World* (London, 1989); P. J. Cain and A. G. Hopkins, *British Imperialism: Innovation and Expansion, 1688–1914* and *British Imperialism: Crisis and Deconstruction, 1914–1990* (London, 1993); Linda Colley, 'Britishness and Otherness: An Argument', *Journal of British Studies*, 31 (1992), 309–29.

[4] Mrinalini Sinha, 'Britishness, Clubbability, and the Colonial Public Sphere: The Genealogy of an Imperial Institution in Colonial India', *Journal of British Studies*, 40 (2001), 491–2, 521.

[5] Paul Gilroy, *The Black Atlantic: Modernity and Double Consciousness* (Cambridge, MA, 1993), 4, 11; Caryl Phillips's writings on this subject include his many novels as well as *The Atlantic Sound* (London, 2001), and *A New World Order: Selected Essays* (London, 2001).

[6] Indian travellers to Britain provide one example. See Antoinette Burton, *At the Heart of the Empire: Indians and the Colonial Encounter in Late-Victorian Britain* (Berkeley, CA, 1998); Antoinette Burton, *Dwelling in the Archive: Women Writing House, Home, and History in Late Colonial India* (New York, 2003); Rozina Visram, *Ayahs, Lascars and Princes: The Story of Indians in Britain, 1700–1947* (London, 1986); Shompa Lahiri, *Indians in Britain: Anglo-Indian Encounters, Race, and Identity, 1880–1930* (London, 2000).

encountered during stopovers en route, even if they felt their colonial distinctiveness upon arrival.[7]

British-Indian families like those Kipling described on board 'the exiles' line' similarly owed their identity to travels to and from the metropole. Ongoing contact with Britain separated those considered white and at least middle class from the socially and racially ambiguous poor whites and domiciled Europeans who shared much in common with mixed-race Anglo-Indians in terms of culture, career opportunities, and socio-economic standing. Despite what often amounted to generations of involvement in the subcontinent, their journeys worked against the possible stigma of mixed ancestry and prevented the loss of their British insider status with its many attendant privileges. None the less, their sense of inclusion within the nation was frequently compromised by outlooks and practices that stemmed from their imperial lifestyle. While their movements between Britain and India combatted the suggestion of racial hybridity, then, they also underscored their cultural hybridity within British society.

As Kipling's poem notes, moreover, Britons on 'the exiles' line' were not limited to men, despite his emphasis on the transmission of Indian service 'from sire to son'. Historians have explored how colonial arenas could easily appear as a man's world, not only because of an imbalanced sex ratio among the British community but also due to the homosocial culture stemming from this. India indeed allowed men ample opportunities to exhibit forms of imperial masculinity ranging from military exploits, governing the 'natives', and exploring unknown lands to leisure activities such as hunting and team games. As John Tosh suggests, the empire could provide an ideal destination where men seeking a 'flight from domesticity' could evade the constraints imagined to pervade bourgeois married life in the metropole.[8] European men in the subcontinent always greatly outnumbered European women, but this study covers the era starting in the later nineteenth century when India had increasingly become a family affair in which 'wife and babe' were also core

---

[7] Angela Woollacott, *To Try Her Fortune in London: Australian Women, Colonialism, and Modernity* (New York, 2001), 34.

[8] John Tosh, 'Imperial Masculinity and the Flight from Domesticity in Britain, 1880–1914', in Timothy P. Foley et al. (eds.), *Gender and Colonialism* (Galway, 1995); and *A Man's Place: Masculinity and the Middle-Class Home in Victorian England* (New Haven, CT, 1999), ch. 8. Other studies of British imperial masculinity include Sinha, *Colonial Masculinity*; Hall, *Civilising Subjects*; Graham Dawson, *Soldier Heroes: British Adventure, Empire and the Imagining of Masculinities* (London, 1994); John M. MacKenzie, *The Empire of Nature: Hunting, Conservation and British Imperialism* (Manchester, 1988); J. A. Mangan, *The Games Ethic and Imperialism: Aspects of the Diffusion of an Ideal* (Harmondsworth, 1986). See also Ronald Hyam, *Empire and Sexuality: The British Experience* (Manchester, 1990), for a more problematic analysis of homosexuality among British men and their sexual relationships with colonized men and women.

participants. Women constituted only a small fraction of the European population during the eighteenth century, but by the time of the 1901 *Census of India* there were 384 females for every 1,000 males. By 1921 the numbers totalled approximately 45,000 women and 112,000 men.[9] Factors colluding to encourage more women to spend part of their lives in the subcontinent included the improvements in transport emerging throughout the Victorian era. Months-long voyages around the Cape of Good Hope were superseded first by the overland route through the Middle East and then by steamships travelling directly to India once the Suez Canal opened in 1869. Going to the subcontinent became more comfortable, much cheaper, and far faster, with the trip between London and Bombay reduced to three weeks.[10]

Greater accessibility went hand in hand with changing ideologies of rule that elevated white conjugality to a new pride of place. Feminist scholarship published since the mid-1980s illustrates the diversity of European women's involvement as travellers, missionaries, teachers, doctors, and activists in India as well as many other British and European colonial contexts.[11] Women's most common overseas roles by far, however, were as wives and mothers. Ann Stoler's comparative analyses convey the cultural and political importance European women acquired in Dutch, French, British, and other colonial arenas, as administrators increasingly came to view interracial sexual liaisons

---

[9] Suresh Chandra Ghosh, *The Social Condition of the British Community in Bengal, 1757–1800* (Leiden, 1970), 58–66; P. J. Marshall, 'British Immigration into India in the Nineteenth Century', in P. C. Emmer and M. Moerner (eds.), *European Expansion and Migration: Essays on the Intercontinental Migration from Africa, Asia, and Europe* (New York, 1992), 183–4; and 'The White Town of Calcutta Under the Rule of the East India Company', *Modern Asian Studies*, 34 (2000), 311; H. H. Risley and E. A. Gait, *Census of India, 1901, Vol. I: India. Part I: Report* (Calcutta, 1903), 394. For 1921 totals see Judith M. Brown, 'India', in Judith M. Brown and Wm. Roger Louis (eds.), *The Oxford History of the British Empire, iv: The Twentieth Century* (Oxford, 1999), 423.

[10] John Murray (ed.), *A Handbook for Travellers in India and Ceylon* (London, 1891), xxix; Peter Padfield, *Beneath the House Flag of the P. & O.* (London, 1981), 23, 52–8.

[11] Relevant studies and collections (among many) that suggest women's wide-ranging imperial possibilities include Margaret Strobel, *European Women and the Second British Empire* (Bloomington, IN, 1991); Sara Mills, *Discourses of Difference: An Analysis of Women's Travel Writing and Colonialism* (London, 1991); Nupur Chaudhuri and Margaret Strobel (eds.), *Western Women and Imperialism: Complicity and Resistance* (Bloomington, IN, 1992); Hillary Callan and Shirley Ardener (eds.), *The Incorporated Wife* (London, 1984); Clare Midgley (ed.), *Gender and Imperialism* (Manchester, 1998); Helen Callaway, *Gender, Culture and Empire: European Women in Colonial Nigeria* (London, 1987); Antoinette Burton, 'Contesting the Zenana: The Mission to Make "Lady Doctors for India", 1874–1885', *Journal of British Studies*, 35 (1996), 368–97; Kumari Jayawardena, *The White Women's Other Burden: Western Women and South Asia During British Rule* (New York, 1995); Vron Ware, *Beyond the Pale: White Women, Racism, and History* (London, 1992); Malia B. Formes, 'Beyond Complicity Versus Resistance: Recent Work on Gender and European Imperialism', *Journal of Social History*, 28 (1995), 629–41.

that produced mixed-race populations as a threat to the stability of their rule.[12] Relative tolerance of British men's relationships with Indian women that lasted through much of the eighteenth century dwindled in the nineteenth, as did official attitudes towards progeny generally known until the early twentieth century as 'Eurasians' and more commonly referred to as 'Anglo-Indians' thereafter. India was only one of many settings where persons of mixed ancestry fell outside the bounds of acceptable bourgeois respectability, both in terms of their lower socio-economic standing and descent from relationships later condemned as immoral and that violated the growing desire for racial exclusivity.[13] As Stoler phrases it, 'the management of sexuality, parenting, and morality was at the heart of the late imperial project . . . [and] shaped the boundaries of European membership'.[14] White women—known in India as memsahibs— became designated as the only appropriate partners for male colonizers, entrusted with upholding a domestic regime that prevented men from 'going native' and allowed the European community to reproduce itself, literally as well as figuratively.

Empire Families positions British children, and family life more broadly construed, as pivotal to perceiving what the white community connected with late imperial India stood for. In so doing it unites family history and imperial history—two fields of study that rarely have converged to date. Few scholars aside from Stoler have considered European children in the colonies in any detail, even those whose work on memsahibs has greatly enhanced our understandings of gender and domesticity among Britons in India.[15] Women's roles as wives rather than as mothers receive the most attention because, as Rosemary Marangoly George encapsulates, 'most English mothers in the colonies sent their children back to England for schooling while themselves remaining

---

[12] Ann Laura Stoler, *Carnal Knowledge and Imperial Power: Race and the Intimate in Colonial Rule* (Berkeley, CA, 2002), 39, 47–58, 64, 70–5; and *Race and the Education of Desire: Foucault's History of Sexuality and the Colonial Order of Things* (Durham, NC, 1995). Other work on later nineteenth- and twentieth-century Dutch and French overseas communities that foregrounds gender issues includes Julia Clancy-Smith and Frances Gouda (eds.), *Domesticating the Empire: Race, Gender, and Family Life in French and Dutch Colonialism* (Charlottesville, VA, 1998); Frances Gouda, *Dutch Culture Overseas: Colonial Practice in the Netherlands Indies, 1900–1942* (Amsterdam, 1995); Elspeth Locher-Scholten, *Women and the Colonial State: Essays on Gender and Modernity in the Netherlands Indies, 1900–1942* (Amsterdam, 2000).

[13] Robert J. C. Young, *Colonial Desire: Hybridity in Theory, Culture and Race* (London, 1995), 95, 121, 180; Kenneth Ballhatchet, *Race, Sex and Class under the Raj: Imperial Attitudes and Policies and their Critics, 1793–1905* (London, 1980).

[14] Stoler, *Carnal Knowledge*, 110.

[15] Mary A. Procida, *Married to the Empire: Gender, Politics and Imperialism in India, 1883–1947* (Manchester, 2002); Alison Blunt, 'Imperial Geographies of Home: British Domesticity in India, 1886–1925', *Transactions of the Institute of British Geographers*, N.S. 24 (1999), 421–40. Margaret MacMillan briefly considers children in *Women of the Raj* (London, 1988), 125–41. See also Claudia Knapman's brief treatment of Fiji in 'The White Child in Colonial Fiji, 1895–1930', *Journal of Pacific History*, 23 (1988), 208–13.

behind with their husbands'.[16] When children enter historical discussions at all they do so briefly and often as infants in light of the widespread medical and social recommendations that they leave India—usually between ages 6 and 8.[17] No sooner are they invoked than they are summarily dismissed from the colonial arena altogether—and from further analysis. But while many were indeed 'sent home', not all invariably underwent this transition so early. Assuming all families could readily afford the costs of journeys to Britain and schooling children there from the start of their formal education overlooks the wide socio-economic diversity among the British community that few scholars have treated adequately.

In two articles published in 1979 and 1983, David Arnold made the distinction between 'how the Raj chose to see itself'—as consisting mainly of civil servants, army officers, planters, and businessmen—and the diverse reality underlying the 'illusion of an essentially elite European community'.[18] Arnold stresses that nearly half the Europeans in late nineteenth-century India fell into the category of 'poor whites'. Most were men who had arrived as soldiers or sailors (occasionally with female dependants, although this remained relatively rare) and turned to other forms of employment instead of returning to Britain once their military service ended. What is more, even those Arnold counts among the more 'elite' occupied differential positions within a complex colonial hierarchy. Beneath the viceroy and provincial governors were Indian Civil Servants (the so-called 'heaven-born'), senior officials in other state employment sectors, and high-ranking army officers, along with Anglican bishops and archdeacons; these comprised what Paul Hockings terms the 'upper class' among Britons in India. The 'upper-middle class' included more junior officials, planters, chaplains, and most army officers, while the 'lower-middle class' encompassed many in trade and commerce (known pejoratively as 'boxwallahs', a term that also referred to Indian itinerant peddlers who carried their wares in boxes) and Protestant missionaries. Wealthier businessmen, while deemed socially inferior to the official sector, were at least its equals in terms of income, however, while subordinate, or 'uncovenanted', officials also might count among the 'lower-middle' group—only some of the countless examples that reveal the impossibility of facile social categorization according

---

[16] Rosemary Marangoly George, 'Homes in the Empire, Empires in the Home', *Cultural Critique*, (winter 1993–4), 98.

[17] Nupur Chaudhuri, 'Memsahibs and Motherhood in Nineteenth-Century India', *Victorian Studies*, 31 (1988), 517–35.

[18] David Arnold, 'European Orphans and Vagrants in India in the Nineteenth Century', *Journal of Imperial and Commonwealth History*, 7/2 (1979), 104; and 'White Colonization and Labour in Nineteenth-Century India', *Journal of Imperial and Commonwealth History*, 12/2 (1983), 133–58.

to occupation. The 'upper-lower', meanwhile, included British Other Ranks of the armed forces and Catholic clergy, along with many other intermediaries or semi-skilled workers in state or private employment, including the railways; the 'lower-lower' described the condition of most (but certainly not all) Anglo-Indians.[19] While not alluding to incomes, the 1891 *Census of India* provides a representative occupational breakdown of a European community that then exceeded 165,000 (compared with 81,000 Eurasians). The military dominated with approximately 85,000, including 67,800 troops, 5,080 officers, and over 11,000 wives and children. Civil employees of the state and their families totalled approximately 10,500 while the railway community amounted to 6,100, leaving well over 65,000 men, women, and children supported by the professions, trade, commerce, planting, missionary work, and a host of other non-official positions.[20]

Although some scholars now have turned their attention to a wider range of the colonial spectrum of British India,[21] the social myopia Arnold described persists among studies focused upon British women and domestic life. Wives of men in the Indian Civil Service continue to command the lion's share of historians' attention, with army officers' wives coming in a distant second. Families of businessmen, planters, missionaries, and other less affluent subordinate state employees and non-officials remain virtually absent in their accounts. This predilection is somewhat understandable given the extent to which archival collections in Britain charting the lives and attitudes of 'women of the raj' and similar topics contain vastly more voluminous and detailed material about the families of well-placed civil and military officers than any other group. Restricting their purview only to those enjoying the highest status largely explains why children are so peripheral to their analyses; such families were indeed those most able to send their offspring away from India at young ages.

---

[19] Paul Hockings, 'British Society in the Company, Crown, and Congress Eras', in Paul Hockings (ed.), *Blue Mountains: The Ethnography and Biogeography of a South Indian Region* (Delhi, 1989), 345. Although Hockings focuses on the highlands region of southern India known as the Nilgiris, his sketch of the British social spectrum applies to the subcontinent more generally.

[20] J. A. Baines, *Census of India, 1891. General Report* (London, 1893), 208, 177. For reasons that are considered in Chapter 2, the numbers of domiciled as opposed to non-domiciled Europeans were consistently obscured given suspicions that many who claimed to be domiciled European were actually Eurasian/Anglo-Indian.

[21] On the non-official and less affluent social sectors of the British community, see Raymond K. Renford, *The Non-official British in India to 1920* (New Delhi, 1987); on businessmen, see Maria Misra, *Business, Race, and Politics in British India, c.1850–1960* (Oxford, 1999); Gordon T. Stewart, *Jute and Empire: The Calcutta Jute Wallahs and the Landscapes of Empire* (Manchester, 1998). Relevant analyses of a somewhat earlier period are Bernard S. Cohn, 'The British in Benares: A Nineteenth-Century Colonial Society', in *An Anthropologist among the Historians and Other Essays* (Dehli, 1987), 422–62; P. J. Marshall, 'The Whites of British India, 1780–1830: A Failed Colonial Society?', *International History Review*, 12 (1990), 26–44.

Chapter 1 evaluates the advice parents received from prescriptive literature that stressed India's potential to harm vulnerable children both through climatic dangers as well as cultural 'contamination' from contacts with Indians, usually the family's servants. While parents who could afford to send their children home almost always did so, prescription cannot simply be conflated with practices and attitudes. Family letters and later recollections provide a more nuanced picture of colonial daily life that illuminates how childhood in India could also be viewed positively—and typically with immense nostalgia—and not solely as replete with dangers to bodies and minds. Moreover, a closer look both at the childrearing patterns shared among the better-off as well as at sources that shed light on the practices of the less powerful and affluent reveals much more about why so many considered it crucial that children leave for Britain at the ages most commonly specified. Ideally, children represented a middle- to upper-middle class community that maintained its racial and cultural distance from the colonized. Their upbringing was meant to reflect their families' comfortable socio-economic standing and status as temporary sojourners in the subcontinent who maintained a secure foothold in the metropole. Considering those *failing* to adhere to this supposedly universal set of practices—usually because family finances necessitated prolonged childhood and schooling in India—reveals the extent to which a white bourgeois identity became predicated upon travels to, and formal education in, Britain, especially for boys.

Chapter 2 turns to the interconnected racial and class implications for children who went to schools for 'children of European descent' at Indian hill stations. As institutional documentation, government reports, and other forms of contemporary and retrospective commentary indicate, the large proportion of Anglo-Indian pupils made these schools undesirable options for most parents who considered themselves superior to this community but found it difficult for their children to partake in one of the key practices that distinguished them from it: attending school in Britain. Europeans who stayed in India and became 'domiciled' in an arena not construed as a white settler society counted among the 'country born'. Indicatively, this term was not a literal one and never became applied to the many Britons born in the subcontinent—estimated to have been about 40 per cent of the adult population near the turn of the century—and sent home to school.[22] Instead, 'country born' was reserved

---

[22] As the 1901 *Census* reported, 'more than one-third of the persons returned as Europeans were born in India; the proportion falls to less than a quarter if we exclude children under 15, all of whom many be assumed to have been born in this country, but it again rises to two-fifths if we exclude the army, which may be taken to be wholly English-born'. *Census of India, 1901*, Vol. I, Part I, 394.

for non-transients, who could include either domiciled Europeans or Anglo-Indians.

If children were educated in India, they were deemed likely to acquire cultural traits such as a 'chi-chi' accent that increased their resemblance to mixed-race persons. Furthermore, boys later found themselves ineligible for the higher sectors of state and commercial employment for which education and examinations in Britain were long crucial criteria for entry, and were consequently restricted to subordinate posts seen as largely Anglo-Indian preserves and that became increasingly Indianized in the interwar years. For this reason parents with limited finances commonly prioritized sending sons to Britain and kept daughters in India longer, given the essential role that male professional qualifications played in determining their future class, and also racial, status. Ancestry and physical appearance were never enough to connote whiteness: in the context of late imperial India, this was constructed along gendered lines and as much by culture, education, class, occupation, and geography as by biology. Whiteness in India reflected empowered status and, as will be seen below, had different meanings upon return to Britain.

Empire Families does not pretend to provide Anglo-Indian or Indian perspectives about their encounters with British private life and family practices. Rather, they emerge here as prominent 'significant others' in stories told by those who considered themselves as part of the expatriate community and occasionally by those who described themselves as domiciled Europeans.[23] While the evidence drawn upon in this book is primarily written and occasionally oral, photographs also illustrate how Britons of different class and occupational backgrounds constructed their relationships with other communities. Photographs of officer-class families commonly include Indians, but almost exclusively domestic servants. In the picture of 'Frances with Ayah' dating from 1922, the young daughter of a civil engineer in the Public Works

---

[23] Anglo-Indians during the late imperial and post-colonial eras are examined in Lionel Caplan, *Children of Colonialism: Anglo-Indians in a Post-Colonial World* (Oxford, 2001); Laura Charlotte Bear, 'Traveling Modernity: Capitalism, Community and Nation in the Colonial Governance of the Indian Railways', Ph.D. diss., University of Michigan (1998); Laura Roychowdhury, *The Jadu House: Intimate Histories of Anglo-India* (London, 2000); Alison Blunt, ' "Land of our Mothers": Home, Identity, and Nationality for Anglo-Indians in British India, 1919–1947', *History Workshop Journal*, 54 (2002), 49–72; Glenn D'Cruz, 'Representing Anglo-Indians: A Genealogical Study', Ph.D. diss., University of Melbourne (1999). I know of no in-depth studies that explore how Indian servants evaluated their employment by British families, but an excellent analysis of Dutch photographs of themselves and their Indonesian servants, and how the latter assessed such representations in the post-colonial era, is Ann Stoler's essay co-written with Karen Strassler, 'Memory-Work in Java: A Cautionary Tale', reprinted in Stoler, *Carnal Knowledge*, 162–203. On white settlers in Zambia and their African domestic workers, see Karen Tranberg Hansen, *Distant Companions: Servants and Employers in Zambia, 1900–1985* (Ithaca, NY, 1989).

Department appears with her nursemaid in a pose suggesting cautious affection exchanged between the two and solicitous guidance on the ayah's part (see Illustration 2). Loyalty and mutual affection counted among the more positive qualities some Britons saw in their servants (regardless of what the reality may have been), in contrast to other portrayals of their Indian staff as a source of cultural corruption and unhygienic habits. Juxtaposing children and servants also worked to underscore the differential power relations dividing them. In a photograph of another engineer's son taken early in the twentieth century, the boy sits elevated in a dandy carried by four men while his ayah stands at attention. The five Indians appear grudgingly resigned to their designated labors revolving around the wants of one toddler, and the scene is devoid of any trace of intimacy (Illustration 3). Whether relations between British employers and Indian employees were friendly, perfunctory, or tinged with hostility, however, continual close proximity did little to problematize the divide between colonizers and colonized. In a photograph entitled 'Christmas 1925', the Collector of the Nilgiris stands with his wife, two daughters, a pony, and a dog in front of their sumptuous home to the right side, while twelve of their servants stand together to the left (Illustration 4). They, and the house, help to underscore their employers' high rank within colonial society, and a great deal more came between the two groups than several yards of space and a row of flower pots.

Dorothy Scott's photograph album from the interwar years yields a very different snapshot of relationships taken from the less lofty heights of the family of an Englishman, Donald Scott, who went to India to take up an appointment in the Post Office. No domestic servants appear here; rather, in Dorothy's description the picture shows 'Mum, Dad, me and three office staff', seemingly her father's Indian colleagues who sit on either side of the nuclear family at the center (Illustration 5). While the Indians were probably Donald's subordinates rather than his equals at work, the image suggests how the associations between Britons, Indians, and indeed those in between took on a completely different character among those earning more modest livelihoods within the less prestigious state services. Donald Scott worked side by side with Britons, Indians, and Anglo-Indians, and his wife, Maisie, was seemingly one of the 'country born' who lacked direct ties to Britain prior to her marriage. Crossovers of many kinds occurred at home and at the office which are absent in representations of colonial elites, exemplified in the wedding photograph of Iris Butler and Gervas Portal taken in 1927 while the bride's father, Montagu Butler, was the Governor of the Central Provinces (Illustration 6). High-ranking civil and military families unite, their members including individuals who attained distinction within metropolitan society as well: Iris's brother Rab, about to embark on his parliamentary career in London, returned to India to attend the wedding in the company of his socially prominent and wealthy wife, née Sydney Courtauld. Indicatively, not one Indian or Anglo-Indian is visible amidst this extended family circle as it underwent a rite of passage intended to reproduce itself along unambiguous racial and social lines—although again a pet dog (sporting a ribbon for the occasion) can be found prominently displayed in the front row.

The importance so many Britons placed upon distinguishing themselves from other communities in India and the often imperfect results of this can be seen in the shifting nomenclature meant to designate groups according to their racial, class, cultural, and geographical orientation. Distinctions drawn between those who might be labelled 'white', 'European', or 'English' in India (all of which were common and frequently interchangeable terms then and now), persons of mixed European and Indian descent, and Indians fail to do justice to the diversity *within* such broadly construed groups as well as the imprecise boundaries between them. 'Indians', for instance, included an endless variety of men, women, and children with distinct regional, ethnic, religious, caste, and class backgrounds, many of whom would have described themselves in terms of their differences rather than their similarities as 'colonized' peoples. More important with respect to the issues dealt with throughout this book, however, are the various names used to distinguish Europeans from those who were partly European and partly Indian. Dr Graham, long in charge of the St Andrew's Colonial Homes at Kalimpong that housed and educated many children of mixed descent, stated in 1934 that when the name 'Anglo-Indian' was substituted for 'Eurasian' in official documents early in the twentieth century 'it meant robbing Britishers, who had served in India, of a title of which they were proud and for which no satisfactory successor seems to have been discovered'.[24] Graham accurately reflected the disparaging sense of entitlement many Britons felt *vis-à-vis* Anglo-Indians, a community widely seen as unworthy of either their privileges or their appellation. Shifting and inexact nomenclature persists up to the present day, with some scholars using 'Anglo-Indian' to describe those of mixed ancestry and others to connote the transient 'white' British.

---

[24] The Very Revd J. A. Graham, 'The Education of the Anglo-Indian Child', *Journal of the Royal Society of Arts*, 83 (23 Nov. 1934), 23. The 1911 *Census of India* saw 'Eurasians' referred to as 'Anglo-Indians' in official discourse, a shift that represented this community's campaign to be defined in ways that emphasized their European ancestry and culture rather than their Indian background. E. A. Gait, *Census of India, 1911, Vol. I: India. Part I: Report* (Calcutta, 1913), refers to 'the use, under the orders of the Government of India, of the term Anglo-Indian as the official designation of the mixed race, instead of Eurasian, their former designation, which was very unpopular amongst them', 139.

In an attempt to minimize this confusion that in itself suggests the indistinct boundaries between them, I use 'Anglo-Indian' throughout this book to describe those of mixed descent unless citing contemporary sources that employ the alternative meaning. I refer to Britons who depicted themselves as exclusively European as 'British-Indians', drawing upon Francis Hutchins's preferred term.[25] 'British-Indian' was not commonly used by contemporaries but it provides necessary clarity; moreover, 'British' is a far more accurate term for those connected with India than 'Anglo', given the large numbers of Scots and Irish as well as the English involved in the imperial enterprise.[26] 'British-Indian' additionally underscores the repetitive journeys between, and alternating experiences in, metropole and colony that proved so crucial to creating and stabilizing both whiteness and middle-class status in India.

Chapters 3, 4, and 5 correspondingly shift to Britain to explore how formative experiences there were as central to shaping British-Indian lives and family trajectories as those in India. What Catherine Hall writes with reference to nineteenth-century Jamaica—that 'the making of colonising subjects, of racialised and gendered selves [took place] both in the empire and at home'— applies equally to British India, albeit in locally specific forms.[27] Restricting our attention to family life as lived on Indian soil tells only half the story of a mobile community and omits half the participants from further analysis. Children, parents on leave, and retirees have traditionally been assigned bit parts in the historiography of British India, quickly ushered off the scene when dispatched home to leave young adults and the middle-aged as virtually the only players in view. By overlooking their pre- and post-working lives scholars have paid insufficient attention to the meanings of ongoing contact with Britain. *Empire Families* now addresses this lacuna by opening up a new metropolitan stage and recasting perennial extras as leading actors in family stories of empire.

The same conditions of travel that accounted for British women's and children's presence in the subcontinent and helped to consolidate white

---

[25] Francis G. Hutchins, *The Illusion of Permanence: British Imperialism in India* (Princeton, NJ, 1967), 101.

[26] The significant roles played by the Scots and the Irish in the British empire (the Welsh, by contrast, were a far less noticeable contingent in India) are discussed further in my 'Haggis in the Raj: Private and Public Celebrations of Scottishness in Late Imperial India', *Scottish Historical Review*, 81/2, no. 212 (2002), 212–39; among other work, see John M. MacKenzie, 'Essay and Reflection: On Scotland and the Empire', *International History Review*, 15 (1993), 714–39; R. A. Cage (ed.), *The Scots Abroad: Labour, Capital, Enterprise, 1750–1914* (London, 1985); Stewart, *Jute and Empire*; Stephen Howe, *Ireland and Empire: Colonial Legacies in Irish History and Culture* (Oxford, 2000); Keith Jeffrey (ed.), *An Irish Empire?: Aspects of Ireland and the British Empire* (Manchester, 1996); Scott B. Cook, 'The Irish Raj: Social Origins and Careers of Irishmen in the Indian Civil Service, 1855–1914', *Journal of Social History*, 20 (1987), 507–29.

[27] Hall, *Civilising Subjects*, 13.

domesticity as an imperial ideal among the colonizers simultaneously worked in opposition to it. Perceptions of India's multiple threats to children in particular led to the fracturing of the domestic sphere, with parents and children becoming separated by thousands of miles for years at a time. Chapter 3 considers how British-Indians dealt with sending children away to the metropole on both practical and emotional levels. While this may have marked families as white and middle-class in contrast to the less affluent and racially suspect domiciled European community, it came at a high price. Historians have charted the centrality that ideals of family intimacy acquired for the British (and especially among the middle classes) by the nineteenth century, but the typical lifestyle among families with ties to India rendered it improbable that they could achieve what so often proved challenging even for their metropolitan social counterparts.[28] Children's departure for Britain, moreover, was only one of many manifestations of what William Beveridge, born in India in 1879, later called a form of 'family life punctuated by separations' that became 'habitual'.[29] Fathers working in the cities and plains regions of India often saw little of their wives and children at certain times of year if they could afford to spend the hottest months in the hills for a combination of health and social reasons; then, when children were sent home mothers who accompanied them could choose to divide their time between India and Britain. Most often, though, children saw little of either parent between furloughs once they left the subcontinent. Instead, they relied upon members of their extended family, paid guardians, and boarding schools to provide what were often recalled as unsatisfying alternatives to the idealized nuclear family.

Lengthy family separations have commonly been described 'the price of empire' that proved hardest to pay. William Beveridge's mother, Annette, bemoaned the emotional havoc wreaked during the course of 'all these vagrant years' when she, her husband, and their children rarely all lived under the same roof but instead were scattered between Calcutta and Darjeeling or between Calcutta and Eastbourne.[30] Their pain, however, has proven historians' gain. Family separations like the Beveridges' generated a wealth of written documentation and some of the most detailed available accounts about British-

---

[28] Key studies include Leonore Davidoff and Catherine Hall, *Family Fortunes: Men and Women of the English Middle Class, 1780–1850* (Chicago, 1987); Leonore Davidoff, Megan Doolittle, Janet Fink, and Katherine Holden, *The Family Story: Blood, Contract and Intimacy, 1830–1960* (London, 1999); John R. Gillis, *A World of Their Own Making: Myth, Ritual, and the Quest for Family Values* (New York, 1996).

[29] LSE, Beveridge Papers, William Beveridge, 'Anglo-Indian Childhood', typescript MS, n.d. [c.1949], 2, 7.

[30] OIOC, MSS Eur C176/23, Annette Beveridge to Henry Beveridge, 8 July 1888.

Indian family practices, anxieties, and aspirations. As William wrote of his efforts in the 1940s to reconstruct family happenings during his father's Indian Civil Service career, the discontinuities their transient lifestyle entailed made 'reliance on memory needless':

My father and mother were separated repeatedly, even when in India, and wrote to one another on every day of being apart, and kept the letters . . . we children began writing in the same way . . . there are literally hundreds of letters by my sisters or myself written before I was ten. I am able today to compare the child that scrappily and vaguely I can remember as myself, with the child whom the documents discover but whom, in most ways, I have forgotten wholly.[31]

Not all families were as prolific as the Beveridges, but many came close and left extensive records of their years overseas in which their times apart are more thoroughly charted than their times together. William's confidence in their accuracy requires qualification, however. While it is essential not to view either contemporary correspondence or memories recorded decades afterwards as telling the 'true' story of imperial family life, both bodies of evidence remain central to this analysis. This study juxtaposes private papers dating from the era of the raj itself with fictional work considering British-Indian childhood and parenting as well as with written and oral retrospective accounts, many of which have emerged since the 1970s. While they fall into a number of genres, 'factual' and 'fictional' texts overlap in many respects, as do colonial and post-colonial accounts, and this book attends to the historically specific conditions informing their production and dissemination. Liz Stanley stresses 'the role played by fictions within the apparent facts of autobiography, of the genre's creation rather than representation of self', an assertion that is equally valid with respect to correspondence and other narratives.[32] Other critics, Joan Scott prominent among them, justifiably have warned scholars against reading such autobiographical texts as evidence of historical reality.[33] Regardless of their limitations and their compliance with the prevailing conventions of letter-writing, composing a memoir or family biography, writing a novel, or recording memories on tape with an interviewer, such sources do, however, convey a great deal about how writers and speakers perceived conditions affecting them at a give point in time. Alessandro Portelli's points about the value of oral

---

[31] LSE, Beveridge Papers, Beveridge, 'Anglo-Indian Childhood', 3–4.

[32] Liz Stanley, *The Auto/biographical I: The Theory and Practice of Feminist Auto/biography* (Manchester, 1992), 3–4, 60.

[33] Joan Wallach Scott, 'Experience', in Judith Butler and Joan W. Scott (eds.), *Feminists Theorize the Political* (New York, 1992), 22–40.

sources apply to other accounts as well: 'they tell us not just what people did, but what they wanted to do, what they believed they were doing, and what they now think they did . . . Subjectivity is as much the business of history as are the more visible "facts". What informants believe is indeed a historical *fact* (that is, the fact that they believe it), as much as what really happened'.[34]

Empire Families, then, explores how British-Indians defined themselves, made sense of their lives, and expressed their hopes, fears, and biases, both among themselves and to others across the high imperial and post-colonial eras. As was seen above, some of their stories stress the drawbacks to the lifestyle they created: the risks to body and character through contact with India's hot climate, indigenous populations, and stigmatized members of the Anglo-Indian and domiciled community that made many send their children away, followed by emotional traumas commonly experienced during the resulting family separations. India could easily become construed primarily as a 'land of regrets' where British participants made continual sacrifices. Kipling's rhetoric in 'The Exiles' Line', for instance, upholds this emphasis when describing such families as forming 'chain-gangs of the East from sire to son'.[35] Clearly, however, their activities in the subcontinent were anything but altruistic, as Benita Parry and Janaki Nair both emphasize.[36] Arguments that British men, women, and children paid the 'price of empire', Nair stresses, consistently 'trivialized the price paid by the colony'.[37] Indeed, the many pleasures they derived from life and work in the subcontinent do much to explain why so many willingly maintained their involvement there not only over the course of much of their lifetimes but also into the next generation. Although some clearly did not find adequate compensation and terminated their ties with India, others grew to relish their imperial lifestyle despite its drawbacks. Time spent in the metropole during school years, furlough, or after retirement often reinforced an awareness of India's rewards among children and adults alike, one dimension of which was the sense of belonging they felt among the expatriate community that was lacking when in the company of other Britons. A story entitled 'A Mother in India' written at the turn of the century by one memsahib, Sara Jeannette Duncan, describes how one woman's imperial contentment overrode anxieties about her estrangement from her daughter after years of separation.

[34] Alessandro Portelli, *The Death of Luigi Trastulli and Other Stories* (Albany, NY, 1991), 50.

[35] On representations of India as a 'land of regrets', see B. J. Moore-Gilbert, *Kipling and 'Orientalism'* (London, 1986), 42–7.

[36] Benita Parry, *Delusions and Discoveries: India in the British Imagination, 1880–1930*, 2nd edn. (London, 1998), 41–57.

[37] Janaki Nair, 'Uncovering the *Zenana*: Visions of Indian Womanhood in Englishwomen's Writings, 1813–1940', in Hall (ed.), *Cultures of Empire*, 238.

Boarding the ship back to India at the end of her husband's furlough came not a moment too soon:

> It was a Bombay ship, full of returning Anglo-Indians. I looked up and down the long saloon tables with a sense of relief and a solace; I was again among my own people . . . I could pick out a score that I knew in fact, and there were none that in imagination I didn't know. The look of wider seas and skies, the casual experienced glance, the touch of irony and of tolerance, how well I knew it and how well I liked it! Dear old England, sitting in our wake, seemed to hold by comparison a great many soft, unsophisticated people, immensely occupied about very particular trifles. How difficult it had been, all the summer, to be interested! . . . Gladly I went in and out of the women's cabins and listened to the argot of the men; my own ruling, administering, soldiering little lot.[38]

For many British-Indians, especially wives and children, life overseas was played out predominantly within fairly circumscribed settings. While these never fully excluded members of colonized society, they often worked deliberately to maximize contacts with their own community. Bungalows and their surroundings—often walled-in compounds—contained many Indian servants, but admitted only selected other representatives of 'native' society, as did social clubs.[39] 'Civil lines', cantonments, and other districts intended to cater to the British, along with the hill stations that became climatic as well as cultural refuges in which British-Indian culture set the tone, also ranked high among the enclaves that British-Indians colonized and from which they derived some comfort and sense of belonging in a land where they constituted a minuscule fraction of the population.[40] Specific geographical positionings within the Indian subcontinent reflect their separation, both spatial and cultural, from much of India, comprising a central dimension of what Partha Chatterjee has described as 'the preservation of the alienness of the ruling group'.[41] As was seen in Sara Jeannette Duncan's story, steamships carrying them to and from home similarly served as microcosms in which British-Indians and their culture appeared predominant, regardless of the existence of 'others'—not only among a diverse group of passengers but also among the crews that included many Indian lascars.

---

[38] Sara Jeannette Duncan, 'A Mother in India' (1903), in Saros Cowasjee (ed.), *Stories from the Raj from Kipling to Independence* (London, 1982), 83–4.

[39] Anthony D. King, *The Bungalow: The Production of a Global Culture* (London, 1984), and *Colonial Urban Development: Culture, Social Power and Environment* (London, 1976); Thomas R. Metcalf, *Ideologies of the Raj: The New Cambridge History of India*, iii.4 (Cambridge, 1995), 177–84.

[40] Dane Kennedy, *The Magic Mountains: Hill Stations and the British Raj* (Berkeley, CA, 1996).

[41] Partha Chatterjee, *The Nation and Its Fragments: Colonial and Post-Colonial Histories* (Princeton, NJ, 1993), 10.

Upon arrival back in Britain many continued to stand out from their surroundings, despite proclaiming themselves to have 'come home'. While returned British-Indians exemplify the extent to which metropolitan Britain was pervaded by peoples, commodities, understandings, and practices that originated in the empire or reflected the nation's range of overseas projects, they also suggest this to have been a differential process, more visible and concentrated in some locations than in others.[42] Children and adults alike often lived in the midst of a peer group sharing links with India or other colonial settings that closely resembled their own, and Chapters 4 and 5 consider arenas where empire families made a particularly strong impression: selected schools, towns, and neighborhoods.

Boys and girls 'sent home to school' commonly found themselves educated alongside others like themselves at institutions well-known among British-Indian parents. Among the best-documented schools with notable British-Indian and other colonial contingents were those for older boys that followed public-school models, including Haileybury, the United Services College, Cheltenham College, and Bedford Grammar School. Records of the Schools for the Sons and Daughters of Missionaries near London (later called Eltham College and Walthamstow Hall) enable a comparison between the educational experiences of male and female children from one occupational sector. Such schools not only attracted a substantial imperial clientele but also played central roles in perpetuating this identity into the next generation by training their pupils for imperial careers. Girls' educational experiences—underdocumented since many schools they attended were small-scale and are now defunct—led some to seek employment overseas as well, but a great many more came to lead imperial adult lives by ultimately marrying men who, as their fathers had done, made their careers in India. Pre-existing family ties with India and school culture worked together in gender-specific ways to make grown children's returns overseas a strong possibility.

---

[42] John M. MacKenzie (ed.), *Imperialism and Popular Culture* (Manchester, 1986). Many studies charting the presence of empire 'at home' pay particular attention to its manifestations in discrete locations, including port cities and specific areas or communities in London, Dundee, Birmingham, or Glasgow, to name a few. See Felix Driver and David Gilbert (eds.), *Imperial Cities: Landscape, Display and Identity* (Manchester, 1999); Jonathan Schneer, *London 1900: The Imperial Metropolis* (New Haven, CT, 1999); Laura Tabili, '*We Ask for British Justice': Black Workers and the Construction of Racial Difference in Late Imperial Britain* (Ithaca, NY, 1994); Woollacott, *To Try Her Fortune*; Burton, *At the Heart of the Empire*; Hall, *Civilising Subjects*; Stewart, *Jute and Empire*. Other scholars, meanwhile, usefully suggest that aspects of empire were, and remain, present within British culture whether they were blatantly manifest or appeared not far below the surface once this was scratched; see for example Julia Bush, 'Moving On—And Looking Back', *History Workshop Journal*, 36 (1993), 183–94.

Many of the towns known as British-Indian educational venues in fact became home—whether temporarily or permanently—to adults back from India on leave or in retirement. Bedford and Cheltenham, along with a number of seaside towns including Eastbourne, Brighton, and Hove, all developed reputations as educational, leisure, and retirement centers that counted many British-Indians among their middle-class child and adult populations. Others chose to spend furlough or retirement in and around London, often settling near other repatriates in neighborhoods like Bayswater or Ealing. In his 1939 novel *Coming Up for Air*, George Orwell—himself born into a British-Indian family, and who had abandoned a brief career with the Indian Police in Burma—provided a thumbnail sketch of the lifestyle and outlooks of returned British-Indians he undoubtedly knew well from the perspective of an outsider, George Bowling. Recalling his first encounter with his future wife Hilda's parents, the protagonist describes his introduction to a 'colony' of repatriates residing in the 'little dark house[s]' in 'those buried back-streets' in Ealing. They comprised 'the poverty-stricken officer class' who, upon retirement, had clustered together to form a subculture obsessed by reduced circumstances ('looking twice at sixpence') and the grander days gone by. Having personal histories and interests that distinguished them from other Britons, they opted to reside where they remained well represented and found others with whom they shared reminiscences, a common argot, and Indian material paraphernalia. To the onlooker, their mode of existence was as insular as it was archaic, forty years behind the times:

I hadn't known till then that there was a considerable Anglo-Indian colony in Ealing. Talk about discovering a new world! . . . It's almost impossible, when you get inside these people's houses, to remember that out in the street it's England and the twentieth century. As soon as you set foot inside the front door you're in India in the 'eighties. You know the kind of atmosphere. The carved teak furniture, the brass trays, the dusty tiger-skulls on the wall, the Trichinopoly cigars, the red-hot pickles, the yellow photographs of chaps in sun-helmets, the Hindustani words that you're expected to know the meaning of, the everlasting anecdotes about tiger-shoots and what Smith said to Jones in Poona in '87. It's a sort of little world of their own that they've created, like a kind of cyst.[43]

In portraying Britain's agents of empire as decayed and dusty in terms of their status, age, and relevance to interwar metropolitan modernity, Orwell clearly intended Ealing's pensioned British-Indians as a critical comment on

[43] George Orwell, *Coming Up for Air* (1939; repr. London, 2000), 138–9, 141. Thanks to Bernhard Rieger for recommending this book to me.

empire more generally. Taken literally, however, his narrative supports other descriptions of returned colonials written both by themselves and others. As E. M. Collingham summarizes, their world proved a self-contained one in many respects, its representatives developing a form of 'Britishness . . . peculiar to themselves' both as a result of the distinctive lives they led in India and their declined significance thereafter.[44] Francis Hutchins aptly described sectors of British-Indian society as constituting a 'middle class aristocracy' to underscore how imperial life allowed them to live 'in a manner well above the station from which they had sprung in England'.[45] Returning to the metropole often proved a letdown since it meant giving up the elevated standing based on class, race, and nationality they had enjoyed in India, enhancing the nostalgia many younger and older repatriates felt for their time overseas.

Coming Up for Air, moreover, suggests how parents' decreased standing and ongoing India-inflected domesticity in metropolitan retirement helped to shape their children's futures. While the daughter, Hilda, married the solidly lower-middle-class George Bowling who resembled her parents financially (if in little else), the son, Harold, 'had some official job in Ceylon', seemingly having chosen to return to relative affluence overseas rather than join the rest of his family in leading a comparatively obscure and drab existence in London's suburbs.[46] While not pursuing the same profession as his father and in opting to resume imperial life in Ceylon instead of India, Harold's path strongly resembled that portrayed throughout non-fictional renditions of British-Indian family trajectories. Although *Empire Families* largely restricts its attention to families active in Britain and India, many in fact spread much further afield as some descendants remained in Britain, some returned to India, and others added to imperial genealogies in other British colonies or spheres of influence. Some parents, as Chapter 5 notes, failed to return to Britain at all when fathers' careers came to an end, opting instead for retirement in African settler colonies, the dominions, or continental Europe because they believed they could live better on their pensions abroad than at home.

Encapsulating how far-flung—and professionally diverse—an extended family could become were the Rices, who maintained connections with empire that lasted well over a century. B. Lewis Rice was the son of a missionary who

[44] E. M. Collingham, *Imperial Bodies: The Physical Experience of the Raj, c.1800–1947* (Cambridge, 2001), 201, 164. Some of these issues are also addressed in Georgina Gowans, 'A Passage from India: British Women Travelling Home, 1915–1947', D. Phil. thesis, University of Southampton (1999).

[45] Hutchins, *Illusion of Permanence*, 107–8. Benedict Anderson makes a similar point in *Imagined Communities: Reflections on the Origin and Spread of Nationalism*, rev. edn. (London, 1991), 150.

[46] Orwell, *Coming Up for Air*, 139.

went to Bangalore in the 1830s; one of his brothers followed in their father's footsteps but he made his own career in the Department of Education, also becoming involved in archaeological research and publication. Lewis Rice married another South India missionary's daughter, Mary Sophia Garrett, in 1869, and their ten children born between 1870 and 1888 all spent part of their childhoods in India prior to starting school in Britain. Of Lewis and Mary's four daughters, all returned to India and three appeared to have married army officers and travelled with them between postings in India, Sierra Leone, and Singapore. (Illustration 7). Of their six sons, only one failed to return overseas, becoming a vicar in England; one joined the Indian Staff Corps after leaving Sandhurst, one entered the Indian Public Works Department, and three entered business or banking that involved periods spent in India, Burma, Japan, Hong Kong, and Singapore. One of the latter ultimately turned to farming in South Africa. Although they retired to Britain in 1906, Lewis and Mary remained active in the family work of empire by looking after some of their grandchildren separated from their parents—grandchildren who, as adults, often remained part of expatriate communities scattered throughout the world until the 1960s. Mary Rice's wedding veil tellingly became worn upon one granddaughter's marriage in South Africa and was then used at a great-granddaughter's christening in Singapore, becoming a symbolic artifact within a migratory family culture that spanned the globe over five generations (Illustration 8).[47]

The opportunities families like the Rices found throughout the formal and informal empire, moreover, suggest that Britain's imperial personnel could draw upon a range of understandings and practices that were shared by colonizers elsewhere at the same time as these necessarily acquired contours specific to distinct settings. Nicholas Thomas correctly emphasizes the necessity of 'localizing colonialism' to avoid generalizations that falsely conflate vastly different colonial projects and actors.[48] In examining British families in India between the late Victorian era and decolonization this book tells a story specific to that arena, yet scholars considering related issues in colonial contexts elsewhere will surely find many of their outlooks and forms of behavior at least partly familiar. Fears about the impact of hot climates and contact with non-Western and mixed-race peoples on Europeans and beliefs about how best to

---

[47] CSAA, Rice Papers, Mary Sophia Rice, 'My Memoirs' (privately published, n.d. [*c.*1920s]). On 'Granny Rice's' travelling veil, see her granddaughter Sheila Bevan's *The Parting Years: A British Family and the End of Empire* (London, 2001), 2. I am grateful to Antoinette Burton for alerting me to Bevan's account.

[48] Nicholas Thomas, *Colonialism's Culture: Anthropology, Travel and Government* (Princeton, NJ, 1994), 2–3.

negotiate these perils without abandoning the imperial enterprise apply to countless other locations, yet never in exactly the same ways. Similarly, British-Indians were not alone among those based overseas in continuing to look towards home to define themselves in racial, cultural, and class terms. The extent to which actual travels to and time spent in Britain, especially for education, bolstered their status as white and relatively elite, however, worked differently for those who saw themselves as temporary sojourners in non-settler societies and those who had put down roots in Australia and in white communities in South, Central, or East Africa.[49]

Additionally, despite the differences within the British-Indian community, *Empire Families* argues that families with comparable financial means but divergent occupational profiles engaged in broadly similar private practices on many levels. Childrearing ideals and methods were never uniform as individual families made their own decisions on how best to evaluate published advice and apply what they considered to be common-sense ideas to their own specific circumstances. Childhood and parenting experiences often differed across gender lines as well, yet also converged at many junctures. Despite the distinct forms of education sons and daughters received, children of both sexes were likely to perpetuate their ties with the subcontinent (or elsewhere overseas) into the next generation yet maintain their foothold—unsteady or unsatisfying though it proved for some—within the metropole. Often they remained part of colonial society until India became independent, while expatriate status for those within the non-official community could extend well past 1947.[50]

In assessing the decades spanning the late Victorian era and independence, this book considers a time when Crown Rule had replaced the East India Company's administration in the wake of the 1857–8 Indian uprising and the raj expanded, diversified, and became consolidated. Concurrently, it faced accelerating challenges as Indian nationalism gained momentum and ultimately brought empire in South Asia to an end. Yet during an era replete with continual changes, British family life as it was played out just prior to decolonization

---

[49] On white settler communities, see Dane Kennedy, *Islands of White: Settler Society and Culture in Kenya and Southern Rhodesia, 1890–1939* (Durham, NC, 1987); Woollacott, *To Try Her Fortune*; Daiva Stasiulis and Nira Yuval-Davis (eds.), *Unsettling Settler Societies: Articulations of Gender, Race, Ethnicity and Class* (London, 1995); Vivian Bickford-Smith, *Ethnic Pride and Racial Prejudice in Victorian Cape Town: Group Identity and Social Practice, 1875–1902* (Cambridge, 1995); J. M. Coetzee, *White Writing: On the Culture of Letters in South Africa* (New Haven, CT, 1988).

[50] Malia Formes considers Britons who remained present in India after independence in 'Post-Imperial Domesticity Amid Diaspora, 1959–79: A Comparative Biography of Two English Sisters from India', paper presented at 'Post-Imperial Britain': 16th Annual Conference of the Institute of Contemporary British History, London, 8–10 July 2002.

retained much that would have appeared familiar to participants over fifty years previously. Concerns about children's physical health, cultural development, and racial identity; the transportation and educational facilities, along with the career entry procedures that made going to Britain not only feasible but also coveted on the grounds of the cultural, class, and racial status that it brought; the separations and the disappointments that time in Britain entailed: the persistence of predominant features within British-Indian lifestyles throughout this era is striking. Like George Orwell's rendition of the time-warped domestic atmosphere prevailing within the 'Anglo-Indian colony in Ealing' in the interwar years, E. M. Collingham's assessment that a distinctive culture was in place among this community by the late nineteenth century that became marked by an increasingly archaic form of continuity well into the 1900s is persuasive.[51] While this book notes changes including those that came about during or as a result of the First and Second World Wars, as well as those connected with the gradual implementation of Indianization policies within state employment sectors, it suggests that the truly decisive break within British family traditions in India came only with independence in 1947.

Post-colonial renditions of raj experiences reveal distinctive historical contours that scholars relying on them need to take on board. *Empire Families* concludes by bridging the gap between the high imperial period and the post-colonial moment with a brief examination of the influential roles that the last generations of former British-Indians have played in documenting, reconstructing, and often mythologizing the nation's imperial past following the end of empire, helping to shape wider public perceptions. Voluminous oral and written accounts of their own and their ancestors' experiences feature prominently in British archival collections, have found publishers, or have become part of media productions imbued with imperial nostalgia. Narratives by and about the better-off dominate these genres, showing that long-term emotional and social investments in British India and the pleasures of empowerment stemming from them did not end with decolonization. Indeed, they remain part of public and private memory in Britain up to the present day.

British-Indian family trajectories, in sum, illustrate how social, cultural, and racial identities depended on a series of migrations that started in childhood and ended only in retirement. Maintaining an imperial lifestyle began with childrearing patterns that encapsulated many of the fears and desires circulating around India's geography and peoples. British-Indians developed an early

[51] Collingham, *Imperial Bodies*, 9, 150–3, 161, 165.

awareness of their colonial privileges, not only during childhood years in India but also after being sent home to school. Despite the disadvantages of an imperial lifestyle, many used the benefits their metropolitan schooling bestowed to rejoin the colonial community as adults, enjoying much higher status than if they had not left India—or if they never returned overseas. The following chapters chart their responses over time to the risks and drawbacks that jostled with pleasures and perquisites that, for many, tipped the balance in favor of maintaining their ties with empire as long as it remained possible.

I

Danger and Pleasure at the Bungalow:
British Children at Home in India

With the publication of *The Secret Garden* in 1911, Frances Hodgson Burnett provided one of the most enduring images of India's impact on British children in popular culture. The novel's heroine, 10-year-old Mary Lennox, arrived in England after early years in the empire had left their mark on both her body and her character:

When Mary Lennox was sent to Misselthwaite Manor to live with her uncle, everybody said she was the most disagreeable-looking child ever seen . . . She had a little thin face and a little thin body, thin light hair and a sour expression. Her hair was yellow, and her face was yellow because she had been born in India and had always been ill in one way or another . . . her mother had been a great beauty who cared only to go to parties and amuse herself with gay people. She had not wanted a little girl at all, and when Mary was born she handed her over to the care of an Ayah, who was made to understand that if she wished to please the Memsahib she must keep the child out of sight as much as possible . . . [Mary] never remembered seeing familiarly anything but the dark faces of her Ayah and the other native servants, and as they always obeyed her and gave her her own way in everything, because the Memsahib would be angry if she was disturbed by her crying, by the time she was six years old she was as tyrannical and selfish a little pig as ever lived.[1]

India's climate, 'native' population, and maternal ineptitude worked together to make Mary unhealthy and domineering, and she was only cured of her defects and debilities when both parents died and she returned to England. There, in the Yorkshire moors and among an upstanding rural folk, she underwent both a physical and spiritual recovery through fresh air, exercise, making friends, and tending her own flower garden. During her metamorphosis, India receded into the background until it became an invisible part of Mary's past,

---

[1] Frances Hodgson Burnett, *The Secret Garden* (1911; repr. Ware, Hertfordshire, 1993), 1.

presumably never to reappear to tarnish her new life. *The Secret Garden*, in short, charts the rescue of a corrupted colonial child by the English climate and an idyllically rendered rural culture, with removal from the Indian site of danger enabling a full erasure of its negative effects.

If India's imprint upon Mary Lennox was portrayed as dire yet easily eradicable once she left, Burnett balanced this verdict on the subcontinent's and England's diametrically opposed effects on children with other possibilities in a novel written six years previously. Sara Crewe, the heroine of *A Little Princess*, also spent her first years in India but suffered none of the consequences stemming from parental negligence, bad health, or servant indulgence that had temporarily 'spoiled' Mary Lennox. Instead, India was a setting of domestic happiness for Sara, who had flourished as a robust, kind, and well-behaved child under the influence of her father's and servants' affections, her mother having died in childbirth. When the need to preserve her good health led her father to send her to a London boarding school, Sara's new life in Britain only made her nostalgic for what she had left behind in India. While Mary Lennox's relatives and acquaintances played central roles in reforming her bad character, Sara encountered far less propitious surroundings when placed in the custody of Miss Minchin, the school's proprietress, whom Sara presciently assessed as 'very like her house . . . tall and dull, and respectable and ugly' upon their first meeting.[2] Her ensuing years at the school entailed a painful separation from her father that ended with his death from fever in India after losing his large fortune.

When the penniless Sara was demoted from favored wealthy pupil to overworked and underfed servant by the cruel Miss Minchin after her father died, her degraded condition in England made her days in India seem even more blissful by comparison. Her chance encounter with Ram Dass, the Indian servant of a British-Indian man who had moved into the house next door to Miss Minchin's school, brought home the contrasts between her privileged early colonial childhood and her poverty and subordination in England since her father's death:

The sight of his native costume and the profound reverence of his manner stirred all her past memories. It seemed a strange thing to remember that she—the drudge whom the cook had said insulting things to an hour ago—had only a few years ago been surrounded by people who all treated her as Ram Dass had treated her; who salaamed when she went by, whose foreheads almost touched the ground when she spoke to

---

[2] Frances Hodgson Burnett, *A Little Princess* (1905; repr. Ware, Hertfordshire, 1994), 13.

them, who were her servants and her slaves. It was like a sort of dream. It was all over, and it could never come back.[3]

Predictably, Sara's future failed to live up to her gloomy imaginings. Ram Dass and the wealthy 'sahib' who employed him signalled her rescue from poverty and mistreatment when the latter proved to be her father's close friend who had long attempted to locate her and inform her that her father's fortune had multiplied rather than disappeared; by the novel's end, he became her devoted guardian and welcomed her into his household. While leaving India meant losing a valued domestic and familial setting and later her financial security—not to mention her elevated status based on race in a setting where 'her servants and her slaves' were seemingly one and the same—these all returned via the same colonial channel, albeit one transplanted onto British soil.

In Frances Hodgson Burnett's literary imagination, then, for the British child India might entail a physically and morally debilitating climate, parental negligence (especially on the part of mothers) or mortality, and exposure to 'natives' that inhibited the development of good character. On the other hand, it might just as readily signify a realm of domestic happiness peopled by loving parents and affectionate servants, whose respect and submissiveness did not necessarily render children 'tyrannical and selfish'. Britain, meanwhile, might either serve as a site of redemption where India's ills could be eradicated, or alternatively become an unwelcoming and lonely place for children devoid of family and bring a decline in the socio-economic status enjoyed overseas. Moreover, vestiges of India could just as readily remain part of repatriated Britons' lives as sink without a trace, exemplified in *A Little Princess* when Sara leaves Miss Minchin to become part of a new 'family' in London consisting of a retired 'sahib' and his Indian servant. Both Britain and India, it seems, might appear as either a blessing or a curse.

Although Burnett neither visited India nor came from a family with imperial connections, her divergent renditions of its effects on British children bear an uncanny resemblance to views expressed among a wide range of commentators writing both during and after the late imperial period.[4] That her fiction should overlap with representations found in medical and colonial housekeeping literature as well as in the private stories of those with firsthand knowledge

---

[3] Ibid., 144.

[4] Ann Thwaite, *Waiting for the Party: The Life of Frances Hodgson Burnett, 1849–1924* (London, 1994). On *The Secret Garden*, see also discussions by Mandy S. Morris, ' "Tha'lt be like a blush-rose when tha' grows up, my little lass": English Cultural and Gendered Identity in *The Secret Garden*', *Environment and Planning D: Society and Space*, 14 (1996), 59–78; Ann Laura Stoler, *Race and the Education of Desire: Foucault's History of Sexuality and the Colonial Order of Things* (Durham, NC, 1995), 149; E. M. Collingham, *Imperial Bodies: The Physical Experience of the Raj, c.1800–1947* (Cambridge, 2001), 98.

of British-Indian childrearing ideals and practices explored below suggests that these were to some extent common understandings among certain sectors of British society, and her widely read novels undoubtedly worked to make such ideas even more familiar still. India was almost universally seen as a risky environment for rearing British children, the biggest threats stemming from its climate and indigenous population. As was the case in both *The Secret Garden* and *A Little Princess*, the Indians children encountered on the most regular and intimate basis were the servants employed in their homes, which most familiarly took the form of a bungalow surrounded by a large enclosed compound.[5] White children's intertwined physical and mental health, morality, racial identity, and cultural development as Britons were all widely deemed jeopardized even within what was often a highly self-contained and protected setting. Few commentators felt comfortable with their staying in India long after the age of 8, and many indeed argued that they should be sent away several years earlier.

After scrutinizing the consensus view that children should leave once they had reached later childhood, this chapter explores a range of understandings concerning not only India's potential dangers but also its pleasures. Although writers had no difficulty identifying reasons why children needed to go to Britain, they might also downplay some of the subcontinent's supposed dangers and instead single out aspects of colonial life for praise and nostalgic recollections rather than as sources of anxiety. The following sections begin by considering the messages conveyed in medical discourse and prescriptive literature on colonial childcare and then move on to evaluate how British families responded to warnings about their children's well-being as a result of their early exposure to India. To what extent did practice correspond with professional advice and widespread ideals? Furthermore, what distinct perspectives on British-Indian childrearing and childhood emerge in contemporary and retrospective accounts, many of the latter dating from the post-colonial period? Lastly, how might children's subsequent metropolitan experiences have colored later memories of their early lives overseas? As this as well as later chapters argue, many British-Indians expressed misgivings about sending children to Britain because it necessitated family separations in tandem with the loss of other cherished aspects of their Indian years. Whatever their regrets, those who could afford to pay for their children's journeys to, and schooling in, Britain found the notion of

---

[5] On the colonial bungalow's spatial form and social significance, see Anthony D. King, *The Bungalow: The Production of a Global Culture* (London, 1984), 14–64; *Colonial Urban Development: Culture, Social Power, and Environment* (London, 1976), 123–55.

voluntarily keeping them in India unthinkable. Not all could partake of Britain's opportunities and sidestep India's hazards, however; as Chapter 2 examines, children whose parents were financially unable to make school years in the metropole possible faced threats to their socio-economic and racial status that many considered far more detrimental than those encountered in early life.

DEBILITY AND DEGENERATION: 'EXPERT' VOICES ON COLONIAL CHILDREN

In 1873 Sir Joseph Fayrer summarized what decades of experience in the Bengal Medical Service had taught him was common wisdom about British childrearing in India:

It has long been known to the English in India that children may be kept in that country up to 5, 6, or 7 years of age without any deterioration, physical or moral, and in the higher classes of life with probably as little, if not less, danger to life than in England; for most assuredly in some respects—as, for example, scarlatina, measles, hooping-cough [*sic*], thoracic complaints, and even dentition—they suffer less in India than in England. But after that age, unless a few hot seasons spent in the hills should enable parents to keep their children in India until a somewhat later age, to do so is always a doubtful proceeding. The child must be sent to England, or it will deteriorate physically and morally—physically, because it will grow up slight, weedy, and delicate, overprecocious it may be, and with a general constitutional feebleness not perhaps so easily defined as recognised, a something expressed not only in appearance, but in the very intonation of the voice; morally, because he learns from his surroundings much that is undesirable, and has a tendency to become deceitful and vain, indisposed to study, and to a great extent unfitted to do so, —in short, with a general tendency to deterioration, which is much to be deprecated, and can only be avoided by removal to the more bracing and healthy (moral and physical) atmosphere of Europe.[6]

Fayrer was far from alone in his pessimistic assessment of India's impact on British children. Indeed, similar and often nearly identical views pervaded writings by members of the British medical community until the 1930s. While Fayrer certainly had not been the first to warn of India's dangers for European children, his work in particular was enlisted by numerous later authors to support their own ideas about childcare in what they termed the

---

[6] Sir Joseph Fayrer, *European Child-Life in Bengal* (London, 1873), 29–30.

'tropics'.[7] Over the following decades, individual writers may have disagreed on minor points, but they never disputed the basic premises that underlay what emerged as a cumulative consensus both on the threats colonial children encountered as well as the best methods of confronting them. Despite considerable medical advances and recourse to preventive measures that greatly increased European chances of survival and good health in India, the subcontinent continued to be discussed as a site of physical and moral risk until the end of empire, particularly for children, whom many considered the most vulnerable members of colonial society.[8]

Contemporary discussions about the extent to which European adults and children could cope with India's hot climate and common diseases reflect a diverse yet interconnected set of understandings about human development, race, culture, and geography as well as the kind of imperial presence Britain hoped to secure in the region. Studies by Mark Harrison and E. M. Collingham chart how a certain degree of medical optimism that Europeans might adapt to the tropics during the later eighteenth and early nineteenth centuries gradually declined, so that by the 1840s most commentators saw India as an inherently pathogenic environment for those hoping to rule it.[9] Much could be done to mitigate India's dangers, writers continually stressed: individuals could do a great deal to prevent their own mortality or constitutional debility through paying careful attention to hygiene and leading a life of moderation, for example, just as official efforts to reform what were condemned as poor sanitary practices by Indians and to fight disease through research and eradication campaigns also might increase the hope that India could be made physically safer for both indigenous peoples and colonizers.[10] Instead of becoming more confident that Europeans might live in the subcontinent with less risk, how-

---

[7] For earlier medical writings mentioning India's risks to children, see Mark Harrison, *Climates and Constitutions: Health, Race, Environment and British Imperialism in India, 1600–1850* (New Delhi, 1999), 103, 143. Later authors invoking Fayrer's views include Joseph Ewart, 'On the Colonisation of the Sub-Himalayahs and Neilgherries. With Remarks on the Management of European Children in India', *Transactions of the Epidemiological Society of London*, 3 (1883–4), 96, 116; Edward John Tilt, *Health in India for British Women, and On the Prevention of Disease in Tropical Climates*, 4th edn. (London, 1875), 101–5; C. R. M. Green and V. B. Green-Armytage, *Birch's Management and Medical Treatment of Children in India*, 5th edn. (Calcutta, 1913), 4, 9–10.

[8] Collingham, *Imperial Bodies*, 90, draws attention to anachronisms contained in medical advice books, some of which were repeatedly reissued with little updating. One example was Sir William Moore's manual that first appeared in 1873 and reached its ninth edition free of substantial changes by 1921; Cuthbert Allan Sprawson, *Moore's Manual of Family Medicine and Hygiene for India* (London, 1921).

[9] Harrison, *Climates and Constitutions*; Collingham, *Imperial Bodies*.

[10] Several key studies include Philip D. Curtin, *Death by Migration: Europe's Encounter with the Tropical World in the Nineteenth Century* (Cambridge, 1989); David Arnold, *Colonizing the Body: State Medicine and Epidemic Diseases in Nineteenth-Century India* (Berkeley, CA, 1993); Mark Harrison, *Public Health in British India: Anglo-Indian Preventive Medicine, 1859–1914* (Cambridge, 1994).

ever, most came to view European acclimatization as either impossible or highly undesirable throughout the later imperial era. That members of the 'master race' might acquire characteristics of indigenous subject populations that would enable them not only to survive but to thrive was unthinkable, yet at the same time an omnipresent fear. Either supposedly innate and fixed racial qualities were said to prevent them from adapting to India's environment and thus necessitate returning to Europe to avoid death or serious deterioration, or else the ability to remain for long periods meant a physical alteration. If the latter occurred, they could find themselves disqualified from European status.

Pervasive anxieties about possible racial mutation for those who endured the specters of heat and disease count among the main reasons why India was not considered appropriate for permanent white settlement. Although some had hoped that the region—especially the newly established stations in the cooler, sparsely populated foothills of the Himalayas and the Nilgiris—might become home to communities of British settlers, studies by Dane Kennedy, David Arnold, and Mark Harrison show that by the mid-nineteenth century most officials firmly opposed a deliberate colonization policy.[11] Europeans might, at best, live there temporarily and possibly suffer few long-term consequences if they exercised extreme caution, but permanent residence entailed a grim future—especially if those in question spent most of their time on the hot plains. As a series of medical writers warned, Europeans who managed not to perish became progressively weaker over time due to repeated bouts of illness as well as prolonged exposure to intense sunlight and extreme temperatures. Surgeon-General Sir William Moore summarized common views in 1891, arguing that the hot climate disturbed the nervous system and caused 'the quality of the blood' to become 'deteriorated'.[12] Even if the effects were not immediately apparent, he and others claimed, their emergence was inevitable. As Joseph Ewart put it in the 1880s, 'though this generation may flourish, ultimate extinction of their progeny looms in the no distant future'; 'the degeneracy of our race', he continued, is never 'so palpably demonstrated as in our children'.[13] 'The profound modification in the European system produced by

[11] Dane Kennedy, *The Magic Mountains: Hill Stations and the British Raj* (Berkeley, CA, 1996), 149–56; David Arnold, 'White Colonization and Labour in Nineteenth-Century India', *Journal of Imperial and Commonwealth History*, 9/2 (1983), 133–58; Harrison, *Climates and Constitutions*.

[12] Sir William Moore, 'Is the Colonisation of Tropical Africa by Europeans Possible?', *Transactions of the Epidemiological Society of London*, 10 (1890–1), 34; for similar views, see G. Montagu Harston, *The Care and Treatment of European Children in the Tropics* (London, 1912), 18–19.

[13] Ewart, 'On the Colonisation', 117, 98. Nearly identical statements later appeared in 'J. P.', *The Care of Infants in India*, 6th edn. (London, 1907), 88.

prolonged heat I regard as hereditarily transmissible', Moore concluded.[14] Lamarckian concepts of human evolution clearly died a slow death in many scientific circles, with physicians linked to the British-Indian community continuing to find them relevant well into the twentieth century.[15]

As a result of inheriting tropically acquired debilities, such writers concluded, Europeans who attempted to remain permanently in India or other 'hot climates' (particularly more recently established colonies in East and Central Africa) were fated to 'die out' by the third generation.[16] Medical authorities remained confident of these claims as late as the 1930s, when Dr G. W. Bray asserted that 'the descendants of early settlers that have survived are never as alert or vigorous as their forefathers in mental and social—as well as physical—characteristics'; as a result, 'the European cannot produce in tropical regions more than three generations of true European blood, as from then on sterility is observed'.[17] Repeated references to 'blood deterioration' and other symptoms of bodily change were equated, whether implicitly or explicitly, with racial decline—not only through physical decay and impending sterility but often racial mixing as well. Moore, for instance, firmly believed that Europeans could only survive in India across the generations via 'an infusion of native blood'.[18] As Dane Kennedy persuasively concludes, 'the specter of degeneration lay less in the threat of physical extinction than in the prospect of miscegenation and the loss of racial identity ... the risks ... precluded the possibility of a European settler population's surviving over several generations *as* Europeans'.[19] The hostile tone pervading medical discussions about racial adaptation via altered blood and visible bodily features—as Andrew Balfour argued in 1921, 'the skin of the European long resident in the tropics undoubtedly darkens ... his descendants tend, though not invariably, to have dark skins'—suggests that many considered extinction as Europeans preferable to survival as mixed-race persons, or those who strongly resembled them.[20]

[14] Moore, 'Is the Colonisation?', 35.

[15] L. J. Jordanova, *Lamarck* (Oxford, 1984), 105–11; Nancy Stepan, *The Idea of Race in Science: Great Britain, 1800–1960* (London, 1982); Peter J. Bowler, *Evolution: The History of an Idea*, rev. edn. (Berkeley, CA, 1983, 1989), 257–68, 274, 285.

[16] David N. Livingstone, 'Human Acclimatization: Perspectives on a Contested Field of Inquiry in Science, Medicine, and Geography', *History of Science*, 25 (1987), 359–94.

[17] Dr G. W. Bray, in Dr A. R. Neligan et al., 'Discussion on the Adaptation of European Women and Children to Tropical Climates', *Proceedings of the Royal Society of Medicine*, 24, Part 2 (1931), 1327–8; see also Sir Aldo Castellani, *Climate and Acclimatization: Some Notes and Observations* (London, 1931), 61, 51.

[18] Moore, 'Is the Colonisation?', 30.

[19] Kennedy, *Magic Mountains*, 33. See also Harrison, *Climates and Constitutions*, 19, 125; Collingham, *Imperial Bodies*, 81, 177–8.

[20] Andrew Balfour, 'Personal Hygiene in the Tropics and Minor Tropical Sanitation', in W. Byam and R. G. Archibald (eds.), *The Practice of Medicine in the Tropics by Many Authorities*, Vol. I (London, 1921), 6.

Given these purported consequences of prolonged residence and permanent settlement and Britain's unwillingness to abandon its presence in a 'hot climate' like India, those writing of the dangers it posed to the colonizers needed to pinpoint ways to mitigate its worst aspects if they were to be taken at all seriously. Time and again they singled out children as those most at risk, but since the presence of British husbands and wives in an imperial arena thousands of miles from the metropole made birth and early childhood in India inevitable many adopted a more constructive approach in suggesting ways to protect children from danger. Sending them away from India at a sufficiently early age was seen as the key to preserving their European attributes that would otherwise deteriorate over time, culminating in their becoming permanent residents whose descendants were doomed to die out. Until they went, however—and provided they *did* ultimately leave before it was 'too late'—many medical commentators assured parents that their offspring might remain relatively safe for their first years if carefully guarded against environmental hazards.

Some advice provided by physicians and others publishing similar childrearing manuals applied to children of all ages and overlapped with recommendations made to adults. Child mortality and morbidity could be reduced, they stressed, given hygienic surroundings, an appropriate diet, and protection from disease-carrying insects and the sun (through special clothing, mosquito nets, staying indoors during the hours of strongest exposure and wearing sun helmets, called sola topis, while outdoors). Similarly, India's ill effects might be tempered if children (as well as adults) spent intervals at the cooler hill stations perceived as healthier than the plains[21] (Illustrations 2 and 9). In other respects, however, views about colonial childrearing were both highly age-specific and spelled out the limits of preventive mechanisms to ensure well-being. While parents could take many precautions to protect children from illnesses, many writers emphasized the range of factors outside their control and whose dangers increased as children grew older. These included both the impact of India's climate as well as contacts with its indigenous population—both of which were, unsurprisingly, difficult to evade in the subcontinent.

Although well aware that those under 5 were far more likely to die in India than were older children, medical writers somewhat incongruously asserted that they were safest during these years.[22] Indeed, as Fayrer had noted and others echoed, some found the relative lack of scarlet fever, diphtheria, tuberculosis, and whooping cough—all common causes of young children's deaths in

---

[21] Joseph Ewart, *Goodeve's Hints for the General Management of Children in India in the Absence of Professional Advice*, 6th edn. (Calcutta, 1872), 28.

[22] On child mortality rates, see Fayrer, *European Child-Life*, 8.

Britain—a reason for optimism about infancy and early childhood in India.[23] The first years of tropical residence were considered the healthiest but were rapidly followed by exhaustion as heat caused both blood and the nervous system to deteriorate.[24] Initial heat-induced 'stimulation', many argued, made children mature too quickly, becoming 'weedy'—with grievous results.[25] Drawing upon evolutionary recapitulation theories that highlighted the importance of infant, child, and adolescent development to assert that the development of a race was mirrored in the maturing of an individual, commentators suggested that European children raised in the tropics could pass through stages of growth too rapidly and thus fail fully to attain capacities deemed specific to the highly evolved Caucasian.[26] In consequence, their development was arrested at a lower level closer to that reached by colonized peoples condemned as physically and mentally subordinate by virtue of race—thus setting in motion the degeneration they subsequently bequeathed to their descendants.

Children thus purportedly faced increasing risks after infancy, but parents were repeatedly assured that they might keep them in India until they were between 5 and 8 (or, alternatively, as late as 10) without severe consequences stemming from accelerated development. European children in India were regularly described in words similar to Fayrer's—'slight, weedy, and delicate, overprecocious'—but writers often believed them able to escape the subcontinent's most harmful effects as long as they were sent to temperate climates well before adolescence.[27] Their reasoning reflects ideas most closely associated with the internationally renowned American scholar G. Stanley Hall, whose *fin de siècle* work envisioned adolescence as the period when humans passed from the childhood state—at which the stage of development was believed to resemble that attained by mature primates and 'savages'—to the more highly evolved state characterizing 'civilized' adults. 'The child comes from and harks back to a remoter past', he asserted, whereas in the adolescent 'the later acquisitions of the race slowly become prepotent . . . the whole future of life depends on how the new powers . . . are husbanded and directed.' Meanwhile,

---

[23] Green and Green-Armytage, *Birch's Management*, 2–4, 7–8; Dr A. R. Neligan, Sir Aldo Castellani, and Bray in Neligan et al., 'Discussion on the Adaptation', 1317–18, 1321, 1328.

[24] Moore, 'Constitutional Requirements', 40; 'Is the Colonisation?', 34–5; Green and Green-Armytage, *Birch's Management*, 10–12, 111.

[25] Ewart, 'On the Colonisation', 116; Balfour, 'Personal Hygiene', 5; Neligan, in Neligan et al., 'Discussion on the Adaptation', 1316. See also Kennedy's discussion in *Magic Mountains*, 130–2.

[26] Stephen J. Gould, *Ontogeny and Phylogeny* (Cambridge, MA, 1977); Gould, *The Mismeasure of Man* (New York, 1981); Stepan, *Idea of Race in Science*; John R. Morss, *The Biologising of Childhood: Developmental Psychology and the Darwinian Myth* (Hove, East Sussex, 1990), 43–8.

[27] Neligan, in Neligan et al., 'Discussion on the Adaptation', 1317–19.

however, 'everything is plastic', and young persons could easily travel down roads that failed to lead to their full potential.[28] For Europeans seen to have most to lose, tropical environments impeding these acquisitions during puberty jeopardized their ability to serve as worthy representatives of the colonizing and superior white race.

While endlessly reiterated anxieties surrounding precocity took many forms, the early onset of puberty concerned medical writers most. Sir Aldo Castellani confidently asserted in the early 1930s that 'after the age of 8, 9, or 10 years, European children, especially boys, do not do well in the tropics, the nervous system suffering principally, and precociousness in sexual matters being of common occurrence'.[29] Yet most others focused primarily on older girls and consistently asserted that menstruation began at an earlier age in British girls in the tropics than in those residing in temperate regions. As a result of the climate's 'stimulating effects', Grace MacKinnon—formerly the medical superintendent of a hospital in Patna—calculated the average age of menarche among Europeans in temperate climates to be 14 or 15 while in India for 'English girls and Eurasians it is 13 to 14, the Eurasian however, tending to be a little earlier than the English'. 'Natives of Madras', meanwhile, began menstruating at 12–13, and 'natives of North India' at 11–14.[30] Although she believed climate a less significant factor than race, her views suggest the suspicion that physical distinctions between races narrowed among those living in the tropics. MacKinnon indicatively saw little difference between English and mixed-race girls in India and implied that in this respect they physically resembled one another more than they did girls in Europe; moreover, both groups together occupied an intermediary position between European girls in Europe and Indians.

The supposed tendency for girls in India—whether English, Eurasian, or Indian—to reach sexual maturity earlier than their counterparts from, and in, Europe was a central aspect of wider discussions of degeneration in hot climates that contemplated changes to Europeans' reproductive capacities and 'nervous systems' concomitantly. Dr Andrew Balfour linked these repercussions of colonial life when asserting that 'both in the male and female there is greater generative vigour in the tropics, but excess in venery is more speedily followed by exhaustion and neurasthenia than is the case in temperate

[28] G. Stanley Hall, *Adolescence: Its Psychology and Its Relation to Physiology, Anthropology, Sociology, Sex, Crime, Religion and Education*, 2 vols. (New York, 1904), i. pp. xiii, xv; see also 31.

[29] Castellani, in Neligan et al., 'Discussion on the Adaptation', 1322.

[30] Grace MacKinnon, 'Diseases of Women in the Tropics', in Byam and Archibald (eds.), *Practice of Medicine*, iii. 2474; see also Fayrer, *European Child-Life*, 21; Castellani, *Climate and Acclimatization*, 59–61; Balfour, Neligan, and Castellani, in Neligan et al., 'Discussion on the Adaptation', 1316, 1320.

climates'.[31] 'Tropical neurasthenia'—a continually discussed but often vaguely defined condition whose symptoms might include extreme irritability, psychological instability, mental breakdown, and a 'lack of emotional control', as MacKinnon phrased it—connoted a deviation from acceptable standards of fitness and propriety for the colonial ruling group.[32] 'Exhaustion', meanwhile, implied an impaired reproductive capacity, which in women became manifest in difficult pregnancies and lactation along with frequent miscarriages.[33] Sterility loomed as the most extreme form of white tropical exhaustion that preoccupied pessimists who believed Europeans would die out because unable to acclimatize to tropical life. The most effective means of preventing these dire outcomes was for members of the colonial community periodically to visit temperate climates, including hill stations in India but more importantly by taking furloughs in Britain. Leaving older children and adolescents behind in the metropole, in short, nipped their potential sexual precocity and its undesirable long-term ramifications in the bud, removing them from the colonial site of danger during the years when they were deemed most physically impressionable.

Medical commentary and other forms of prescriptive literature on colonial childrearing, however, did not restrict warnings about India to the effects of its climate and diseases on the body. Indeed, children's mental, moral, and physical development were inseparable in the eyes of physicians and lay writers alike, and were seen to stem as much from India's geography as from detrimental human interactions. As R. S. Mair put it in his 1874 *Medical Guide for Anglo-Indians*, 'the child commonly grows up delicate, pale and flabby, comparatively feeble in mind and body; often timid and unstable, and but seldom able to compete on equal terms, either physically or mentally, with those who have been brought up in England'. The causes of their multiple bodily and character weaknesses he considered 'obvious': '1st, The unquestionably enervating, and generally deteriorating effect of constant exposure to a high temperature. 2nd, The unavoidable contact with native servants'.[34] For Mair as well as countless other writers throughout the late imperial era, the social and physical threats children faced in India converged in the figure of the Indian domestic servant.

[31] Balfour, 'Personal Hygiene', 5.

[32] MacKinnon, 'Diseases of Women', 2475.

[33] Castellani, in Neligan et al., 'Discussion on the Adaptation', 1327; MacKinnon, 'Diseases of Women', 2471–2. See also Ann Laura Stoler, *Carnal Knowledge and Imperial Power: Race and the Intimate in Colonial Rule* (Berkeley, CA, 2002), 73.

[34] R. S. Mair, *Medical Guide for Anglo-Indians* (London, 1874), 127–8.

Large retinues of household staff are a well-known aspect of British-Indian culture, and it was common for families in the middle and upper colonial sectors to employ between ten and twenty Indians, if not more, in their homes[35] (Illustrations 3 and 4). Hiring substantial numbers of servants allowed the better-off to distinguish themselves not only from most of those they ruled but also from Europeans (and Anglo-Indians) who possessed less wealth and status; many who did so also claimed it necessary because Indian caste restrictions on performing specific types of work meant that a large staff was needed to complete the range of tasks employers demanded.[36] The comparatively low cost of Indian labor also made employing a number of retainers possible even for the less affluent, enabling a lifestyle drastically different than Britons of similar means in the metropole could achieve—a topic considered further in Chapter 5. The spectacle and luxury of the well-staffed domestic sphere was perceived to have its drawbacks, however, as it entailed exposing most aspects of home life to the gaze and potentially harmful influence of the colonized. As Raleigh Trevelyan wrote of his childhood with his parents in Kashmir in the 1920s, 'we seemed never to be *alone*'.[37] Since the colonial environment and its indigenous peoples were so commonly depicted by the British as disease-ridden, overtly lascivious, and conducive to bodily illness as well as immorality for Europeans in contact with them, it is unsurprising that many observers found the ubiquitous practice of employing numerous Indians to live and work in such close proximity to British families a mixed blessing.[38] By virtue of their constant presence in the family circle, Indian servants epitomized racial and cultural difference for many Britons, particularly women and children who often had

[35] Collingham, *Imperial Bodies*; Margaret MacMillan, *Women of the Raj* (London, 1988); Mary A. Procida, *Married to the Empire: Gender, Politics, and Imperialism in India, 1883–1947* (Manchester, 2002), 66, 81–105.

[36] For insight into the concept of British imperial rule as parade and spectacle, see Bernard Cohn, 'Representing Authority in Victorian India', in Eric Hobsbawm and Terence Ranger (eds.), *The Invention of Tradition* (Cambridge, 1983), 165–209; David Cannadine, *Ornamentalism: How the British Saw Their Empire* (London, 2001). On shifting ideas about the Indian caste system, see Nicholas B. Dirks, *Castes of Mind: Colonialism and the Making of Modern India* (Princeton, NJ, 2001).

[37] Raleigh Trevelyan, *The Golden Oriole: A 200-Year History of an English Family in India* (New York, 1987), 5.

[38] Among many excellent studies analysing colonizers' attitudes about and attempts to regulate indigenous peoples' health, sanitation, and sexuality and segregate 'unhealthy' subject peoples from 'vulnerable' European communities, see Philip Curtin, 'Medical Knowledge and Urban Planning in Tropical Africa', *American Historical Review*, 90/3 (1985), 594–613; John W. Cell, 'Anglo-Indian Medical Theory and the Origins of Segregation in West Africa', *American Historical Review*, 91/2 (1986), 307–35; David Arnold (ed.), *Imperial Medicine and Indigenous Societies* (Manchester, 1988); Arnold, *Colonizing the Body*; Kennedy, *Magic Mountains*; Kenneth Ballhatchet, *Race, Sex and Class Under the Raj: Imperial Attitudes and Policies and Their Critics, 1793–1905* (New York, 1980); Philippa Levine, 'Venereal Disease, Prostitution, and the Politics of Empire: The Case of British India', *Journal of the History of Sexuality*, 4/4 (1994), 579–602; Sander L. Gilman, *Difference and Pathology: Stereotypes of Sexuality, Race, and Madness* (Ithaca, NY, 1985).

limited contact with other colonized groups. As such, they played central roles in literature about British-Indian medical issues, housekeeping, and childrearing, personifying the perceived dangers of daily life in the subcontinent.

Indians employed in British homes, especially female nursemaids (ayahs) and wetnurses (dais), were repeatedly accused of enhancing the bodily risks children already faced from the climate and regional diseases. Bungalows inhabited by the family, Harston's handbook stressed in 1912, should be situated at least half a mile from any Indian homes to decrease the possibility that 'infected natives' would transmit their own ailments to British offspring. Indians seemed as much a threat as the insects that transmitted dengue fever, he implied, since 'in epidemic times children should be kept from frequenting native houses, and be protected as much as possible from mosquitoes'.[39] Kate Platt's *The Home and Health in India and the Tropical Colonies* dating from 1923 similarly outlined measures for protecting and distancing the bungalow from the unsanitary 'low standards' prevailing in the servants' quarters.[40] Alongside their poor hygiene, servants in direct contact with their employers' children were perceived to jeopardize their health through a combination of what another writer labelled 'ignorance, prejudice, and carelessness'.[41] Potentially fatal ailments including diarrhoea, dysentery, and cholera were indeed preventable, commentators insisted, if servants handled food preparation and feeding differently. Milk and water in particular needed to be boiled and carefully stored, but instead 'natives [were] in the habit of diluting the milk with water, which may have been contaminated by the cholera bacillus', as Harston put it. In reciting a litany of hazards he lingered over a tirade that linked the 'abomination' of rice-eating—'that bane of tropical dietary, as far as European children are concerned'—to diarrhoea:

[Native] nurses are in the habit of living mainly upon rice themselves, and they naturally conclude that what is good for their own children must necessarily be good for the European child . . . It enters into the soup, which is thickened with congee water; . . . the native nurse, unless closely watched, will dilute the milk with the same abomination . . . and will often give the child a spoonful or two of soft rice and congee water out of her own bowl of food.[42]

Alongside opting for contentious feeding practices (whether deliberately or unknowingly), ayahs as well as dais also were said to try to put their charges to sleep using opium—another childcare method frowned upon for cultural rea-

---

[39] Harston, *Care and Treatment*, 65, 100.
[40] Kate Platt, *The Home and Health in India and the Tropical Colonies* (London, 1923), 18, 20–1.
[41] 'J. P.', *Care of Infants*, 54.
[42] Harston, *Care and Treatment*, 121, 151–2.

sons even when it did not commonly result in children's death or long-term debility.[43]

Indian servants in British households, including the majority whose duties did not center on childcare, caused concern not only for their effect on children's bodies, however; they were feared as a source of negative cultural influence as much as they were castigated for poor sanitation and carelessness. Moreover, just as many medical writings saw India's climate as having an increasingly detrimental effect as children grew older, so too did commentators consider intimate exposure to indigenous society and customs to become more dangerous as children matured and grew more impressionable. Kate Platt's manual, for instance, admitted that 'the Indian ayah has many good points; she surrounds her charges with an atmosphere of love and devotion and has infinite patience', but quickly moved on to warn her readers that 'too much should not be expected of her. Her standard of truth and sincerity . . . differs from ours as much as her standard of personal cleanliness. The training in obedience, straightforwardness, and self-control, so essential to a child in the earliest years of life, is not to be obtained from her.'[44] Outside Britain, children thus could fail to acquire the character attributes that would qualify them as legitimate representatives of the 'ruling race', adopting habits and desires that British adults condemned in their place. Servants' overindulgence made children demanding authority figures in ways deemed inappropriate for those whose age meant they should be submissive, orderly, and obedient themselves. As Flora Annie Steel and Grace Gardiner stressed in their long-popular and con-tinually reissued *The Complete Indian Housekeeper and Cook*, lack of discipline lay at the heart of common misbehavior. 'It is no unusual thing', they noted,

to see an English child eating his dinner off the floor, with his hands full of toys, while a posse of devoted attendants distract his attention, and the *ayah* feeds him with spoon-fuls of *pish-pash*. Appetite is no doubt variable in Anglo-Indian children, but it is pos-sible that a little more pomp and circumstance, and a wholesome conviction that food is not forthcoming except *at* meal-times, would induce Sonny or Missy Baba to treat dinner with graver circumspection. Where, save in India, do we find sturdy little tots of four and five still taking their bottles and refusing to go to sleep without a lullaby?[45]

Servants' submissiveness not only created children who resembled the fic-tional Mary Lennox—'self-indulgent and capricious tyrant[s] on a small scale',

[43] Platt, *Home and Health*, 128. Collingham's work charts how opium use, formerly more acceptable among Britons in India, increasingly became frowned upon as the nineteenth century progressed. Anxieties that servants would give children opium were well entrenched by the 1850s. Collingham, *Imperial Bodies*, 31, 96.

[44] Platt, *Home and Health*, 138.

[45] F. A. Steel and G. Gardiner, *The Complete Indian Housekeeper and Cook* (1888; repr. London, 1917), 87.

as Edmund Hull put it in his 1871 handbook for Europeans in India—but also caused children to develop strong affection for them that many writers considered equally problematic.[46] The attraction children could have for their Indian caretakers resembled the affinity that could develop in middle- and upper-class families elsewhere as well, a theme that Leonore Davidoff, Ann Stoler, and other scholars have explored in metropolitan British and other colonial contexts. In Victorian Britain, Davidoff argues, working-class nurses and maids fulfilled nearly all the daily requirements of their employers' offspring below school age. Young children often had little informal contact with either parent as they were fed, bathed, and disciplined by servants. This relationship provided an early and intimate exposure to working-class mores, and it was not uncommon for adults writing about their childhood to express a lingering love for the women with whom they had once spent the majority of their time. Contacts with working-class female servants allowed a partial view of the habits and living conditions of their social and economic inferiors, 'windows . . . into the outside world' which did not win parental approval.[47]

Colonial conditions did not, however, mirror those prevalent in Britain. In addition to class divisions between servants and the families employing them, understandings of racial, caste, and religious difference entailed further distinctions. British commentators frequently cited such factors as evidence of the supposedly unbridgeable gap between ruler and ruled during the late imperial era, but children's early exposure to Indians and the delight they seemed to take in these relationships was feared to undermine the divide. Developing affection for, and learning habits from, Indian servants during a time when they were ideally meant to inculcate characteristics that reinforced a superior status was repeatedly singled out as one of the most contemptible results of colonial childhood.[48] As Hull warned his readers, 'by being constantly with native servants, children pick up the "ways" of those who often belong to all but the lowest class of natives. Human nature is highly imitative; child nature especially so; the tendency being always to copy what is bad than what is good'.[49] Attitudes were clearly contradictory: signs of egalitarianism between children and servants were harshly condemned, but so too were instances of children's tyran-

---

[46] Edmund C. P. Hull, *The European in India; or, Anglo-India's Vade Mecum* (London, 1871), 135.

[47] Leonore Davidoff, 'Class and Gender in Victorian England: The Diaries of Hannah Cullwick and A. J. Munby', in *Worlds Between: Historical Perspectives on Gender and Class* (New York, 1995), 109–12; quote taken from 112. See also Leonore Davidoff, Megan Doolittle, Janet Fink, and Katherine Holden, *The Family Story: Blood, Contract and Intimacy, 1830–1960* (London, 1999), ch. 6; Peter Stallybrass and Allon White, *The Politics and Poetics of Transgression* (Ithaca, NY, 1986), 149–70.

[48] See Stoler's discussions in *Carnal Knowledge*, especially ch. 5, and *Race and the Education of Desire*, 99, 147, 149, 164.

[49] Hull, *European in India*, 135.

nical behavior that stemmed from an empowered standing. Whichever the case, corruption was the outcome. Maud Diver, an Edwardian-era novelist and observer of British-Indian society, similarly felt that children became more 'apt to suffer harm in body and mind' once they became more impressionable. 'It is less easy to keep the eager, all-observant little minds fearlessly upright in an atmosphere of petty thefts and lies, such as natives look upon as mere common-sense', she asserted; staying in India too long set them back considerably in 'the race of life'.[50]

One of children's main conduits into Indian customs as practiced by family servants came through learning Indian languages as a result of spending so much time in the company of native speakers. Young children's ability to understand and converse in 'Hindustani' or other tongues with more ease than English was both feared and detested by many authors of prescriptive childrearing texts. Just as India was believed to have undesirable effects on children's bodies that made them 'grow too fast' physically, cultural interactions with Indians were another cause of the 'precocity' much deplored in British colonial children. Hull lamented their 'premature experience of mastery' in their dealings with Indians and felt the vernacular languages they learned caused them to 'lose much of the innocence of childhood', since 'the language of the vulgar in India is corrupt, and interspersed with obscenity to an extent almost incredible'.[51] Platt similarly saw colonial children as typically devoid of 'the naturalness of childhood', their precocity owing much to their ability to understand Indian conversations at home. 'The Indians themselves live very near to nature, and the events of birth, marriage, and death, as well as the primitive emotions, are discussed openly and without reticence', she complained, adding that 'their gossip about the doings of their sahibs and mem-sahibs . . . are not conducive to the moral welfare of children'.[52]

Some medical explanations of why girls supposedly reached puberty earlier in India linked morally corrupting servants with the physically corrupting effects of a hot climate. In Grace MacKinnon's discussion of the ages of menarche among girls in India, she noted the views of other practitioners who felt that 'certain mental states can hasten the oncoming of menstruation' and that 'the early appearance of menstruation in Indian girls was largely due to their unwholesome early surroundings and their precocious knowledge of sexual matters'.[53] As Louise Jackson suggests in her work on sexually abused girls in

---

[50] Maud Diver, *The Englishwoman in India* (Edinburgh, 1909), 42–4.
[51] Hull, *European in India*, 135–6; also Tilt, *Health in India*, 106.
[52] Platt, *Home and Health*, 139, 142.
[53] MacKinnon, 'Diseases of Women', 2474.

Victorian England, 'precocity' was a term used in lieu of child sexuality and 'suggested abnormal and premature development; it indicated that not all children were sexual but that the harmful acquisition of sexual knowledge could impede natural growth and development'.[54] Conceptualizations of childhood as a time of innocence that took form during the Enlightenment and became increasingly entrenched thereafter had as their antithesis the child stamped as 'corrupted', 'fallen', or simply 'old beyond their years'.[55] British children whom India's climate and general 'unwholesomeness' predisposed to a mutually constitutive sexual maturity and knowledge of immorality counted among those who could, it was feared, undercut these childhood ideals, and needed to be saved from these multiple hazards with racial implications.

Knowledge and regular use of Indian languages spoken by those deemed racial and social inferiors not only led to cultural corruption and precocity, commentators warned; it also inhibited children from perfecting their mother tongue.[56] Under such inauspicious conditions, the English children learned was feared to be that which was pejoratively termed 'chi-chi': the accent and turns of phrase said to be characteristic of those of mixed European and Indian ancestry as well as Indians who spoke English as a second language. Hull castigated those parents who 'point with pride to Johnny's or Charley's progress in Tamil or Hindustani' on these grounds, proposing instead that it was 'far better to keep them totally in ignorance of so muddy a stream . . . The nasal twang and shrill unmusical tone of voice so generally found in native women of the lower orders give a most unpleasing peculiarity of tone and pronunciation, often noticed in Anglo-Indian children.'[57]

Flawed English could originate either from speaking mainly Indian languages or 'broken English' with Indians, or if parents employed European or mixed-race nursemaids who had been brought up and educated at schools in India. Both Steel and Gardiner in the 1880s and Platt in the 1920s told readers of the potential hazards awaiting their children under such circumstances, the former arguing that 'though some young girls from the Sanawar and Mayo

---

[54] Louise A. Jackson, *Child Sexual Abuse in Victorian England* (London, 2000), 86; see also 17, 56–8, 95, 136.

[55] Anne Higonnet, *Pictures of Innocence: The History and Crisis of Ideal Childhood* (London, 1998); Peter Coveney, *The Image of Childhood, the Individual and Society: A Study of the Theme in English Literature*, rev. edn. (Harmondsworth, 1967); Hugh Cunningham, *Children and Childhood in Western Society Since 1500* (London, 1995).

[56] Discussions of language and its perceived relationship to national identity include Benedict Anderson, *Imagined Communities: Reflections on the Origin and Spread of Nationalism*, rev. edn. (London, 1991); Stoler, *Carnal Knowledge*, ch. 5; Brian Doyle, *English and Englishness* (London, 1989); Robert Colls, *Identity of England* (Oxford, 2002), 286–91, 351–2, 360–1.

[57] Hull, *European in India*, 136.

schools have proved quite satisfactory, the general run of girls brought up in India have a strong *cheechee* accent, and are lazy, careless, and independent'.[58] Platt expressed almost identical views nearly fifty years later, suggesting either direct borrowing from what had long been the paradigmatic colonial house-keeping manual or unchanged social and racial attitudes, but quite probably both:

A girl born and bred in India, and brought up in an institution or orphanage, may make a very satisfactory nurse, if well supervised. Some of these are of pure English extraction and some are of mixed parentage. To both the objection of accent applies, for the Eurasian accent is very infectious and small children quickly adopt it.[59]

Debility and falling short of 'English' qualities might thus derive just as much from 'infectious' social contacts as from the hot climate and disease. Significantly, for some commentators 'infectious' accents could just as readily be transmitted by poorer members of the European community 'born and bred' in India and persons of mixed descent as by 'natives'. Chapter 2 further explores how a 'chi-chi' accent served as one of the key signifiers of class, cultural, and ultimately racial identity, placing the child within a nebulous intermediate category—encompassing 'domiciled', less-affluent Europeans and Anglo-Indians—between colonizers and colonized.

Such adamant convictions about India's many perils for children of the colonizing community made barriers to these diverse forms of infection considered essential. Writers encouraged mothers to find a European nanny or governess—preferably one who had not been 'born and bred in India'—to assist with childcare, since they were believed to provide a more regimented as well as hygienic environment along with greater exposure to metropolitan British 'ways' than children would receive from Indians, mixed-race, or domiciled European servants.[60] Imported nannies and governesses were difficult to obtain in India, however; demand exceeded supply, and they received much higher salaries than did Indian servants.[61] Employing these women was one marker of a family's social standing and wealth and was beyond the means of many British-Indians. Regardless of their ability to employ white child-minders, however, medical and social commentators considered the active

---

[58] Steel and Gardiner, *Complete Indian Housekeeper*, 166.

[59] Platt, *Home and Health*, 137.

[60] Steel and Gardiner, *Complete Indian Housekeeper*, 164; 'J. P', *Care of Infants*, 54; Platt, *Home and Health*, 138.

[61] Some families hired nannies in Britain and paid their passages to India, an even more costly option. See BLARS, Z186/14 and Z186/15, Evelyn Chaldecott to Mrs Cochrane Forster, 27 Jan. 1915; OIOC, MSS Eur C176/19, Annette Beveridge to Henry Beveridge, 19 May 1886.

participation of mothers themselves to be essential for proper childrearing (fathers' domestic roles, such as they might be, never entered their discussions). Yet widespread perceptions of their unwillingness to give adequate attention to their children's needs made memsahibs some of the most criticized figures in this genre of writing. White women's primary roles in the colonies, as Stoler and other scholars have outlined, included not only bearing white children but also preserving the physical and moral well-being of their families, and many were accused of falling far short of these domestic ideals.[62]

Prescriptive literature demanded a high level of maternal vigilance both over their children as well as the Indians employed to look after the family. Steel and Gardiner epitomized the attitude that 'no one can take the mother's place, as regards the loving and constant watchful care of her little ones'.[63] Mothers were called upon to ensure that the household was as hygienic as possible through constantly policing Indians deemed prone to 'low standards' and taking many sanitation procedures into their own hands. Harston's diatribe against ayahs who fed children rice and contaminated beverages noted above made it clear that mothers bore the ultimate responsibility for children's welfare. 'Lest it should be thought that the writer is prejudiced against native nurses', he stressed that 'it is only on account of imperfect supervision usually accorded [them] by mothers in the tropics, that such frequent warnings are necessary'.[64] Some writers even attributed many instances of child mortality to mothers' failings. In 1913 the authors of one manual went so far as to tell readers that 'whether your child is to live or to die in your far-off home . . . lies largely in your own hands'.[65] Steel and Gardiner tried to convince women to nurse their own infants if they were able (rather than choosing either a wetnurse or bottle feeding) since 'the cause of half the deaths of young babies and the delicacy of many who survive, is the growing objection of mothers to nursing their children, "they seem to consider it a trouble" ', and prioritizing 'selfish and social demands on their time' instead.[66] Platt similarly argued that 'it is the duty as well as the privilege of every mother to feed her own child', but if 'Indian

---

[62] Stoler, *Carnal Knowledge*, ch. 3; *Race and the Education of Desire*, 135, 140, 154; Margaret Strobel, *European Women and the Second British Empire* (Bloomington, IN, 1991); Nupur Chaudhuri, 'Memsahibs and Motherhood in Nineteenth-Century India', *Victorian Studies*, 31/4 (1988), 517–35. On metropolitan contexts, see Anna Davin, 'Imperialism and Motherhood', *History Workshop Journal*, 5 (1978), 9–65.

[63] Steel and Gardiner, *Complete Indian Housekeeper*, 175.

[64] Harston, *Care and Treatment*, 152–3.

[65] Green and Green-Armytage, *Birch's Management*, 5.

[66] Steel and Gardiner, *Complete Indian Housekeeper*, 164; see also Mair, *Medical Guide*, 6; 'J. P.', *Care of Infants*, 54.

foster-mothers' became necessary for women unable to breastfeed they 'need continual supervision'.[67]

Women who neglected their children and failed to oversee the Indians who looked after many of their needs hurt themselves as well as their offspring, writers warned. A writer in the early 1930s claimed that the psychological damage European women experienced in hot climates was aggravated by 'the evil trinity of late nights, alcohol and ennui' that they should sidestep by substituting these with childcare activities.[68] Inept maternal behavior not only left children with those believed to provide inappropriate sexual and cultural knowledge, as Platt had suggested, but women's social activities away from home might in and of themselves lead to transgressions that would then be conveyed to their children through servants' 'gossip about the doings of their sahibs and mem-sahibs'. In short, mothers' 'neglect' not only left children more susceptible to illness and unsavory servants' talk but also might provide additional material to be imparted in lurid tales that harmed their 'moral welfare'.

COMPARING PRESCRIPTION AND PRACTICE: FAMILY RENDITIONS OF CHILDREARING AND CHILDHOOD

In medical and housekeeping texts on British-Indian childrearing, mothers were commonly condemned as a weak link accentuating the already high level of risk their vulnerable children faced in problematic climatic and cultural surroundings. None the less, memsahibs' attitudes and behavior were in fact what largely determined daily domestic routines. How closely did their understandings, priorities, and practices correspond with the overwhelmingly dire images contained within the texts discussed above? Moreover, how did those who underwent a colonial upbringing evaluate its effects? The following pages consider the limitations of prescriptive texts as a tool of analysis by exploring how participants' own renditions of childrearing and childhood work both to uphold as well as contradict such portrayals. While the meanings attributed to growing up in British India derived in part from ideas about the region's potential dangers for white children, these alternate with depictions of its harmless and enriching pleasures highly valued by those who experienced them.

No absolute division separates the ideas conveyed in prescriptive writings from depictions of personal experiences in India. Medical commentary and

---

[67] Platt, *Home and Health*, 82, 84.
[68] Bray, in Neligan et al., 'Discussion on the Adaptation', 1332.

other published childcare guidelines worked in a symbiotic relationship with private renditions of raising British children in India, largely because many of the experiences and understandings of 'experts' overlapped with those of their readers. Physicians penning such texts normally had spent at least part of their careers in India and commonly enlisted this to enhance the authority of their views, while other commentators from outside the medical profession—Steel, Gardiner, and Diver among them—also had lived in India for long periods.[69] Moreover, such writers had imbibed the social and cultural attitudes of British-Indian society that surpassed formal medical expertise; few physicians attempted to 'prove' their assertions about India's effects on children and instead considered their statements to be colonial common sense. Terminology found in most prescriptive texts was typically free of scientific precision and overlapped with lay descriptions of children's condition and the threats they encountered. Medical experts continually proclaimed European children in India to be 'pale, flabby, and have an unhealthy appearance'; 'slight, weedy, and delicate'; 'listless'; and lacking 'the all-round physiological tone, physical robustness, muscular rotundity, hardness, plumpness, and rosy complexions of children of the same class in this country [Britain]'. Vaguer still were views that children simply indicated 'a certain something wanting' or 'a general constitutional feebleness not perhaps so easily defined as recognised'.[70]

Such comments closely resembled those written in both the colonial and post-colonial periods by those observing either their own or other British-Indian children. 'Pale' was how children often appeared in the hot plains regions, while time at a hill station or going to Britain made them 'strong' with red, rosy cheeks. In the 1880s Annette Beveridge described her young son, Herman, as 'much better and rosy already' several days after coming to Darjeeling from Calcutta, while upon taking her children back to England she told her husband Henry how 'they have never looked half so well. They have firm cheeks and are really robust looking'—unlike 'the poor Calcutta children'.[71] Near the turn of

---

[69] These writers' professional links to India are indicated on the frontispieces of their works cited above. Among others, Fayrer had long been in the Bengal Medical Service and became personal surgeon to Viceroy Lord Mayo and later President of the India Office Medical Board; Mair had been the Deputy Coroner of Madras; Green was surgeon to the Eden Hospital, Professor of Calcutta University, and a Lieutenant-Colonel in the Indian Medical Service while Green-Armytage also worked at the Eden Hospital as an IMS officer; Platt was Principal of the Lady Harding Medical College and Hospital for Women in Delhi; and Moore was Honorary Surgeon to the Viceroy. Others including Castellani and Balfour were key figures in the field of tropical medicine in Britain. On these themes see also Harrison, *Climates and Constitutions*, 67–8, 211.

[70] Mair, *Medical Guide*, 5, 130; Hull, *European in India*, 134; Green and Green-Armytage, *Birch's Management*, 9; Ewart, 'On the Colonisation', 115; Neligan and Castellani, in Neligan et al., 'Discussion on the Adaptation', 1316, 1321; Fayrer, *European Child-Life*, 30.

[71] OIOC, MSS Eur C176/63, Annette Beveridge's 1887 diary, entry for 13 Mar.; MSS Eur C176/17, Annette Beveridge to Henry Beveridge, 26 Aug. 1884.

the century William Bannerman, an officer in the Indian Medical Service, described a visit to Simla to his daughter in Edinburgh, writing that the cooler, elevated location gave 'the children . . . such nice red cheeks just like yours, not like poor wee Rob or Pat [his sons] in Bombay'.[72] Positive transformations wrought by the hill stations were similarly conveyed in the 1922 *Newman's Guide to Darjeeling and Neighbourhood*, whose author proclaimed that children 'brought up from the plains of Bengal suffering from anaemia, flabby, pale, peevish . . . soon become sturdy and cheerful, looking the picture of health, and with their cheeks simply radiant with colour'.[73] Nearly identical indices of good or bad health recur in one mother's 1979 rendition of taking her daughters back to England in the 1930s, when 'we didn't realise how pale they were until we compared them with British-bred children who seemed to be perpetually blushing'.[74] In these assessments, little distinguishes the language of professionals and amateurs, both of whom drew upon personal experiences and predilections in evaluating children's bodily condition.

Hints of common ground in popular and professional discourses on colonial childhood raise questions about the degree to which parents (particularly mothers) read this material and followed its advice as they raised their families. Few parents had access to the most recent medical journals, but most authors examined here wrote expressly for a popular readership. Childrearing strictures in advice literature have never been the equivalent of parental actions, however, and in many cases they bear little resemblance to practice. Indeed, the adamant tone writers adopted may have reflected their underlying awareness that those they hoped would respond to their work behaved differently, whether through ignorance, indifference, or open defiance of their exhortations.[75] Taken to extremes, such texts may not even have resembled widespread childrearing values but simply manual-writing styles.[76] On the other hand, Nancy Armstrong considers domestic novels and conduct books as genres that created a context for viewing certain practices as normal behavior and in so doing helped to reshape it, thereby working 'both as the document and as the agency of cultural history'.[77] Armstrong's points about the likely interplay

---

72 NLS, Bannerman Papers, Dep. 325/II, William Bannerman to Day Bannerman, 14 Oct. 1903.

73 *Newman's Guide to Darjeeling and Neighbourhood* (Calcutta, 1922), 55.

74 CSAA, Dench Papers, Mrs M. O. Dench, 'Memsahib', typewritten manuscript (1979), 60.

75 Stoler, *Carnal Knowledge*, 99; Christine Doran, '"Oddly Hybrid": Childbearing and Childrearing Practices in Colonial Penang, 1850–1875', *Women's History Review*, 6/1 (1997), 29–46, which argues that medical practitioners often had little impact on European childrearing methods in colonial Malaya.

76 Jay Mechling, 'Advice to Historians on Advice to Mothers', *Journal of Social History*, 9/1 (1975), 44–63.

77 Nancy Armstrong, *Desire and Domestic Fiction: A Political History of the Novel* (Oxford, 1987), 23, 59, 65–6; see also her 'The Rise of the Domestic Woman' in Nancy Armstrong and Leonard Tennenhouse (eds.), *The Ideology of Conduct: Essays on Literature and the History of Sexuality* (New York, 1987), 96–141.

between texts, actions, and values are persuasive, yet Rosemary George's more extreme suggestion that women's colonial novels and guidebooks 'were written and read as representations of the truth about British India and as such became self-fulfilling prophecies' appears unwarranted.[78] While neither contemporary allusions to childrearing practices in particular families nor later recollections of British-Indian childhood and parenting provide a complete or necessarily accurate picture of actual behavior or the reasons behind it, personal narratives do allow for an exploration of the concerns that participants did, or did not, voice during different periods. These were just as likely to resemble as diverge from themes stressed by advice literature.

Several women's letters, diaries, and subsequent recollections indicate the diverse ways individuals might communicate their views on, and experiences of, preserving children's physical health in India as well as how family decisions to send children away from sites of danger came to be made. Born in India in 1845, Mary Rice lived there until she was 9 and later returned and married an Inspector of Schools in 1869 (Illustrations 7 and 8). Over the next two decades she bore ten children, who all survived infancy to be sent to Britain during childhood. When writing her memoir in the 1920s she periodically mentioned their health but distinguished between each child's particular condition and perceived needs. Some proved less fit than others; the more delicate were taken to Britain upon a doctor's advice while the others remained in India longer and spent the hottest months in the hills. Mary Rice's references to her children's well-being, however, rarely attributed specific ailments to 'tropical' factors. In many instances they suffered illnesses common among children throughout Britain and Europe, and she wrote far more of her fear of chicken pox, measles, and whooping cough than of the possibility of malaria or other more 'Indian' maladies.[79] If indeed she was familiar with the dire prognoses and warnings given in colonial medical and housekeeping manuals on the problems particular to British-Indian childrearing, her recollections in old age provided no hint of how she interpreted, followed, or rejected such advice.

Annette Beveridge's letters and diaries provide a second example dating from the late nineteenth century. After marrying and having four children during the late 1870s and early 1880s, her writings regularly alluded not only to the ailments they suffered but just as commonly to her perpetual anxieties of what might befall them. Like Mary Rice she expressed concerns about colds, teething problems, and other afflictions her children would have encountered

---

[78] Rosemary Marangoly George, 'Homes in the Empire, Empires in the Home', *Cultural Critique*, (winter 1993–94), 119.

[79] CSAA, Rice Papers, Mary Sophia Rice, 'My Memoirs', n.d. [*c.*1920s], 28, 33, 42, 46.

regardless of where they lived, but she differed by singling out the Indian environment as the cause of the illnesses she dreaded most. Accounts of prickly heat and dysentery peppered her diaries, and the threat of cholera always seemed around the corner. She herself nearly died from cholera, and she periodically noted the deaths of her friends' young children from it. Yet her views about whether illnesses were preventable in India fluctuated with time and experience. Having taken her three oldest children back to England to begin school in 1884, she and her husband took the unusual step of bringing them back to India two years later because of the misery brought by separation. Although Calcutta was the source of endless health worries, she deemed it safe for her children to spend the three coolest months of the year there and the other nine in Darjeeling, where they lived with two governesses and received periodic visits from their parents. This arrangement proved successful until William became ill with 'latent malarial fever' at the age of 11 and hovered near death for two months. Convinced that he had contracted it in Calcutta, Annette told her husband that 'we will not have any of the children in the plains of Bengal again', and immediately initiated plans for them to leave India permanently. Not even the hills, it seemed, could provide any sense of security in the wake of their close call.[80]

Several descriptions of early twentieth-century and interwar childrearing further suggest the diverse ways health anxieties could find expression, and which depended more on individual experiences and dispositions than on the historical moment of writing. Ann Butler's letters from the early 1900s reveal little about any serious illnesses that may have befallen her four children; instead, her few comments about health concern her infant son she called 'Tweedle' (soon after nicknamed Rab) being 'queer again'; periodic headcolds and new teeth; and a query as to whether a spare mosquito net would be available for one of their babies when they returned to their bungalow after several months' absence, but 'never mind if not'.[81] By far the most extended family discussion of a physical ailment concerned Rab's broken arm after falling off a pony; as he recalled later in life, the broken arm worried his father endlessly as it threatened to impinge upon his athletic performance once he began public

[80] OIOC, MSS Eur C176/13, Annette Beveridge to Henry Beveridge, 20 Sept. 1882; MSS Eur C176/55, Annette Beveridge's 1879 diary, entries for 16 May, 13 June, 14 June, 23 July; MSS Eur C176/19, Annette Beveridge to Henry Beveridge, 'Tuesday 19th' [May 1886]; MSS Eur C176/25, Annette Beveridge to Henry Beveridge, 1 Nov. 1889.

[81] OIOC, MSS Eur F225/22, Ann Butler to Montagu Butler, 27 May 1903; MSS Eur F225/26, Ann Butler to Montagu Butler, 29 May 1910; MSS Eur F225/31, Ann Butler to Montagu Butler, 9 June 1917.

school in England.[82] Ann's daughter Iris, who later married and had two children in India in the 1920s and 1930s, was equally reticent about health concerns; her renditions of both childhood and motherhood in India recorded in the 1970s did little more than note how British nannies and mothers were careful to ensure that milk and water were boiled and food was protected from flies. In addition, although Iris considered one of her daughters to have been 'delicate' enough to be taken back to England for two years, they then brought her back to India until school age. England's restorative effects, it seems, enabled children not only to recover but to return to India without cause for undue parental anxiety.[83] Like the Beveridges and the Rices, moreover, both Ann and Iris spent time at Simla, Darjeeling, Murree, and other hill stations, presumably viewing this as an adequate way to combat many potential child illnesses.

Ann Butler's and her daughter's descriptions of health precautions, such that they are, share much in common with many other accounts recorded after decolonization. Many who either raised children or were born in India and looked back from the vantage point of the later twentieth century said little about either personal or family illnesses or precautions taken against them. Downplaying India's perceived threats to the well-being or even survival of British families might reflect the decreased mortality rates among the British in the twentieth century or, alternatively, the subsequent obsolescence of many fears common in the late imperial era. Additionally, they might just as easily be attributed to preventive measures being so commonplace as to become largely unremarkable. For women like those in the Butler and Rice families, moreover, health concerns and precautions may well have appeared banal and unworthy of extensive discussion because their own parents had lived in India and made the range of colonial household and childrearing procedures a normal feature of daily life for generations.

Many post-colonial accounts note, but rarely dwell upon, annual interludes in the hills, the insistence that children wear topis in the sun, the use of mosquito nets over beds, measures taken to preserve hygiene in the home, and the need to ensure that food preparation methods killed bacteria; such preventive measures were *de rigueur* among most of the British community in India until independence.[84] Many parents presumably considered these precautions effec-

---

[82] OIOC, MSS Eur F225/25, Ann Butler to Montagu Butler, 22 July 1909; R. A. Butler, *The Art of the Possible: The Memoirs of Lord Butler* (London, 1971), 7, 10.

[83] CSAA, Portal Papers, Iris Portal, 'Song at Seventy', typescript manuscript, n.d. [*c.*1975], 6, 63, 65; CSAA, MT20, transcribed interview with Iris Portal by Mary Thatcher, 15 Oct. 1974, 6, 12.

[84] CSAA, Donaldson Papers, Barbara Donaldson, 'India Remembered', typewritten manuscript (1983), 5; taped interviews by author with Margaret Ramsay-Brown, 23 May 1995; Theon Wilkinson, 12 July 1995; Enid Boon, 23 April 1995; 'Questionnaire on British Children and Family Life in India Before 1947', compiled by author, completed by Jack Sewell, Peter Cashmore, Rachel Taylor, and Peter Clark, 1995.

tive, but others writing both during and after empire could exhibit anxieties similar to those expressed in prescriptive literature as a result of bad experiences. Annette Beveridge counted many bereaved parents among her social circle and saw her own child close to death after attacks of cholera or other 'fevers', and this in itself may account for her panic about climate and disease. Had any of Mary Rice's ten children died in India, perhaps she too would have devoted more of her memoir to India's risks to the young. Many narratives that do not otherwise discuss India's potential to harm children in detail none the less periodically refer to children's deaths (or brushes with death) from rabies, often contracted from the family's pet dog, or the risk of being bitten by poisonous snakes.[85] Until the end of empire, enough children died from causes to which they would not have been subjected in Britain to make ongoing apprehensions about their safety a feature of family stories. Another woman's recollections of growing up in India in the 1940s stressed that her mother was 'fanatical about health and cleanliness in the kitchen', particularly following her sister's death from malaria.[86] Individual proclivities and experiences appear to account more for such attitudes than the timing of the narrative. Furthermore, while reading published childcare guidelines may well have influenced family behavior, deeply entrenched practices among the colonial community undoubtedly had just as much, or more, of an impact than advice provided in books.

Despite some similarities between concerns expressed by families living in India and by the authors of prescriptive literature, personal accounts diverge sharply in one crucial respect. No one describing their own family experiences even hinted that childhood years in India could result in long-term or irreversible physical damage unless children actually died. Hereditarily transmitted tropical debilities, permanent deterioration or degeneration, or possible sterility never featured in either contemporary or retrospective accounts of personal life. Indeed, as many parents had been born in India and presumably preferred to see themselves as free from the stigmas of degeneration, they might easily take heart from their own and wider family experiences when deciding how to raise their children. Whether personal stories reveal considerable anxiety about children's well-being or said little on the subject, they assumed that taking children away from the site of risk would erase any ill effects.[87] Hill

---

[85] NLS, Dep. 325/V, Helen Bannerman to Janet Bannerman, 2 Nov. 1906; 325/VI, William Bannerman to Day Bannerman, 24 Dec. 1909; George Roche, *Childhood in India: Tales from Sholapur*, Richard Terrell (ed.), (London, 1994), 32.

[86] 'Questionnaire on British Children and Family Life in India Before 1947', compiled by author, completed by Mrs Geraldine Hobson, 1995.

[87] This view was supported by many scientists as well, as Nancy Stepan suggests in 'Biological Degeneration: Races and Proper Places', in J. Edward Chamberlin and Sander L. Gilman (eds.), *Degeneration: The Dark Side of Progress* (New York, 1985), 103.

stations could strengthen the 'delicate' and provide the requisite rosy cheeks by removing children from the risks of the Indian plains in the short term, while leaving them in Britain by later childhood would complete the restoration process.[88] As M. M. Kaye recalled of entering boarding school in England in the 1920s, her schoolmistresses proclaimed that 'anyone could see that I came from India since I was much too thin, skinny and sallow for my age and clearly in need of "building up" ', but consoled her mother that 'she would see a remarkable change in her little daughter after a few months of good English food, fresh milk, sea-bathing and bracing air'.[89]

In exhibiting such confidence that Britain could restore children to full health and roll back any damages India might have inflicted, participants parted company with medical commentators who prophesied 'indelible' permanent bad effects.[90] Instead, they might take heart from reassurances such as those from the writer who envisioned a Mary Lennox-like metamorphosis: 'few sights are more pleasing than to see these puny, pallid, skinny, fretful little ones *converted, by British food and British meteorology,* into fat and happy English children'.[91] As long as children escaped death in India, then, they were usually salvageable upon arriving home. In the meantime protective measures and proper adult supervision might ensure survival. Still, those playing the leading roles in childrearing—mothers and servants—were the same figures continually accused of inadequacies in prescriptive literature, while contacts with Indians in the home were largely denigrated as inconducive to desirable cultural formation as well as physical safety. Do personal narratives support these negative depictions, or do they tell a different story?

Just as most of the comments pertaining to children's health seen above reflect maternal rather than paternal points of view, so too were family letters discussing servants involved in childcare penned almost exclusively by mothers. In an era when domestic servants were a ubiquitous presence in British middle- and upper-class homes both in the metropole and overseas, mothers never questioned that persons other than themselves would play some role—and often a considerable one—in attending to their children's daily needs. Few would have understood employing Indian ayahs or involving other servants in childcare as negligent (as some medical and childcare commentary examined above suggested), yet women did often express concerns about their children's contacts with 'natives'. Nupur Chaudhuri's analysis of mid- to late-

---

[88] Collingham, *Imperial Bodies*, 99; Kennedy, *Magic Mountains*, 130–4.
[89] M. M. Kaye, *The Sun in the Morning: My Early Years in India and England* (New York, 1990), 321–2.
[90] Green and Green-Armytage, *Birch's Management*, 9; Platt, *Home and Health*, 139.
[91] 'J. P.', *Care of Infants*, 88; emphasis added.

nineteenth-century parental fears about children mixing with Indian servants provides clear evidence that some British women exhibited considerable racial hostility towards their domestic staff.[92] Yet memsahibs' attitudes and responses about Indian caregivers and their impact on children reveal ambiguities and complexities that require greater attention given the key position servants occupied both in colonial and post-colonial accounts of British-Indian family life.

Annette Beveridge's correspondence with her husband as well as her diary entries provide one example of how a late-Victorian memsahib might by turns fear and praise servants, attempting at times to limit her children's interactions with them but considering them harmless at other junctures. Anxieties about servants included her fear—ultimately defused by the family doctor—that the ayah had given her baby a sleep-inducing 'narcotic', along with periodic injunctions that the children should steer clear of certain servants who were 'dirty'. Yet even her worries about hygiene and social interaction could become tempered with humor. As she wrote in her diary in 1880, her 3-year-old daughter, Letty, 'having been told not to talk to the punkah wallah as being dirty, she addressed a few words to him . . . and returning to me said "He has bathed" '.[93] Letty, or Laetitia—whose middle name Santamani reflected her parents' interest in Sanskrit—spoke to the punkah wallah (fan puller) in Bengali; Annette frequently noted the new words and phrases her children learned and seemed equally pleased with their acquisitions in Indian languages as those in English. For several years her son William was referred to as 'Bhaia', meaning 'brother', in family circles following Letty's example. Watching the children playing with servants and taking them to the occasional local fair (mela, or tamasha) were ordinary features of daily life, and Annette was just as likely to describe individual servants as inoffensive companions, or as 'good', 'faithful', and 'dedicated', as she was to criticize some as 'dirty'.[94] When she insisted that her children leave India permanently in 1889 it was due to her fears of illness and death rather than any determination to curtail their exposure to servants or other Indian social sectors (Illustration 10). Indeed, their transition from Darjeeling to Eastbourne the following year was made with the help of Churgi, who

---

[92] Nupur Chaudhuri, 'Memsahibs and Their Servants in Nineteenth-Century India', *Women's History Review*, 3/4 (1994), 549–62, and 'Memsahibs and Motherhood', 530–2.

[93] OIOC, MSS Eur C176/56, Annette Beveridge's 1880 diary, entries for 25 April and 4 Nov.

[94] OIOC, MSS Eur C176/12, Annette Beveridge to Henry Beveridge, 3 Oct. 1881; MSS Eur C176/13, Annette Beveridge to Henry Beveridge, 20 Sept. 1882; MSS Eur C176/14, Annette Beveridge to Henry Beveridge, 31 Aug., 10. Sept., and 29 Sept. 1882; MSS Eur C176/126, Annette Beveridge to Letty Beveridge, 18 Jan. 1886.

temporarily accompanied them as their cook and kitmagar (table servant) and joined in the children's games of cricket.[95]

Annette Beveridge thus expressed many positive sentiments about her family's proximity to Indians, yet at the same time she was (and remains) well known for adamant views about Indian inferiority. As she demonstrated publicly while participating in the campaign against the Ilbert Bill in 1883 (which, had it passed, would have enabled Indian judges to try Europeans in courts of law), she considered Indians as 'uncivilized' on many levels and found the notion that they might exercise power over Europeans unthinkable.[96] Writing to Henry (who did not share her opinions), she argued that 'the real fact is—the substance of England in India—that race for race superiority is on our side. Breed is breed in men and horses.'[97] Such firm convictions undoubtedly do much to explain why, despite her willingness to condone or even encourage some interaction between her children and their servants, she also insisted upon hiring white governesses as well. When she wrote to Henry from London of her decision to bring the children back to India for several years, she felt assured that keeping them in Darjeeling most of the year in tandem with having them spend most of their time in the company of European governesses instead of anyone too closely connected with India would protect them. 'We must keep up English ways as much as possible and this can be much better done by an imported person than by an Anglo-Indian who has lived in the country. Besides we must have someone capable of giving good elementary teaching', she wrote.[98] Somewhat ironically, the method she chose to 'keep up English ways' was by bringing 'Fraulein', who would continue to teach the children the German they had long since begun to study, along with an English nursery governess. 'Imports' from Britain or Europe, it seemed, could be preferable not only to ayahs but also to white women in India who, by having 'lived in the country', might offer English ways in even a more diluted form than did Germans—at least in the eyes of a woman who lacked British-Indian ancestry herself. Annette Beveridge, it might be added, never raised the possibility of employing a Eurasian woman to provide childcare.

[95] OIOC, MSS Eur C176/134, Lettie Beveridge to Henry Beveridge, 21 Sept. 1890; Lord Beveridge, *India Called Them* (London, 1947), 323, 325, 329.

[96] Mrinalini Sinha, *Colonial Masculinity: The 'Manly Englishman' and the 'Effeminate Bengali' in the Late Nineteenth Century* (Manchester, 1995), 58–61; Barbara Ramusack, 'Cultural Missionaries, Maternal Imperialists, Feminist Allies: British Women Activists in India, 1865–1945', in Nupur Chaudhuri and Margaret Strobel (eds.), *Western Women and Imperialism: Complicity and Resistance* (Bloomington, IN, 1992), 122–4; Vron Ware, *Beyond the Pale: White Women, Racism and History* (London, 1992), 121–47, 161–3.

[97] OIOC, MSS Eur C176/17, Annette Beveridge to Henry Beveridge, 22 Sept. 1884.

[98] OIOC, MSS Eur C176/19, Annette Beveridge to Henry Beveridge, 24 May 1886.

Nannies or governesses from Britain or Europe could act as effective barriers between children and Indian domestics, and many mothers valued them both on these grounds and for the increased leisure time they enjoyed as a result. Employing white women, however, did not always mean that mothers categorically distrusted all members of their Indian staff. Near the turn of the century Ann Butler brought a Scottish nanny to India in part because she disliked leaving her children exclusively with an ayah and, as she put it, 'feel terrified to answer an advert. fr. a Eurasian nurse'.[99] But despite having a nanny as well as an ayah whose duties pertained exclusively to childcare, Ann still refused to contemplate a trip away with her husband unless their head bearer, Gokal— singled out as exceptional—remained in charge at home. 'I would not leave the children alone in this house without him', she told Montagu.[100] With a nanny in addition to a senior Indian servant she fully trusted, she had the luxury of an active social life that seemingly freed her from anxiety about her children's health and social surroundings. As her daughter Iris recalled during the 1970s, their nanny and Gokal were 'great allies' in coordinating the other servants' work as well as the children's daily routine, placing limits on their interactions with more junior Indian household staff.[101] Rab Butler concurred, adding that 'we did not have an Indian enclosed childhood such as Kipling describes in *Something of Myself*. . . We did not learn to speak the vernacular freely and the Indian scene was filtered through Nanny's stringent personality.'[102] How this circumscribed contact with most Indians affected their wider perceptions of colonized society is open to interpretation. In retrospect Iris preferred to describe how family visits to shrines, witnessing Diwali celebrations, visits from Indian friends of her parents, and hearing stories of Indian gods and heroes made acceptance 'natural and ever-lasting'; no notion of superiority 'ever entered our heads', she stressed.[103] One of her mother's letters from 1910 provides a different perspective, however: 'Iris last night, eluding the ayah who had been attempting for some 10 minutes to undo her dress, [said] "I hate being dragged about by these natives." '[104]

For Iris and the many others reminiscing during the later twentieth century, the passage of time in tandem with the arrival of the post-colonial era both

[99] OIOC, MSS Eur F225/22, Ann Butler to Montagu Butler, 27 May 1903.

[100] OIOC, MSS Eur F225/24, Ann Butler to Montagu Butler, 21 Dec. 1908.

[101] CSAA, Portal, 'Song at Seventy', 4, 7, 70; CSAA, MT20, transcribed interview with Iris Portal by Mary Thatcher, 15 Oct. 1974, 5.

[102] Butler, *Art of the Possible*, 7.

[103] CSAA, Portal, 'Song at Seventy', 4, 9.

[104] OIOC, MSS Eur F225/26, Ann Butler to Montagu Butler, 10 Aug. 1910.

work to shape interpretations of domestic relationships between British children and their family's Indian staff. Post-colonial accounts of British-Indian childhood have historically specific contours, but like both Iris and Rab Butler those describing their early colonial years also utilized prior narratives to frame their recollections. Rudyard Kipling's renditions of his childhood in Bombay in the late 1860s not only count among the most familiar accounts of British-Indian childhood but also, as will be examined in greater detail in Chapter 3, provided a model to which others turned in his wake—even when, like Iris and Rab, they invoke Kipling's childhood as a means of showing contrasts between his and their own.

Kipling's autobiographical writing—including his 1888 short story 'Baa Baa, Black Sheep' but especially his 1935 memoir *Something of Myself*—contained what became the classic elements found throughout subsequent recollections. Kipling described being in India until the age of 5 as a time of warm, colorful, and affectionate surroundings, where he felt fully at home in a culturally diverse environment:

My first impression is of daybreak, light and colour and golden and purple fruits at the level of my shoulder. This would be the memory of early morning walks to the Bombay fruit market with my *ayah* and later with my sister in her perambulator . . . Our *ayah* was a Portuguese Roman Catholic who would pray—I beside her—at a wayside Cross. Meeta, my Hindu bearer, would sometimes go into little Hindu temples where, being below the age of caste, I held his hand and looked at the dimly-seen, friendly Gods.[105]

Evening walks by the sea, also in the company of his ayah and sister, seeing palm and banana trees, Arab dhows, and Parsis 'wading out to worship the sunset' also appear prominently among his memories. Parsi funeral practices taking place in the Towers of Silence near the family home was forbidden knowledge, some of which he came to learn from his ayah. In *Something of Myself*, the key figures in Kipling's first years are Indian people and surroundings rather than either of his parents, who are kindly but peripheral facets of daily life, as was the language they spoke. 'In the afternoon heats before we took our sleep', he wrote, '[my ayah] or Meeta would tell us stories and Indian nursery songs all unforgotten, and we were sent into the dining-room after we had been dressed, with the caution "Speak English now to Papa and Mamma". So one spoke "English", haltingly translated out of the ver-

---

[105] Rudyard Kipling, *Something of Myself* in Thomas Pinney (ed.), *Rudyard Kipling: Something of Myself and other Autobiographical Writings* (Cambridge, 1990), 3.

nacular idiom that one thought and dreamed in.'[106] For Kipling, being 'below
the age of caste' could open doors to Indian life that remained closed to most
British adults (either because they were unwilling to try to gain entry or were
refused access), and he dealt with this theme in greater depth in his novel *Kim*.
According to his sister Alice, he drew some of his inspiration for the story of a
working-class British boy who grows up with the ability to wander freely
between the two societies from his own childhood recollections. 'Mother
used to say that, like Kim, he was "Little friend of all the world" and that's
what the Indian servants in Bombay called him before we came home', she
reflected.[107]

Kipling's renditions of British-Indian childhood count among the many
accounts that bear little resemblance to fears about health and cultural
identity expressed by some parents as well as the authors of prescriptive
childrearing texts. Instead, they focus largely on the affectionate relationships
they developed with Indian servants and the delight they took in exposure
to Indian society and culture outside as well as inside the home, finding
such contacts enriching rather than harmful to body or mind. By the
post-colonial period it had become increasingly common for Britons to call
their childhood years in India 'magical' and, often explicitly citing Kipling's
narrative precedents, attribute this to the climate, geography, indulgence
by Indian servants, and their opportunities for exploring indigenous
culture.[108] In *Two Under the Indian Sun*, their 1966 memoir about growing
up in India just prior to and during the First World War, Jon and Rumer
Godden outlined how 'the Bengal year' was celebrated in their home,
allowing the children to participate in Hindu and Muslim as well as Christian
holiday festivities. Like Kipling, the Goddens claim to have enjoyed access
to local people and customs through their servants, who represent the
kindness, receptivity, and knowability of Indian society.[109] Literary critic
Benita Parry's brief analysis of the Goddens' work concludes that 'a childhood
in India could spare the British that overpowering sense of alienation and
confusion' characterizing much writing about the subcontinent. 'Why', she
asks, 'were so very few Englishmen able to make the imaginative leap to

---

[106] Ibid., 4.
[107] Alice Macdonald Fleming, 'My Brother, Rudyard Kipling (I)', in Harold Orel (ed.), *Kipling: Interviews and Recollections*, Vol. I (London, 1983), 10; originally published in *Kipling Journal*, 14 (Dec. 1947), 3–5.
[108] CSAA, MT46, transcribed interview with Mrs Veronica Bamfield by Mary Thatcher, 10 Sept. 1981, 4–6.
[109] Jon and Rumer Godden, *Two Under the Indian Sun* (1966; repr. New York, 1987), 84–111.

comprehend India in its own terms, to respond to her unique pulse of existence, her particular imaginative and intellectual quality?'[110]

Britons recalling colonial childhood after decolonization often make claims similar to Parry's, suggesting that their age allowed them to develop unique insights into India that most adults lacked. Regardless of any familiarity with ways of life outside the British community, however, many recollections indicate that contacts with servants or other Indian social sectors largely worked to create and reinforce a white, middle-class, British imperial identity in children. Leonore Davidoff's analysis of children's relationships with family servants in Victorian Britain argues that personal intimacy did not erase notions of the 'otherness' of the British working class. Contrasts between class standards of acceptable cleanliness, hygiene, speech, and other mores caused children to recognize their cultural differences from their nurses and other domestics, even while retaining special affection for them. Regardless of servants' strong influence on their daily lives, children became aware of the gap separating them and realized that their future would take them from the nursery into their parents' social world.[111] Art historian Griselda Pollock's reflections on her upbringing in South Africa in the 1950s support Davidoff's assertions in an overseas setting where racial inequalities rested alongside class distinctions to enhance still further the divisions between children and household staff. Seeking to recontextualize her affections for her African nursemaid with the benefit of hindsight, Pollock stresses how their relationship was predicated upon her own inclusion in a privileged and exploitative white society. Because 'the child, however innocent, is being formed as a bearer of the dominant order of *whiteness*', she quickly sensed the higher value placed upon the physical and social attributes she shared with her parents.[112] Pollock thus comprehended her beloved nurse only in the capacity their surroundings allowed, in which the woman was known to her only as 'Julia'—a name not her own, bestowed by her employers. The sense of difference from racially and socially disempowered servants that white children learned took place under circumstances that largely foreclosed 'knowledge' that might lead to 'comprehension'—of Africa, in this instance— 'in its own terms'.

---

[110] Benita Parry, *Delusions and Discoveries: Studies on India in the British Imagination, 1880–1930* (Berkeley, CA, 1972), 66–7. In a related context, Ashis Nandy has argued that highly relevant interpretations of imperialism may be culled from those living on the margins of colonial society, including children, in *The Intimate Enemy: Loss and Recovery of Self Under Colonialism* (Delhi, 1983).

[111] Davidoff, 'Class and Gender', 112.

[112] Griselda Pollock, 'Territories of Desire: Reconsiderations of an African Childhood, dedicated to a woman whose name was not really "Julia" ', in George Robertson et al. (eds.), *Travellers' Tales: Narratives of Home and Displacement* (London, 1994), 78.

In late imperial India many factors impeded children's intimacy with Indians, regardless of how much these relationships were either feared or extolled by various commentators. Some remember how parental disapproval of their access to Indian culture created barriers which were imposing even when partly breached. Monica Clough's analysis of her upbringing on a Travancore tea estate in the 1920s explored her mother Marjorie's attempts to insulate her from the health and cultural threats of indigenous life from a post-colonial perspective, and she sought to distance herself from her mother's attitudes both when a child and in the present. Entrusted to the care of a Tamil Christian ayah—indeed, some parents appeared to prefer ayahs who were Roman Catholic converts, perhaps believing them either more distanced from most of Indian society or better acquainted with Western culture—Clough recalled the limitations her mother placed on permissible interaction with 'Mary ayah', Mary's husband Anthony, and their 'world':

Mary bought me bangles when the travelling bangle-pedlar came, fragile glass in rainbow colours, but Marjorie would not let me wear them much; too Indian. She would have desperately disapproved if she knew that I sometimes cajoled Mary into getting me a bazaar penny worth of jaggery (black molasses toffee—like sugar) . . . Mary didn't often break the rules, but found the great preoccupation with hygiene hard to fathom. I think the racial hostility which must have existed somewhere, and the fear which my mother must have had of all this was rationalized into a preoccupation with Germs . . . True the risks were very great . . . Close contacts with Indian children were forbidden, and Indian food and water . . . We still got malaria now and then . . . But 'don't touch, it's come from the bazaar' and 'let me wash it in Pinky' (permanganate) . . . was I think a defensive beyond the needs of sanitation.[113]

Despite her mother's injunctions, Clough none the less befriended Mary's niece and entered the servants' compound although it was off-limits, along with the bazaar, 'full of spices and saris and blankets and rice and chillies and sugar, and not a place for little girls . . . the bazaar men were uniformly lewd'. If her trespassing was discovered, 'Ayah and Anthony got blamed, which was hard for me to bear'.[114] Curiosity, attraction, and the thrill of disobeying her mother made the risks worthwhile, and enabled her to assert a more enlightened attitude later that seemingly enhanced the pleasure of reliving her experiences in the early 1980s.

In a setting where parents and other adult members of colonial society continually reminded children of their distinctions from the colonized even while

---

[113] CSAA, Clough Papers, Mrs M. F. Clough, 'A Childhood in Travancore, 1922–1931', typewritten manuscript (1983), 25.
[114] Ibid., 47, 27.

they placed them in their care, it would have been difficult for children not to internalize at least some, if not all, of their values, even if they later claimed to have more tolerant views about India and Indians. By becoming aware of their own privileges and status *vis-à-vis* the Indians they encountered—or learning to 'appreciate the full significance of their "race" ', as Nancy Paxton phrases it— the divides their parents had tried to impose became reinforced by an emerging sense of belonging to the British community.[115] For Clough, a key turning-point came when she began to learn to read English and tried, unsuccessfully, to teach her ayah: 'I discussed quite seriously with [Mary] why she couldn't or wouldn't [learn to read], and I began to see that my destiny, education, and advantage, was going to take me beyond her horizons.'[116] For Jon and Rumer Godden, the memory of riding through the local bazaar on ponies in the company of their servant, Guru, exemplified the many occasions through which they grew to recognize their comparative privileges, when 'the difference between us and the milling thousands of Indians round us, all added up to a princess quality'.[117]

Servants themselves, meanwhile, may well have been fond of their em—ployers' children (or, alternatively, have merely tolerated them to avoid dis-missal), but they were necessarily aware of the distinctions dividing them and the importance of childcare that accorded with parental wishes (Illustration 3). A poem written by Mrs A. B. Shoosmith about her 1920s childhood described how her family's bearer encouraged her to replicate traditions prevalent within British-Indian society and not Indian, in this instance through insisting she wear 'the topi' as protection from the sun while outdoors:

> It's such a bother when they say
> 'Put your topi on'.
> Not one minute out all day
> Without a topi on.
>
> .   .   .
>
> But when the bearer says to me,
> 'All Sahibs putting on
> Little Sahib like big Sahib, see?'
> I put my topi on.[118]

---

[115] Nancy L. Paxton, *Writing under the Raj: Gender, Race, and Rape in the British Colonial Imagination, 1830–1947* (New Brunswick, NJ, 1999), 168.

[116] CSAA, Clough, 'A Childhood', 81.

[117] Godden, *Two Under*, 30.

[118] CSAA, Mrs A. G. Shoosmith, 'Poems of Childhood in India', autograph manuscript, No. 25, 'The Topi', n.d.

Shoosmith's rendition of how she became persuaded to wear her sun helmet—
that by doing so she, the 'little Sahib', would be included in the ruling group of
'all Sahibs' through joining in one of their most visible distinguishing practices—strongly suggests which community she already counted herself within.[119] Moreover, her poem highlights the role servants could play not in
'corrupting' British children by encouraging them to 'go native' in their habits,
but rather in maintaining their distinctions from colonized peoples.

Positive images of Indian servants come not only from those recalling childhood but can also be found in many post-colonial narratives of parenting as
well. While some references to fears about servants' poor hygiene, their potential to corrupt children culturally, and the possibility that they might give children opium persist in more recent accounts, these often become superseded by
discussions of servants as loyal protectors of British families. Lady Anderson's
stories of motherhood in the 1920s epitomize the ways Indian domestic staff
came to be praised for their childcare methods from a late twentieth-century
vantage point. One anecdote tells how the Muslim bearer took her sons for
morning walks to the 'Sahib's Court', where 'the Mali and the Chowkidar
(both Hindus) would open the doors and the Chota Sahibs were made to stand
before the portrait of the King Emperor, and told to "Salute the King!" Here
there was a focus of loyalty for them all!' Another episode highlighted her
gratitude to her ayah, and by extension many other Indian servants across the
colonial period, for offering special protection in the face of manifold potential
threats:

Jankhi Ayah once put me to shame . . . to my horror a small black wriggling creature
fell on to the baby's pillow, and I jumped back—but Ayah jumped forward and
snatched the baby out of his cot. It was only a lizard—but I know we had both thought
it a krait. Not all Ayahs were [like] Jankhi, though friends have told me of other
instances of such devotion. In the days of the Mutiny many women and children were
saved by their servants. Let the memory of them not be forgotten.[120]

In contrast to colonial-era texts that commonly pinpointed servants as a probable source of cultural and bodily harm to British-Indian families, for Lady
Anderson—and indeed many others in the aftermath of empire—servants
become a port in many storms. Her memories are pervaded by real and

---

[119] Dane Kennedy, 'The Perils of the Midday Sun: Climatic Anxieties in the Colonial Tropics', in John
M. MacKenzie (ed.), *Imperialism and the Natural World* (Manchester, 1990), 118–40; Francis A. De Caro and
Rosan A. Jordan, 'The Wrong *Topi*: Personal Narratives, Ritual, and the Sun Helmet as Symbol', *Western
Folklore*, 43/4 (1984), 233–48; Bernard S. Cohn, 'Cloth, Clothes, and Colonialism: India in the Nineteenth
Century', in *Colonialism and its Forms of Knowledge: The British in India* (Princeton, NJ, 1996), 149–60.

[120] CSAA, 'Women in India: Replies to Questionnaire', Lady Anderson, n.d. [late 1970s or early 1980s].

imagined dangers that she and other Britons before her faced in India, almost interchangeably encompassing poisonous snakes, the rebels of 1857, and, by extension, the nationalists who made the interwar years she revisits a time when Indians wanting to 'Salute the King!' became increasingly rare. Servants here work to protect British children and parents alike from physical harm, or are configured as comforting respites from challenges to British security and authority being mounted from the world outside the bungalow. As this book explores further in its conclusion, loyal and affectionate domestic staff who 'knew their place' thus count as central figures in post-colonial accounts that celebrate the colonizer–colonized relationship, helping to justify British nostalgia for imperial India in an era when the recent history of a successful independence struggle made expressing fond memories of participation in the raj an uncertain enterprise.[121]

'A HALCYON TIME': INDIAN CHILDHOODS, METROPOLITAN TRANSITIONS, AND THE GARDEN METAPHOR

Nostalgia about the subcontinent features prominently in memories of British-Indian childhood, and is far more pervasive in the post-colonial era than when Kipling published his now standard accounts. Chronological and spatial distance from the settings of colonial childhood as well as the end of empire determine the contours of recollection, as does the cultural significance long given to childhood as a period of life central to shaping the adult individual. Carolyn Steedman proposes that between the late eighteenth and early twentieth centuries the Western notion of what constituted the 'self' gradually coalesced into 'the idea that the core of an individual's psychic identity was his or her own lost past, or childhood'.[122] Imperial India became central to the identity of many who spent their first years there, but was an aspect of the self shaped equally by rupture. Fred Davis links nostalgia with passage through the life cycle, stressing that 'nostalgia thrives on transition, on the subjective discontinuities that

[121] Retrospective British assessments of Indian servants share common features with both post-colonial Dutch memories of Javanese servants as well as white representations of mammies in the American South after the Civil War. See Stoler's account (co-written with Karen Strassler) in *Carnal Knowledge*, ch. 7; Grace Elizabeth Hale, *Making Whiteness: The Culture of Segregation in the South, 1890–1940* (New York, 1998), ch. 3; Cheryl Thurber, 'The Development of the Mammy Image and Mythology', in Virginia Bernhard et al. (eds.), *Southern Women: Histories and Identities* (Columbia, MO, 1992), 87–108.

[122] Carolyn Steedman, *Strange Dislocations: Childhood and the Idea of Human Interiority, 1780–1930* (London, 1995), 4.

engender our yearning for continuity'.[123] British-Indian childhood nostalgia, however, stemmed just as much from a combination of geographical, social, and cultural transitions as from growing older. For men and women alike, the cherished position that early colonial life occupies in memory is inseparable from the prism of subsequent events through which they viewed it. By highlighting the disparities between their lives before and after departure—what Iris Portal called 'the violent and abrupt contrast faced by every British child transferred from east to west'—time in India acquires a particularly idyllic cast.[124] Moreover, it made many eager to return after they finished school to rejoin the world they regretted leaving behind.

Traumatic adjustment to the metropole after 'going home' constitutes the basis of most adult analyses of childhood overseas, making Indian days appear 'magical' and imagined as 'real childhood' by comparison with their British aftermath. Rumer Godden summarized that going back to England marked 'the end of our childhood';[125] her memoir written with her sister Jon filtered details of their carefree life in Bengal through its disparities with the strictness, straitened financial circumstances, and the general gloom pervading their grandmother's house in London.[126] Such accounts link times that were happy—in India—with the period of life they call 'childhood', which ended not upon reaching a specific age but rather upon their arrival in the metropole. George Roche described his days in India as 'a halcyon time for small boys who did not have to worry about anything'; 'of all my memories I hold those of my childhood in India the most dear'. Conversely, his memoir tells relatively little about his subsequent boarding school days in England, 'an experience I prefer to forget'.[127] Deeply ensconced cultural tendencies to view childhood as an ideally blissful time perhaps help to explain why some former British-Indian children appear unwilling to deem their later experiences in Britain worthy of occupying the sacred mental space to which it lays claim.[128]

When asked in 1995 about 'the first thing that comes to mind when you think about being in India as a child', Margaret Ramsay-Brown's response drew together facets of her social and natural world that characterized many other accounts. She emphasized 'the amount of freedom that one had; the warmth

[123] Fred Davis, *Yearning for Yesterday: A Sociology of Nostalgia* (New York, 1979), 49, 55.

[124] CSAA, Portal, 'Song at Seventy', 12.

[125] Rumer Godden, *A Time to Dance, No Time to Weep* (New York, 1987), 3.

[126] Jon and Rumer Godden, *Two Under*, 11, 14, 18–19, 23, 66.

[127] Roche, *Childhood in India*, pp. 31, xvi.

[128] Cunningham credits Rousseau with first articulating the notion that childhood could be the best time of life and worthy of immense nostalgia, a view that became enhanced under Romanticism. *Children and Childhood*, 66–7, 76–8.

with which one—I don't mean climatic warmth, but the warmth with which one was surrounded really by—by servants, one's family, everyone that one met . . . the colour, the quality of light, the space'.[129] For many, Britain proved the antithesis of all these pleasurable qualities. Like Burnett's Sara Crewe, children leaving India often exchanged warm and familiar human relationships—both with family and servants—for a life with relatives they scarcely knew, strangers, or long stretches at boarding schools, as Chapters 3 and 4 explore. Freedom was replaced by regimentation, and an elevated social and racial status by a new awareness of their family's limitations, as Chapter 5 considers, while the climatic warmth and brightness of Indian skies, flowers, and general surroundings was substituted by a land seen as cold and grey. In short, they left behind what until then had been their home for a nation meant to be 'home' but feeling the opposite. M. M. Kaye arrived at the docks of Tilbury after the First World War to find a 'depressing foreign country', a 'wet, flat, dark-grey country with its black, oily river, ugly buildings and drably clad dock-workers . . . so different was it from the crowded docks at Bombay in the blinding Indian sunlight, the noise, the heat, the hurrying coolies and the colours—the brilliant clashing colours'. Like the Goddens she mocks the idea of attachment to the national 'home' to which she is meant to belong, describing time in Britain as a period of 'exile'.[130] High expectations built up by their parents frequently ended in disappointment. For Kay Mosse, the singing birds and flowers she was promised were rewarded by 'unending greyness', birds with 'ugly feathers with no bright colours', and 'small, colourless' flowers that made her long 'for all my bright Indian flowers, the tall really yellow sunflowers and all the others'.[131] She had yet to develop the appreciation for English nature deemed central to national identity, and bringing her home 'for her education', as she put it, was clearly meant to instill what were construed as appropriate values and not simply entail attending a school.[132] Undergoing an indoctrination in the attributes of national, class, and racial affiliation, however, simultaneously encouraged affection for the colonial settings children left behind.

Women's and men's recollections of colonial childhood have much in common on many levels, but some accounts explicitly provide gendered interpretations. Born in 1888, John Rivett-Carnac described Indian years as a time of freedom when having 'plenty of Indian servants to order about and look after one' instilled the thrill of masculine authority and outdoor adventure. The son

---

129 Margaret Ramsay-Brown, interview by author, tape recording, 23 May 1995.
130 Kaye, *Sun in the Morning*, 311, 319; Jon and Rumer Godden, *Two Under*, 11, 199.
131 CSAA, Mosse Papers (1983), Kay Mosse, 'Home', typewritten manuscript, n.d., 1–4.
132 Ibid., 1; also see Paxton, *Writing under the Raj*, 168.

of an Indian Police officer, he grew up in a heavily forested region and spent his days setting traps for wild animals, shooting birds, and bird-nesting; servants as well as the Indian Police staff subordinate to his father not only taught him hunting skills but gave him 'a feeling of confidence and superiority'. For Rivett-Carnac, memories of servants' bedtime stories and domestically situated intimacy are dwarfed by the taste of male empowerment at an early age:

There were many servants and many police officers and orderlies always around who treated me as if I was an adult, rather, with the same respect as they treated my father. The result was that I . . . got a great idea of my own importance . . . You felt . . . rather as if you were a school prefect talking to small boys at a public school.

Upon returning to England and attending first St Bede's School and then Eastbourne College, he promptly found the tables turned. Because limited family finances postponed his entry into metropolitan educational institutions until he was nearly 13, 'I had to start at my prep school in the bottom class with six and seven year old boys, and it took me about six years, five or six years, to catch up'. A hierarchy based on a combination of race and his father's rank was replaced, in Eastbourne, by one based on age and the impediment of entering school late. When he ultimately returned to India to follow his father into the Police, these measures of status remained inseparable, but again worked in his favor. No longer a perpetual new boy or fag, he readily resumed the role of prefect: 'the ordinary mass of Indians, one thought them rather as small prep schoolboys who would do what they were told to do', he summarized.[133]

Women's evaluations of the contrasts between Britain and India, meanwhile, often employ the image of the garden as a means of delineating differences between the two settings. Perhaps because of their gendered associations with the 'female' realms of home and domesticity, gardens feature prominently in women's memories of bungalow surroundings and intimate relationships, subjects which scarcely enter John Rivett-Carnac's narrative dominated by shooting and power relations within male-only arenas of socialization. For women, the garden recurs as a symbolic physical and social space for children, the site where their bodily and cultural development could take decisive turns in either positive or contemptible ways. Carolyn Steedman's research compellingly positions gardens as both 'an organizing metaphor for a particular kind of relationship between the child and the universe' as well as 'a place of actual healing and nurture', an understanding upheld in Frances Hodgson Burnett's depiction of a Yorkshire garden as the place enabling Mary Lennox's

[133] OIOC, MSS Eur T55, John Rivett-Carnac, transcribed interview, n.d., *c.* early 1970s, 1, 4–10.

recuperation from India's physical and spiritual damages.[134] Yet this view of the garden as an idealized metropolitan space in which children born in the empire could be reclaimed, however, was contested as much as it was upheld within British-Indian reminiscences.

Unlike Burnett's glowing descriptions of this form of domesticated nature, British-Indian women looking back exhibited considerably less enthusiasm. M. M. Kaye enlisted the garden metaphor to underscore her dislike and sense of exclusion. Immediately after disembarking at Tilbury she recalled seeing urban working-class neighborhoods through the train window, where 'everything in sight, including the drizzle and the dingy lines of washing that hung limply in many of the tiny, rubbish-strewn back gardens, seemed to be permeated with soot'. Her first excursion to Kensington Gardens brought her into contact with drastically different social surroundings but proved equally off-putting:

So *this* was what the British called a 'garden'! . . . Acres and acres of grass . . . Trees of the type one could not climb; neat flowerbeds that bore notices forbidding the public to pick flowers; a plethora of sooty laurel scrubs . . . and, dotted about in pairs, innumerable iron chairs on which one could not seat oneself without a watchful park attendant hurrying up to collect a small sum for the privilege of doing so.[135]

For Kaye, Kensington's strict layout and many prohibitions could not compete with the beauties as well as the freedom to enjoy the 'flower-scented tangle' of gardens she knew in India. Significantly, in Kaye's memoir English gardens she could enter such as Kensington were not symbolic extensions of idealized middle-class domestic spaces;[136] for her and others, the metropole provided no such family settings she could call her own. Gardens she saw belonged to others or constituted part of urban public culture, and in the case of Kensington felt exclusionary given the restrictions placed upon where visitors could go. If gardens served as a means of representing childhood happiness, affectionate human relationships, and a sense of belonging to their surroundings, those in Britain easily paled in comparison to their Indian counterparts. Recollections of India, on the other hand, commonly juxtaposed visions of 'my beloved Ayah', 'my baby brother', 'our lovely garden', and 'walking with my father in the evening', making the garden a central stage for scenes of human

---

[134] Carolyn Steedman, *Childhood, Culture and Class in Britain: Margaret McMillan, 1860–1931* (New Brunswick, NJ, 1990), 82, 97; on gardens, see also Morris, ' "Tha'lt be like a blush-rose" '; Simon Pugh, *Garden, Nature, Language (Cultural Politics)*, (Manchester, 1988).

[135] Kaye, *Sun in the Morning*, 315–16; 318.

[136] Leonore Davidoff and Catherine Hall, *Family Fortunes: Men and Women of the English Middle Class, 1780–1850* (Chicago, 1987), 17, 188–92, 370–5.

intimacy that vanished once children were 'left behind', often alone, in the metropole.[137]

While India nearly always appears in a more favorable light than Britain, comparisons none the less remain laced with ambiguity. Alongside negative portrayals of Britain's greyness, regimentation, or even pollution as conveyed through depictions of domesticated nature, some recollections, while not glorifying English gardens, still praise them for providing the security and protection colonial variants lacked. Monica Clough remembered how 'safe' she felt as a young girl during her family's furlough, finding it 'amazing to be allowed, encouraged, to leap into piles of dead leaves; in South India dead leaves harboured snakes and all sorts of noxious insects'. Living on the tea estate had made her wary of playing outdoors, even in the garden, following an encounter with a nest of baby cobras under the tree where she played with her dolls, a 'ghastly parody of Beatrix Potter'.[138] While the garden adjoining the colonial bungalow was generally somewhat sheltered from outside influences or literally walled in, it nevertheless exposed children to nature and culture perceived to bring both peril and temptation.

Correspondingly, even writers who described childhood loneliness and alienation in Britain after being sent away from India largely viewed this practice as desirable, or at least unavoidable. Many who returned to India, married, and had children of their own never questioned the inevitability of sending the next generation back to the metropole to repeat the family pattern. For all the emotional drawbacks associated with children's removal from the family circle and familiar natural and cultural surroundings, later childhood and adolescence in Britain remained the preferred means of passing white middle-class attributes on to their descendants. Most adults who themselves described unpleasant years in Britain retrospectively concurred that white children were best removed from India's uncertainties and dangers during a time of life characterized by vulnerability, instability, and an underdeveloped identity. Rumer Godden's novels—*The River* (1946) and *The Peacock Spring* (1975) in particular—explore the subcontinent's fascinations and joys yet simultaneously underscore its threats, employing the symbolism of the family garden to delineate these pleasures and dangers. Despite drawing heavily upon her own nostalgia, they also support the argument that those brought up in India faced perpetual cultural and physical risks.

[137] CSAA, 'Women in India: Replies to Questionnaire on Childhood', Mrs K. L. Perry-Keene, 4 June 1981; see also Mrs R. A. Tewson, 27 July 1982.
[138] CSAA, Clough, 'A Childhood', 73, 52.

The River provides a dramatic example of the combined lure and threat of a British family's garden in Bengal. Amid the lush but domesticated beauties within the walled space, tragedy lurked as the 6-year-old son played with all the animals he found there, driven by an insatiable curiosity in his explorations within the garden's confines. He discovered a cobra nearby, enticed to the garden wall because the local villagers placed food offerings at the shrine on the opposite side. The garden wall was broken by a tree, symbolizing its permeability and the openness of the garden and the British family within it to indigenous animal and human elements outside, despite clear intentions to limit the children's interactions. Once he located the cobra the boy could not be dissuaded from trying to lure it to his side of the wall, using saucers of milk and a whistle in imitation of the snake charmers whose performances he had witnessed. His prying soon brought the inevitable, the cobra killing him in a matter of minutes after it struck. Disaster descended with rapidity and finality even in a guarded space, suggesting the threat Indian nature (assisted by the villagers at their shrine) posed to children not wise enough to sense the presence of imminent dangers in a seductive setting.[139]

Godden's anxieties about India's influence on young Britons extended beyond her story of child mortality told in *The River* to her rendition of the cultural and sexual dangers for adolescent girls in *The Peacock Spring*. Written in the 1970s and taking place long after Indian independence, the novel centered on many issues of concern during the later imperial period, particularly that of adolescent instability in an uncertain setting. It began when two sisters, Una and Hal, left their English boarding school to live in Delhi with their divorced father, Sir Edward, a high-ranking United Nations official. His insistence on bringing them worried his friends, one of whom told Una, 'you and Hal are young; no one knows what you may do next, not even yourselves . . . in a strange country like this'.[140] Sir Edward's behavior provided another textual rendition of the bad-parenting theme, his selfish motives for bringing the girls becoming evident when they learned their Anglo-Indian governess was actually his fiancée; her teaching position merely provided a respectable pretext for cohabitation. Neglected by both her father and governess, 15-year-old Una began admiring Ravi, their young chota mali (assistant gardener), from the verandah. Once their mutual sexual attraction became clear, it was only a matter of time until they consummated their relationship.

---

[139] Rumer Godden, *The River* (1946; repr. Calcutta, 1991), 14–15, 19–20, 25, 43, 61, 75–8.
[140] Rumer Godden, *The Peacock Spring* (1975; repr. Harmondsworth, 1987), 104.

In *The Peacock Spring* as in *The River*, Godden again portrayed an Indian garden as a place of magical beauty that also underscored the vulnerability of young Britons theoretically contained within its walls. Ravi the chota mali, paid by his employer to tame Indian nature in accordance with English tastes, instead served as Una's conduit into 'Indian life' and sexual maturity, with many key moments of her passage transpiring in lush gardens. Ravi and the garden he tended formed an eroticized organic whole: '[Una] heard a rustle, as if creepers had been pushed aside; then, behind her, a warmth; there was another soft movement, as of muslin clothes . . . Then a hand came over her shoulder; it was a brown hand on a strong wrist that wore an amulet . . . [holding] another [peacock] feather.'[141]

The biological and social uncertainties of adolescence along with a remiss parent combined to make Una crave physical contact with one who was desired and accessible. Una's sexual initiation with Ravi followed his attempt to comfort her when she became upset about her father and governess by singing her to sleep with a nursery rhyme, 'Nini, baba, nini', or 'Sleep, baby, sleep'.[142] Godden's use of this lullaby as the prelude to Una's lost virginity—and subsequent pregnancy—is particularly suggestive of the novel's firm roots in colonial culture. 'Nini, baba, nini' was commonly sung to British children by their ayahs; its appearance here as sexual foreplay suggests how, taken to extremes, children's interaction with Indians might lead to what was widely considered to be the worst outcome of contacts between colonizer and colonized.[143] Moreover, it underscores Una's youth and childlike innocence at the very moment when she is sexually desirable to, and desiring of, an Indian servant.

In *The Peacock Spring*, Rumer Godden thus explored themes that also recur in her autobiographies of youth in late imperial India. While they evoke a fondly recalled idyllic landscape peopled with kindly, accessible Indians, dangerous or sordid qualities lurk close to the surface. Ravi was soon discredited for self-centered, authoritarian behavior, making Godden one of a long stream of white Western writers who stressed the dire consequences of interracial sexual relationships that were likely to produce mixed-race children. The union between Sir Edward and the Anglo-Indian governess was repeatedly condemned as a mistake doomed to fail, as was Una's romance with Ravi. Actions such as Una's are condemned on the grounds of both her age and ignorance, her education in England having been curtailed before she could fully learn

[141] Ibid., 106–7.

[142] Ibid., 179.

[143] See references to this nursery rhyme as recorded by Mrs Sherwood in 1807 in Hilton Brown (ed.), *The Sahibs: The Life and Ways of the British in India as Recorded by Themselves* (London, 1948), 200–1.

cultural lessons considered appropriate for those of her nationality, class, and gender and pass her unpredictable teenage years in controlled surroundings. Her eventual miscarriage and her father's discovery of her relationship with Ravi brought what Godden implied was the best possible outcome to the unfortunate results of parental thoughtlessness: the novel concluded with the sisters' safe return to school in England, where Una could be partly restored following her unwholesome Delhi experiences. Even a writer such as Godden here acquiesced to socialization in British schools, although her memoirs provided detailed descriptions of her own happy Indian childhood, professions of sympathy and friendship with many Indians, and dismal memories of being in Britain as an adolescent. Regardless of India's many appealing qualities, it posed sufficient imagined threats to make her fiction uphold many of the fears and advice long highlighted by prescriptive childrearing literature. Dangers represented by snakes and adolescent sexual encounters in the garden stood in marked contrast to the idealized English garden and overall environment signifying safety, health, innocence, and proper cultural nurture for children in the metropole.

Regardless of arguments stressing the need to protect children from the multiple hazards of colonial life and remove them from India altogether by later childhood, many families could not afford to play entirely by these rules. Barriers to the subcontinent's threats such as visiting the hill stations and hiring white nannies to partake in childcare and partly inhibit children's contacts with Indian servants may have been a widespread recommendation and ideal, but many parents simply lacked the funds to comply. Families like the Butlers and Beveridges who did follow many of these prescriptions were supported by fathers earning Indian Civil Service salaries, but those with less lucrative careers had to accommodate their domestic life to their income level in ways that diverged from what many commentators presented as the norm. The colonial community's diversity thus prevented its members from turning children's early departure for Britain into the universal practice it was commonly imagined to be.

    Chapter 2 now turns to the alternatives to sending children home at young ages and the implications of their not leaving. Staying in India 'too long' typically meant beginning formal education in the subcontinent instead of the metropole, and the risks that accompanied schooling within India were central to the adamant insistence that children needed to go at precisely this time of life. Moreover, they account for some of the inconsistencies within medical recommendations and common understandings. Although older girls were imagined to face greater physical and sexual risks than did boys if they stayed, families prioritized sending boys back to Britain sooner because of the gender-specific implications of imperial schooling options. Children of both sexes, however, saw their class, cultural, and racial identity threatened if they did not acquire the attributes that time in Britain provided. Failing to make the journey home and spend at least some of their formative years in Britain threatened to place them outside the transient white community and within the socio-economic sector occupied by both 'domiciled Europeans' and Anglo-Indians. Contacts with Indians and a hot climate were not seen as the primary dangers they faced; rather, the greater peril stemmed from the intermediary racial and social groups of which children grew more likely to become part through the company they kept, both during and after Indian schooling.

2

'Not Quite Pukka': Schooling in India and the Acquisition of Racial Status

Looking back upon her schooling during the 1930s and 1940s, Hazel Innes Craig described being sent to school in Britain after an early childhood in Calcutta, where her father worked in commerce. The outbreak of the Second World War, however, led to her unexpected return to India, where she remained for the duration of hostilities. Enrolling as a boarder at Mount Hermon School in Darjeeling introduced her to a new racial discourse that reflected perceptions of her schoolmates' backgrounds: 'I became familiar with such remarks as "chi-chi" and "fifteen annas" . . . the former referring to the sing-song, almost Welsh accent of the "Anglo-Indian" community at large; and the latter a joke for not being quite pukka or 100%, for everyone knew sixteen annas made a rupee.'[1] For a child who before the war had experienced what many commentators suggested was the inevitable departure for Britain, going to Mount Hermon not only demonstrated the possibility of other educational paths within India but, more importantly, their complex implications. As one of many schools in India that had been founded to educate 'children of European descent', Mount Hermon's intake was diverse: it enrolled both British and Anglo-Indian children, Americans (having been established by American methodist missionaries), some Indians, and a handful of other nationalities. Yet in Craig's account Anglo-Indians predominated culturally, symbolized by a 'chi-chi' accent; moreover, given that 'eight annas' was one of many derogatory terms applied to Anglo-Indians, her reference to 'fifteen annas' is revealing. Attending the school meant that children who otherwise

---

[1] Hazel Innes Craig, *Under the Old School Topee* (London, 1990), vi.

seemed 'pukka'—meaning genuine, authentic, or superior—risked appearing less than '100%' and lacked at least one anna of potential value within the racial currency of British India.

Although wartime conditions were distinct in certain respects, throughout the later imperial period returning to Britain for schooling was never a foregone conclusion for all children from colonial society. Many writers discussing childrearing in British India emphasize that white colonial families sent children home for their education—a course greatly facilitated by both steamship travel and the opening of the Suez Canal in 1869. When they allude to the possibility of attending school in India at all, they stress that the 'children of European descent' doing so were almost exclusively Anglo-Indian. Although education in Britain was indeed considered optimal by most parents, many found the cost of the journey and school fees upon arrival prohibitive and therefore needed to contemplate local alternatives, at least temporarily. Ignoring children variously named as 'European', 'English', 'British', or 'white' as part of the constituencies of schools located in the subcontinent corresponds to the historical neglect meted out to Britons in India who fell beneath the higher socio-economic sectors.

Such silences reveal just how tenuous claiming a white, or 'pukka', identity could prove if a family failed to raise children according to supposed norms, usually due to limited incomes. Scholars exploring the history of white racial status across a range of American, European, and colonial arenas stress how white people's hegemonic political, socio-economic, and cultural position has resulted from, and been reinforced by, elaborate mechanisms designed to maintain and police boundaries which divide them from less-privileged groups. Defining who counted as white in multi-racial societies was central to this process, because racial identity historically has depended on a shifting set of subjective criteria rather than a fixed group of innate characteristics.[2] As Ruth Frankenberg summarizes, 'whiteness is above all a *social* construction, but

---

[2] Verena Martinez-Alier, *Marriage, Class and Colour in Nineteenth-Century Cuba: A Study of Racial Attitudes and Sexual Values in a Slave Society* (Ann Arbor, MI, 1989); Angela Woollacott, *To Try Her Fortune in London: Australian Women, Colonialism, and Modernity* (Oxford, 2001); Ann Laura Stoler, *Race and the Education of Desire: Foucault's History of Sexuality and the Colonial Order of Things* (Durham, NC, 1995); *Carnal Knowledge and Imperial Power: Race and the Intimate in Colonial Rule* (Berkeley, CA, 2002); Catherine Hall, *White, Male and Middle Class: Explorations in Feminism and History* (New York, 1992); Vron Ware, *Beyond the Pale: White Women, Racism, and History* (London, 1992); Richard Dyer, *White* (London, 1997); David R. Roediger, *The Wages of Whiteness: Race and the Making of the American Working Class* (London, 1991); Ruth Frankenberg, *White Women, Race Matters: The Social Construction of Whiteness* (Minneapolis, MN, 1993); Matthew Frye Jacobson, *Whiteness of a Different Color: European Immigrants and the Alchemy of Race* (Cambridge, MA, 1998).

one whose disciplinary practices work forcefully to maintain the fictive biological "alibi" of race'.[3]

In late British India, childhood and specifically schooling experiences were fundamental aspects of racial categorization, with schools becoming crucial spaces in which interdependent racial and class identities were brought to the surface and often reconstituted. Ancestry and physical appearance played important roles, but acted in combination with the cultural attributes and academic credentials children acquired alongside the geographical location of their school to influence perceptions of their racial status. These were subsequently enhanced by their occupations and incomes once they completed their education. Racialization occurred in gender-specific ways, however, necessitating a comparison of how young women and men came to be included in, or excluded from, 'pukka' circles. If the latter occurred, it was not through their resemblance to Indians but rather their growing similarity to members of the stigmatized mixed-race community. Those who did not achieve an indisputably white standing—perhaps by only the slightest of margins—elucidate what its main components were under these specific historical conditions. Going to the metropole for their education signified and helped to perpetuate a coveted racial and class identity, while completing their schooling in India was likely to place them within the ranks of the 'domiciled' or 'country born', who included less-affluent Europeans and Anglo-Indians alike. Whether those of European descent were metaphorically valued at 8 annas or 15 annas, they amounted to the same small change in the realm where the rupee ruled.

SCHOOLS FOR 'CHILDREN OF EUROPEAN DESCENT' AND THE UNCERTAINTY OF RACIAL DIVIDES

Schools intended for children of British parentage in India, whether wholly British or partly of Indian descent, began to open in the second half of the eighteenth century with the expansion of the community connected with the East India Company's diversifying interests. As studies by Christopher Hawes and Durba Ghosh illustrate, the small numbers of European women in India led British men from throughout the social spectrum to form sexual relationships with Indian women, sometimes legalized by marriage but more often remain-

---

[3] Ruth Frankenberg, 'Introduction: Local Whitenesses, Localizing Whiteness', in Ruth Frankenberg (ed.), *Displacing Whiteness: Essays in Social and Cultural Criticism* (Durham, NC, 1997), 28.

ing on an informal basis.[4] Many also either intermarried or cohabited with descendants of earlier Portuguese, Dutch, or French communities who remained after Britain's own ascendancy in the subcontinent. While a small minority of the children born of these unions were sent back to Britain for their education if their fathers were army officers or Company officials, many more remained in India whether they were descended from officers or, as was more likely, from the military rank and file. Schools and orphanages opened in the larger British settlements to provide non-natives with a basic English-language, Christian education. Founded by missionaries and religious orders or funded by private and Company donations, many proved ephemeral institutions, but among the earlier ventures that survived and prospered were the La Martinière Colleges in Calcutta and Lucknow. Established in 1840 and 1836 respectively through the bequest of the French soldier of fortune Claude Martin, they counted among the most prestigious boys' schools for Europeans and 'Eurasians'—as they were known throughout the nineteenth century—in the plains.[5] Well-known girls' schools were founded by the Loreto nuns of Ireland in many cities and also in the Himalayan foothills beginning in the 1840s.[6] St George's College for boys was opened by Capucins near Mussoorie in 1853 and was taken over by the Irish Brothers of the Order of St Patrick in 1894.[7]

These Roman Catholic initiatives signalled the advent of many more schools in the Himalayan foothills and later in the Nilgiris further south. Dane Kennedy has outlined how British hill stations—Simla, Darjeeling, Mussoorie, Murree, Naini Tal, Ootacamund, and Kodaikanal prominent among them—developed for health and recreational purposes after the mid-nineteenth century, in the process becoming increasingly favored as educational venues for European-descended children.[8] When Sir Henry Lawrence established asylums for British soldiers' children and orphans beginning in 1847, he believed the temperate climate of isolated hill settings to offer the best hope for children debilitated by early years spent in the heat of the plains and the 'unwholesome' moral atmosphere prevailing in army barracks.[9] In the wake

---

[4] Christopher Hawes, *Poor Relations: The Making of a Eurasian Community in British India, 1773–1833* (Richmond, Surrey, 1996), chs. 1 and 2; Durba Ghosh, 'Colonial Companions: Bibis, Begums, and Concubines of the British in North India, 1760–1830', Ph.D. dissertation, University of California, Berkeley (2000); Durba Ghosh, 'Making and Un-making Loyal Subjects: Pensioning Widows and Educating Orphans in Early Colonial India', *Journal of Imperial and Commonwealth History*, 31/1 (2003), 1–28.

[5] Chandan Mitra, *Constant Glory: La Martinière Saga, 1836–1986* (Calcutta, 1987).

[6] Mother Mary Colmcille, *First the Blade: History of the I. B. V. M. (Loreto) in India, 1841–1962* (Calcutta, 1968).

[7] SGCM, *Right Reverend Dr Delany and the Brothers of St Patrick* (Wellington [Nilgiris], 1955), 48–50.

[8] Dane Kennedy, *The Magic Mountains: Hill Stations and the British Raj* (Berkeley, CA, 1996), 134–46.

[9] *The Lawrence Military Asylum* (Sanawur, 1858).

of the Indian rebellion of 1857–8, climatic understandings and greater accessibility paved the way for hill towns to become the predominant locations for European education in the subcontinent.[10]

Following the 'Mutiny' and the shift from Company to Crown Rule, representatives of the Church of England and government alike drew attention to the population of poorer Europeans and Eurasians that increased in tandem with the expanding civil, military, and commercial colonial infrastructure. Existing educational facilities providing a Christian moral and English scholastic training within India could accommodate only a fraction of the growing numbers of children whose parents could ill afford school fees in India, let alone contemplate sending them to Britain. Bishop Cotton of Calcutta voiced the dangers that descendants of Europeans might present to the stability of colonial rule in the future, despite their loyalty to the British during the recent uprising. Cotton considered it 'nothing less than a national sin to neglect a class who are our fellow Christians and fellow subjects, whose presence in India is due entirely to our occupation of the country, but who, unless real efforts are made for their good, are in great moral and spiritual danger'. Poor Europeans and Eurasians posed a threat not only to themselves, but also appeared likely to jeopardize Indian opinion of the British more generally—a crucial consideration given the widespread nature of the recent uprising and its devastating consequences. 'The conduct and character of the Christians settled among them must have the most direct influence upon their estimate of Christianity and Western civilization', Cotton stressed. 'If a generation calling itself Christian, and descended wholly or partly from European parents, grows up in ignorance and evil habits, the effect on the heathen and Mahommedan population will be most disastrous.'[11]

Bishop Cotton's views soon encouraged Governor-General Lord Canning to issue a minute in 1860 advocating government grants-in-aid both to support existing schools and to encourage their proliferation. As it emerged, these schools long received only sporadic state assistance and continued to depend largely upon financing from private resources and religious bodies. None the less, the ideologies and priorities foregrounded by Cotton and Canning in the immediate aftermath of revolt and the advent of Crown Rule paved the way for further non-official initiatives and, by the 1880s, led to regulated government grants to institutions that adhered to successive Codes of Regulations for

---

[10] H. N. Mathur, 'Education of European and Eurasian Children in India, 1860–1894', *Indian Historical Records Commission: Proceedings* 31, Part II (1935), 113–20.

[11] Bishop Cotton, cited in *Cottonian*, 32 (1934), 33.

European Schools.[12] Given the increasing numbers of both Europeans and Eurasians in India, Canning emphasized that 'if measures for educating these children are not . . . aided by the Government, we shall soon find ourselves embarrassed in all large towns and stations with a floating population of Indianized English, loosely brought up, and exhibiting most of the worst qualities of both races'. Moreover, he hoped to ensure the ongoing cultural and political loyalty of persons of partial Indian ancestry to the Crown as well as bolster their utility as state employees, since they 'serve the Government more efficiently than the Natives can . . . and more cheaply and conveniently than Europeans'.[13]

In his minute, Canning, like Bishop Cotton before him, envisioned two types of schools for children whose families could not pay for education in Britain. Boarding establishments in the hills were seen as optimal for those who could afford the added expense, while cheaper day schools on the plains— where most Europeans and Anglo-Indians lived—could provide for those unable to leave home. Many of the new institutions founded in the hills in the decades following Canning's minute indeed counted among the 'higher class' schools. Among the boys' schools were the Bishop Cotton School at Simla, founded under Anglican auspices in 1863, and St Joseph's College at Darjeeling, established by Jesuits in 1888. Girls' schools that also accepted younger boys included the Presentation Convent High School at Kodaikanal, begun by the Irish Presentation nuns in 1916, and the Queen's Hill School at Darjeeling, opened in 1895 by the Women's Foreign Missionary Society of the American Methodist Episcopal Church. The latter expanded to include older boys and changed its name to Mount Hermon School in 1930. Yet these more socially prestigious establishments shared their location with others for the orphaned or otherwise destitute that either charged only minimal fees or accepted children free of charge. Like the Lawrence Military Asylums preceding it, the Christian Training School and Orphanage was opened at Mussoorie by nonconformists in 1888, later becoming known as Wynberg Allen School and educating both girls and boys. The St Andrew's Colonial Homes at Kalimpong founded in 1900 served a similar constituency.[14]

---

[12] Viceroy Lord Lytton again reviewed the state of European and Eurasian education in 1879, which led to a formalized policy of grants-in-aid and to official Codes of Regulations for European Schools in the 1880s. See Austin A. D'Souza, *Anglo-Indian Education: A Study of its Origins and Growth in Bengal up to 1960* (Delhi, 1976), 108–19; OIOC, V/24/4429, Sir Alfred Croft, *Review of Education in India, 1886* (Calcutta, 1888), 294–8.

[13] OIOC, V/26/861/2, *Committee upon the Financial Condition of Hill Schools for Europeans in North India, Vol. II: Evidence and Appendices* (Calcutta, 1905), 'Minute by Lord Canning, dated the 29th October 1860', 335.

[14] Dick B. Dewan, *Education in the Darjeeling Hills: An Historical Survey: 1835–1985* (New Delhi, 1991).

Just as the hills became home to schools for children ranging from the poorest to those whose families could afford tuition and boarding fees in India but not in Britain itself, no absolute divide emerged to keep those of wholly or partly European ancestry either in distinct institutions or regions. From the later nineteenth century to the present day, many writers have attempted to assign pupils to schools in distinct geographical settings according to perceptions of their 'race'. In 1860, Cotton and Canning both imagined that hill schools were most essential for children of pure European ancestry, while Eurasians could more readily remain in the hot plains climate since they possessed the 'advantage' of native blood.[15] Dane Kennedy's study supports this view, suggesting that 'Anglo-Indians were not welcome at most of the better [hill] schools', helping to make the hills 'nurseries of the ruling race', while David Arnold's work on schooling and orphanages for 'poor whites' similarly positions them as a category that retained some distinction from Anglo-Indians, at least in the nineteenth century.[16] In contrast, other commentators both during and after the late imperial era largely omit European children from the hill schools' constituencies on the grounds that nearly all left India to be educated in Britain, labelling both hills and plains schools for those of European descent 'Anglo-Indian schools' by the interwar years.[17] Despite their divergent conclusions, the divide between Europeans 'pure and mixed' persists. Reality, however, proved far less willing to respect such dichotomous classifications, which became increasingly blurred by the early twentieth century.

As successive government Codes of Regulations for European Schools laid out, the 'Europeans' such hills or plains institutions were meant to encompass included 'any person of European descent, pure or mixed, who retains European habits and modes of life'.[18] Although the British men and women in charge of such schools often exhibited considerable biases against mixed-race children, few institutions of any size or longevity appeared to have succeeded in excluding them for long. For reasons that will be explored further below, this

---

[15] Ibid., 335–6. See also OIOC, V/24/4429, 296.

[16] Kennedy, *Magic Mountains*, 141; David Arnold, 'European Orphans and Vagrants in India in the Nineteenth Century', *Journal of Imperial and Commonwealth History*, 7/2 (1979), 106, 108. My conclusions differ from Kennedy's suggestion that the hill schools' social composition shifted between the nineteenth and twentieth centuries.

[17] D'Souza, *Anglo-Indian Education*; Noel P. Gist and Roy Dean Wright, *Marginality and Identity: Anglo-Indians as a Racially-Mixed Minority in India* (Leiden, 1973); Evelyn Abel, *The Anglo-Indian Community: Survival in India* (New Delhi, 1988).

[18] OIOC, V/27/861/3, *Code of Regulations for European Schools in Bengal for the Year 1884–85* (Calcutta, 1884), 1. Later editions of the Code as well as other official reports defined 'Europeans' using similar and usually identical wording.

was particularly the case at boys' schools. Indeed, many originated during the same era when a combination of improved shipping and the expansion of boys' public school-style education in the metropole both began to siphon off a greater portion of their prospective male clientele whose families had adequate funds to perpetuate their British links. As the governors of the Bishop Cotton School at Simla discussed only three years after it opened in 1863, 'it is not at all likely that parents with ample means will avail themselves of the School to any great extent; rather it is likely that we shall have fewer applications for admission from such classes as the facilities for sending boys to England increase'.[19]

Given the stronger pull of Britain, boys' schools that tried to maintain their social, and implicitly racial, exclusivity did so at considerable risk. The fall of the Mussoorie School for boys served as a warning. Dating from 1835 and reputed to be the first school for Europeans in the hills, it flourished into the 1870s when a government report described it as thriving without public assistance by charging a fee 'higher than that of any other school in India'. Fathers including Public Works Department, Police and army officers, planters, merchants, and other government officials paid Rs. 550 annually for each boy's tuition and board.[20] Yet by the time a detailed government report on the hill schools emerged in 1904 and 1905, the Mussoorie School was listed as 'in abeyance' and never ultimately reopened. Probable reasons for its demise included parents' unwillingness to pay high fees to educate their sons in India, regardless of their potential schoolmates' respectable pedigrees and the school's healthy location. Shorter voyages between Britain and India were partly responsible, as was the expansion of what one observer called 'the smaller English public schools'—by which he meant the second-tier public schools or their imitators. Bedford, a school this book considers further in Chapter 4, was cited as one of several common metropolitan educational destinations where the fee for boarders 'was no higher if as high as at our hill schools'.[21] Schools in India competed at their peril, and most seem to have made few efforts to do so. Perennially short of funds and relying on the patronage of families with limited educational budgets who often opted for British counterparts at the first opportunity, attempting to limit or exclude Anglo-Indians or charge

---

[19] BCSS, *Board of Governors Minute Book, Bishop Cotton School, Simla, 1863–c.1900*, 75.

[20] OIOC, V/27/861/1, A. J. Lawrence, *Report on the Existing Schools for Europeans and Eurasians Throughout India* (Calcutta, 1873), 100–1.

[21] OIOC, V/26/861/2, evidence given by the Revd G. A. Ford, 34.

excessive fees rendered it even more difficult to guarantee financial solvency and survival.[22]

By the early twentieth century, then, the class of families arguably more likely to have enrolled their children in earlier decades now opted for educational facilities in Britain. As the former Archdeacon of Lucknow put it:

> no considerable number of the children of English gentlemen are educated in India at all. The sons and daughters of officers of superior rank, of planters, and of gentlemen generally, are commonly sent home to England when the school time comes . . . Here and there an officer's son, and more often an officer's daughter will be found in an Indian school; but the number of these children is never likely to be large, while all attempts to found an Indian Eton seem foredoomed to failure.[23]

Britain's attractions, however, did not curtail the presence of either boys or girls described as Europeans at schools in India, despite limiting their numbers. Given the 'population permanently domiciled in this country, whose ties with England are loosened', the 1904–5 government report asserted, 'when all who can afford to send their children home have done so, there remains a solid and increasing body of the population who must send their children to school in the hills'.[24] The 'dividing line' between families sending children to school in India and those opting for the metropole was seen as largely financial, deriving from fathers' subordinate standing within either state or non-official employment sectors. One school principal summarized: 'the parents, who are English . . . belong to a lower social grade. Such parents may be engaged in trade or commerce in Calcutta . . . or they may be employees of the various railway or steamer companies, or they may belong to the lower ranks of Government service'.[25] 'English' parents like these who could not afford education in Britain, however, jeopardized their children's very inclusion in this community. Leaving India for a metropolitan education became a rite of passage that positioned an individual within the transient, sojourner, better-off community marked as 'European', whereas schooling in the subcontinent indicated a domiciled, poorer, and racially ambiguous status.

---

[22] More prestigious hill schools such as the Bishop Cotton School and St George's College respectively charged boarders Rs. 28 and Rs. 23 a month in the 1870s, while by 1908 the best hill schools were said to cost between Rs. 300 and Rs. 500 annually (equivalent to £20 and £33). OIOC, V/27/861/1, 106, 120; Revd O. D. Watkins, 'The Education of European and Eurasian Children in India', in *Pan-Anglican Papers, Being Problems for Consideration at the Pan-Anglican Congress, 1908: Church Work among those Temporarily Residing in Distant Lands* (London, 1908), 6.

[23] Watkins, 'Education of European', 3–4.

[24] OIOC, V/26/861/1, *Committee Upon the Condition of Hill Schools for Europeans In Northern India, Vol. I: Report* (Calcutta, 1904), 2.

[25] OIOC, V/26/861/2, 191, evidence given by W. H. Arden Wood, Principal, La Martinière College, Calcutta.

Socio-economic divides failed to mirror racial distinctions during the late imperial era. David Arnold's work on India's 'poor white' population, which encompassed nearly half of the European community in the subcontinent by the end of the nineteenth century, charts its emergence through British rank-and-file soldiers and sailors staying in India—becoming 'domiciled'—instead of returning to Britain once their military service ended. Studies by Laura Bear and Lionel Caplan further delineate how domiciled Europeans increasingly converged with the Anglo-Indian community to form an 'interstitial group' between more senior Europeans and Indians in terms of their social and occupational standing. Most found jobs in the same sectors as the Anglo-Indians, with the railway becoming the largest employer. They also worked alongside men newly arrived from Britain (who sometimes brought female dependants with them) to take up subordinate appointments in posts, telegraphs, customs, public works, and in the Indian Medical Department as well as other state-run divisions. Others filled intermediary positions in the growing private sector including on tea estates and in commercial firms. Many also became linked to Anglo-Indians by marriage.[26] By the last decades of British rule, individuals of mixed British and Indian ancestry were rarely the children of European men and Indian women, more commonly having either two Anglo-Indian parents, or alternatively one Anglo-Indian and one European parent.

Partly because India did not count among the overseas imperial destinations Britain promoted as appropriate for permanent white settlement, however,[27] those who lost touch with Britain were commonly equated with the racially mixed by colonial elites. Regardless of their actual ancestry, they experienced the same disadvantages as the Anglo-Indian community, in effect falling outside the bounds of whiteness with its many attendant privileges. More affluent Britons in India who counted themselves among the temporary sojourners practiced a form of what John Hartigan has termed 'intraracial othering' with reference to the contemporary United States, in this instance by consigning domiciled Europeans to a racial category deemed inferior because of their inferior class status and geographical rootedness in the subcontinent.[28] As

---

[26] Arnold, 'European Orphans', 104–14; David Arnold, 'White Colonization and Labour in Nineteenth-Century India', *Journal of Imperial and Commonwealth History*, 9/2 (1983), 148–53; Laura Gbah Bear, 'Miscegenations of Modernity: Constructing European Respectability and Race in the Indian Railway Colony, 1857–1931', *Women's History Review*, 3/4 (1994), 531; Lionel Caplan, *Children of Colonialism: Anglo-Indians in a Postcolonial World* (Oxford, 2001), 25–30; Lionel Caplan, 'Cupid in Colonial and Post-Colonial South India: Changing "Marriage" Practices Among Anglo-Indians in Madras', *South Asia*, 21/2 (1998), 6–7.

[27] Arnold, 'White Colonization', 145–54; Mark Harrison, *Climates and Constitutions: Health, Race, Environment and British Imperialism in India, 1600–1850* (New Delhi, 1999); Kennedy, *Magic Mountains*, 149–56.

[28] John Hartigan, Jnr, 'Unpopular Culture: The Case of "White Trash"', *Cultural Studies*, 11 (1997), 317.

Ann Stoler summarizes, because of the ways poorer whites merged with the racially mixed socially across a range of colonial contexts, 'in practice these persons were often treated as indistinguishable, one and the same', and were nearly always considered a 'problem' by the more affluent Europeans, for they 'called into question the very criteria by which Europeanness could be identified'.[29]

Those whose travels to and from the metropole provided them with a more secure classification were highly sceptical about the origins of individuals who were domiciled in India but claimed to be descended exclusively from Europeans. Given the multiple stigmas attached to mixed ancestry, many felt that these persons deliberately obscured even the slightest degree of Indian heritage. Civil servants in charge of the Census of India issued repeated warnings about the limitations inherent in the demographic data they collected concerning Europeans and Eurasians/Anglo-Indians. The 1891 Census report stated that 'the distinction between the three races is very shadowy, and there is a tendency for Eurasians to enter the European group, and for native Christians to be returned as Eurasians'.[30] Alongside the community's interracial origins it was, on the one hand, said to be infiltrated from 'below' by Indians who had converted to Christianity, and, on the other, accused of fraudulent assertions of purely European status—in effect producing an atmosphere in which all ancestral claims were open to speculation.[31]

Census-making constituted a prime example of colonial authorities' desire to identify, categorize, and therefore more effectively to control the populations they governed overseas. Benedict Anderson highlights the 'passion for completeness and unambiguity' and 'intolerance of multiple . . . blurred, or changing identifications', which, by their very existence, belied the far more complex colonial conditions which made such classification schemes so appealing in the first place.[32] Attempts to document the populations resident in India became even more unsettling when British officials were forced to confront the ways 'Europeans' themselves confounded straightforward categorization. Reports analyzing Census returns from the late nineteenth century until

[29] Stoler, *Race and the Education of Desire*, 107.

[30] J. A. Baines, *Census of India, 1891. General Report* (London, 1893), 178.

[31] The purported tendency for Indian Christians to 'pass' as Anglo-Indians through adopting European dress, names, and other 'modes of life' was often criticized by members of the mixed-race or domiciled European community concerned to maximize their affinities to white European culture. See for example 'One of the Community', *The Euro-Asian' or 'Anglo-Indian': A Burma Brochure* (Rangoon, 1910), 2.

[32] Benedict Anderson, *Imagined Communities: Reflections on the Origin and Spread of Nationalism*, rev. edn. (London, 1991), 164–6. See also Bernard S. Cohn, 'The Census, Social Structure, and Objectification in South Asia', in *An Anthropologist Among the Historians and Other Essays* (New Delhi, 1987), 224–54; Nicholas B. Dirks, *Castes of Mind: Colonialism and the Making of Modern India* (Princeton, NJ, 2001).

the 1930s repeatedly described data concerning the European and mixed-race populations as 'unreliable' or 'unsatisfactory', illuminating as they did how European self-definition *vis-à-vis* other groups revealed itself to be both constructed and mutable. By the time of the 1931 Census report, officials had developed elaborate means of estimating the extent of Anglo-Indian duplicity when registering their affiliation, thereby simultaneously illuminating and attempting to rectify the difficulties in defining who was a European in India. Noting 'the tendency of Anglo-Indians who are not handicapped by excessive pigmentation to return themselves as Europeans', the compiler calculated that 30,000 Anglo-Indians should be deducted from the total number of European British Subjects. 'The numbers of those born and *remaining* in India . . . *excluding as they must do* the great majority of Europeans, seem to be much too high to represent only the unmixed domiciled Europeans', the 1931 report claimed.[33]

Views like these suggest that skin color, other physical markers, and birthplace provided insufficient proof of an individual's European or Anglo-Indian status. Although domiciled Europeans were popularly known as the 'country born', this distinction could also apply to most children of the highest-ranking British families in India if interpreted literally—as simply having been born in the subcontinent. Instead, 'remaining in India' was the decisive feature distinguishing the 'domiciled' who were racially suspect from the 'real' Europeans who were able to pay for travels that allowed them to maintain contact with Britain. Behavior and lifestyle made possible mainly by wealth thus determined racial categorization as much as ancestry, which could prove defiantly indeterminate.[34] Education in the subcontinent was a central element within the process by which Europeans in India became defined as 'domiciled' there and downgraded as indistinguishable from the racially mixed.

The ways children attending schools for those of 'European descent, pure or mixed' could elude a concrete racial definition is illustrated in *Scabby Dichson*, a novel written in the 1920s by Richard Blaker. Providing a thinly disguised portrait of the Bishop Cotton School at Simla the author had attended, its characters express attitudes concerning domiciled Europeans and Anglo-Indians common among the transient British community of the time, focusing

---

[33] The report then re-evaluated the 'real' number of Anglo-Indians as 168,400, thus reducing the European population to 125,500. See J. H. Hutton, *Census of India, 1931, Vol. I-India. Part I.-Report* (Delhi, 1933), 426; emphasis added.

[34] As Verena Martinez-Alier extrapolates from her study of nineteenth-century Cuba, 'racial classifications in Western societies from the eighteenth century onward collapsed phenotype and genotype with socio-cultural status, being applied not only to the "savages" abroad but also to social inferiors at home'. *Marriage, Class and Colour*, p. xvi.

upon perceptions of one orphaned pupil's unascertained racial heritage. Dichson's symbolic status as one lacking knowable parentage allows British adults who meet him to question his background and guess whether he was fully European—as he claimed—or of partial Indian ancestry. In one scene, an admiring schoolmaster describes Dichson to an Indian Police officer, saying that he 'seems quite one of us, somehow. Makes one wonder what sort of people he comes from. He says Dutch . . .' In angry disbelief, the Policeman replies, 'Dutch my grandmother! . . . That is an old dodge among that sort. They're always claiming outlandish ancestry—usually Spanish or Portuguese—when there's a touch of the old brush in them somewhere.'[35] Asserting descent from continental Europeans that was symbolized by foreign surnames suggested partial Indian ancestry even more strongly than simply claiming British forebears, since few Dutch, Portuguese, or French women had accompanied men from their respective nations to India in the seventeenth and eighteenth centuries.[36] Although earlier generations of Britons had perpetuated the tradition of sexual liaisons with Indian women and thus multiplied the pre-existing population of mixed descent, the subsequent arrival of greater numbers of British women allowed those claiming wholly British descent some benefit of the doubt—albeit often not much.

Given the scepticism about ancestral claims, British observers commonly turned to other indicators in their efforts to unmask the evasive Anglo-Indian. Certain physical attributes—often extremely minute—were popularly deemed viable 'proofs' of mixed-race heritage, particularly in individuals whose outward appearance otherwise suggested 'genuine' Europeanness. Carlo Ginzburg has traced how the conviction that 'though reality may seem to be opaque, there are privileged zones—signs, clues—which allow us to penetrate it' proliferated throughout Western European culture in the late nineteenth and early twentieth centuries. Techniques believed capable of distinguishing art forgeries from original paintings, Ginzburg argues, bore resemblance to both the evaluation of 'symptoms' in Freudian psychoanalysis and to Sherlock Holmes's crime-solving methods, all being based on 'the hypothesis that apparently negligible details could reveal profound phenomena of great importance' to those with sufficient expertise.[37] As the Census reports implied, self-styled

[35] Richard Blaker, *Scabby Dichson* (London, n.d. [*c.*1920s]), 34–5. Blaker is mentioned as an old boy of the Bishop Cotton School, Simla in the school magazine. *Cottonian*, 29 (Dec. 1932), 7.

[36] On the diversity of European origins within the group which came to comprise the Anglo-Indian community, see Hawes, *Poor Relations*, 1–2; Caplan, *Children of Colonialism*, 22–5; Caplan, 'Cupid in Colonial', 5.

[37] Carlo Ginzburg, 'Clues: Roots of an Evidential Paradigm', in *Clues, Myth, and the Historical Method*, trans. by John and Anne C. Tedeschi (Baltimore, MD, 1989), 123–4.

connoisseurs seeking to distinguish 'real' Europeans from potential impostors existed in abundance in India, often turning to supposed bodily signifiers of racial identity. In Blaker's novel, another British official attempted to ascertain Dichson's ancestry by 'peering at the back of his neck for a clue as to the essential colouring of his subcuticle'.[38] Forays into racial decoding often entailed a focus on more specific attributes, however, some of which attained transnational salience in cultures where white concern about racial 'passing' among disempowered groups was rampant.[39] Werner Sollors explores how fingernail pigmentation—'the bluish tinge in the halfmoon'—became a dominant 'mark' through which whites in Britain, India, France, Germany, the Caribbean, and especially the United States sought to certify 'blackness', especially in individuals who otherwise showed no 'signs' of non-European descent. Belief in the clues provided by fingernails (or alternatively by skin, hair, or eyes) Sollors argues, exemplifies the 'wish for verisimilitude' pervading efforts to 'decide the undecidable'.[40]

'Telltale nails that tell nothing' was often the outcome of such scrutiny, just as Dichson's neck failed to divulge his ancestry.[41] Bodily attributes believed to suggest Indian blood often proved infuriatingly absent or deeply hidden, causing racial detectives to go beyond 'the false promise of the visible' by turning to cultural indicators as a means of recognizing Anglo-Indians.[42] The man peering down Dichson's neck also 'listen[ed] to his vowels with an etymologist's absorption' to ascertain the boy's 'chi-chi' accent—another stereotypical marker of the Anglo-Indian who allegedly spoke English differently from those with stronger metropolitan connections.[43] Just as accent was an important marker of class, cultural, and regional background in Britain, in India 'chi-chi' English took on an additional layer of racial connotations, attesting to its speakers'

---

[38] Blaker, *Scabby Dichson*, 81.

[39] 'Passing' has recently received attention from scholars focused on the United States, including Gayle Wald, *Crossing the Line: Racial Passing in Twentieth-Century U.S. Literature and Culture* (Durham, NC, 2000); Vikki Bell, 'Show and Tell: Passing and Narrative in Toni Morrison's *Jazz*', *Social Identities*, 2/2 (1996), 221–36; Harryette Mullen, 'Optic White: Blackness and the Production of Whiteness', *diacritics*, 24/2–3 (1994), 71–89.

[40] Werner Sollors, *Neither Black Nor White Yet Both: Thematic Explorations of Interracial Literature* (New York, 1997), 154, 158. Rudyard Kipling used fingernail pigmentation as the physical mark that did most to undermine a woman's attempts to pass as British in his story 'Kidnapped', in *Plain Tales from the Hills* (1888; repr. Oxford, 1987), 98.

[41] Sollors, *Neither Black Nor White*, 158. Judith R. Walkowitz also discusses visual markers of racial difference in her study of Olive Christian Malvery, an Anglo-Indian woman in early twentieth-century London. See 'The Indian Woman, the Flower Girl, and the Jew: Photojournalism in Edwardian London', *Victorian Studies*, 42/1 (1998/1999), 3–46.

[42] Amy Robinson, 'It Takes One to Know One: Passing and Communities of Common Interest', *Critical Inquiry*, 20 (1994), 716.

[43] Blaker, *Scabby Dichson*, 81.

failure to attain 'the cultural competencies which the conferral of European status required', as Stoler puts it.[44] 'Chi-chi' was also a common derogatory term for Anglo-Indians, making those speaking in this manner tantamount to being racially mixed themselves in the eyes of many observers from Britain.[45] Because its racial overtones derived from what was explicitly learned behavior as opposed to any inherent biological quality, the possibility that their children would emerge even from 'higher-class' hill schools speaking 'chi-chi' ranked high on many parents' lists of reasons for avoiding such educational venues at all costs.[46]

Indeed, 'chi-chi' accents, Anglo-Indian companionship, and hill schools in India easily became fused in narratives detailing the risks British children faced if they could not leave for the metropole during their school years. In their memoir *Two Under the Indian Sun*, Jon and Rumer Godden looked back upon the five additional years they spent in India after the outbreak of the First World War led their parents to bring them back from Britain for the conflict's duration. Until they were 12 and 13, they and their two younger sisters remained at home in Narayangunj, where their father worked for a steamship company. Arranging for their education proved a trial, since governesses their parents deemed acceptable proved hard to find and even harder to retain in a household with four unruly children. English governesses came and went before their parents hired an Anglo-Indian nanny, only to discharge her when the children 'caught her chi-chi accent'.[47] In desperation, their aunt living with the family stepped in to teach the girls because, they later surmised, 'there was no one else; in those days, English children of any family did not go to the hill boarding schools where the children were chiefly Anglo-Indian. There was a

[44] Stoler, *Race and the Education of Desire*, 12; Lynda Mugglestone, *'Talking Proper': The Rise of Accent as Social Symbol* (Oxford, 1995).

[45] In 1903, 'cheechee' was defined as 'a disparaging term applied to half-castes or Eurasians . . . Said to be taken from *chi* (Fie!), a common native (South Indian) interjection of remonstrance or reproof, supposed to be much used by the class in question. The term is, however, perhaps also a kind of onomatopoeia, indicating the mincing pronunciation that often characterizes them . . .' See Col. Henry Yule and A. C. Burnell, *Hobson-Jobson: A Glossary of Colloquial Anglo-Indian Words and Phrases*, William Crooke (ed.), (New Delhi, 1968, repr. of 2nd 1903 edn.), 186. Letters written by the wife of an Indian Forest Service officer in 1922 indicatively refer to 'chi-chi' as an 'appalling accent' and one of its speakers as 'only a chi-chi boy', with whom she hoped their own sons would have limited contact. OIOC, MSS Eur D931/11, Enid Dawkins to Clinton Dawkins, 12 April 1922; 18 April 1922.

[46] On parental dislike of 'chi-chi' accents and hesitation to send children to school in India because of this 'threat', see Kennedy, *Magic Mountains*, 141–2; M. M. Kaye, *The Sun in the Morning: My Early Years in India and England* (New York, 1990), 194–5. The 1904–5 government report cited one commentator who asserted that 'some parents object to the low class of boys found in a certain proportion of Indian schools, and to their nasty accent'. See OIOC, V/26/861/2, 40, evidence given by the Most Revd Dr Charles Gentili, O.C., Archbishop of Agra.

[47] Jon and Rumer Godden, *Two Under the Indian Sun* (New York, 1966; repr. 1987), 33–5.

curious fear of—was it contamination—and there was the accent, "chi-chi", hallmark of the country bred'.[48]

'English' children who attended school in India had much in common with their mixed-race peers—so much so that countless Britons whose higher incomes enabled journeys home refused even to acknowledge schooling in India as a possibility for their offspring. In many instances, parental desire to distance themselves and their children from inclusion within the constituencies of schools in India was such that, in the words of one *fin-de-siècle* observer, 'all those who are able to scrape the money together will send their children to England', no matter how hard the sacrifice.[49] Like the Godden family during the First World War, many parents needing to postpone their children's entry into British schools simply had them taught in the home until they left, usually by either a governess or their mother. While home education was largely conducted on an *ad hoc* basis, some families turned to the correspondence lessons administered by the Parents' National Educational Union in England.[50] Private methods effectively ensured that children's contacts with other groups were largely restricted to Indians, especially servants, as opposed to Anglo-Indian and domiciled European children.

Significantly, when parents voiced fears about their children's companions if they attended a school intended for those 'of European descent', they unfailingly neglected to single out the Indian pupils who often attended alongside Europeans and Anglo-Indians. Institutions accepting government grants for European schools had the option of admitting a limited number of Indians, with the maximum proportion varying over time but generally falling between 15 and 25 per cent of their total enrollment. By the 1920s and 1930s many schools indeed welcomed Indians (especially those who were Christian) because their fees could prove an invaluable means of increasing limited operating budgets.[51] British parents appeared unconcerned about their children mingling with 'natives' at school and focused their reservations on

---

[48] Ibid., 63.

[49] OIOC, V/26/861/2, 196, evidence given by the Very Revd A. Neut.

[50] The PNEU was founded by Charlotte Mason in 1887, and its correspondence course enrolled an increasing number of families living in the empire. On its domestic origins, see George K. Behlmer, *Friends of the Family: The English Home and its Guardians, 1850–1940* (Stanford, CA, 1998), 146–60; on its overseas clientele, see 'The PNEU in India', *Parents' Review*, 28 (1917), 667–77; 'Letters from PUS Families in the Dominions', *Parents' Review*, 35 (1924), 389–425; 'Problems of the Family Separated by the High Seas', *Parents' Review*, 48 (1937), 335–54, 583–608. The PNEU's 'rigorously English' curriculum is described in CSAA, Clough Papers, Mrs M. F. Clough, 'A Childhood in Travancore, 1922–1931', typewritten manuscript (1983), 80, 55.

[51] See for example OIOC, V/24/4432, R. Littlehailes, *Progress of Education in India, 1922–27: Ninth Quinquennial Review*, Vol. 1 (Calcutta, 1929), 226.

Anglo-Indians, just as those who decided to educate their children in the home could exhibit similar differential attitudes. In the Godden household, prohibitions on mingling with Anglo-Indians included not only dismissing the children's nanny but also placing their next-door neighbors' children off-limits as potential playmates; instead, Jon and Rumer recalled spending much time in the company of Indian servants with parental approval.[52] For the daughters of a man whose commercial occupation placed the family below the higher civil and military colonial circles in terms of income and status, Indian domestic staff posed less of a threat than members of other intermediary groups who came too close for comfort. By staying in India until they approached adolescence, it became all the more important for them to appear distinct from others who were similarly, yet more irrevocably, 'country bred'. Foremost among the probable reasons for this selective anxiety was the belief that their children were more likely to develop 'undesirable' traits that increased their resemblance to others who shared European ancestry but were of lower status than to become similar to those who fell outside the realm of the 'European descended' altogether.

Perceptions of racial status depended not only upon readings of bodily, cultural, and socio-economic qualities but also were tied to evidence (or lack thereof) of ongoing contact with Britain. In 1928, as Donald and Maisie Scott prepared for their 10-year-old daughter to transfer from her day convent school near their home in Quetta to board at St Denys's School in the hill station of Murree, Donald wrote to ask a favor of his brother's family in England. By making his career in the Posts and Telegraphs Department he had grown well aware of the qualities that enhanced his status within a subordinate occupational sector that also employed many domiciled Europeans, Anglo-Indians, and Indians, and he searched for ways his daughter might socially profit from stronger ties to Britain than many of her schoolmates could claim:

Dorothy is going up to school in a fortnight's time and I should like her to get a letter occasionally . . . say once a month. It will be a treat for her and also an advantage. In India, the land of snobbery, it is a great thing to have relations in England, and since Dorothy is so very meek and mild in the ordinary way I would like to give her a chance of boasting among her new friends about her cousins 'at Home'. A few days ago we had a call from the matron of the convent in Quetta where Dorothy went to school on our return from leave and she was saying how one morning she was told 'A child has come to school, who has come direct from England' and she got so excited that she ran off at once into the school to have a look . . . that will give you an idea of the feelings on the

---

[52] Jon and Rumer Godden, *Two Under*, 107–9.

subject in India. It has been a great advantage to me in my career to be able to boast myself of English birth and education and I am very sensible of the advantages of it. All horrible snobbery of course, but we live in a snobbish world.[53]

Dorothy Scott in many respects was a typical example of a hill-school pupil in the interwar period. Her father worked in an occupation and earned an income that made choosing schools in India logical. The family revisited Britain rarely due to the journey's expense—indeed, ten years could elapse between long leaves in Britain—and he found the £6 a month that covered her educational expenses as a boarder difficult to afford.[54] Within her father's letters and her later memoir her mother's ancestry is not specified beyond Dorothy's allusion to a 'Latin temperament' inherited from her maternal grandparents; this alongside her own and her mother's appearance in photographs most likely positioned her as an Anglo-Indian in the knowing eyes of observers within the colonial community[55] (Illustration 5). Playing up her father's British background and her own fleeting contact on furlough, however, ideally allowed her to lay claim to a non-domiciled status. By the standards of European schools in India this made her a rarity, a child 'direct from England', with all its racial and social connotations. Letters from her father's family, by providing ongoing tangible evidence of her ties to home, were intended to testify to her heritage and credit several additional rupees to her racial account—pushing her further away from 8 annas and closer to the 15 that commonly marked the upper limits for children at hill schools. While Donald Scott's family were but precariously positioned within the transient sector, his own origins, their rare trips to Britain, and ultimately their permanent return once he retired none the less helped them to maintain an unsteady foothold within a higher-status racialized group—regardless of his wife's ancestry, his restricted income, and the site of his daughter's school. However, as the following pages argue, this would have proved more difficult had Dorothy Scott been a boy or had brothers who were similarly educated in India. Any of the professional advantages Donald Scott enjoyed thanks to 'English birth and education' would have been lost for his sons had they not followed in his footsteps, direct family links to the metropole notwithstanding.

---

[53] OIOC, MSS Eur D1232/3, Donald Scott to Bert Scott, 3 Mar. 1928.

[54] OIOC, MSS Eur D1232/5, Donald Scott to Bert Scott, 19 Feb. 1929.

[55] OIOC, MSS Eur D1232/14, Dorothy Langham (née Scott), typescript manuscript, 'Missie Baba and Family', n.d., 266.

BOYS' SCHOOLING AND THE CLOSING OF CAREERS

Founded during the same decades when public schools in Britain both expanded in number and consolidated their prominence as middle-class and elite male educational settings, many Indian schools for boys of European descent turned to them for cultural inspiration. This was particularly true at institutions in the hills seeking to build a reputation for catering to the highest classes of families not able to start their sons at metropolitan schools.[56] Their administrators often sought (largely unsuccessfully) to limit the proportion of day boys in order to maintain a boarding-school character. They hoped this not only would denote a higher social level through requiring families to pay additional boarding fees but also enhance the daily regime characterized by the house system, prefects, and the centrality of team games.[57] Boys' hill schools, however, found their public-school aspirations compromised on nearly every level. Cricket, one of the key features of English public-school life, failed to acquire prominence at many Indian hill schools despite the best efforts of teachers and headmasters to conquer pupils' apathy, partly because the sloping and gravelly landscape made it difficult to play. Instead, hockey proved most popular among pupils, one of many ways in which such schools diverged from their sources of inspiration.[58]

Alongside distinctive games priorities, neither their scholastic curricula nor the future social and employment prospects they could offer made them comparable to more elite forms of metropolitan schooling. Boys typically studied English, Latin, Scripture, maths, and history alongside more utilitarian subjects which deviated sharply from a 'classical' public-school-style education. Urdu replaced Greek, and boys could also take physical science, chemistry, bookkeeping, shorthand, accounting, mechanical drawing, and surveying.[59] These vocational courses were stepping stones to posts similar to those most of their fathers had held in the lower levels of the public services and colonial commercial sectors, where most worked as clerks or in a restricted managerial capacity. The domiciled European and Anglo-Indian populations had long been allotted a substantial quota of the positions available in certain subordi-

[56] In 1925, St George's College at Mussoorie claimed that it was 'intended for the education of European boys whose parents can afford to give their sons a high-class training in India. It is conducted after the model of the best English Public Schools'. *Manorite* (1925), 68.

[57] BCSS, 'Notes of the 56th Meeting, 2 April 1870', 'Notes of the 60th Meeting, 26 May 1871', *Board of Governors Minute Book, Bishop Cotton School, Simla, 1863–1900*, 177–84; 200–2; *Cottonian*, 32 (1934), 30–41; OIOC, V/27/861/1, 122–3.

[58] *Manorite* (1920), 27–8; *Manorite* (1923), 36.

[59] OIOC, V/26/861/1, 17–19.

nate, or 'uncovenanted', branches of state employment, particularly those connected with the transport, communications, and engineering sectors.[60] At the turn of the century, the government departments men most commonly entered after leaving European schools in India included the Public Works Department, Survey, Police, Opium, Salt, Customs, Telegraph, Postal, the Indian Medical Department (the subordinate branch of the Indian Medical Service), and the Secretariats. Many others found work on the railways or in the commercial, tea, jute, indigo, or mining sectors.[61]

Through quotas in specific occupational sectors, the state thereby provided jobs for less-privileged Europeans and Anglo-Indians without compromising the exclusivity of superior state services, which were recruited only in Britain until after the First World War. Men of European descent educated in India were thereby barred from appointments offering the highest incomes, prestige, and chances for promotion. The road to covenanted, officer-grade careers in India passed through Britain; men unable to claim the assets of metropolitan schooling and to take entrance examinations there faced far more limited occupational prospects (termed 'subordinate' or 'uncovenanted') and a correspondingly liminal racial and socio-economic status. Yet such men enjoyed considerable advantages compared with Indian candidates: they commonly received their appointments on the strength of a school certificate upon completing their Senior Cambridge examination, while Indians required university training to win comparable positions.

Beginning in the late nineteenth century, however, a number of gradual shifts occurred that came to be viewed as 'the closing of careers' for boys of European ancestry educated in India. Some of what were formerly the best appointments for European-descended men with Indian credentials were downgraded in status. In many government departments (including Finance, Superior Traffic, Superior Accounts, Police, Opium, Public Works, and Forestry) the number of desirable vacancies filled in Britain increased after the formation of the Provincial Services in 1892. Thereafter, the higher gazetted posts were filled only by men applying from Britain and applicants in India were restricted to lower ranking appointments, causing boys leaving school in the subcontinent to face more limited possibilities than before.[62] The

---

[60] Hawes, *Poor Relations*, 42–54; Laura Charlotte Bear, 'Traveling Modernity: Capitalism, Community and Nation in the Colonial Governance of the Indian Railways', Ph.D. diss., University of Michigan (1998); Caplan, *Children of Colonialism*, 26–30.

[61] OIOC, V/26/861/1, 14–15; Mark Naidis, 'British Attitudes Toward the Anglo-Indians', *South Atlantic Quarterly*, 62/3 (1963), 418–21.

[62] OIOC, V/26/861/2, 201, evidence given by Major E. H. Atkinson, R. E., Principal, Thomason College, Rurki.

redistribution of higher status occupations in the Public Works Department (PWD) exemplified this trend. Prior to the opening of the Royal Indian Engineering College at Cooper's Hill outside London in 1871, most PWD engineers received their training at the Thomason College of Civil Engineering at Roorkee in North India, which dated from 1848. Competing for places at Roorkee had been restricted since 1882 to 'Pure Natives of India' and 'Statutory Natives of India', a category which encompassed domiciled Europeans and Eurasians. After 1892, Roorkee-trained engineers became designated as 'Provincial Engineers', while men who had attended Cooper's Hill and consequently were recruited in Britain constituted the 'Imperial Engineers'. Roorkee graduates thereby received less pay, fewer promotion opportunities, and worked for a branch of service subordinate to that populated by Cooper's Hill graduates.[63]

Indianization of the public services, moreover, further eroded domiciled European and Anglo-Indian employment prospects.[64] As Mrinalini Sinha suggests in her analysis of debates surrounding the reorganization of the civil service in the late 1880s, many of what appeared to be government concessions to Indian demands for increased access to state employment bore little substantive fruit until the end of the First World War. But although the state acceded to pressure from men of European descent resident in India and retained many of the biases in their favor in specified subordinate services, they constantly feared losing privileges and demanded 'more than equal treatment as ' "natives of India" '; instead, they called for preferential treatment as ' "European British Subjects" '.[65] Retaining existing advantages—let alone gaining additional concessions—they felt they were owed due to their racial origins proved difficult, however, in the face of increasingly vocal Indian demands in conjunction with the ongoing recruitment of higher grade, covenanted officers by examinations held only in London.

Following a number of smaller incremental changes, the most substantial transformation in state recruitment policies came in 1919, when the Montagu-

---

[63] OIOC, P/T 724, *Historical Retrospect of Conditions of Service in the Indian Public Works Department* (All-Indian Service of Engineers, n.d. [c.1925]), 2; OIOC, V/26/861/2, 39, evidence given by the Revd Father Norman; Brendan Cuddy and Tony Mansell, 'Engineers for India: The Royal Engineering College at Cooper's Hill', *History of Education*, 23/1 (1994), 107–23; Raymond K. Renford, *The Non-Official British in India to 1920* (New Delhi, 1987), 234–5, 271.

[64] Richard Symonds, 'Eurasians Under British Rule', in N. J. Allen et al. (eds.), *Oxford University Papers on India*, Vol. 1, Part 2 (Delhi, 1987), 33–5; Lieut.-Col. H. Gidney, 'The Status of the Anglo-Indian Community Under the Reforms Scheme in India', *Asiatic Review*, 21/68 (1925), 657–62; Sir Henry Gidney, 'The Future of the Anglo-Indian Community', *Asiatic Review*, 30/101 (1934), 27–42.

[65] Mrinalini Sinha, *Colonial Masculinity: The 'Manly Englishman' and the 'Effeminate Bengali' in the Late Nineteenth Century* (Manchester, 1995), 105, 127–30.

Chelmsford reforms led to the Government of India Act giving Indians a vastly greater proportion of public service posts than they had enjoyed previously. Many subordinate positions previously reserved for the European-descended community were now thrown open to Indian competition.[66] Although domiciled Europeans and Anglo-Indians both qualified to compete as 'Statutory Natives of India', most were ill prepared to challenge Indians to enter the posts they had traditionally held. As the report on the *Progress of Education in India, 1917–1922* summarized, most men of European descent lacked the collegiate and professional education that had become necessary prerequisites for many more jobs than before:

The temptation offered by the high rates of pay obtainable by a lad who has passed the Senior Cambridge examinations has in the past lured most Anglo-Indian boys straight from school to work . . . the adoption of a policy of Indianisation in the public services revealed the fact that the number of Anglo-Indians qualified for admission to the superior services . . . was woefully small.[67]

As it emerged, the same financial limitations that caused boys to attend school in India rather than Britain prevented many from acquiring additional formal education beyond the Senior Cambridge examination even when changed times made this essential to win many subordinate state posts. At institutions that catered to poorer and orphaned pupils like the Wynberg Allen School at Mussoorie, administrators continually expressed anxiety about the prospects of their school-leavers who were hard-pressed to complete secondary school, let alone afford further study.[68] But at the nearby St George's College, staff hoped that enough boys with some family resources could be encouraged to remain at school for two additional years to complete Intermediate examinations. With these added credentials, they could qualify for better jobs than before, or alternatively transfer to Indian universities and complete their degree two years later.[69] Armed with these assets, they could thereby better compete with Indians to attain not only subordinate, uncovenanted posts but also the officer-grade appointments whose entrance examinations were now held in India as well as in Britain.

---

[66] The 1919 Act divided responsibility for administration at the provincial level, allowing for increased Indian involvement in areas such as education, public health, public works, and local self-government—precisely the areas where Anglo-Indians and domiciled Europeans had previously enjoyed the most advantages in securing employment. For a brief summary, see Philip Woods, 'The Montagu-Chelmsford Reforms (1919): A Re-assessment', *South Asia*, 17/1 (1994), 31–2.

[67] OIOC, V/24/4432, J. A. Richey, *Progress of Education in India, 1917–1922: Eighth Quinquennial Review*, Vol. 1 (Calcutta, 1923), 198–9.

[68] *Excelsior*, 1/2 (1937), 6.

[69] *Manorite* (1929), 47; *Manorite* (1931), 37; *Right Revd Delany*, 48–9.

For the small minority of domiciled European and Anglo-Indian boys with the academic capital to hold their own against Indian competitors, the inter-war period opened up senior-level professional opportunities for those who had never left India that were previously possible only for those who could travel to Britain. Indianization paradoxically worked to favor a select number of European-descended 'domiciled' men—who were, after all, 'Statutory Natives' as much as they were 'European British Subjects'—even while for the majority it rendered attaining traditional appointments vastly more problem-atic. Officer-class employment prospects that remained in the realm of fantasy for earlier generations who lacked British education became possible for those with sufficient resources and determination to persevere with their education in India. Basil La Bouchardière, whose father had made his career in the subor-dinate Indian Medical Department, attended St Joseph's College at Darjeeling between 1921 and 1929, later earning a BA in History at the Deccan College in Poona. This enabled him to compete to enter the Indian Police as an officer, which he succeeded in doing in 1936. Yet despite achieving what would have required metropole-based endeavors in an earlier period, he still considered his Indian domicile to have hindered him *vis-à-vis* his British colleagues:

> I put myself down as a domiciled European . . . when I applied for the Police . . . I therefore excluded myself from all those [overseas] allowances which were payable to the English-born applicant. So although I got officer grade, I was domiciled here . . . And then later on, there was a discreet discrimination drawn between the postings. They got the best postings, I got the less posting . . . there was this thing, you know, that he . . . he is British and I am country born.[70]

Within services like the Police, domiciled European and Anglo-Indian men who collectively made up the 'country born' faced similar disadvantages as Indian officers because of having been recruited in the subcontinent. Objec-tions to receiving the same professional treatment as Indian colleagues due to the wish to be accorded equality with British recruits were widespread, how-ever. Had Basil or others like him finished their education in, and entered government service from, Britain, they might claim British domicile and thus the privileges stemming from connections with the metropole. Lacking these assets made claims for affiliation with the British and distinction from Indians worth little, particularly in light of the long-standing British biases against the 'country born' seen as racially as well as socially inferior.

---

[70] Basil La Bouchardière, interview by author, 20 April 1995.

Domiciled men without the additional qualifications Basil had attained expressed even stronger resentment about British prejudices (while justifying their own) when reflecting upon their careers. James Staines, born in 1909 and enrolled at St George's College between 1917 and 1925, left soon after passing his Cambridge school certificate examination and was unable to continue his studies because his father's once thriving leather goods business in Cawnpore had gone into decline. In his autobiography *Country Born*, Staines remembered that

> it was my father's intention to send me to England for further education, to obtain what he called a hall-mark, but that was in the good old days of Staines & Co. Those earlier plans began to take on a dreamlike quality as the family fortunes declined from year to year until the reality became that he found it hard to keep me at Manor House [St George's], especially for the final two years, let alone send me abroad.[71]

Leaving St George's at 16 with minimal credentials and becoming a railway ticket collector, he considered this a last resort because of the 'snobbish attitude towards working on the railway' he had acquired at school. Other comments indicate that this perspective derived from his desire to distance himself from the Anglo-Indians heavily represented within the railway work force:

> The way I pronounced English notwithstanding, I was British by descent, outlook and upbringing . . . However, because we were domiciled in India, and more particularly because we were educated there, whether we liked it or not, we were dubbed Anglo-Indian . . . in the last few years of the Raj, [Anglo-Indian] was corrupted into embracing all of European descent, whether of mixed blood or not.[72]

Like Basil La Bouchardière, James Staines claimed to be of pure European ancestry and thus a domiciled European, recounting in his memoir multiple tales of discrimination by the transient, covenanted Britons with whom he felt he deserved to share the privileges of whiteness. He left his railway post at the earliest opportunity to work for Burmah-Shell in Calcutta, but found that his marginal country born status inhibited advancement in non-official commercial work as well, giving him and others schooled in India lower pay and more limited prospects for promotion than covenanted staff recruited in Britain.[73]

Staines's book is a catalogue of resentments about his treatment by 'my fellow whites' who placed him outside their racial and social circles by virtue of his

---

[71] James Richard Staines, *Country Born: One Man's Life in India, 1909–1947* (London, 1986), 57.
[72] Ibid., 87.
[73] Ibid., 220, 255–8, 261.

geographical affiliations and lack of metropolitan credentials which, in their eyes, implied dubious heritage and entitlement to privileges.[74] Anger at British refusals to consider him their equal rests alongside his own wish to elevate himself above other members of the domiciled community who were of mixed descent, not to mention above Indians. His attitudes suggest the extent of the internal diversity pervading every group that identified itself as linked to the British by descent, whether of transient, sojourner status identified as white, domiciled European, or Anglo-Indian. Indeed, the unwillingness of some who emphasized their own exclusively European ancestry to make common cause with the Anglo-Indians was a recurring refrain among leaders of that community in the early twentieth century and interwar era.[75]

Because of the career disadvantages faced by the domiciled, many parents unable to send their sons to Britain as young children tried to pay for what one contributor to the 1904–5 government report called 'a finishing English education' for their last several years of schooling.[76] Location and career entry procedures were their main considerations, commentators believed, not the quality of instruction. As one school principal put it, parents 'do not always send [boys] to the best schools; sometimes, they send them to schools which are probably less efficient than are some schools in India . . . At any rate such boys educated in England are not debarred from competing on equal terms with English boys for Indian appointments'.[77] The report summarized that of 660 boys recorded as leaving hill schools the previous five years, 220 had gone to England, generally making the transition in mid-adolescence.[78] At the Bishop Cotton School, Simla, a substantial minority of boys consistently left in order to finish school in Britain, making many of the former pupils described in the school magazine's 'Old Cottonian Notes' anything but 'old' in terms of their years.[79] One writer described conditions in 1914 that had long affected domiciled men of 'pure European extraction' and of 'mixed descent' alike, and that remained largely unchanged until the end of British rule. 'The disadvantages they labour under are identical in most instances', he stated, but if parents could afford to send sons to Britain they 'have the pleasure of receiving their

[74] James Richard Staines, *Country Born: One Man's Life in India, 1909–1947* (London, 1986), 283.

[75] Caplan stresses Anglo-Indians' class heterogeneity, also drawing attention to community leader Sir Henry Gidney's disdain at the reluctance of many claiming to be 'pure Europeans' to unite with other Anglo-Indians to promote their mutual interests. *Children of Colonialism*, 7, 21, 78; see also OIOC, P/T 592, A. N. Gordon (ed.), *About the Domiciled Community* (Madras, 1914), 91.

[76] OIOC, V/26/861/2, evidence given by J. I. B. Cockin, Archdeacon of Lucknow, 31.

[77] Ibid., evidence given by W. H. Arden Wood, Principal, La Martinière College, Calcutta, 191.

[78] OIOC, V/26/861/1, 12.

[79] BCSS, '254th Meeting, 15 Mar. 1909', in *Board of Governors Second Minute Book, Bishop Cotton School Simla (1901–29)*, 118; *Cottonian*, 3/2 (1921), 12.

offspring back as officers in the Army or officials in the Civil Service and the Departments, purified from the terrible sin of being reared and taught in the land of their birth. The fortunate youth returns, gilded as it were, to be accepted as sterling metal.'[80]

In effect, schooling in Britain created a member of the white middle classes—either pure 'sterling metal', or at least one sanctioned as 'genuine'. Education in India, on the other hand, placed an individual within the racially *amorphous* realm of the 'country born' which included both domiciled Europeans and Anglo-Indians, valued at between 8 and 15 annas.[81] New opportunities to enter state services at the officer level from within India after 1919 affected relatively few men of European descent and applied mainly to Indians; in any case, they were deemed inadequate compensation for the long-resented 'closing of careers' over the previous decades. Given the continuing racial, social, and cultural value of metropolitan credentials, the more prestigious European schools for boys reported that a significant number of their pupils went to Britain for further education and examinations until the Second World War restricted overseas travel.[82]

GIRLS' EDUCATION, SOCIAL GRACES, AND THE MEANINGS OF WOMEN'S EMPLOYMENT

Many of these concerns about the racial and social standing accorded to children who attended schools in India were voiced with respect to boys alone. The attributes signifying 'whiteness' or 'Europeanness' and membership in a desirable colonial class category in terms of culture, occupation, and income derived from the type of schooling male offspring experienced and the subsequent careers for which they were thereby made eligible—or, more problematically, ineligible—if they attended school in India and did not complete their education in Britain. For girls, however, although Indian schooling might also suggest mixed racial heritage in tandem with straitened family finances, these risks were not perceived to be as great as those their brothers faced in similar circumstances. Consequently, parents having an income that allowed for some

---

[80] OIOC, P/T 592, Gordon (ed.), *About the Domiciled*, 1, 5, 3.

[81] See OIOC, P/T 722, the Revd O. Younghusband, *The Domiciled Community in India* (n.p., n.d.), 6, who described how children of Englishmen became domiciled in India when their parents could not afford to send them 'home' and educated them in India instead.

[82] *Manorite* (1925), 33–5; *Manorite* (1931), 5–6; BCSS, '331st Meeting, 31 May 1926', in *Board of Governors Second Minute Book, Bishop Cotton School, Simla*, 318.

degree of educational choice commonly sent sons to Britain for either all or at least the final years of their schooling and subsequent professional training, while daughters remained in India longer or perhaps until they had completed their studies. While 35 per cent of the boys leaving hill schools went to Britain for additional education during the five years preceding the report published in 1904 and 1905, only 18 per cent of girls did the same.[83] Correspondingly, the report asserted that 'the girls' schools contain rather a larger sprinkling of children of the upper middle class than the boys' schools'. A more expensive and prestigious girls' hill school such as Auckland House at Simla consequently was said to extend into a slightly higher social stratum than did the neighboring Bishop Cotton School for boys.[84] One educator summarized that 'tradesmen are the richest people who send their daughters to be educated in India. The highest classes socially, which do the same, are probably planters, merchants, District Superintendents of Police, Solicitors, Engineers, and Railway Officers'.[85]

Within many non-official sectors of the colonial community in addition to the covenanted branches of state employment, then, daughters could spend many of their schooldays and perhaps their entire education in India, often enabling their brothers to study in Britain with the money their parents saved. This gender distinction in schooling based upon limited finances characterized the colonial community for decades, and can be illustrated by John and Janet Erskine's experiences in the early 1940s. Children of a tea planter, they both attended the Presentation Convent High School in the hill station of Kodaikanal, but in John's case this was only because he could not be sent to Britain due to the travel restrictions imposed by the Second World War. After the war, he attended Ampleforth College in Yorkshire, but Janet remained at the convent because, as she later explained, 'I couldn't have been [in England] at the same age. It was very expensive sending John to England. And it was also *very* important to all families that the sons should go to public school . . . Daughters are *never, ever* . . . so important.'[86]

Most parents placed greater emphasis upon boys' education in Britain because of the specific professional implications discussed above. Although daughters might also subsequently enter salaried employment, the most common assumption was that the majority would soon marry and engage in

---

[83] OIOC, V/26/861/1, 12.

[84] Ibid., 11; OIOC, V/26/861/2, 58, evidence given by Miss Pratt, Headmistress, Auckland House, Simla.

[85] OIOC, V/26/861/2, 21, evidence given by the Revd Mother Mary Gonzago, Mother Provincial of the Loreto Order in India.

[86] John Erskine and Janet de Vries (née Erskine), interview by author, 17 April 1995.

unwaged domestic labor; thus, most parents and educators paid far less attention to providing girls with British academic credentials or instruction geared towards particular careers than boys. Schools for orphaned girls or those from poorer families devoted more attention to their pupils' future ability to earn a living than those catering to families who might support daughters until they married with greater ease. At these institutions, girls could leave with vocational training in fields ranging from dressmaking, nursing, and teaching to office skills including shorthand, typewriting, and bookkeeping.[87]

For girls attending schools catering to the more affluent families educating daughters in India, their basic scholastic instruction resembled that typically offered at boys' schools, although they were unlikely to have studied subjects like chemistry, physical science, or Urdu in favor of botany and French. For girls who were not trained with vocational skills as their main goal, a significant portion of their time at school was spent studying subjects valued on cultural grounds alone. As was the case at many schools in Britain, artistic subjects and knowledge of social graces that connoted gentility figured prominently on parents' and educators' agendas for girls at European schools in India. Music lessons were extremely popular, as were painting, drawing, and ornamental (as opposed to functional) needlework.[88] Lessons in elocution and the cultivation of accents which were not 'chi-chi' appear with especial prominence in descriptions of female education.[89] Alongside music and elocution, dancing and 'deportment' were integral features of girls' education at the Presentation Convent at Kodaikanal.[90] School magazines from the 1940s placed great emphasis on dancing, gymnastics, and musical events, stating in one issue that 'the Physical Culture and Dancing Competitions and Performances of 1945 may form the point of departure for stating the school's intentions and aims . . . bearing and carriage being the features of the Gentlewoman of the Twentieth Century'.[91]

Although girls attending schools like the Presentation Convent typically did so because their families could not afford schools in Britain, educators and undoubtedly their clients as well had considerable faith that 'accomplishments'

---

[87] *St Andrew's Colonial Homes Magazine*, 3/4 (1903), 61; *Excelsior*, 1/2 (1937), 6; *Excelsior*, 1/4 (1939), 42; Ruskin Bond, *A History of Wynberg Allen, Mussoorie* (Mussoorie, 1988), 9, 14.

[88] On musical instruction, see for example *Blue and Gold*, 1/1 (1924), 11; *Blue and Gold*, 1/5 (1929), 8, 12, 37; *Blue and Gold: Queen's Hill School*, 1/6 (1931), 3.

[89] *Blue and Gold* (1929), 21; *Blue and Gold*, 1/1 (1924), 5.

[90] Janet de Vries (née Erskine) and Jane Turner (née Erskine), interview by author, 17 April 1995.

[91] *P.C.K.'s Own* (1945), 12–13. See also *P.C.K.'s Own* (1944), 14–16, and *P.C.K.'s Own* (1946), 1–5, on the importance of examinations in music as part of girls' education. Many thanks to Jane Turner for lending me copies of these magazines.

might allow pupils to become 'Gentlewomen of the Twentieth Century' despite the impediment presented by education in a colonial setting. Both in the metropole and in India, these cultural lessons had long been believed well worth their price and the time spent perfecting them. In 1905, for instance, the headmistress of one of the more exclusive girls' schools in the Himalayan region noted 'a feeling in the parents' minds that however well educated their sons are they can scarcely hope to rise to any position of importance; whereas, for a well educated and attractive girl there are many possibilities'.[92] Implicitly, girls' earning potential was not foremost among these 'possibilities' in comparison with their ability to fit into desirable colonial socio-economic strata and attract husbands from respectable circles. Until the end of British rule, European women continued to be outnumbered by European men, despite their increased presence; thus, schooling in India as such did not bar a woman from marrying a man well placed within the colonial occupational hierarchy, especially if her parents were well connected. This form of adult success was seen to be more dependent upon acquiring genteel cultural attributes that girls might attain *without* leaving India; for boys, opportunities to reach these same elevated levels in colonial society were contingent upon careers to which British educational and examination structures constituted the far more likely point of entry.

None the less, however high in the hierarchy of European schools a given institution may have ranked and however 'genteel' its curriculum, schooling in India still exposed girls to cultural attributes of the 'country born' that implied inclusion within the mixed-race contingent at these locales. Foremost among these was speaking with a 'chi-chi' accent, regardless of efforts schools made to steer students in 'purer' linguistic directions. Letters that Jean Martin wrote to her parents in 1942 while she and her sister Alie were enrolled at Auckland House School in Simla attempted to reassure them that 'I try to talk carefully, and I don't think we'll come home speaking chee-chee. It's really surprising how little of it there is in school.'[93] Her parents clearly did not consider themselves domiciled Europeans, even though their daughters had attended a series of schools in India. Her father had come from Scotland to work in the jute industry in Bengal and later returned there upon retirement; in between, he and his wife apparently made their daughters aware of the importance of

---

[92] OIOC, V/26/861/2, 46, evidence given by Miss Holland, Principal and Proprietress, Hampton Court School, Mussoorie.

[93] PKCA, MS 72/2, Jean Martin to Mr and Mrs George Martin, 3 May 1942.

avoiding cultural traits which might suggest a non-European, non-transient status.[94]

Even if the possibility of learning 'chi-chi' English was reduced, a racially mixed peer group might subject girls to other potential dangers. By the 1940s, some girls' schools permitted their pupils a limited degree of interaction with members of the opposite sex attending selected boys' schools in the vicinity, and older girls at Auckland House occasionally attended sporting events and dances at the Bishop Cotton School. Seventeen-year-old Jean Martin's letters refer to these encounters and support the view that the boys attending hill schools were often of lower social status and were more likely to be—or resemble—Anglo-Indians, again through reference to boys' accents. 'Admittedly the B.C.S. boys speak worse than Auckland House, but not all of them', she wrote. 'There were—I think—a majority of Europeans at the social . . . There was a Scotsman, or rather, Scots boy there, who was one of Alie's admirers, his name was Willie something, and they were great pals!'

Jean's comment alludes to several features of schools in India causing anxiety among families concerned to define themselves as exclusively European in origin. The boys Jean and Alie met at the dance at the Bishop Cotton School were mainly European, but Jean could not be sure of this; 'I think' appears as an afterthought underscoring the need for guesswork, with her continual allusions to 'chee chee' possibilities compromising any racial certainties. In addition, interaction among the adolescent pupils at boys' and girls' schools provided the opening, however narrow, for subsequent encounters which could take on more undesirable sexual connotations. Because the Martin girls stayed with their aunt in Simla and attended school as day scholars, they were freer to interact with Bishop Cotton boys than would have been possible as boarders. Still, their guardian tried to ensure that any boys with whom they mingled after school hours were acceptable companions on racial grounds:

The Scotsman, Willie, who danced with [Alie] at the B.C.S. social, and a pal of his . . . managed to get out an invitation [to us] to go to tea and the pictures . . . Alie asked Auntie if we could go, and she said certainly, if they weren't Anglo-Indian, and if we were sure they were nice boys. I think they are and at least they *are* English.[95]

When older girls attended school in India, meetings with boys were closely monitored with vigilant attention given to issues unlikely to have arisen in

94 PKCA, MS 72, death notice of George Martin in the Dundee *Courier and Advertiser*, 27 Nov. 1984. Jean Martin (born in 1925) and her sister Alie attended the Loreto Convent, Darjeeling, the Bhatpara District European Private School (where her parents lived near Calcutta), and ultimately Auckland House School, Simla.
95 PKCA, MS 72/2, Jean Martin to Mr and Mrs George Martin, 14 June 1942.

Britain. In India, the fact that Willie and his friend were presumably 'nice boys' in terms of behavior and class was secondary to whether they were 'English'— or, in this instance, Scottish—and not Anglo-Indians who appeared otherwise at first glance. Maintaining female sexual respectability by policing girls' social interactions with boys was fundamental to preserving a European identity, particularly as mixed-race women were popularly perceived as morally disreputable by many Europeans.[96]

Thus, with careful attention to their peer group and cultural attainments, girls might be shielded from the aspects of Indian schooling deemed most pernicious. Still, if their families could afford it, girls, like boys, were sent to schools outside of India for at least the last several years of their education to gain prestigious cultural credentials, but rarely to win career qualifications. Janet Erskine, for instance, later spent one year at school in England and another in Belgium because 'it was not considered good to finish your schooling in India . . . you were branded as being "country bottled"'. She left India, however, for the sake of promoting family status in unremunerative ways, recalling how 'my father was quite insistent at one point that daughters should not even have to earn their own living . . . he considered . . . that it was a slur on him that I should think of [it]'.[97]

The genteel cultural forms connoting European status that girls' schools sought to instil in their pupils and the comparative lack of concern about career opportunities thus made girls' education in India a more acceptable option than was the case for boys of similar backgrounds. None the less, they remained in racial and social jeopardy. Parents and educators typically anticipated only a brief period of paid employment at most between school and marriage, but if female school-leavers did indeed work they were often placed within the social category dominated by Anglo-Indians. If they subsequently trained as teachers and taught in schools similar to those they attended, they, like men trained and recruited within India, were paid less than their counterparts with British institutional credentials who were defined as 'European'.[98] As in Britain, women's paid employment might compromise social status and

---

[96] Bear, 'Miscegenations', 533, 539–40; Benita Parry, *Delusions and Discoveries: India in the British Imagination, 1880–1930*, 2nd edn. (London, 1998), 85; Caplan, *Children of Colonialism*, 63–6, 76–7; Lionel Caplan, 'Iconographies of Anglo-Indian Women: Gender Constructs and Contrasts in a Changing Society', *Modern Asian Studies*, 34/4 (2000), 869, 872–3. Related themes are examined in the context of wartime Britain in Sonya O. Rose, *Which People's War?: National Identity and Citizenship in Wartime Britain, 1939–1945* (Oxford, 2003).

[97] Janet de Vries (née Erskine), interview by author, 17 April 1995.

[98] OIOC, V/26/861/2, 35, 51, 58, evidence given by Miss S. A. Easton, Lady Principal, and Miss R. A. Sellers, Assistant Lady Principal, Wellesley Girls' School, Naini Tal; Miss Birrell, Principal and Proprietress, Ayrcliff High School, Simla; Miss Pratt, Headmistress, Auckland House School, Simla.

respectability well into the twentieth century, but by the interwar period the meanings attached to middle-class single women's work in the metropole and among the colonial community in India had become increasingly divergent.[99] One retired Indian Army officer living in Britain and writing in the mid-1930s described the many 'employments filled by better-class girls nowadays', including teaching, nursing, working in London department stores, and as typists or receptionists. The modern young woman, he wrote, had 'never heard of except in caricature, the Victorian or Edwardian miss with one principal and several minor accomplishments and a fixed root in the home till the right man came along. She is up and doing.'[100] While paid work outside the home for unmarried middle-class women had slowly shed some of its stigma in Britain, however, British women in India doing the types of jobs he mentioned faced inclusion within the category of the racially mixed—in effect judged by much of the company they kept. Many of the occupational categories common among women in India—most notably nursing and secretarial work—were fields filled mainly by those perceived to be Anglo-Indians.[101]

Furthermore, if women decided to use an education in 'genteel accomplishments' to earn a living, as Rumer Godden did in the 1920s by opening a dancing school in Calcutta, they might find the doors of 'respectable' British circles virtually slammed shut. 'In Calcutta's then almost closed society, "nice girls" did not work or try to earn their living', Godden recalled. 'There were women doctors, school inspectors, matrons of hospitals, missionaries, but they did not rank as "society", whose girls should stay at home, perhaps do some charity work or amateur acting or painting, strictly unpaid; anything else was taboo.'[102] Even highly educated women professionals who had been trained in Britain could encounter social discrimination within the more elite sectors of the colonial community. Women engaged in many less prestigious but more common occupations for which schools in India qualified them could well find themselves placed within socially as well as racially liminal spheres labelled as 'Eurasian' or 'Anglo-Indian'. Teaching ballet posed this risk, as Godden

---

[99] On the long-problematic nature of paid employment for 'respectable' women in nineteenth- and twentieth-century Britain, see Martha Vicinus, *Independent Women: Work and Community for Single Women, 1850–1920* (Chicago, 1985); Deirdre Beddoe, *Back to Home and Duty: Women Between the Wars, 1918–1939* (London, 1989); Sandra Burman (ed.), *Fit Work for Women* (London, 1979); Angela John (ed.), *Unequal Opportunities: Women's Employment in England, 1800–1918* (Oxford, 1986).

[100] 'Mauser', *How to Live in England on a Pension: A Guide to Public Servants Abroad and At Home* (London, 1934), 87.

[101] Caplan, 'Iconographies', 883–5; Caplan, *Children of Colonialism*, 30–2; Gist and Wright, *Marginality and Identity*, 65–6; Naidis, 'British Attitudes', 420; Kenneth Ballhatchet, *Race, Sex and Class under the Raj: Imperial Attitudes and Policies and their Critics, 1793–1905* (New York, 1980), 138.

[102] Rumer Godden, *A Time to Dance, No Time to Weep* (New York, 1987), 86.

discovered, because Calcutta's 'schools of dancing were run almost exclusively by Eurasians'.[103] Should women engage in paid work out of choice or economic need, the surest means of preserving the interrelated attributes of female respectability and European status was by laboring within the confines of the European bourgeois domestic sphere. Those employed as governesses or private teachers in British homes were far less likely to be viewed as 'country born' and of dubious racial descent than were those working in more public capacities, such as in schools, hospitals, or offices. In the same manner as schooling in India suggested limited financial and therefore racial capital, subsequent work, if undertaken, could well enhance the perception of these characteristics.

PERSISTENT REJECTIONS AND DENIALS: WARTIME SCHOOLING ALTERNATIVES

In the last decades of imperial rule, losing a secure claim to European status achieved by ongoing contact with Britain became increasingly detrimental. Members of the Anglo-Indian and domiciled European community saw many employment privileges the government had previously accorded them in certain fields eroded as the British responded to Indian nationalist demands for greater participation in state sectors. Indian competition for jobs concerned domiciled European and Anglo-Indian men more directly than women, making metropolitan educational credentials all the more important for them. Men and women alike, however, were affected by this interstitial community's increasingly marginal position in the years prior to decolonization. Both sexes experienced racial definition through their employment status after leaving school, with women's claims to be European becoming enhanced if their financial condition made paid work outside the home unnecessary.

Whiteness or European status in late colonial India was therefore far more than an innate biological condition. Rather, it depended upon individuals displaying a gender-specific combination of cultural, behavioral, occupational, and class markers deemed characteristic of a privileged racial identity. Regardless of their ancestry, children who failed to acquire certain attributes during their 'formative years' might be denied inclusion in European society. Whiteness was thus an extremely fragile construct, and parents often worried far more about children slipping into the realm *between* colonizer and

---

[103] Rumer Godden, *A Time to Dance, No Time to Weep* (New York, 1987), 86.

colonized than they did about their possibly 'going native' through contact with Indians. The racial border between Europeans and Indians was considered far more difficult to cross than that which separated transient Europeans from the domiciled community in which less affluent Europeans merged with the racially mixed. Adamant parental refusals to entertain any notion of educating their own children at schools in India remained common up until decolonization, even at times when the outside factors inhibiting voyages to Britain made contemplating local alternatives a logical temporary measure.

Family responses to the First and Second World Wars marked two key instances when hostility towards or disavowal of schools in India surfaced most prominently. Like Jon and Rumer Godden's recollections of being taught by their aunt instead of attending a hill boarding school, letters written by Evelyn Chaldecott, the wife of an Indian Army officer, illustrate the makeshift arrangements that came into play when global circumstances delayed sending a child away. Having planned to send their son Gilbert to England to start at a preparatory school when he was 8, the Chaldecotts found that wartime travel restrictions postponed his return until he was 10. In letters to her mother in Bedford, Evelyn chronicled her many failed attempts to have him taught in India; governesses proved unreliable and short-lived, and she was equally dissatisfied with the small private schoolrooms where Gilbert had lessons alongside a handful of other officers' children. Feeling that she lacked the ability to teach him herself, she also found it 'rather tiresome' to look after him and resented having to limit her social engagements at the Club when governesses were absent. Her continual references to his misbehavior and 'imperious ways' with his ayah made 'I shall be glad to settle Gilbert at school' a persistent refrain in her correspondence. Boarding schools in the hills were an obvious short-term solution, yet were condemned for enrolling too many pupils who were 'rather mixed'.[104] Despite her palpable impatience to be rid of Gilbert and her fears that his haphazard lessons would make him fall behind his peers when he finally did return to England, Evelyn never contemplated sending him away for more formal instruction at pre-existing schools within India.

It was 1919 before Evelyn at last located what she described as 'the only place in India that I know of that I would send Gilbert to' for what were to be his last months in India: a 'war school' founded specifically for families like themselves

---

[104] BLARS, letters from Evelyn Chaldecott to Mrs Cochrane Forster, Z186/19, 14 Feb. 1915; Z186/156, 8 Nov. 1917; Z186/162, 5 Jan. 1918; Z186/74, 11 April 1916.

whom travel restrictions had detained against their will. Opened in the hill station of Naini Tal and enrolling only about twenty boys, the school was only intended to last until its pupils could leave India once passages became available. It owed its appeal to its founder, Mr Milsted, being 'very particular who he takes': 'only gentleman's sons', Evelyn insisted.[105] Deftly tapping into widespread parental disinclination to patronize racially and socially 'mixed' establishments, Mr Milsted advertised his own school as the only viable alternative given their predicament. As his promotional leaflet emphasized, he offered

the best equivalent to that home school life they would have had but for the war: the right kind of development in congenial surroundings. My own experience is that this can be so only when boys associate with the 'right stuff' and when they can be given individual attention in work, in games, in health . . . Such is not possible in a big school in India . . . The boys are being educated with a view to prepare them for entrance to a Public School at home, when they can get there. They are all delightful British boys and are being kept absolutely as such in tone, character, manners, and ideas . . . It is obviously essential that the 'other boys' should be of the right sort and I have limited the numbers to secure this end.

Fees totalling Rs. 185 a month effectively barred the less affluent from attempting to enrol. As final 'proof' of his school's social (and implicitly racial) exclusivity, Mr Milsted concluded his circular by highlighting that pupils' fathers included army officers as well as men in the Indian Medical Service—in other words, well above the subordinate occupational sectors who patronized other schools in which boys were manifestly not 'the right stuff'.[106]

Similar biases against schools for those of 'European descent' re-emerged during the Second World War, yet not all parents rejected them like Evelyn Chaldecott had a generation earlier. Once again, many children were unable to travel home when they reached school age, while others, like Hazel Innes Craig, uncharacteristically left their British schools when wartime dangers made India appear the safer option. Like Craig who attended Mount Hermon, many such 'evacuees' entered the higher status hill schools for the war's duration. Boys' schools such as St George's College at Mussoorie, the Bishop Cotton School at Simla, and St Paul's School at Darjeeling all experienced a tremendous influx of pupils in the early 1940s who had previously attended schools in Britain, as did many other boarding schools in the Himalayan

---

[105] BLARS, Evelyn Chaldecott to Mrs Cochrane Forster, Z186/198, 10 Mar. 1919; Z186/205, 30 April 1919.
[106] BLARS, Z186/197, W. P. S. Milsted, 'War School, Naini Tal, 3 March 1919: A School to prepare boys for entrance to Public Schools at home'.

foothills and the Nilgiris.[107] Admissions registers of the Bishop Cotton School illustrate the contrast between the negligible numbers of pupils born in Britain or who had previously gone to school there prior to the war and the situation prevailing in 1940 and 1941. In those two peak years its total enrollment doubled: 171 new boys entered, 36 of whom had been born in Britain and 81 of whom had recently left metropolitan schools. In effect, the situation long prevailing at Bishop Cotton, whereby a noticeable proportion of boys left after several years to go to Britain, had been reversed. The profiles of the new boys entering after the outbreak of war who had been born or schooled in Britain reveal more fathers in prestigious professions—including men in the Indian Civil Service, army officers, other covenanted government officials, and merchants and planters—than had ever been the case before.[108]

Not all British parents whose children returned to India during the war proved equally willing to enrol them in schools with a long history of educating 'children of European descent', however. Long-standing objections to these institutions and their mainly 'country-born' pupils were so deeply ensconced that many families did not consider them plausible options even when international conditions otherwise made them logical temporary choices. Like the Chaldecotts had done, many parents in the early 1940s opted for newly opened 'war schools', none of which was intended to last once the conflict ended and passages home could be arranged. Among these were the Sheikh Bagh Preparatory School in Srinagar, run by the missionary Eric Tyndale-Biscoe, open from 1940 to 1946; the Hallett War School in Naini Tal, lasting from 1941 to 1944; and the New School, established in Calcutta and later moved to Darjeeling, dating from 1940 to 1944.

Parents selecting special war schools and those in charge of opening and running them voiced a number of reasons why they were chosen instead of the countless schools already available. References to the pre-existing schools' inability to cope with the wartime influx of children returning from Britain abound, as do suggestions that their curriculum was inappropriate for children meant to continue their education in Britain at the earliest opportunity. The

---

[107] St George's College had a record number of new boys in 1942; SGCM, St George's College, Log Book, entry for 10 Mar. 1942 and *Manorite* (1942), 3. On boys from Britain coming to St Paul's School in Darjeeling during the war, see *St Paul's School, Darjeeling: Commemorative Volume, 1823–1973* (n.p., 1974), 94, as well as Theon Wilkinson, interview by author, 12 July 1995, on his transfer there from Radley College. On schools in the Nilgiris during wartime, see John Erskine, Janet de Vries (née Erskine), and Jane Turner (née Erskine), interview by author, 17 April 1995, who recalled that there 'were hundreds, literally hundreds of us [British "evacuees"] in Indian schools' then.

[108] BCSS, *Admissions Register, 1879–*, 115–21; '370th Meeting, 10 Aug. 1940', in *Board of Governors Third Minute Book, Bishop Cotton School, Simla, 1930–58*, 225; *Cottonian*, 43 (1943), 4, 39–42; *Cottonian*, 51 (Nov. 1944), 2.

deciding factor for most, however, remained the children's prospective peer group.[109] The New School effectively restricted its clientele to well-off British families through prohibitively high fees, its exclusivity rapidly earning it the sobriquet 'Harrow on the Hooghly'.[110] As such, families from social sectors traditionally utilizing schools in India because they were more affordable than British variants were dissuaded from trying to enrol their children. In any case, a 1990s rendition of its origins suggests that they would likely have been turned away for the same reasons that the New School's patrons had founded a separate institution:

The existing English-speaking schools, several of which, like St Paul's in Darjeeling, were of a high standard, could not absorb many [British children]. In any event a lot of parents would not even consider them mainly because they did not wish their offspring to acquire the local singsong 'chi-chi' accent which in those days would have been a significant disadvantage both socially and in a career. A new school would have to be founded.[111]

In rejecting these educational environments, however, parents also neglected the academic advantages that more firmly established schools offered. Instead, they opted for rapidly contrived makeshift arrangements which, in the case of 'Harrow on the Hooghly', entailed a limited and inexperienced teaching staff and lessons taught in ill-adapted buildings and classrooms.[112] Yet from the perspective of the New School's clientele these children's wartime education could be hailed as a success won in the face of unpropitious circumstances.

As this rendition of the need for the New School suggests, the stigma of the 'chi-chi' accent remained a touchstone within rationalizations of why schools for those of 'European descent' were better left alone until the end of British rule. 'Chi-chi' English alongside the prospect of social and professional drawbacks serve as convenient substitutes for explicitly invoking parental desires to distance their children from racially ambiguous pupils at other available institutions. Post-colonial accounts of family life among the more affluent sectors of British-Indian society tread along well-established paths when explaining how children came to receive a metropolitan education. Typical among the

---

[109] OIOC, MSS Eur R214/37, Revd R. C. Llewelyn [Principal of the Hallett War School, Naini Tal], interview by Mrs E. D. Cornish, tape recording, 27 Sept. 1982; Craig, *Under the Old School Topee* (London, 1990), 93–7.

[110] John Lethbridge, *Harrow on the Hooghly: The New School in Calcutta and Darjeeling, 1940–1944* (Charlbury, Oxfordshire, 1994), 15; Margaret Martyn, *Married to the Raj* (London, 1992), 45.

[111] Lethbridge, *Harrow on the Hooghly*, 10–11.

[112] Ibid., 13–16; Martin, *Married*, 45, 50–1; Craig, *Under the Old*, 94, 96.

ready excuses were that while there were 'one or two' schools British children might have attended, 'it was not possible to get the standard of education in India that would be available . . . in independent schools in Britain'.[113] Alternatively, 'there were a few that existed, but they weren't patronized except by the children of the domiciled community . . . [and] didn't measure up to the standards of . . . British educational institutions'.[114] Others simply omitted the scores of hill schools from the historical record altogether, with the exception of the war schools:

I was left behind [in England] for ever at about 8 . . . and so was my brother . . . we always knew we would be because all children were and I think it's very silly because afterwards in the war, Second World War, we got our girls out and they started a school in Naini, they could have done that all this long time.[115]

Consigning the educational offerings for Europeans in the subcontinent to oblivion upholds the false impression of a largely uniform colonial society that scholars who continue to focus largely on Indian Civil Service or army officers' families have still not succeeded in fully overturning. Claiming that 'all children' were sent to Britain places the many families who could not afford to do so outside the pale of the 'pukka' community. Those making compromises by sending sons but not daughters, or only children considerably older than 8, encounter similar neglect, allowing the racial and social ramifications of their partial participation in supposedly ubiquitous colonial practices to remain unaddressed. Such elisions, however, work to uphold another colonial paradigm, that of family sacrifices as a result of children being 'left behind for ever'. Suggesting this was undertaken out of necessity because there were 'no schools' for them in India denies the extent to which sending children to Britain was a choice based on class and racial ideologies and aspirations.

Chapter 3 now turns to parent–child separations and the distinctive relationships that emerged when nuclear family life became conducted on a transcontinental basis. Despite the emotional difficulties that resulted, sending children to Britain allowed those born in India to remain being seen as a class, and a race, apart from the 'country born'. Upon boarding the steamships to embark upon a new phase of life in the metropole, they enhanced their foothold among the transient British community and watched the distance grow between themselves and the domiciled.

---

113 CSAA, Portal Papers, Mrs Iris Portal, 'Song at Seventy', typescript manuscript, n.d. [c.1975], 114.
114 OIOC, MSS Eur T18, Sir John Cotton, transcribed interview, n.d. [c.1973], 46.
115 CSAA, MT45, Mrs Joan Davis, transcribed interview with Mary Thatcher, 24 Aug. 1981, 1. Mrs Davis's father was an army officer and her husband was in the Indian Forest Service.

3

Separations and the Discourse
of Family Sacrifice

Nearly all discussions of British family life in India from the mid-nineteenth to the mid-twentieth centuries stress how important most parents felt it was to send their children back to Britain for their education. Perceptions of the dangers that children were believed to face in India and that supposedly increased as they approached adolescence—including physically and culturally threatening contacts with India's climate and indigenous and mixed-race populations, as discussed in previous chapters—acted in combination with Britain's strong attractions as an environment for childrearing. Families whose livelihoods derived from imperial life and work reaffirmed a white, British status by demonstrating sufficient affluence to pay for children's journeys to and school fees in Britain while simultaneously avoiding educational options in India that were racially and socially problematic. Leaving the subcontinent enabled children to benefit from exposure to Britain's climate, culture, and schooling provisions, factors that, taken together, inculcated highly coveted forms of cultural and career competence connoting whiteness and respectability. As the next chapter illustrates, education in Britain—either at a public school or at an institution strongly resembling one—was especially crucial for boys as their stepping stone into professions that brought a higher socio-economic (and racial) status both in Britain and overseas in adulthood. Girls' experiences, meanwhile, could differ greatly, because few families prioritized preparing them for future careers.

Sending children to Britain, however, came at a high price despite the assets resulting from it. Until the government provided many of its officers in India with a limited allotment of free passages for themselves and their families in the interwar era, the cost of paying for children's journeys home constituted a significant drain on their income. Upon arrival, schooling costs varied greatly depending on where children lived and studied but were often substantial. In the 1880s, for instance, Henry and Annette Beveridge left their son William and daughters Letty and Jeannette (usually called 'Tutu') at a small school in Southport for £30 a month, while between the 1910s and 1920s Montagu and Ann Butler paid well in excess of £100 a year for each of their four children's school fees and additional living and holiday expenses.[1] Since both fathers worked in the Indian Civil Service they could afford such rates, but for families supported by less high-ranking professions British schooling might need to be postponed and was ultimately achieved only with great financial difficulty.

For all the socio-economic differences dividing the families who either might readily afford to educate children in the metropole or could barely achieve this aim because of limited incomes, they none the less shared another cost more equitably. Sending children to Britain proved an emotional as well as a financial sacrifice because of the lengthy separations that resulted. The quest for a secure racial and class status clashed with the cultural ideals of domesticity and family intimacy that had become dominant values among many British social sectors and especially within the middle classes by the mid-Victorian period, as John Gillis has argued in his work.[2] Jonas Frykman and Orvar Löfgren's assessment that what changed in Swedish bourgeois family life in the nineteenth century was not the composition of families and households but rather 'the emotional and psychological structure of family relations' fore-grounding an ideology of love applies equally to the British middle classes.[3] Deviation from an increasingly entrenched model was widely depicted as a source of great emotional trauma both for parents and children who typically had no direct contact with one another for several years at a time. If, as Leonore Davidoff, Megan Doolittle, Janet Fink, and Katherine Holden assert, British children's identities were formed predominantly within a familial rubric (which might take a variety of forms), then British-Indian children in the metropole were commonly defined in terms of their *lack* of family.[4] A number of commentators tellingly saw colonial children long separated from their parents as analogous to orphans, indicating that parents' life and work in the

---

[1] Lord Beveridge, *India Called Them* (London, 1947), 266; OIOC, MSS Eur F225/27, Ann Butler to Montagu Butler, 22 May 1911; MSS Eur F225/33, Ann Butler to Montagu Butler, 22 July 1921.

[2] John R. Gillis, 'Ritualization of Middle-Class Family Life in Nineteenth Century Britain', *International Journal of Politics, Culture and Society*, 3/2 (1989), 213–35; 'Making Time for Family: The Invention of Family Time(s) and the Reinvention of Family History', *Journal of Family History*, 21/1 (1996), 4–21; *A World of Their Own Making: Myth, Ritual, and the Quest for Family Values* (New York, 1996).

[3] Jonas Frykman and Orvar Löfgren, *Culture Builders: A Historical Anthropology of Middle-Class Life*, trans. by Alan Crozier (New Brunswick, NJ, 1987), 153, 118.

[4] Leonore Davidoff, Megan Doolittle, Janet Fink, and Katherine Holden, *The Family Story: Blood, Contract and Intimacy, 1830–1960* (London, 1999), 55.

empire led to the temporary death of nuclear family life. David Livingstone, for example, was said to have proclaimed that 'nothing but the conviction that the step will lead to the glory of Christ would make me orphanise my children' during the course of extended absences in Africa to pursue his calling as a missionary and explorer.[5] Children parted from their parents for years at a time did resemble orphans in certain respects as boarding school staff, other relatives, and non-familial guardians took on enhanced roles as surrogate childrearers.

What might be termed a discourse of family sacrifice runs through countless family letters, fictional works, and other contemporary commentary on British life in the empire, and features even more prominently in reminiscences dating from the later twentieth century. This discourse relies heavily upon how British-Indian family culture differed from lifestyles *imagined* to prevail among families of similar standing without overseas connections. As John Gillis, Paul Thompson, and others have noted, the field of family history has long been dominated by efforts to reconstruct the quantifiable families people have, as Gillis puts it, 'lived with', and not 'the symbolic families, the family myths, stories, and symbols, they have *lived by*'.[6] Throughout stories of British-Indian family life, the disparity between its members' condition and the 'normal' (meaning nuclear) British family characterized by cheerful domesticity and parent–child togetherness was repeatedly bemoaned, thus casting into relief the family models many chose to 'live by'.

But just how different were these imperial family dynamics from those common in families of the same social level based solely in Britain, and how normal was the model of nuclear family life they could not achieve when children left India? Scholars including Linda Nicholson as well as Davidoff and her co-authors stress the problems not only with viewing the nuclear family as co-extensive with a single household, but more broadly with accepting concepts such as the 'traditional family' as a standard rather than a false, idealized universality that remained elusive for many. After all, British households both at home and in the empire commonly included not only other kin but also persons not related by blood, including servants or lodgers.[7] As Chapter 1 revealed,

[5] WHSA, Newspaper Cuttings Book, Dr David Livingstone, cited in 'The Children of Venture', *Baptist Times* (10 Feb. 1922); also see 'Concerning some "Grass Orphans"', *Outward Bound* (Jan. 1921), 299.

[6] Gillis, 'Making Time for Family', 7; Paul Thompson, 'Family Myth, Models, and Denials in the Shaping of Individual Life Paths', in Daniel Bertaux and Paul Thompson (eds.), *International Yearbook of Oral History and Life Stories, Vol. II: Between Generations: Family Models, Myths, and Memories* (Oxford, 1993), 13–38; Raphael Samuel and Paul Thompson (eds.), *The Myths We Live By* (London, 1990); and Tamara K. Hareven, 'Recent Research on the History of the Family', in Michael Drake (ed.), *Time, Family and Community: Perspectives on Family and Community History* (Oxford, 1994), 37–8.

[7] Davidoff et al., *Family Story*, 86, 243, 268; Linda Nicholson, 'The Myth of the Traditional Family', in Hilde Lindemann Nelson (ed.), *Feminism and Families* (New York, 1997), 27–42.

when in India many children spent considerable time with Indian servants—perhaps more than with their parents—and accordingly developed affection for them that complemented or competed with parent–child intimacy. Rather than being characterized by their autonomy, relationships between parents and children in any family took shape with reference to wider household, kinship, and friendship networks, the neighborhood, and other forms of community within which they operated.[8] Moreover, as is well known, the practice of sending children away to boarding school was widespread not only among British-Indians but also among middle-class and elite Britons who had no direct links overseas. In families throughout the social spectrum, meanwhile, children could be separated from their parents and either institutionalized or placed in other homes as a result of parents' death, abandonment, or a range of other factors.[9]

When compared to other Britons, British-Indian families did indeed function within a distinct set of geographical and cultural parameters, even if they shared some aspects of their lifestyle with others who lacked overseas ties. Still, their assertions of uniqueness underscore how central myths of the 'normal' family could be for those who failed to live up to these ideals. As Jeffrey Weeks suggests, 'the family is a potent trope even in the hands of those whose adherence to a traditional model is dubious', and one might add that it might in fact be *especially* powerful among such individuals.[10] The way British-Indians commonly described their family life as a deviation from an ideal none the less constitutes a key example of what Ken Plummer has called 'narrative truth'.[11] The culture of storytelling, Plummer argues, not only draws upon the wider culture in which writers and speakers live; once accounts are recorded they in turn work to shape the worlds both of storytellers and the audiences using them to interpret their own lives. Over time, British-Indians drew upon a growing range of prior narratives and used these to help make sense of their own experiences of childhood and parenting in the context of the late imperial and ultimately the post-colonial era.

---

[8] Ellen Ross, *Love and Toil: Motherhood in Outcast London, 1870–1918* (Oxford, 1993); Rayna Rapp, Ellen Ross, and Renate Bridenthal, 'Examining Family History', in Judith L. Newton, Mary P. Ryan, and Judith R. Walkowitz (eds.), *Sex and Class in Women's History* (London, 1983), 243–4; Barry Reay, 'Kinship and Neighborhood in Nineteenth-Century Rural England: The Myth of the Autonomous Nuclear Family', *Journal of Family History*, 21/1 (1996), 93, 99.

[9] Lynn Abrams, *The Orphan Country: Children of Scotland's Broken Homes from 1845 to the Present Day* (Edinburgh, 1998).

[10] Jeffrey Weeks, 'Pretended Family Relationships', in David Clark (ed.), *Marriage, Domestic Life and Social Change: Writings for Jacqueline Burgoyne, 1944–88* (London, 1991), 227.

[11] Ken Plummer, *Telling Sexual Stories: Power, Change, and Social Worlds* (London, 1995), 35, 38, 171

This chapter argues that what developed as a dominant mode of emphasizing family sacrifices stemming from separations incurred in the course of imperial service can be seen in letters between parents and children as well as in other sources dating from the late nineteenth century, but grew much stronger and became more frequently expressed over time. Rudyard Kipling's published renditions of his childhood after leaving India and his parents had a tremendous impact on how other British-Indians subsequently structured their recollections, with writers and speakers often explicitly describing their own pasts in terms of the paradigm he had done so much to create. As Roger Chartier succinctly asserted, 'representations of the social world themselves are the constituents of social reality', and Kipling often appears, I argue, as powerful a force in shaping many later autobiographical accounts as any childhood realities these adults had experienced.[12] Discourses of family sacrifice, then, had roots in the imperial era itself but continued to evolve up to and during the post-colonial era, as those looking back from the cultural climate of the later twentieth century have enhanced and consolidated now-dominant renditions of imperial childhood and family life. Indeed, emotions that earlier generations may not have been as likely to discuss openly or perhaps even feel consciously are now commonly found in retrospective accounts recorded by older people. While sometimes silenced, expressions of sentiment were none the less far from absent in contemporary writing. Before turning to these issues, however, this chapter first considers what family letters coupled with later recollections tell us about the alternative forms of family life British-Indians relied upon, and what these meant, once members of the nuclear family were divided by thousands of miles.

IMPERIAL FAMILIES DIVIDED AND RECONSTITUTED

Children leaving India for Britain normally encountered one or more of the following living and educational arrangements. Since many men employed in India were not permitted to marry early in their careers or voluntarily chose to wait until better able to support a family, some fathers reached retirement age and returned to Britain while children were quite young, thus curtailing family separations at an early stage. In other cases, children might grow up in

---

[12] Roger Chartier, 'Intellectual History or Sociocultural History?: The French Trajectories', in Dominick LaCapra and Steven L. Kaplan (eds.), *Modern European Intellectual History: Reappraisals and New Perspectives* (Ithaca, NY, 1982), 41.

Britain in homes to which fathers never returned, headed by widowed mothers. More frequently, however, nuclear families were divided on a less permanent basis, with some members residing in India and others in the metropole. Mothers sometimes accompanied children home and remained with them in Britain for much of their time at school, and in this instance the 'divided family' entailed the father working in India but only seeing his wife and children every several years while on furlough. Eric Blair/George Orwell's early family life exemplifies two of these possibilities. His father, Richard Blair, had already served in the Opium Department for over twenty years when he married Ida Limouzin—the daughter of a teak merchant in Burma and eighteen years his junior—in 1896. Their first two children, Marjorie and Eric, were born in India, but in 1904 Ida settled with them in England. Aside from Richard's home leave in 1907 (when another daughter was conceived), he did not see his family again until he retired in 1911.[13]

For Ida Blair, the choice between living in India with her husband and remaining in Britain with the children may not have been a difficult one given how relatively little time Richard had left to serve prior to retirement. Other women who were closer to their husbands in age had to make a geographical and familial decision that lasted considerably longer and typically entailed not only pain but a guilty conscience, since the burden of choosing which family members to prioritize rested on their shoulders. In 1909 Maud Diver summarized their dilemma in melodramatic terms not uncommon in discussions of British-Indian family dynamics in *The Englishwoman in India*. Women faced 'the rival claims of India and England; of husband and child. Sooner or later the lurking shadow of separation takes definite shape; asserts itself as a harsh reality; a grim presence, whispering the inevitable question: "Which shall it be?"'[14]

Most women appear to have opted primarily for India and their husbands, their choices perhaps influenced by anxieties about male infidelity during prolonged absences. Children sent to Britain thus experienced long periods apart from both parents, and this was widely portrayed as far more challenging than when only fathers were absent. As will be seen below, relationships between children and their fathers were far from meaningless for many families; literal distance did not always bring emotional distance. In other instances, however, mothers' absences in particular were seen as the main reason why children's family life fell short of widespread ideals. Recent scholarship by John Tosh, Lynn Abrams, Megan Doolittle, and John Gillis has shed more light on the role

---

[13] Bernard Crick, *George Orwell: A Life* (London, 1980), 5–7.
[14] Maud Diver, *The Englishwoman in India* (Edinburgh, 1909), 37.

of fathers in the domestic realm and examines the relevance of their interactions with children—areas of family life that long received little attention by historians as a result of the emphasis placed upon motherhood. Fathers, Gillis summarizes, were 'at the threshold of family life, never at its center', whereas in contrast, as Abrams puts it, 'a family without a mother was not deemed to be a family in any real sense'.[15] Men spent long periods on their own in India if their wives chose to reside mainly with the children, but their possible loneliness when bereft of family received considerably less attention than women's and children's.[16]

In India-connected British families mothers were well aware of the implications of separations from their children, and despite the fact that they often spent much of their time in India many none the less attempted to balance the periods with husbands and children. Memsahibs commonly were the most well-travelled members of their families because they were free to migrate between Britain and India as much as family finances and personal inclination permitted, in sharp contrast to their husbands, whose professional responsibilities restricted such movements to periods of long leave. Wives of well-paid Indian Civil Servants like Annette Beveridge and Ann Butler gave steamship companies like the P. & O. substantial custom, perhaps spending six months or a year with their children in Britain and then returning to India for a year or two prior to the next journey; their husbands, meanwhile, could experience five-year intervals between visits. Despite their more privileged position in this regard, women regularly alluded to misgivings and heartbreak when reflecting on their circumstances. As Ann Butler wrote in several letters to her husband when she was in England with the children, 'I can't stand a year again [of separation from him]. And yet I can't stand being away from the boy'; she continued later, 'for if I have the children and am with you the other half of me is gone again'. Still, she realized that 'it is far and desperately worse for you, who are without either half' while she was away.[17]

Ann never seemed to reconcile herself to dividing her time between continents as well as husband and children, but Annette Beveridge managed a tem-

---

[15] Gillis, *World of Their Own Making*, 179, 124; Lynn Abrams, ' "There was Nobody like my Daddy": Fathers, the Family and the Marginalisation of Men in Modern Scotland', *Scottish Historical Review*, 78/2: No. 206 (Oct. 1999), 237; John Tosh, *A Man's Place: Masculinity and the Middle-Class Home in Victorian England* (New Haven, CT, 1999), 2, 79–101; Megan Doolittle, 'Missing Fathers: Assembling a History of Fatherhood in Mid-Nineteenth-Century England', Ph.D. thesis, University of Essex (1996).

[16] See, however, allusions to men's experiences of 'the cruellest disruptions of domestic ties' by Sir George Trevelyan, *The Competition Wallah* (1864; repr. London, 1907), 127–8; 'The Indian Civil Service: Part I— What It Is', *Fraser's Magazine* (Oct. 1873), 435.

[17] OIOC, MSS Eur F225/27, Ann Butler to Montagu Butler, 'July 1911'; n.d. 'Wednesday night'.

porary solution to her own dilemma in 1886 upon returning to England alone nearly two years after leaving their three children (aged 4, 5, and 7) at a small school in Southport with their German governess. Her reunion with them revealed disappointing arrangements at the school that, along with being apart from their parents, put the children in 'low spirits' and made 'Fraulein' refuse to return. 'Letty does want her mother!', she wrote to Henry in Calcutta. 'She is a darling but she has sad moods as tonight when she told me she was afraid something was going to happen. She says with her dear hand on my shoulder . . . "There is no-one like mother" to comfort her. I see she cannot speak or think of my going without tears.' Annette seemed as unwilling to undergo another lengthy separation as her children, at least not immediately. 'Tutu asked me which I liked best to be with of my family halves . . . I said that I was sad when away from either. They often ask me when you will come.' She searched for alternatives:

I had an inspiration last night . . . it solves so many hard problems. I see you separated from your children and deprived of their charm. I see anxiety and the torture of parting before them and me. Letty feels it very much and so do the others, I think. They do not however dwell on it as she does . . . it shot through me that I would give ourselves the happiness of having them with us and unsay my declared resolution that I would never take them back . . . They have been at home three years and are strong and well. They could I believe remain three months in Calcutta without hurt and spend the rest of the year in Darjiling . . . I think they could stay out some three years without harm to education. I had a good governess with Fraulein . . . you would have them and they would learn to know you and would be within easy reach . . . We could spend all the holidays with them.[18]

Henry was more than happy to agree to these proposals, and Annette and the children soon returned to India. However, their choice was a luxury which entailed paying for the children's passages as well as protecting them from the climatic dangers Annette feared by arranging for them to live in the hills most of the year with two governesses employed to teach them—an option that, ironically, perpetuated distance despite enabling more frequent parental visits. While many other families experienced similar qualms about separations, few either could or would follow the Beveridges' example by bringing children back overseas once they had left.

When both parents were away in India, as was most often the case, it was common for an entire network of kin (and, to a lesser extent, family friends) to

---

[18] OIOC, MSS Eur C176/19, Annette Beveridge to 'My dearest Henry', 9 May 1886.

become enlisted in the task of British-Indian childrearing. Families with many members living overseas depended heavily upon those at home on a permanent basis in addition to those who had already retired from imperial work or were in Britain for extended leaves to take part in childcare activities. Children might live with guardians either year-round if they did not attend boarding school, or during school holidays if they did. Parental recourse to a circle of helpful relations when raising their offspring *in absentia* could substantially reduce the expense of leaving children in Britain by limiting the cost of boarding fees and even the price of their instruction. Girls in particular were more likely than boys to live with members of their extended family on a long-term basis and be taught at home by a governess or a relative, often alongside female cousins; alternatively, they might attend day schools nearby. Such an arrangement could last through the level of primary education or longer, depending upon their parents' priorities, incomes, and the ongoing willingness of family or friends to look after them.

One instance when relatives stepped in to fill the parental void is illustrated in the Talbot family correspondence. An officer in the Indian Political Service between 1873 and 1900, Adelbert Talbot and his wife Agnes had three daughters and a son born between 1873 and 1880. After their return to England their eldest two daughters, Guendolen and Muriel, initially stayed in the home of an aunt and uncle before attending a small girls' boarding school in the early 1880s. Their aunt prided herself upon fulfilling her family responsibilities with both the devotion and duty she deemed necessary to those parted from their parents, writing to Adelbert:

How strange it seems that the time is drawing to a close for the dear children to leave us! They have found Woolstone thoroughly a home and will always I think have a happy remembrance of these three years—certainly I can conscientiously say that they have been far more anxiously and affectionately watched over than had they been elsewhere . . . They fret a good deal at the thought of leaving me at Woolstone, but like all children will settle down in their new life in a few months. Muriel . . . scarcely remembers her mother, which must always be the case when separated before five years.[19]

This account of the recourse to the extended family in lieu of actual parental presence highlights the ideals of providing children with a place they considered 'thoroughly a home' and where they were treated 'affectionately', suggesting both the cultural importance placed upon these conditions of childhood by both the letter's writer and readers. The tone with which their aunt assessed her three-year commitment to the girls was self-congratulatory, however, implying

---

[19] OIOC, MSS Eur E410/65, Mary Coventry to Adelbert Talbot, 15 Dec., n.d. [*c.*1880].

that she had cared for Guendolen and Muriel as much from a sense of family obligation as from affection. Clearly, she considered her period *in loco parentis* to have drawn to a close, reminding Adelbert and Agnes that they could depend upon individual relatives in only a limited capacity. Like many other British-Indians, the Talbots therefore relied upon a combination of family members and boarding schools to raise their children over the course of more than a decade of separation. An alternating circle of their children's many aunts and uncles performed a variation on what anthropologist Micaela di Leonardo has termed 'kin work', assisting their absent parents by providing them with a place of residence as well as—possibly—a caring environment both prior to attending boarding school as well as during school holidays later.[20] Kindness was certainly no guarantee, however. As the adult reminiscences of the Talbots' youngest daughter, Esmé, reveal, she was sent to stay with different relations at the age of four and was regularly beaten by her aunt when falsely accused of her cousins' misdeeds. When she was older, she learned that when her great-aunt 'came down to see how I was getting on found me very neglected and my clothes shabby and torn'.[21]

No matter how affectionate or otherwise, no one within the Talbots' circle of kin aspired to be permanent parental replacements for the duration of four childhoods. The two elder daughters lived with different aunts and uncles than their younger sister did several years later, while their brother, Addy, appears to have begun preparatory school at Temple Grove without ever residing with family. The four siblings were seldom reunited even during their school holidays and instead were divided among various households; alternatively, they occasionally simply remained in the custody of school staff. When compared with staying with hesitant or hostile relations, non-familial arrangements were sometimes preferable. Once Esmé Talbot's unhappy time with her aunt ended, she never attended a boarding school but instead was sent to stay with a 'gentleman farmer' and his wife, who wanted to take in a girl of the same age as their daughter so that they might share the services (and costs) of a governess. She later recalled that the couple 'were kindness itself to me all the three years I was with them. Maud was like a sister to me and we became very fond of each other. How happy I was!'[22] Esmé's sphere of intimacy during this period was completely reformulated to encompass a combination of persons not related to

---

[20] Micaela di Leonardo, 'The Female World of Cards and Holidays: Women, Families, and the Work of Kinship', *Signs: A Journal of Women in Culture and Society*, 12/3 (1987), 440–53; see also Carol B. Stack and Linda M. Burton, 'Kinscripts', *Journal of Comparative Family Studies*, 24/2 (1993), 157–70.

[21] OIOC, MSS Eur D1222/1, Esmé Mary Dew (née Talbot), 'Our Affairs', n.d. [c.1943], 8–10.

[22] Ibid., 11.

her by blood (but who became 'like a sister') in addition to some, but not all, members of her natal family—even excluding some living relatively close by. As she described it, 'I saw very little of my sisters during the three years from seven to ten, when they were at school, so we were almost strangers, but my brother and I became fast friends [because he came to the family she lived with for his school holidays] and that to some extent satisfied one's need for a family of one's own.'[23]

The Talbots were not alone in opting to leave children with guardians who were not relatives, although this seems to have been less common than recourse to the extended family.[24] Some parents in India found close friends at home willing to look after children during school holidays, and who in fact proved far more amenable to the idea than were members of the family. Indeed, although Annette Beveridge was unsatisfied with the conditions her children experienced at their boarding school, she reserved only the highest praise for the way friends cared for them over holidays: 'the children are perfectly at home there and Mr and Mrs Turner kindness itself', she reported.[25] Parents in India might also turn to acquaintances they had known overseas who had returned to Britain. One army officer described how he and his wife found a guardian for their children in the 1870s after word of their needs spread throughout the intertwined circles of distant relations and Indian connections. 'At last we heard from Uncle Alick Robertson of a Mrs Whitlock, widow of great Sir George Whitlock's brother', he recalled. 'Her husband had been in the same regiment of Madras cavalry as Major Robertson had been, and was a truly estimable woman. We resolved, therefore, to leave the three in [her] care.'[26] In this instance, a wider British-Indian network spread over two continents largely replaced 'kin work' when blood relatives were either unavailable or unwilling to help look after children divided from their parents. All parties undoubtedly benefited from this intra-communal arrangement, as widows commonly sought additional income from taking in children and parents still overseas might feel more comfortable leaving their offspring with those they knew by reputation and who presumably could empathize with the situations imperial families faced.

[23] OIOC, MSS Eur D1222/1, Esmé Mary Dew (née Talbot), 'Our Affairs', n.d. [c.1943], 15.

[24] Nupur Chaudhuri, 'Memsahibs and Motherhood in Nineteenth-Century India', *Victorian Studies*, 31/4 (1988), 534–5.

[25] OIOC, MSS Eur C176/19, Annette Beveridge to 'My dearest Henry', 9 May 1886. Letters that Alice Turner and the Beveridge children wrote to Annette in 1885 about holiday visits attest to the pleasure they all experienced with the arrangement; OIOC, MSS Eur C176/121.

[26] CSAA, Grove Papers, typewritten copy of the untitled autobiography of Major-General Henry Leslie Grove, n.d. [c.1890s], 40.

Beyond taking advantage of friends and a wider British-Indian community based in Britain, another option for parents was to turn to strangers. Personal accounts as well as advertisements that prospective caregivers placed in English-language Indian newspapers attest to this practice, but it appears that those who resorted to it on a year-round basis were a small minority.[27] Children who did stay with families their parents did not know personally were most likely to have done so only during their time away from boarding school, when some joined others in a similar position at what were known as 'holiday homes'. None the less, imperial childrearing by strangers has achieved greater notoriety than the level of actual recourse to it merited, thanks largely to the popularity of Rudyard Kipling's writings on this theme that resonate with particular strength in late twentieth-century reminiscences. The following pages consider Kipling's adult renditions of his childhood experiences and their unique imprint upon those discussing their own early lives in his wake. These set the stage for a more detailed exploration of what distinct genres from different eras do and do not reveal about imperial family practices and their impact when parents and children were separated for long periods.

THE KIPLING PARADIGM AND RETROSPECTIVE ANALYSES

Born in Bombay in 1865, Rudyard Kipling is one of the best-known 'children of the raj'. While much of his literary output concerned India-connected Britons, he dealt with his own early childhood experiences in two works in particular: his short story 'Baa Baa, Black Sheep', dating from 1888; and his autobiography *Something of Myself,* begun in 1935 not long before his death. Penned nearly five decades apart, his accounts of childhood in India (introduced in Chapter 1) and its aftermath in England may not be literally accurate—after all, the first is a work of fiction, and the second, like any memoir, cannot be proved to mirror either his actual childhood experiences or how he felt about them at

---

27 Some who advertised their services lived in Bedford, which, as later chapters illustrate, had a significant British-Indian population. They may have been connected with this community themselves, or were simply familiar with its needs. Representative listings include 'Bedford Home and Education. A Widow Lady offers to take entire charge of a few Children'; or, 'A Lady in Bedford offers a happy Home for Anglo-Indian Children, Boys or Girls, with every school advantage. Moderate terms, including holidays', *Times of India, Overland Weekly Edition,* 7 April 1900, 20.

the time.[28] None the less, these writings are not only the main source of evidence that remains about his early life, but more importantly have been read as 'truth' by many after publication and frequently invoked as a standard of comparison by others looking back on their own imperial childhoods.

'Baa Baa, Black Sheep' and *Something of Myself* begin on Indian soil, but they quickly turn to images of children being taken back to Britain and left with complete strangers when their parents returned overseas. What happened to Kipling and his younger sister Alice (known more familiarly as 'Trix') at the ages of 5 and 3 respectively happened to children called Punch and Judy in 'Baa Baa, Black Sheep': they were left as paying boarders in the Southsea home of Sarah and Pryse Agar Holloway and their son, referred to respectively as 'Aunty Rosa', 'Uncle Harry', and 'Harry' in the short story. Punch and Judy's parents are shown to be deeply troubled by their lack of prior acquaintance and knowledge about the people they have chosen as guardians, by the fact that five years will pass before they are reunited, and by the anxiety that they soon will be forgotten by children so young. As both texts delineate, their worst fears were largely realized.

These two renditions of Kipling's five years in Southsea with his sister in the 1870s describe a period that, for him, was one of unmitigated misery. This was somewhat less true for Alice, who was treated far more affectionately by the Holloways than he. Still, both had 'lost all their world', and he (or, Punch) in particular is shown as 'cast without help, comfort, or sympathy upon a world which is new and strange to him'.[29] The Holloways' home became the 'House of Desolation' in the story, 'an austere little villa' where a 'cold wind' had ominously welcomed them.[30] Calling these guardians 'Aunty' and 'Uncle' ironically served to emphasize that these were not members of their own family, but rather fictive kin with no obligations other than to provide food and shelter for a fee, and ensure some form of rudimentary education. The children were repeatedly portrayed as abandoned by their parents and in many ways like orphans. Writing shortly after her brother's death, Alice recalled their experience as 'like a double death . . . we felt that we had been deserted, "almost as much as on a doorstep" '.[31] Significantly, in another fictional work— *The Light*

<hr/>

[28] C. E. Carrington, ' "Baa Baa, Black Sheep": Fact or Fiction?', *Kipling Journal* (June 1972), 7–14. Other discussions of Kipling's childhood experiences include Ashis Nandy, *The Intimate Enemy: Loss and Recovery of Self Under Colonialism* (Delhi, 1983), 64–70; Zohreh T. Sullivan, *Narratives of Empire: The Fictions of Rudyard Kipling* (Cambridge, 1993), ch. 2; Andrew Lycett, *Rudyard Kipling* (London, 1999), 22–50.

[29] Rudyard Kipling, 'Baa Baa, Black Sheep', in Thomas Pinney (ed.), *Rudyard Kipling: Something of Myself and Other Autobiographical Writings* (Cambridge, 1990), 143.

[30] Ibid., 141; Rudyard Kipling, *Something of Myself*, in Pinney (ed.), *Rudyard Kipling*, 7.

[31] Mrs A. M. Fleming, 'Some Childhood Memories of Rudyard Kipling, by His Sister', *Chambers's Journal*, (March 1939), 171.

That Failed, dating from 1890–1—Kipling described a home and atmosphere so similar to his other renditions of the Holloways' house in Southsea that it cannot have been coincidental, and in this case the two children taken in really were orphans.[32] That they were made to feel like intruders is summarized most succinctly in 'Baa Baa, Black Sheep', when Punch overheard them referred to as 'strangers' children'.[33]

In numerous ways, all the warmth—physical as well as social—that characterized Kipling's memories of his first years in India in the company of caring parents and devoted Indian servants had disappeared; instead, in Southsea an initially unpromising scenario and unfamiliar set of cultural (and largely evangelical) codes became even worse when 'Uncle Harry', with whom he had better relations, died. Thereafter, he (and/or Punch, now called the 'Black Sheep') was subjected to a steady and increasing stream of abuse, both physical and mental, inflicted by 'Aunty Rosa' and her adolescent son. In 'Baa Baa, Black Sheep' Punch was never shown to have any real release from 'Aunty Rosa' and her son's grasp; Kipling only noted in passing that 'holidays came and holidays went and Black Sheep was taken to see many people whose faces were all exactly alike'.[34] In his autobiography, however, he not only elaborated on the times spent away from the House of Desolation but gave them considerably greater importance. He spent each December in the home of his mother's sister, Aunt Georgy, her husband, the artist Sir Edward Burne-Jones, and their children; there, he wrote, 'I had love and affection as much as the greediest . . . could desire'.[35] His month on parole provided fun, love, and an extended family, following which the inevitable return to Southsea became all the worse by virtue of the stark contrast. He felt bereft of family once again; to return to 'Baa Baa, Black Sheep', there was 'no one to help and no one to care' when Punch faced torment from Aunty Rosa and her son.[36]

Surely his parents, and his Aunt Georgy and her family, all cared very much, but in his autobiography they long remained ignorant of the problems with this childcare arrangement and his sufferings there. For Punch 'the weeks were interminable and Papa and Mamma were clean forgotten'; alternatively, the memory of them 'became wholly overlaid by the unpleasant task of writing them letters, under Aunty Rosa's eye, each Sunday'.[37] Under these circumstances, letters could not reveal true feelings; nor did he feel able to tell

---

[32] Rudyard Kipling, *The Light That Failed* (1891; repr. London, 1909), 1–14.
[33] Kipling, 'Baa Baa', 147.   [34] Ibid., 159.   [35] Kipling, *Something of Myself,* 9.
[36] Kipling, 'Baa Baa', 157.   [37] Ibid., 159, 156.

his Aunt Georgy of his experiences in Southsea. As he explained in his autobiography, after his time there ended and the problems had become known:

the beloved Aunt would ask me why I had never told any one how I was being treated. Children tell little more than animals, for what comes to them they accept as eternally established. Also, badly-treated children have a clear notion of what they are likely to get if they betray the secrets of a prison-house before they are clear of it.[38]

Ultimately, of course, Kipling was freed from the House of Desolation. Family friends visiting the children detected that all was not well, and when he was 10 years old his mother returned from India and took him and his sister away (although later on his sister returned, reflecting her somewhat more positive interactions with Mrs Holloway). When compared with these accounts the next years he spent at school—the United Services College, which will be examined in the next chapter—are portrayed far more positively, most memorably perhaps in his novel *Stalky & Co.*[39] In 'Baa Baa, Black Sheep', he concluded by writing of their mother's guilt about her son's bad experiences and her efforts to re-establish affectionate relations with the children for whom she had become but a dim recollection, and she apparently succeeded in regaining their love and trust. In these two texts, bonds between parents and children (and, specifically, between mother and child) prove extremely resilient, enduring the challenges imposed by five years of separation during which the children suffered poor treatment and believed no one could prevent it.

Kipling was neither the first nor the last writer to describe the emotional dimensions of imperial family separations, but his accounts made the most lasting public impression, in part because of his ongoing literary reputation and in part because of how explicitly he conveyed both the experience and its effects.[40] Kipling's recurring presence in subsequent autobiographical writings about parent–child separations makes it impossible fully to dissociate their 'reality' from his precedent. Leonard Woolf suggested something similar about Kipling's impact when he wrote about his brief period as a civil servant in early twentieth-century Ceylon, commenting, 'the white people were also in many astonishing ways like the characters in a Kipling story. I could never make up my mind whether Kipling had moulded his characters accurately in the image

---

[38] Kipling, *Something of Myself*, 11.

[39] Rudyard Kipling, *The Complete Stalky & Co.* (1899; repr. Oxford, 1991).

[40] Kipling himself also claimed to have textual models of children's lives in Britain after leaving India, citing Mrs Ewing's story 'Six to Sixteen' which he had read as a boy when the piece appeared in *Aunt Judy's Magazine* in the early 1870s; see *Something of Myself*, 6.

of Anglo-Indian society or whether we were moulding our characters accurately in the image of a Kipling story.'[41] Kipling's role in shaping subsequent
narratives of British-Indian childhood rarely resulted in writers and speakers
claiming experiences identical to his. Rather, his tales of the House of Desolation and parental absence became a standard of comparison as well as contrast,
providing a useful point of reference for narrators describing particular
instances when their own lives deviated from imagined childhood 'norms' prevailing in Britain—in short, when they most felt like outsiders, or 'black sheep',
themselves.

Some references to Kipling surface in reminiscences of living with guardians
who, while not unkind, still invite comparison with the Holloways of Southsea. An army officer's daughter born just before the First World War described
her first years away from India in an interview dating from the early 1980s,
recalling:

we, my other sister and my brother and I, were left at home with guardians. The
guardians were sort of relations but that was not the only reason that we went to them
because they were professional guardians and this was a very common situation. Very
often the guardians, as ours were, were country parsons and took in children for the
holidays . . . They were . . . very kind to us and I don't think they ever betrayed the
boredom they must often have felt with us. They had a child who disliked us very much
but it wasn't at all a sort of Kipling/Baa Baa Black Sheep situation at all, she disliked us
and we disliked her and I don't blame her because she had three people introduced into
her family, it must have been very difficult for these children of guardians you know.[42]

With hindsight, this woman was able to reflect that British-Indian childhood
might be a trying experience for those who accepted newcomers into their
homes as well as for the children placed in an unfamiliar environment apart
from their own natal families. None the less, words such as 'boredom' and 'dislike' resonate strongly, as does her emphasis that these were not merely distant
relations who cared for them out of good will but rather 'professionals' who
undoubtedly benefited financially from the arrangement.

This woman's comments do not clarify whether she and her siblings stayed
with this family for an extended period or whether they came only during
school holidays, but 'professional guardians' such as these often did their best
business when children attending boarding school had to leave at the end of the

---

41 Leonard Woolf, *Growing: An Autobiography of the Years 1904–1911* (New York, 1961), 46, cited in Nancy
L. Paxton, 'Disembodied Subjects: English Women's Autobiography under the Raj', in Sidonie Smith and
Julia Watson (eds.), *De/colonizing the Subject: The Politics of Gender in Women's Autobiography* (Minneapolis,
MN, 1992), 387.
42 CSAA, MT 46, transcribed interview of Mrs Veronica Bamfield by Mary Thatcher, 10 Sept. 1981, 4.

term. Another man recalled that the woman with whom he spent his times away from school while growing up in the 1930s was 'a lady who specialized in colonial brats'. In this enterprise, children often were not catered to on a one-to-one basis but instead experienced a group custodial arrangement that resembled boarding school, despite the absence of lessons and the replacement of an institutional with a household setting. His time in the company of this woman was not remembered negatively, however; he was, in fact, explicitly anxious to distance her from Kipling's 'Aunty Rosa':

The lady who took overseas children was a good hearted Irish lady with a grown-up family and a moustache. I imagine she took us for the holidays to supplement her income . . . I remember her with affection; it was nothing like Rudyard Kipling's 'Baa Baa, Black Sheep', thank God.[43]

The novelist M. M. Kaye conveyed a similar attitude when looking back on her childhood in the 1920s, when she and her brother and sister spent their time away from boarding school in the home of an unmarried school friend of her mother's. A sense of duty coupled with economic necessity brought this woman to act in the capacity of 'honorary aunt':

poor Bee eked out her small income by looking after the left-behind children of friends and relatives whose work tied them to India. The trouble was that she did not know the first thing about children. And did not want to! However, that was something Mother never realized; she merely knew that Bee could be trusted to look after us—which she did with something of the manner of a head-warder at Borstal—and that she needed the money . . . indeed we really were grateful . . . we had enough sense to realize that we could have been in much worse hands—just look at what happened to poor little Rudyard Kipling, for example . . .[44]

   In these accounts, holiday guardians encompassed persons from outside the children's extended family, distant relations, and parental acquaintances, some of whom were called 'aunt' or 'uncle' as was the case in Kipling's work. Fictive kinship designations that could just as readily apply to seemingly reluctant carers acting out of duty as to tyrannical 'Aunty Rosas' suggest that 'real' aunts and uncles might be just as likely to fail in their role as affectionate parental substitutes. After all, Esmé Talbot's worst childhood memories concerned the years when she was physically mistreated by her aunt, not when she lived in the home of the 'gentleman farmer'. Although Kipling's autobiography reserved nothing but praise for his Aunt Georgy and her family for opening up their home to

   [43] Peter A. Clark, letters to author, 18 June 1995, 17 July 1995.
   [44] M. M. Kaye, *The Sun in the Morning: My Early Years in India and England* (New York, 1990), 369, 379.

him at Christmastime and other families (like the Butlers) similarly extolled the treatment children received from their parents' siblings, other renditions of British-Indian family divisions turn to Kipling's childhood misery when reflecting on holidays spent with members of their extended family.[45] An auto-biographical novel published in 1993 by Richard Rhodes James shows children growing up during the interwar era who left school for the holidays to visit an alternating succession of aunts, resigned to their sporadic kinship obligations but showing little enthusiasm. Described as 'orphans of the Raj, paying the price of Empire by a separation from parents', the children's status as outsiders who lack an adequate family structure receives in-depth treatment. Time and again they 'join[ed] a family not [their] own in a house that was not theirs', whether it was that of 'Aunt Mary', 'Aunt Maud', or 'Aunt Mabel'. The elder daughter, noting the 'shuffling of aunts', cynically asked, 'Which M this time? . . . Perhaps they've tossed up for it.' Their mother in India, meanwhile, was greatly concerned by their predicament yet also relieved that it was a far cry from the worst-case scenario that had become common colonial currency through Kipling. She 'always had at the back of her mind the dreadful tale of the misplacement of the young Rudyard Kipling in the house of horror when his parents returned to India. She was thankful that she had avoided that. The dear aunts. What would we do without aunts?'[46] 'Real' aunts may not always have provided the emotional sustenance that adult reminiscers demanded, yet they fare well in comparison to the ever-looming spectre of the—partly—fictive 'Aunty Rosa'.

A final and particularly evocative example of Kipling's omnipresence in the structuring of memory about British-Indian childhoods appeared in Alan Ross's *Blindfold Games* published in 1986.[47] Born in the early 1920s in Calcutta where his father worked in the coal-mining industry, Ross was sent to England when he was 7 to attend several prep schools and later Haileybury. He provides a lengthy description of the household he left behind in Calcutta, in which the 'family' he remembered encompassed (and indeed foregrounded) those not related by blood:

When my Indian childhood came to an end and I was sent to England—the first step in an alienation from all family life—it was for [a] composite house that I mourned.

[45] R. A. Butler, *The Art of the Possible: The Memoirs of Lord Butler* (London, 1971), 8–9.

[46] Richard Rhodes James, *The Years Between: A Tale of the Nineteen Thirties* (Bishop Wilton, York, 1993), 43, 122, 195.

[47] Ross long edited the *London Magazine* and was described as a 'poet, writer, and cricket devotee' in his obituary. 'Alan Ross', obituary, *Guardian*, 16 Feb. 2001, 24.

The bearers with whom secret alliances were joined against parental injunctions . . . the mali alongside whom I would squat while he watered and weeded; the various drivers and kitmagars with whom I played cards on the verandah . . . It was this . . . surrogate family whose loss I found most hard to bear . . . Through those boarding-school years what was most loved and familiar was oceans away, though it was the brown hands that I craved, and not the alternately distant and crowding affection of parents.[48]

As Chapter 1 outlined, memories of childhood in India (including Kipling's) commonly highlighted close relationships with servants; for Ross, Indians' role as his 'surrogate family' underscored his attenuated emotional ties with his parents even before he left India and that became weaker still once he went to England. School holidays with a series of guardians (usually clergymen's families) turned him into a 'strangers' child' and brought forth comparisons between his own youth and Kipling's. 'At the age of seven', he wrote,

I became one of the breed that Uncle Harry, kind, dying, and put-upon, termed 'strangers' children' in Kipling's story 'Baa Baa, Black Sheep' . . . Strangers were always good to me, but in the proportion that I felt at home with them so did I feel less part of my own family. As a 'stranger's child' you may get affection, but you do not often get the physical expression of love that a child gets from its own parents. However kindly you are treated, you never lose the feeling of being a 'paying guest'. There may be no family quarrels to disturb you, but you learn to become anonymous. When the time came, the prospect of seeing my parents again, and having to own emotional allegiance to people I could scarcely remember, became increasingly embarrassing. Before long it was my parents who appeared to be strangers.[49]

What can be gleaned collectively from these references to Kipling's accounts of parent–child separations across the empire? Kipling provided many of the dominant motifs later narrators incorporated into evaluations of their own early lives, but they did not invoke his paradigm at random. Rather, Kipling emerges when they recount the points at which their childhoods diverged most sharply from those of other 'normal' children of their social level whose parents were not overseas. Although, as the next chapter considers, the general parameters of Kipling's subsequent boarding-school experiences also resembled those of many other British-Indian offspring in that he attended a school in the company of many others like him with parents in the empire, those who later discuss this phase of their lives do not commonly invoke *Stalky & Co.* or his other writings about the United Services College.[50] Since boarding-school education prevailed among many sectors of Britain's upper middle and middle

---

[48] Alan Ross, *Blindfold Games* (London, 1986), 17–19.
[49] Ibid., 68–9.
[50] Kipling, *Something of Myself*, and 'An English School', in Pinney (ed.), *Rudyard Kipling*, 15–24, 181–97.

classes (and particularly among boys) throughout this era, British-Indian children's distinctiveness became most apparent during school holidays when their schoolmates with parents in Britain went home. As John Gillis and other scholars of middle-class family culture have argued, by the late nineteenth century holidays had become some of the most symbolic occasions when families celebrated idealized conceptions of themselves, with most holiday rituals now focused on family gatherings rather than on a wider social community.[51] Most children experienced Christmas and summertime in a nuclear family setting, regardless of the months they may have spent away at school. Some British-Indian children, like Kipling, may have joined a loving extended family circle in their parents' absence, but many others recall alienation as outsiders in other people's homes, and it is at this juncture when their stories commonly turn to 'Baa Baa, Black Sheep' or *Something of Myself.* Few seem to have suffered from guardians as cruel as 'Aunty Rosa', but even well-intentioned aunts, uncles, and grandparents as well as other warmly recalled caretakers often could not fulfil the high expectations of intimacy culturally demanded of them, particularly at times of year when society at large revelled in such forms of feeling and personal interaction. In these accounts, a sense of alienation from family is inseparable from the widespread idealization of nuclear family relationships.

Another quality these Kipling-inflected reminiscences share is their timing. All date from the 1980s and 1990s, reflecting in part the large quantity of British personal narratives of involvement in India that were written or gathered by archives during these years. However, this cluster of accounts also suggests that the combination of childhood experiences and sentiments Kipling considered had a particular resonance for people who looked back upon the last decades of the raj from the standpoint of late-twentieth-century conditions and attitudes. To what extent would sources dating from the imperial era itself written *during* the period of family separation either resemble or diverge from retrospective post-colonial versions? Letters exchanged between parents and children provide different perspectives both on how they responded to their circumstances and how they developed new ways of maintaining their relationship once parted. Although British-Indian children were often compared to orphans given their parents' long-term absence and their resulting need for other kin and non-kin to step into the breach, divided families none the

---

51 Gillis, *World of Their Own Making*, 98–107. For a bourgeois French context which suggests similarities between British and other Western European middle-class family cultures, see Anne Martin-Fugier, 'Bourgeois Rituals', in Michelle Perrot (ed.), Arthur Goldhammer (trans.), *A History of Private Life, Vol. IV: From the Fires of Revolution to the Great War* (Cambridge, MA, 1990), 285–307.

less had their own dynamics, both material and emotional, appropriate to imperial circumstances.

LONG-DISTANCE INTIMACY: FAMILY LETTERS AND IMPERIAL RELATIONSHIPS

Families split between Britain and India throughout the late imperial era benefited from a well-established postal service linking Britain with the empire which, despite the distance separating them, enabled parents and children to maintain a regular correspondence. Letters took about three weeks to reach their destination, and composing them was a common weekly ritual (although in many families fathers wrote less frequently and left maintaining regular contact with the family to their wives—an important aspect of the 'kin work' women performed).[52] As John Tosh has pointed out, physical separation and geographical mobility prompted families 'to articulate so much that they normally took for granted' in letters that thereby shed light on writers' priorities and values.[53] Separations thus could generate uniquely detailed textual evidence about the ways families discussed their feelings and structured their lives over time, yet letters cannot be said to provide a complete picture of their writers' lives and attitudes. Instead, they reveal the conventions of letter-writing and most commonly contained sentiments and information deemed socially acceptable to convey to their designated readers, making it necessary to consider what individuals felt both willing and able to communicate through this genre.[54]

For parents and children divided for years at a time yet who valued both retaining and building family affection, letters became treasured not only for the thoughts and news written in them but as a tangible reminder of an absent loved one regardless of their contents.[55] Parents who left very young children in Britain often had to wait until they learned to write before hearing from

---

[52] Di Leonardo, 'Female World'. On the ways that women similarly played leading roles in colonial family letter-writing rituals in a Danish missionary family divided between Denmark and South India, see Poul Pedersen, 'Anxious Lives and Letters: Family Separation, Communication Networks and Structures of Everyday Life', *Culture and History*, 8 (1990), 8–9; on correspondence as a means of analyzing American female intimacy, see Carroll Smith-Rosenberg, 'The Female World of Love and Ritual: Relations between Women in Nineteenth-Century America', *Signs: Journal of Women in Culture and Society*, 1/1 (1975), 1–29.

[53] John Tosh, 'From Keighley to St-Denis: Separation and Intimacy in Victorian Bourgeois Marriage', *History Workshop Journal*, 40 (1995), 204–5.

[54] See especially Rebecca Earle (ed.), *Epistolary Selves: Letters and Letter-Writers, 1600–1945* (Aldershot, 1999).

[55] Gillis, *World of Their Own Making*, 77–8.

them directly, and in the meantime relied on secondhand accounts from the adults caring for them. When children took their first steps in mastering basic correspondence, their letters became evidence that they had not forgotten the parents who had ceased to be part of their everyday world. In the Talbot family's late-Victorian correspondence, the children's aunt's comment that Muriel 'scarcely remembers her mother, which must always be the case when separated before five years' touched upon a fear that both Agnes and Adelbert repeatedly conveyed. Agnes encouraged 6-year-old Guendolen in her early efforts to write during her first years in England, stressing that 'I can't tell you how pleased I am to get your letters darling they are my greatest comfort. I like to know that my little girls think of me and remember me now that I am so far away.' She strove to reinforce her daughter's memories of the time when they were together, and thus of her very existence, when describing her journey up into the highlands to Mount Abu:

We came up to Aboo on Monday morning. I was carried up that hill in a chair by four men and Addy sat on my lap. I thought of the day I came up six years ago, when I had a very tiny little baby on my lap, wrapped up in a white shawl. Do you know who that little baby was? . . . You must not forget all those nice visits we paid together.[56]

Annette Beveridge wrote to her youngest daughter in a similar tone that tried to reinforce memories of family togetherness that undoubtedly were becoming dimmer for a 5-year-old. 'Some day [Papa] will come home and you will have great games in the garden with him again like you used to have at Keavil', she promised, adding insistently, 'Do you remember?'[57]

Alongside reminding young children of themselves and the times they once shared together, parents' letters rarely allowed children to forget what they left behind in India. Annette regularly passed on servants' greetings, writing 'Mama's old ayah was calling on me lately and was asking after you all . . . the old bearer often asks after you all and he is fond of looking at the photographs'. The Beveridge children reciprocated, with 6-year-old William ending one letter 'I hope you are quite well. With love and kisses your loving Willie. I send my love to the ayah and the old servants.' Recollections of people were thereby reinforced, as was children's familiarity with Indian vocabulary and colonial domestic practices. 'I remember Willie had forgotten what a punkah was, but I daresay Letty remembers them', Annette continued.[58] The letters Helen and

---

56 OIOC, MSS Eur E410/21, Agnes Talbot to Guendolen Talbot, 15 March [1879].

57 OIOC, MSS Eur C176/120, Annette Beveridge to 'My dear little Tutu', 2 Oct. 1885.

58 OIOC, MSS Eur C176/116, Annette Beveridge to 'My dear Letty, Willie, and Jeannette', 30 Oct. 1884; MSS Eur C176/121, 'Willie' to 'My dear Mamma and Papa', 11 Feb. 1885.

William Bannerman wrote to their four children living with their aunt in Edinburgh between 1902 and 1917 during William's years in the Indian Medical Service reveal similar efforts to keep children aware of the colonial environment they once inhabited. Helen—known today for her historically controversial children's book *The Story of Little Black Sambo*—was a talented amateur illustrator and included a watercolor miniature depicting events, objects, and people that were part of her daily round in each weekly letter.[59] Visual prompts accompanied anecdotes such as one she recounted to her youngest son, Rob, about encountering an Indian beggar, who said ' "Sahib, Sahib, paisa do", the way they always do'.[60] Rob evidently knew Hindi well enough to make an English translation unnecessary, and reading his mother's letter may have bolstered fading knowledge of it. By including selected Indian phrases in her letter, Helen also reiterated her son's insider status within a geographically divided British-Indian community that he did not fully leave behind once in Scotland.

The Bannerman children also received continual updates about their parents' social lives as well as William's medical research. Many British-Indian children retained and enhanced their awareness of what work and leisure in India entailed, which may indirectly have influenced their own decisions to return as adults. Twelve-year-old John Watson showed avid interest in his father's conflated career and recreational pursuits as an army officer in a letter to his mother from prep school in 1886, which asked 'Has Father caught the outlaws? I hope he has. Will Father have any chance to shoot a Gir lion while he is trying to capture those outlaws in the Gir forest?' While his father apparently pursued both Indian people and wildlife with a rifle, John proceeded to capture them in pen and ink during drawing lessons at school. 'I draw out of my head very often stags, lions, tigers, panthers etc.', he related. 'I like stags and tigers much the best I often draw Indians'. In his later career in the Indian Medical Service, he undoubtedly adapted readily to the hunting culture that dominated the leisure agenda in many British circles.[61]

Through letters, parents not only described their daily activities but often tried to ensure that, despite their everyday absence, children grew up sharing their values and learned approved forms of behavior. These too might reflect their imperial family circumstances, such as when Helen and William

---

[59] For biographical information on the Bannerman family as well as a charitable analysis of Helen's fiction for children, see Elizabeth Hay, *Sambo Sahib: The Story of Little Black Sambo and Helen Bannerman* (Edinburgh, 1981).

[60] NLS, Dep. 325/VI, Helen Bannerman to Robert Bannerman, 24 Sept. 1909. 'Sahib, Sahib, paisa do' translates as 'Sir, Sir, give me money'.

[61] OIOC, MSS Eur F244/18, John W. Watson to 'My darling Mother', 14 Feb. 1886; n.d. [1885].

Bannerman discussed religious activities. Along with recounting their diverse forms of involvement with the Free Church of Scotland in Bombay and Madras, they convinced their daughters to do their own part in philanthropic work on behalf of its missions. Janet and Day gave up their pocket money in order to sponsor an Indian child at a missionary school, which, as their mother put it, provided 'a way for you to stretch out your hand to India, and help to bring [a child] into God's kingdom'.[62] The tone the Bannerman letters took was not always contingent upon the interdependent metropolitan and colonial settings in which the family operated; at many junctures they inquired about issues that concerned bourgeois parents regardless of overseas links. 'How many threepennies have you got in your wee bank?', Helen asked 8-year-old Rob, thus encouraging the practice of saving.[63]

In the Talbots' correspondence, meanwhile, both Adelbert and Agnes played active roles in the attempt to enforce appropriate behavior in their children. Religion infused their exhortations to some extent, with Adelbert warning his daughters against disobeying their relatives during visits, despite the inhospitable atmosphere the girls encountered over many holidays. 'I am sure that if you seek *God's* help in fighting against this or any other temptations you will win the victory', he thundered, before linking their future decorum to the tenor their relationship would take once he returned to England:

Next to the fear of offending God who is all pure and holy, should come the wish not to do anything of which your parents need feel ashamed for you and this will I trust induce you to keep your promises most faithfully in future so that when I come home I may feel that my own little girls are all that I should wish them to be.[64]

Adelbert played his role as a strict patriarch inconsistently, but when he did exert moral pressure on the children it most commonly concerned either their handling of precarious relationships with the extended family upon which they relied so heavily, or alternatively their educational progress.

Both Adelbert and Agnes Talbot continually stressed the importance of learning, and it is in this respect that their long-distance advice to (and pressure upon) their children becomes most gender-specific. Although Adelbert's letters to his only son, Addy, do not survive, he repeatedly discussed his progress through prep school and then Eton when writing to Guendolen and presumably did the same with Addy himself. Whether his son came at the top of his

62 NLS, Dep. 325/II, Helen Bannerman to Janet Bannerman, 7 Jan. 1904; see also Dep. 325/I, William Bannerman to Day Bannerman, 14 Mar. 1903.

63 NLS, Dep. 325/VII, Helen Bannerman to Robert Bannerman, 8 April 1910.

64 OIOC, MSS Eur E410/3, Adelbert Talbot to Guendolen and Muriel Talbot, 4 May 1885.

class or won prizes was of overriding importance, particularly since these accomplishments ultimately won him scholarships that saved the family considerable expense and even more crucially led to his admission into the Indian Civil Service.[65] Addy was pushed towards achieving a high-status form of masculinity by his absent father, and both parents similarly stressed how important it was for their daughters to acquire appropriately feminine qualities. Although Adelbert and Agnes praised Guendolen's scholastic successes, they also feared she might 'overdo it' in preparing for examinations and 'injure your health'; instead, they encouraged her and Muriel in their music lessons and in developing the non-academic skills seen as appropriate for late-Victorian young women of their social class.[66] 'You will not be a Girton or Newnham girl I hope', Adelbert told Guendolen when she was 16; her mother soon reminded her where her priorities should lie:

I am sending a recipe from the Lady for red hands, you can easily get one of the those loofahs and try the effect and also some gloves and almond paste . . . Do *please* dear girl try and sit up and not stoop as I hear you do it will spoil your looks so much and though you will never be a beauty you will be a very nice ladylike looking girl if you hold yourself well . . . Remember, indeed I think nice sympathetic manners showing good breeding, make many more friends than merely good looks . . . I don't wish you like those two Major girls whose minds have been trained but not their bodies.[67]

Parents like the Talbots who appeared so conscientious about their children's development but were worryingly unable to witness it on a regular basis relied on reports from other family members as well as what they could discern from their children's letters themselves. Along with containing news about their children's daily lives apart from them, letters were highly valued on a material level. Their very existence and regularity attested that parent–child relationships had not been fully severed despite the impediments posed by time and geographical distance; moreover, they provided parents with indications not only of children's activities and inclinations but also tangibly allowed them to chart their educational progress from the moment they first learned to put pen to paper. Parents may have been unable to hear how well their daughters played the piano, or see how their sons performed in the classroom or on the playing

[65] OIOC, MSS Eur E410/2, Adelbert Talbot to Guendolen Talbot, 24 May 1884; MSS Eur E410/3, Adelbert Talbot to Guendolen Talbot, 23 Jan. 1885; MSS Eur E410/4, Adelbert Talbot to Guendolen Talbot, 14 June 1889.

[66] OIOC, MSS Eur E410/4, Adelbert Talbot to Guendolen Talbot, 6 Sept. 1889; MSS Eur E410/21, Agnes Talbot to Guendolen Talbot, 18 Nov. [n.d.].

[67] OIOC, MSS Eur E410/4, Adelbert Talbot to Guendolen Talbot, 15 Aug. 1889; MSS Eur E410/27, Agnes Talbot to Guendolen Talbot, 30 Nov. 1889.

field, but could (and did) comment on the quality of children's handwriting, spelling, and overall composition upon receiving a letter.[68] Annette Beveridge, for instance, could read just how much German and maths William had learned from their governess when he wrote 'Liebe Mama und Papa . . . Fräulein ist sehr zufrieden mit mir. Ich mache gute Fortschritte in der deutschen Sprache und ich rechne gern. Hier ist ein Additionsexempel . . .'[69] Parents also asked children to enclose their examination papers and copy books as additional evidence of their progress. Annette was clearly pleased with what she found:

We were delighted to see that Letty has learned so much in one year as we see in her examination paper and I will tell you why I was so pleased. You know that your father works very hard to get rupis to have you taught and taken care of and so when I see that you are all learning so much I am glad; I think "All dear Papa's hard work is being made use of by his children".[70]

Such visible testament of their progress, it seems, made the financial (if not the emotional) sacrifices the family incurred during the course of imperial service worth while.

Children regularly sent their parents not only examples of their academic work but also other items that symbolized both their development and their ongoing affection. Letters were often accompanied by small gifts, particularly handicrafts. The Beveridge children's handkerchiefs, penwipers, and knitting sent to their parents were appreciated nearly as much as evidence of their scholarly progress.[71] For Helen Bannerman, the hand-made bookmark her daughter Janet sent was valued both as an indication of her needlework skills as well as a token of affection and remembrance. 'It is very well worked and must have taken you a long time to do, and I like it very much for it means that my daughter loves me though we are so far away', she told her.[72] Other gifts from her children had an even more potent range of meanings. She thanked Janet and Day for the piece of heather they sent during their summer holidays in the Scottish Highlands because it reminded her of her homeland and her absent children simultaneously. The heather 'smelt so sweet, when we shut

[68] OIOC, MSS Eur E410/21, Agnes Talbot to Guendolen Talbot, 7 July [n.d.]; MSS Eur E 410/1, Adelbert Talbot to Guendolen Talbot, n.d.

[69] OIOC, MSS Eur C176/121, 'Liebe Mama und Papa' from 'Euer Sohn Willie', 2 Mar. 1885. This passage means 'Dear Mama and Papa, Fräulein is very pleased with me. I am making good progress in the German language and can add well. Here is an example of my sums.'

[70] OIOC, MSS Eur C176/120, Annette Beveridge to 'My dear children', 9 Sept. 1885.

[71] Ibid.

[72] NLS, Dep. 325/I, Helen Bannerman to Janet Bannerman, 26 June 1903.

our eyes we could almost fancy we were on the moor at Aviemore, with the sun shining, and the heather stretching away in front of us', she wrote. 'I sometimes pin a bit of it in part of my dress at night', she continued, thereby turning the gift into a source of physical connection with both its givers and their environment.[73]

Family exchanges in the form of letters and other items thus perpetuated connections both between people and places. Parents vicariously came into contact both with their distant children and their homeland when the post arrived from Britain; similarly, children remained connected with India not only through their parents' stories of familiar surroundings but also materially. Along with Christmas and birthday gifts, parents periodically sent children Indian objects such as the peacock feathers, saris, and bangles that reached Guendolen and Muriel Talbot, the coins and lizards' eggs the Beveridge children received, or the tiger skull that Jack Butler requested.[74] Every letter, moreover, inevitably had a stamp attached, enabling British-Indian children to become avid stamp collectors if they chose. William Beveridge's early letters to his parents repeatedly provided a tally of his collection that included a complete 'Government of India' set as well as stamps from letters his parents posted from ports of call when they sailed back and forth.[75] As objects inherent in the process of postal communication throughout this era, stamps (like the letters themselves) provide perhaps the most succinct material illustration both of the divisions between family members and the means by which these were bridged.

Of all the items enclosed within family letters, photographs of their writers had by far the greatest meaning. Like letters' written contents, photographs provided recipients with updates of their subjects' development as it manifested itself in their physical appearance along with fulfilling a wide range of other cultural functions. Exchanging photographs, as Elizabeth Edwards has discussed, became a means for 'distant kin to participate in the experience and intimacy of rites of passage', at once illustrating and sustaining group cohe-

---

[73] NLS, Dep. 325/I, Helen Bannerman to Day Bannerman, 2 Oct. 1903. For a longer discussion of the Bannermans and their Scottish cultural practices while in India, see my 'Haggis in the Raj: Private and Public Celebrations of Scottishness in Late Imperial India', *Scottish Historical Review*, 81/2, No. 212 (Oct. 2002), 212–39.

[74] OIOC, MSS Eur E410/1, Adelbert Talbot to 'My dear children', 5 Dec. 1882; MSS Eur E410/34, Guendolen Talbot to Adelbert Talbot, 24 May 1884; MSS Eur E410/32, Guendolen Talbot to Adelbert Talbot, 29 June [n.d.]; MSS Eur C176/120, Annette Beveridge to 'My own little Tutu', 6 Aug. 1885; OIOC, MSS Eur F225/36, Ann Butler to Montagu Butler, 1 April 1925.

[75] OIOC, MSS Eur C176/121, 'Liebe Mama und Papa' from 'Euer Sohn Willie', 2 Mar. 1885; LSE, BPIIa/15, Annette Beveridge to 'My dear little Sonnie', 19 June 1885 and 17 Oct. 1885.

sion.[76] British-Indians' running commentary on family photographs suggests that they were central to the long-distance idealization of family relationships, both in their capacity as constructed images of those they depicted and in how they were treated by their recipients.

Both the Beveridge and the Talbot letters describe eagerly awaiting the arrival of new photographs as well as the response upon receiving them. Annette Beveridge scrutinized every aspect of a group portrait taken of her children in 1885, attempting to discern as much about their personalities and how they were treated as was possible from a single image. She wrote to Letty:

Today we have been made so very happy by seeing the photograph which Miss Lewin sent . . . I think you all look very well and very much as though every one was as good to you as possible. Sonnie looks saucy, is he a saucy boy? You look as though you had something difficult to think about and a little serious but still our own dear little daughter. As for Tutu, she is very nicely taken and sat very still and we like her very much. She looks rather too tall we think.[77]

Annette's response to the picture conveyed many of her hopes and fears about the children parted from her. Were they well treated? Well behaved? The same as she remembered? Or, more worryingly, more serious and 'too tall', indications that they might be unhappy and that their childhoods were all to rapidly passing her by? Similarly, the Talbots' letters illustrate high expectations that could just as easily be followed by disappointment as by delight when photographs finally arrived. When she was 17 Guendolen wrote of her and her sister's response to receiving her parents' most recent portrait, 'we do not like it on the whole, both of you look so awfully stern . . . I think you have both altered a great deal . . . I daresay you will find us quite different too. Esmé certainly you will hardly recognise.'[78] Adelbert replied, 'I shall look forward to getting the photographs of you for I suspect you are all as altered as you think us . . . Muriel with her hair up will be a strange creature to look upon as compared with my recollections of her . . . of course you are both in long dresses by now, you at any rate.'[79] Parents ageing more rapidly than expected or children leaving their childhoods behind proved disturbing news to those

[76] Elizabeth Edwards, 'Photographs as Objects of Memory', in Marius Kwint, Christopher Breward, and Jeremy Aynsley (eds.), *Material Memories* (Oxford, 1999), 233–4. On the meanings of family photographs, see also Jo Spence and Patricia Holland (eds.), *Family Snaps: The Meaning of Domestic Photography* (London, 1991); Julia Hirsch, *Family Photographs: Content, Meaning and Effects* (New York, 1981); Annette Kuhn, *Family Secrets: Acts of Memory and Imagination,* new edn. (London, 2002); Brian Lewis and Colin Harding (eds.), *Kept in a Shoe Box: The Popular Experience of Photography* (Bradford, 1992).

[77] OIOC, MSS Eur C176/120, Annette Beveridge to 'My dearest little Letty', 12 June 1885.

[78] OIOC, MSS Eur E410/38, Guendolen Talbot to Adelbert Talbot, 28 Aug. 1890.

[79] OIOC, MSS Eur E410/4, Adelbert Talbot to Guendolen Talbot, 21 Sept. 1890.

who wanted evidence that family relationships, conveyed visually, were unchanged.

In place of idealized, familiar, and loving images, what recipients found thus might be too 'stern', too 'serious', or scarcely recognizable. None the less, while photographs might bring disappointment as indisputable evidence of estrangement after years of separation, they could also function as icons in their capacity as the closest physical manifestation of those far away. Photographs served not only as images that might underscore unfamiliarity but also as tangible, fetishized, material substitutes for those who were absent.[80] As Guendolen Talbot told her mother, 'I kiss your picture (and Papa's too) goodnight and goodmorning'; 'I often look at your picture; when I feel nasty and unhappy I often kiss the whole family round'.[81] The Beveridge children also kissed their parents' pictures, while their own likeness that reached India was, literally, greeted by members of the household. 'The servants like it too and the ayah made a salaam to it', Annette told them.[82]

Both photographs and the letters that contained them, then, became material means of sustaining relationships between separated parents and children, providing updates about the lives of those far away and in the process illustrating a range of family ideals and daily realities. In some instances letters are emotionally explicit and provide similar renditions of family sacrifice as those appearing in retrospective accounts. Guendolen Talbot's letters to her parents repeatedly demonstrate her early appreciation both of how family life 'should' be and how her own failed to match what she perceived as normality. She described her disappointment following holidays spent with reluctant relatives or their schoolmistresses—'so horrid without you and Papa', she told her mother.[83] Yet her longing to be with her parents mingles with statements suggesting she had forgotten how any other form of family life might feel. As she wrote at the age of 11:

I feel as if you were kind of locked up toys that one could not have you don't seem to be real out there only a name. You seem like some beautiful thing one caught a glimpse of now and then. I love you *very very* much you know. I have grown quite used to hardly seeing you now. It seems as ordinary as eating one's dinner. Somehow we are not like other children a bit I don't think. It is almost odd to hear other children talking of their parents as being always with them something too nice for us to enjoy. I seem almost to

---

[80] Edwards, 'Photographs as Objects', 224–6, 236.

[81] OIOC, MSS Eur E410/33, Guendolen Talbot to Agnes Talbot, 26 Nov. 1883; 2 Dec. 1883.

[82] OIOC, MSS Eur C176/120, Annette Beveridge to 'My dearest little Letty', 12 June 1885.

[83] OIOC, MSS Eur E410/31, Guendolen Talbot to Agnes Talbot, 5 Mar. [n.d.]; MSS Eur E410/36, Guendolen Talbot to Agnes Talbot, 5 Aug. 1888.

ache with longing for you. But for your letters and love I should hardly know I had you dear Mama.[84]

For Guendolen, separation had—disquietingly—become normality, and her mother's letters (as well as her photographs) were all that made her 'real'.

ARTICULATIONS AND SILENCES: COMPARING CONTEMPORARY AND RETROSPECTIVE STORIES OF SEPARATION

Outpourings like Guendolen Talbot's suggest strong feelings about family and intimacy that were undoubtedly sincere, but at the same time many of her and other writers' letters examined above depict their authors in ways that correspond to broader social conceptions of what their designated family roles should entail. Guendolen, her parents, and others perform the parts of the dutiful, loving daughter or conscientious, affectionate parent admirably, and it is difficult to distinguish between their awareness of culturally approved behavior and sentiment and their actual attitudes. Letters reflect a consciousness from a very early age of the feelings deemed appropriate to relate, and it is highly probable that much remained unwritten or was reshaped to fit expectations. Few children or parents conveyed such sentiments in as much detail as Guendolen, however. Letters often say far less about family pain and sacrifice than do later recollections, instead focusing almost exclusively on routine daily activities. Silence about separation, intimacy, and possible unhappiness suggests an alternative, yet equally revealing, set of responses to British-Indian family lifestyles to more effusive communications.

While a considerable number of family letters survive to document the ramifications of parent–child separations, countless others either were not preserved or possibly were never even written in such substantial numbers. Many British-Indians may have been far less diligent correspondents, or simply wrote letters their descendants deemed unworthy of saving or donating to archives. Would these letters, or the lack of them, have reflected weaker family bonds or sentiments that were less intensely felt? Many parents may well have felt less devoted to their offspring than the writers discussed earlier. Evelyn Chaldecott's letters to her mother from India about her young son Gilbert noted in the last chapter continually chronicled his misbehavior, her difficulties in finding a

---

[84] OIOC, MSS Eur E410/34, Guendolen Talbot to Agnes Talbot, 2 Mar. 1884.

governess to care for and teach him, and her annoyance that the First World War postponed his return to Britain to start school by several years. Had her letters to Gilbert once they were finally separated also survived, would they have indicated a different range of emotions that contrasted with her previous desire to send him away, or would they have appeared as perfunctory, obligatory compositions?

Similarly, many letters written by those who claimed to be distressed about being apart from their parents or children also focus mainly on everyday affairs rather than feelings about absence. Ann Butler may have written to her husband about how hard she found it to live apart from either him or her children, yet her letters to her son Rab once she was back in India largely contain cheerful accounts of their comings and goings.[85] Presumably she either saw little point in reminding him of a painful situation she felt unable to change, or simply managed to put her misgivings about separations largely into the background. Many clearly found it helpful to resign themselves to circumstances they considered inevitable, and this possibly became easier the longer families remained involved in India. Iris Portal (née Butler) recalled that she and her many schoolmates who were also 'orphans of the Empire' accepted their fate stoically (at least in retrospect); despite her memory of having been 'overcome by weeping' when her mother left her at school and writing letters begging her to return, she stressed that being left behind 'seemed more than natural because I had been brought up on tales of Grandfather and Grandmother Smith at Serampore, and how they sent their children home in batches to live with The Aunts'. When she left her own daughters in England twenty years later, it seemed 'normal to me as I was the third generation'. Albeit still painful, for her this form of childrearing had become 'a matter of course'.[86]

Children's letters to their parents, meanwhile, most commonly say little about their response to separation beyond closing with standard phrases such as 'I miss you' or 'when are you coming home?' Even Guendolen Talbot and the Beveridge children—who appeared so unhappy with their life in England away from their parents that they were allowed to return to India for several years— wrote mainly about more prosaic subjects rather than their emotional state. Moreover, while Guendolen clearly felt free to communicate her views not only about separation but also criticisms of her schoolmistresses in her letters, other children may well have been more inhibited from such seemingly frank discus-

---

[85] Trinity College, Cambridge, R. A. Butler Papers, RAB A67, letters from Ann Butler to Rab Butler, 1916–19.

[86] CSAA, Portal Papers, Iris Portal, 'Song at Seventy', typescript manuscript, n.d. [c.1975], 18–19, 114.

sions of unhappiness. Just as Kipling described Punch grudgingly writing to his parents 'under Aunty Rosa's eye', other adults looking back have also alluded to censorship, whether direct or indirect, from schoolteachers or guardians. 'I cried every night for a whole term after my mother left . . . my letters to [her] were returned by the staff to be re-written if I had complained, so she never knew', recalled one woman in the 1980s.[87] Another man described similar restrictions at his prep school, where letters became a compulsory writing exercise. 'We could have complained of our misery to our parents, but it was not politic to do so when Miss Fanny, Miss Lizzie or Miss Polly would have read every word we wrote to check our spelling and punctuation', he remembered.[88]

Children's environment coupled with an awareness of what constituted suitable subject matter largely accounts for the contents and tone of their communications. Some young British-Indians may have failed to allude to turmoil caused by separation because they were hindered from doing so, but others simply might have grown accustomed to their circumstances and considered them unworthy of substantial comment. Boys attending preparatory or public schools were the least likely to write of any dissatisfactions with the dynamics of imperial family life. Not only did they live in settings where family ties and sentiments were actively marginalized but they also shared family separations with every other pupil boarding at the school—at least during term. Letters like those Addy Talbot, John Watson, or Rab Butler wrote to their parents instead largely reflect the gender- and class-specific values and attributes both their families and their schools intended them to cultivate. They relate their class ranking in academic subjects, stress how assiduously they prepared for upcoming examinations, and provide running commentary on their own and their schools' athletic accomplishments.[89] For them even more than for girls like Guendolen Talbot, long stretches without family (and, perhaps, without considerable thought devoted to family) could readily become 'as ordinary as eating one's dinner', and hence largely undiscussed.

For many children and adolescents of both sexes and indeed their parents as well, emotional dimensions of family separations may have come under

---

[87] Betsy Macdonald, *India . . . Sunshine and Shadows* (London, 1988), 8.

[88] George Roche, *Childhood in India: Tales from Sholapur*, Richard Terrell (ed.), (London, 1994), 84. On children's writings as reflections of their social environment and how their structure and contents indicate adult guidelines and expectations, see Carolyn Steedman, *The Tidy House: Little Girls Writing* (London, 1982), 69, 74–8.

[89] OIOC, MSS Eur E410/63; OIOC, MSS Eur F244/18; Trinity College, Cambridge, RAB D48/6 and D48/9.

deeper scrutiny only in retrospect. During the era when sending children away from India was widely viewed as an unavoidable experience, lengthy reflection on its ramifications may have appeared unnecessary for most involved in this form of childrearing. Changed times, however, not only made this form of upbringing increasingly unfamiliar but also offered new cultural frameworks for evaluating the effects of British-Indian family life. Near the end of British rule in India and even more in subsequent decades, so much that had made British-Indian childhoods characterized by long separations typical within their social circle altered beyond recognition. The many who have discussed painful experiences in the later twentieth century did so in the wake of widescale decolonization; in an era when air travel had long since replaced lengthy steamship journeys to enable British children whose parents live overseas—working in business or as diplomats, for example—who attend boarding schools at home easily to rejoin their families during holidays; and, when years away at boarding schools had become a somewhat less common experience for affluent and middle-class families in Britain, irrespective of overseas ties. Looking back through these lenses, what once was an ordinary (albeit commonly resented) lifestyle among empire families might resonate more strongly in memory and be subjected to a different kind of analysis than long had commonly been the case.

Just as importantly, post-war British society witnessed an explosion of discussion about early childhood experiences, including separation from parents, from a psychological standpoint. Interest in the psychological dimensions of childhood was relatively slow to develop in Britain, but began to spread gradually beyond professional circles in the interwar era and proliferated further during and after the Second World War.[90] Investigations into the turmoil suffered by working-class children separated from their parents in the course of long-term hospitalization, other forms of institutionalization, or as a result of wartime evacuation did much to put concepts like 'maternal deprivation trauma' on the map.[91] 'Separation anxiety' and related ideas became even more familiar terrain during the 1950s and after, most famously through widely read

---

[90] Cathy Urwin and Elaine Sharland, 'From Bodies to Minds in Childcare Literature: Advice to Parents in Inter-war Britain', and Deborah Thom, 'Wishes, Anxieties, Play, and Gestures: Child Guidance in Inter-war England', in Roger Cooter (ed.), *In the Name of the Child: Health and Welfare, 1880–1940* (London, 1992), 174–99, 200–19; Denise Riley, *War in the Nursery: Theories of the Child and the Mother* (London, 1983), chs. 3 and 4; Harry Hendrick, *Child Welfare: England, 1872–1989* (London, 1994), ch. 5.

[91] John Macnicol, 'The Evacuation of Schoolchildren', in Harold L. Smith (ed.), *War and Social Change: British Society in the Second World War* (Manchester, 1986), 5–7, 26–7; Abrams, *Orphan Country*, chs. 2 and 5; Anna Freud and Dorothy Burlingham, *Infants Without Families* and *Reports on the Hampstead Nurseries 1939–1945* (London, 1974).

books by John Bowlby.[92] Professionals commonly focused their investigations on working-class 'problem' families and said little about middle- or upper-class childrearing practices that also led to separation from parents, but because their basic arguments became so well known it is plausible that they informed the significant additions made to the discourse of imperial family sacrifice in the post-colonial era.

Moreover, British-Indian narratives dating from the later twentieth century also bear the imprint of a cultural atmosphere in which publicly expressing emotions has gained greater acceptability. While work on emotions as a topic of historical inquiry remains in its early stages, historians are increasingly suggesting ways of situating specific modes of feeling and articulating sentiment within the contours created by particular societies and epochs. 'Emotion and emotional expression interact in a dynamic way', William Reddy summarizes, supporting arguments voiced by some psychologists that the very act of exhibiting a feeling may largely create the experience of it.[93] If read in this light, feelings about painful family separations recorded in the aftermath of empire either might have originated during the period of separation itself, or alternatively have emerged much later when circumstances facilitated them. As Martin Francis's work explores, British society was characterized as ideally governed by emotional self-restraint and reserve until well into the twentieth century, and the longevity of this attitude perhaps partly accounts for the cluster of recollections of British-Indian family sacrifices voiced only in the 1980s and 1990s.[94] Kipling's much earlier analyses of his own difficult experiences not only may have decisively molded post-colonial memories but also convinced some people that verbalizing their own unhappiness was acceptable, given his well-respected precedents.

With earlier expressions of family pain stemming from imperial social practices now joined by a substantial body of post-colonial versions, it becomes possible to chart how ideas of family sacrifice have evolved and coalesced since the late imperial era and found expression within a range of textual as well as

---

[92] John Bowlby, *Child Care and the Growth of Love* (Harmondsworth, 1953); *Attachment and Loss, II: Separation Anxiety and Anger* (Harmondsworth, 1975).

[93] William M. Reddy, *The Navigation of Feeling: A Framework for the History of Emotions* (Cambridge, 2001), pp. xii, 104, 143 See also Barbara H. Rosenwein, 'Review Essay: Worrying About Emotions in History', *American Historical Review*, 107/3 (2002), 821–45; Hans Medick and David Warren Sabean, 'Introduction', in Hans Medick and David Warren Sabean (eds.), *Interest and Emotion: Essays on the Study of Family and Kinship* (Cambridge, 1984), 3.

[94] Martin Francis, 'Tears, Tantrums, and Bared Teeth: The Emotional Economy of Three Conservative Prime Ministers, 1951–1963', *Journal of British Studies*, 41 (2002), 354–87.

oral genres. While expressions of feeling take historically specific forms, on many levels depictions of family separations show considerable continuity. From the late imperial period until the present those voicing their sentiments invariably stressed anguish and resentment; those not sharing such views may well have remained silent in light of the cultural value placed on family intimacy throughout the period. Imperial circumstances created families that fell short of widespread ideals, and commentators have consistently depicted both parents and children as martyrs. M. M. Kaye stressed in 1980 how

weeping mothers took their children down to the great trading ports of Calcutta, Madras and Bombay, and handed them over . . . to be taken 'Home' and brought up by relatives, or in many cases . . . by strangers. Such separations were one of the saddest aspects of the Raj . . . India was littered with the graves of children, and as a result those who survived infancy were sent home and often did not see their parents again until they were almost grown up.[95]

Although parents often spent little time with their offspring before they left India and delegated most childcare duties to servants, and then refused even to contemplate keeping them overseas, neither a possible lack of commitment nor any freedom of choice is acknowledged. As a contributor to the *Calcutta Review* put it in 1886, this 'loosening of the sacred family bond' was 'the saddest, yet *inevitable* result of Indian life'.[96] Whether real or imagined, India's dangers were enlisted to turn the agents of imperialism into its victims. In the process, the discourse of family sacrifice is used in the attempt to justify British rule because it illustrated a dedication to the subcontinent despite these 'costs'. Writing in 1888, Annette Beveridge argued that 'our separations are expiation enough for holding the country', while Richard Rhodes James's novel conveys almost identical views over a century later.[97] During her journey back to India after yet another parting from her children, the mother asks herself, 'Was it worth it? Were one's children an acceptable sacrifice? Did the Indians know how much it cost us to govern them? There was little evidence that they thanked us.'[98] For those confronted with detractors both during and after the era of British rule, the price of empire paid by families is offered as proof of selflessness as opposed to self-interest.

[95] M. M. Kaye (ed.), *The Golden Calm: An English Lady's Life in Moghul Delhi* (Exeter, 1980), 49.

[96] J. E. Dawson, 'Woman in India: Her Influence and Position', *Calcutta Review*, 83 (165), 1886, 349, emphasis added; cited in Indrani Sen, 'Between Power and "Purdah": The White Woman in British India, 1858–1900', *Indian Economic and Social History Review*, 34/3 (1997), 371.

[97] OIOC, MSS Eur C176/23, Annette Beveridge to Henry Beveridge, 8 May 1888. See also *Glimpses of Anglo-Indian Life Here and At Home* (Madras, 1901), 2, 22–4.

[98] Rhodes James, *Years Between*, 234.

So much ado about family sacrifice, albeit clearly sincere, largely (and perhaps conveniently) sidelines an equally central dimension of the British-Indian experience: imperial opportunity. If suffering from the 'inevitable' problems India posed to Britons—including jeopardized health, cultural and racial belonging, and family bonds—were the whole story, it would be difficult if not impossible to explain why families often perpetuated ties to the subcontinent into the next generation. As it stands, many sons and daughters chose both to return and remain overseas following their parents' retirement, and raised their own children in ways that mirrored their own upbringing despite having experienced the problems of family separations firsthand. India clearly offered them as many opportunities as drawbacks, and years spent in Britain did much to reinforce an awareness of these. Children sent away from India often looked back on the world they had lost with considerable nostalgia, as Chapter 1 explored, and this made many eager to return later. British experiences in and of themselves, however, were just as likely to render India attractive. For adults as well as children, returning to the metropole often brought dissatisfaction with their reduced socio-economic and cultural standing in a homeland from which they had grown estranged, and Chapter 5 considers how furlough and retirement experiences might increase the appeal of overseas life. But as the next chapter argues, children's metropolitan schooling in tandem with pre-existing family links account just as much for the likelihood of their return to the empire. For many young British-Indians, happy memories and the promise of privileges that education in Britain qualified them to enjoy were enough to offset any regrets and sufferings. In choosing to perpetuate family traditions of Indian-based careers and marriages—where residence overseas was interspersed with schooling, furloughs, and retirement at home—their 'abnormal' family lifestyle increasingly appeared to be merely a specific form of imperial normality.

4

Sent Home to School: British Education, Status, and Returns Overseas

Illustrating British-Indian children's experiences after they were sent home entails entering the endlessly varied realm of middle-class schooling in the metropole. Once they left India, they either attended boarding schools of many descriptions or studied while living with their mothers, retired parents, other relatives, or non-familial guardians. Children's education in Britain was not solely determined by their imperial background, and was equally moulded by their age, parents' priorities and income, and especially gender. As argued previously, however, many factors converged to make the school years of those with family links overseas distinct. This chapter outlines a range of typical patterns of British-Indian schooling, all of which were deemed likely to create higher-status adult opportunities than if children remained in India. Girls' and younger boys' educational experiences are often poorly documented at the institutional level, making personal narratives crucial to understanding both the structure and effects of their time in Britain. A number of schools with strong traditions of catering to older boys with imperial backgrounds, on the other hand, left ample records to suggest the main reasons why many pupils left Britain again upon completing their education.

Economic limitations often lay behind parents' educational choices as well as their children's ultimate returns overseas. Parents able to afford children's passages home and British school fees were usually middle class but often far from affluent, and schools that provided sons with the credentials to embark upon well-paid imperial occupations at an affordable price proved highly popular among this community. Enhanced career prospects that mainly applied to boys, coupled with pre-existing family traditions in the empire, account for the widespread tendency for young men *and* women to go back to India—or to a different overseas destination—after completing their education. School and family influences worked together to prolong family connections with India and the empire more generally.

GENDER, CLASS, AND SCHOOLING POSSIBILITIES IN BRITAIN

Sending boys away from the family to boarding school at young ages was common among many sectors of the British middle and upper classes during this era, regardless of whether their parents lived overseas or at home. The typical pattern for their sisters differed greatly, however, and girls whose parents were in India appear much more likely to have attended boarding school for long periods than their socio-economic counterparts with parents in Britain. As Regenia Gagnier's work suggests, the divergent family and school settings and cultures girls and boys respectively encountered were decisive in shaping gendered British middle-class subjectivities.[1] In the late-Victorian and Edwardian periods many girls were still largely taught in the home by mothers, governesses, or other female relatives, or in small, privately run schoolrooms in the neighborhood. Others attending larger institutions run on more formal lines often were sent to day schools rather than away as boarders, while those who did go away to school might only be gone for a year or two to complete their education.[2]

Ideologies of domesticity partly accounted for gender differences in schooling, but financial considerations were equally responsible if not more so. Because most parents did not train their daughters to pursue paid occupations, they often chose to economize by keeping them at home or at day schools in order to devote most of their available funds to sons' schooling, boarding, and career preparation. Virginia Woolf asserted in *Three Guineas* in 1938 that 'a sum of £100 may be taken as the average [spent on the total education of educated men's daughters] in the nineteenth century and even later', while most such families' resources were earmarked for 'Arthur's Education Fund' to make sons

---

[1] Regenia Gagnier, *Subjectivities: A History of Self-Representation in Britain, 1832–1920* (New York, 1991), 171–219.

[2] Carol Dyhouse, *Girls Growing Up in Late Victorian and Edwardian England* (London, 1981), 3, 41; Deborah Gorham, *The Victorian Girl and the Feminine Ideal* (Bloomington, IN, 1982), 20–2, 73–5; Joan N. Burstyn, *Victorian Education and the Ideal of Womanhood* (London, 1980); M. Jeanne Peterson, *Family, Love, and Work in the Lives of Victorian Gentlewomen* (Bloomington, IN, 1989), 35–57; Joyce Senders Pedersen, 'Schoolmistresses and Headmistresses: Elites and Education in Nineteenth-Century England', *Journal of British Studies*, 15/1 (1975), 135–62; Barbara Caine, *Destined to be Wives: The Sisters of Beatrice Webb* (Oxford, 1986), 43–50.

eligible for high-status careers.[3] As Martha Vicinus has outlined, long after the reformed and academically inclined girls' schools such as Cheltenham Ladies' College had become established and respected features of the educational landscape for daughters of relatively affluent families, many girls whose brothers had received an expensive boarding-school upbringing saw their own instruction limited to governesses or day schools without high academic pretensions which continued to style themselves 'Schools for the Daughters of Gentlemen'.[4] This tendency remained visible into the interwar period, albeit with a distinct decline in home education in favor of day schools. To take an Edwardian example from outside the colonial community, Vera Brittain initially had home lessons with a governess and then attended a local day school for the 'daughters of gentlemen' prior to several years at boarding school—a pattern she described as ubiquitous in provincial middle-class society. While her boarding school was more academically oriented than the day school, most families patronizing both wanted their daughters to gain social credentials and marry 'well' and placed little importance on scholarship.[5]

Notions of female respectability, then, combined with economic considerations to make girls less likely than boys to spend long periods away from their families at boarding school. British-Indian girls experienced this more often than other girls of their class in Britain, but they too were far more likely than their brothers to live with aunts, uncles, grandparents, or other guardians largely on these grounds. In families where mothers decided to live apart from their husbands in order to be in Britain with the children, sons may have gone to prestigious boarding schools while daughters lived with them. This was the case in Enid Boon's family in the 1920s during her father's Indian Civil Service career. Her brother boarded at Lancing College, but she and her sisters resided with their mother in Eastbourne and attended St Winifred's School as day pupils. Her school was chosen largely because of its convenient proximity to their home, she recalled; 'actually it was on the same road . . . so we could just walk there and back'.[6] Academic considerations were unlikely to have influenced her parents' choice. As one former pupil later wrote, parents with higher ambitions sent their daughters to schools like Cheltenham Ladies' College or

---

[3] Virginia Woolf, *Three Guineas* (1938; repr. London, 1977), 263, 11–12. Her reference to 'Arthur's Education Fund' derives from Thackeray's novel *Pendennis*.

[4] Martha Vicinus, *Independent Women: Work and Community for Single Women, 1850–1920* (Chicago, 1985), 165–7.

[5] Vera Brittain, *Testament of Youth: An Autobiographical Study of the Years 1900–1925* (1933; repr. London, 1988), 27–54.

[6] Enid Boon, interview by author, 22 April 1995.

Roedean. Few girls left St Winifred's to go to university; those who did continue their education did a domestic science course or attended art school or a secretarial college, but far more were trained for marriage alone.[7]

St Winifred's enrolled up to 150 girls (both boarders and day scholars) in the interwar era, but many schools catering to families seeking this form of socially acceptable education for their daughters were much smaller and informal establishments. This was particularly true in earlier decades. The Talbot family's schooling choices for their children in the 1880s and 1890s illustrate a number of wider and long-lasting trends. While Addy, the only son, was a boarder at two of England's most expensive and prestigious boys' schools—first at Temple Grove preparatory school and then at Eton—Guendolen and Muriel attended two different schools that only enrolled about twenty girls of all ages. The first, located in Harrow, was run by Mrs and Miss Davies, an Indian Army officer's widow and her daughter, and catered to a combination of day pupils from the neighborhood and British-Indian girls whose parents may well have learned of the school through prior colonial acquaintance with the proprietresses or by word of mouth in India. With the Davies's, Guendolen and Muriel experienced an intimate setting where British-Indian children's concerns were well understood. Guendolen felt able to convey the pain she suffered due to her parents' absence to an empathetic listener, writing that 'I told Miss Davies and she said she felt like that when her father was in India'.[8] Their second school, run by the 'Miss Coopers', also educated a select number of girls including the daughters of a family friend in India.[9] While Guendolen never developed affection for the Miss Coopers like she did for Miss Davies, both schools none the less functioned more as quasi-familial 'homes' than scholastic establishments. Indeed, Adelbert and Agnes Talbot presumably saw little difference between sending their daughters to reside with relatives or other guardians and sending them to schools of this description, since their youngest child Esmé lived first with an aunt and uncle and then with another family. In both households, she was taught—badly, as she later recalled—only by governesses, who most likely possessed similar 'qualifications' as the Davies or Coopers.[10]

Both schools Guendolen and Muriel Talbot attended resembled countless other small-scale private establishments for girls as well as younger boys that relied heavily upon families based overseas for their clientele. Advertisements

[7] Mrs D. E. Winsland, 'St Winifred's', *Eastbourne Local Historian*, 92 (summer 1994), 22–3.

[8] OIOC, MSS Eur E410/34, Guendolen Talbot to Agnes Talbot, 2 March 1884.

[9] OIOC, MSS Eur E410/30, Guendolen Talbot to Agnes Talbot, 19 Aug., n.d. [*c*.1888].

[10] OIOC, MSS Eur D1222/1, Esmé Mary Dew (née Talbot), 'Our Affairs', typescript account, n.d. (*c*.1943), 7–14.

in the *Times of India* illustrate how many schools actively sought to tap into the colonial market by promoting features likely to appeal to this audience. Representative listings for boys' schools at the turn of the century include 'Boys from 8 to 14 prepared for Public Schools . . . Dry, bracing climate, suitable to Boys from India or the Colonies'; 'Private Tuition and Home for Delicate and Backward Boys. Married Tutor . . . only son of the late R. H. Hollingbery, formerly Asst. Secy., Financial Department, Calcutta, prepares a few gentlemen's sons (ages 7–15) for Public Schools . . . most healthy place for delicate boys'; and 'Colonial Boys received for 35 Guineas per annum. May remain during the holidays.' Girls' schools described themselves similarly but emphasized musical offerings, French lessons, and riding opportunities rather than their success in training pupils for more advanced education or paid work. Bourne School, Parkstone, Dorset, for instance, recommended itself as

a high class school for daughters of gentlemen, where girls enjoy, within proper limits, the best influences of Public School Life . . . only 2½ miles from the centre of Bournemouth . . . considered by medical authorities the Best Possible Climate for Children From the Tropics. Special Reductions for Daughters of Officers on Foreign Service.[11]

Gendered forms of social respectability, provisions for the holidays, and the promise of an appropriate climate for 'delicate' children from the 'tropics', then, were their key selling points. Some educators, moreover, played up their own colonial backgrounds as a possible additional inducement to parents who needed to choose a school but, through ignorance and distance, relied on this form of promotion.

    Many who ran such schools may have cultivated their imperial catchment because they lacked a strong reputation among families closer to home. Writing in the 1870s in *At Home on Furlough*, Charles Lawson described British-Indian parents like himself as easy prey for the 'money-grubbing and unscrupulous adventurer who calls himself a schoolmaster . . . [for those] who have no mercy, or no special qualifications for the duties they undertake.'[12] Annette Beveridge encountered these difficulties when selecting schools for her children in the 1880s. Initially, she sent William and his two younger sisters (accompanied by their German governess) to a school known as Bingfield educating nineteen small children run by a casual acquaintance. This woman quickly saw the advantage of expanding her accidental colonial intake, writing

11 *Times of India* (Overland Weekly Edition), 7 April 1900, 19–20.
12 Charles A. Lawson, *At Home on Furlough*, 2nd ser. (Madras, 1875), 304.

'if you should hear of any Anglo-Indian children for me I shall be very glad and I could make some special arrangement for holidays. It is the not knowing what will happen to them in vacation that is the real difficulty.'[13] Annette found such basic provisions insufficient and removed the children from the school during her next stay in England, citing the poor quality of the food, other parents' complaints, and the children's unhappiness and young ages as reasons for bringing them back to India.[14] Several years later she decided to rent a house in Eastbourne and educate the children at private day schools, but again found the choice daunting, since 'there are seventy schools here and some very shady people keep some of them'.[15] Ultimately, she selected a prep school for William called Kent House, and 'Miss Little's School'—another name for St Winifred's—for the girls.

As these diverse accounts suggest, many British-Indian children attended school in Eastbourne or similar south coast towns. Seaside resorts, as the next chapter explores, attracted many British-Indian families throughout this era for their climate, schools, and socially respectable leisure offerings for families on holiday and for retirees. Among the many small girls' and boys' preparatory schools scattered along the coast, children from overseas often found them-selves in the company of others like themselves. George Roche, for example, described the school he attended at St Leonards-on-Sea after the First World War as a 'bleak prep school with other unfortunate boys whose fathers manned the British Empire beyond the seas', run by 'three spinsters'.[16] Similarly, during the 1910s and 1920s Rab Butler and his younger brother attended 'The Wick' in Hove while their sisters Iris and Dorothy studied at a neighboring school called Conamur. Each enrolled about fifty children, some of whose families their parents knew in India.[17] As Iris later wrote, 'many of my companions were also orphans of the Empire, and there was always great excitement when "the Mail" came in'.[18] Word of mouth clearly accounted for the large overseas contingents at some small schools regardless of their location. M. M. Kaye recalled that most of the fifty or sixty children at her school— 'The Lawn' in Clevedon, Somerset—had parents in India. Originating 'as a

[13] OIOC, MSS Eur C176/123, Fanny Lewin to Annette Beveridge, 21 Oct. 1885.

[14] OIOC, MSS Eur C176/19, Annette Beveridge to Henry Beveridge, 30 April 1886. See also Lord Beveridge, *India Called Them* (London, 1947), 241, 278.

[15] OIOC, MSS Eur C176/135, Annette Beveridge to Henry Beveridge, 1 Feb. 1891.

[16] George Roche, *Childhood in India: Tales from Sholapur*, Richard Terrell (ed.) (London, 1994), 84.

[17] OIOC, MSS Eur F225/27, Ann Butler to Montagu Butler, 24 Sept. 1911; MSS Eur F225/30, Ann Butler to Montagu Butler, 7 Dec. 1915.

[18] CSAA, Portal Papers, Iris Portal, 'Song at Seventy', typescript manuscript, n.d. [c.1975], 18.

home-from-home, plus a certain amount of basic education, for three or four small children whose parents, like Kipling's, were compelled to leave them behind in England for years at a time', it evolved into 'a full-scale boarding school whose pupils could, if necessary, stay on . . . during the holidays'.[19]

Whether British-Indian children studied in the company of others from overseas, or—as was just as often the case—in schools where there were only a few or no other children with parents in the empire, family correspondence and adult recollections typically constitute the only evidence that remains of their schooling experiences. Many small boys' preparatory schools and even more residential girls' schools were short-lived enterprises, most often lasting only through the working lives of their founders.[20] All the aforementioned establishments—the Davies' and Coopers' schools, Bingfield, St Winifred's, Kent House, Conamur, 'The Wick', and 'The Lawn'—have long since closed, and seemingly left no public records of their brief histories upon their demise. When children attended larger schools that have survived and possess ample documentation of their past, on the other hand, they formed an invisible minority. This was particularly the case for children who lived with relatives and attended school as day pupils rather than boarders, when evidence of their ties to India might not even appear in admissions registers that listed only local addresses and guardians.

Given that many families economized by educating daughters in this manner, girls' educational years in Britain are particularly underdocumented. By the early twentieth century, however, girls who attended larger private day schools typically received a more academic education than those who went to small establishments that prioritized inculcating 'ladylike' social graces. British-Indian parents who valued girls' scholastic accomplishments were always in the minority, but the few who did may have provided daughters and sons with similar schooling experiences as a result. William and Helen Bannerman's two sons and two daughters all lived with William's sister and attended prestigious Edinburgh schools (the boys at the Edinburgh Academy and the girls at St George's High School) during the Edwardian era and the First World War

---

[19] M. M. Kaye, *The Sun in the Morning: My Early Years in India and England* (New York, 1990), 341.

[20] Donald Leinster-Mackay's work shows that many English boys' preparatory schools originated in the mid- to late nineteenth century in the wake of the expansion of the public school system for older boys as parents increasingly sought more directed early training and socialization prior to their sons' public-school entry. Many schools were thus still in their infancy, often closing when their founders died or retired. *The Rise of the English Prep School* (London, 1984).

as day pupils.[21] Both parents actively encouraged their younger daughter Day in her hopes to follow her father into the medical profession. Letters from India recounting William's experiments in snakebite and plague research laboratories appear to have sparked her initial scientific enthusiasm, which her family then cultivated throughout her secondary education.[22] Helen wrote to Janet, 'tell [Day] if she is very good and industrious . . . and writes to Dad interesting letters like the one about the amoebas, that when Dad comes home he will bring his good microscope with him, and will let her see things through it'.[23] Day's preparation benefited directly from her father's Indian network of medical acquaintances, through whom he procured and shipped first a monkey skeleton and then a human skeleton for her to study. 'If you are going to be a medical student this will be a great help to you', he told her.[24]

Despite some evidence of a shift towards greater parental interest in girls' academic accomplishments, British-Indian girls educated like Janet and Day Bannerman remained rare throughout this era. Few larger, longer lived, and academically reputable girls' schools show evidence of catering to empire families, not even Bedford High School or Cheltenham Ladies' College, which were both located in towns with substantial British-Indian communities. Although it is likely that both did educate some and simply did not specify overseas backgrounds in their records because pupils lived with relatives locally, many parents still preferred their daughters to receive a more traditional education at smaller and—in the case of Bedford High School with its relatively low fees—more exclusive establishments.[25] As its headmistress wrote in 1932, parents long remained '[timid] about these new large schools for girls. They feared the infection of bad accents and bad manners, and above all the forming of friendships in these "mixed" schools with girls whose parents they

---

21 Evidence of British-Indian children's experiences at Scottish schools has been difficult to trace. Given that Scotland had a weaker tradition of boarding education than England, Scottish children whose parents were in India may have been more likely to reside with relatives as the Bannerman children did; many others, particularly boys, attended boarding schools in England which may have been chosen because of their reputation for catering to overseas families.

22 NLS, Dep. 325/V, William Bannerman to Day Bannerman, 27 Oct. 1906; Helen Bannerman to Day Bannerman, 6 Nov. 1906; Dep. 325/VII, William Bannerman to Day Bannerman, 16 April 1910; Dep. 325/X, William Bannerman to Day Bannerman, 4 Oct. 1911.

23 NLS, Dep. 325/VI, Helen Bannerman to Janet Bannerman, 12 Nov. 1909.

24 NLS, Dep. 325/VII, William Bannerman to Patrick Bannerman, 26 Feb. 1910; Dep. 325/XII, William Bannerman to Day Bannerman, 6 Feb. 1913.

25 The admissions registers of Bedford High School and Cheltenham Ladies' College list relatively few girls whose fathers were or had been employed overseas. However, in both the *Cheltenham Ladies' College Magazine* and BHS's magazine the *Aquila* (see respectively Cheltenham Ladies' College Archives and Bedford High School Archives), there are many references to former pupils going to India, suggesting that some may have been from families with prior imperial connections that were unrecorded when they began school.

did not know'.[26] In consequence, many British-Indian families in Bedford continued patronizing now defunct day schools 'for the daughters of gentlemen', often run by widows with similar links to the empire.[27] Cheltenham Ladies' College, on the other hand, was socially exclusive, but its higher fees coupled with a more academic and games-oriented curriculum may have discouraged many local British-Indians from enrolling their daughters.

Given the dearth of material concerning small, defunct schools for girls or younger boys as well as many of the larger institutions where British-Indians were in the minority, most of the schools having extensive documentation of such children's overseas backgrounds were boys' public schools or those that followed public-school models. Long singled out as nurseries of empire for their role in creating empire builders, boys' public schools simultaneously acted as nurseries of British national identity for those born overseas, as did other institutions patronized by such families. Haileybury College, the United Services College, Cheltenham College, and Bedford Grammar School were among the most prominent centers of education for older British-Indian boys. Their records suggest how, and why, many embarked upon imperial careers themselves after their schooldays ended, thereby perpetuating multigenerational patterns of family life split between Britain and its overseas territories. But before turning to them, two other schools' substantial histories provide a unique opportunity to compare how boys and girls from the same family background lived and studied in Britain: the Schools for the Sons and Daughters of Missionaries located near London.

SCHOOLS FOR MISSIONARIES' CHILDREN

Walthamstow Hall was one of the few girls' schools catering for overseas British families to survive and leave substantial documentation of its pupils' backgrounds and school culture.[28] Founded in 1838 and initially known as the

---

[26] K. M. Westaway (ed.), *A History of Bedford High School* (Bedford, 1932), 39. On the history of BHS see also Mary Felicity Hunt, 'Secondary Education for the Middle Class Girl: A Study of Ideology and Educational Practice, 1870 to 1940, With Special Reference to the Harpur Trust Girls' Schools, Bedford', Ph.D. thesis, University of Cambridge (1984). On parental fears of social mixing at larger girls' schools, see Sara Delamont, 'Distant Dangers and Forgotten Standards: Pollution Control Strategies in the British Girls' School, 1860–1920', *Women's History Review*, 2/2 (1993), 233–51; *Knowledgeable Women* (London, 1989).

[27] Joyce Godber and Isabel Hutchins (eds.), *A Century of Challenge: Bedford High School, 1882–1982* (Biggleswade, 1982), 367–9; Beryl Irving, 'Edwardian Schooldays', *Bedfordshire Magazine*, 9/67 (1963–4), 95.

[28] The Royal School at Bath for army officers' daughters also enrolled many girls with parents abroad in the nineteenth and early twentieth centuries, but its records were not made available to me. However, see Honor Osborne and Peggy Manistry, *A History of the Royal School for the Daughters of Officers of the Army, 1864–1965* (London, 1966), 87, 103.

'Home and School for the Daughters of Missionaries', it provides an in-depth illustration of how girls born in India might live and study in Britain. Just as importantly, it enables their experiences to be compared with those of their male counterparts, since a corresponding School for the Sons of Missionaries—later renamed Eltham College—was established in 1842.[29] Both institutions began with small numbers of pupils whose parents worked as Protestant evangelical missionaries overseas (most commonly in India, Africa, or China), and their main priority was to supply affordable education as well as a year-round place of residence for children lacking other relations with whom they could live or visit during school holidays.[30] Their fees reflect parents' limited resources; for instance, the maximum annual cost for a missionary's daughter to attend Walthamstow Hall was £15 in 1858 and £24 in 1912, and missionaries' sons were charged comparably modest rates.[31] Many families ultimately paid less if extenuating circumstances persuaded school authorities of their special needs. After the directors voted to admit lay day pupils and boarders in the late nineteenth century, the higher fees they generated helped to offset the artificially low amounts for missionary children.[32] Despite the increasing numbers of lay pupils at both institutions, however, their administrators continued to stress that 'the education and arrangements [would] be carefully planned with a view to foreign service, whether missionary or not', thus prioritizing the needs of both missionary and other colonial families until

[29] On the schools' development, see Elsie Pike and Constance E. Curryer, *The Story of Walthamstow Hall: A Century of Girls' Education* (London, 1938); WHSA, *A Ship's Log* (Sevenoaks, 1988); ECA, Owen Kentish, 'The Past History of Eltham College and its Present Position: An Address Delivered to the Members of the Eltham College Parents' Association on 8th March, 1932'; Clifford Witting, *The Glory of the Sons: A History of Eltham College, School for the Sons of Missionaries* (London, 1952).

[30] Most pupils were affiliated with either the London Missionary Society or the Baptist Missionary Society, but smaller numbers had parents working on behalf of the General Baptist Missionary Society, the Free Church of Scotland Missionary Society, the Irish Presbyterian Missionary Society, the British and Foreign Bible Society, and the China Inland Mission. WHSA, *Report of the Institution for the Education of the Daughters of Missionaries, Walthamstow Hall, Sevenoaks* (hereafter *Report of the Institution*), 1886, 18–20.

[31] WHSA, *Report of the Institution*, 1858, 7; 1912, 8. Missionaries paid between £18 and £21 annually for each son's education and board in 1899; see ECA, *The Home and School for the Sons and Orphans of Missionaries, Blackheath: Report and List of Subscribers* (hereafter *Report*), 1899, 22.

[32] ECA, *Report*, 1887, 6; WHSA, *Report of the Institution*, 1886, 6, 9. Walthamstow Hall subsequently grew from an enrollment of only 43 missionaries' daughters in 1865 to 162 girls in 1922, of whom 72 were boarders from missionary families, 82 were day girls, and 8 were lay boarders. WHSA, *Report of the Institution*, 1865, 10–22; Board of Education, Kent, 'Report of Inspection of the School for the Daughters of Missionaries, Walthamstow Hall, Sevenoaks, held on 18th, 19th and 20th October 1922', 2. Even more dramatically, the boys' school increased from 58 missionaries' sons and 20 day scholars in 1880 to over 400 pupils in 1932, of whom the vast majority were day boys without missionary connections. It relocated from its original premises at Blackheath to larger grounds at Eltham, renamed itself Eltham College, and refashioned its identity as a minor public school in the interwar period. ECA, *Report*, 1881, 8–9; *Elthamian*, 3/12 (1941), 404–5; Kentish, 'Past History of Eltham College', 3; Witting, *Glory of the Sons*, 97.

well after the First World War.[33] Although missionary children constituted the vast majority of their overseas contingents, the schools aimed to provide an environment geared towards the perceived physical, moral, and familial circumstances shared by children from colonial backgrounds regardless of their parents' professions.

Given the low fees many parents paid, supplementary donations from participating missionary societies were essential for running schools which faced perennial financial difficulties. Extensive propaganda designed to raise funds provides important insights into both the purposes the schools served and the ideologies that lay behind them. Britons supporting overseas missions repeatedly were reminded of these institutions' critical role in furthering wider evangelical goals. A 1923 newspaper article soliciting funds summarized what many other reports had stated for decades, arguing that many missionaries would be prevented from pursuing their modestly paid vocations unless the schools furnished both a subsidized home and education for the children they sent back to Britain. Comparing the incomes of missionary parents with those of other overseas families, this writer in the *Huddersfield Examiner* stressed that 'when the Government sent out a Civil Servant to India they could pay a sufficient salary to enable him to send his children to the best schools, but the missionary societies could only spend the money the churches allowed them . . . There were missionaries who could not afford to continue their work, unless their children were cared for as they were at these two schools.'[34]

As this book demonstrates, missionaries were not alone in their struggle to pay for the British schooling that conferred numerous signifiers of respectability; many other parents in both official and non-official sectors of Indian employment found it equally challenging to give their children a metropolitan education. Moreover, spokesmen on behalf of the missionary schools felt it necessary to remove British children from India, Africa, or other overseas regions for reasons that echoed those expressed by countless lay commentators, merely stressing religious factors as part of broader arguments against keeping children overseas. They portrayed the schools as sites for reforming children whose health and cultural development supposedly had been jeopardized by the climate, 'heathen' populations, and lack of appropriate schools where their parents lived. One of many statements outlining this combination of hazards appeared in a letter aimed at young readers of the *Christian World* in 1880:

---

[33] WHSA, *Report of the Institution*, 1886, 7; 1916, 4, 15–18.

[34] WHSA, Newspaper Cuttings Book, 'Missionaries' Children: Local Appeals for Support for Schools', *Huddersfield Examiner* (13 Jan. 1923); see also 'Institution for the Education of the Daughters of Missionaries', 1879; *Report of the Institution*, 1896, 12.

Heathen lands are often very unhealthy—so hot that little English children cannot live there without getting very ill, and even if they did keep well there are no nice schools for them to go to, and the people around would be always teaching them to do and say wicked things. So when the missionaries' little children get about five years old, they begin to grow so pale and languid, that it is felt they must be sent home to England to get strong and be taught.[35]

Transferring children to Walthamstow Hall and the School for the Sons of Missionaries thus allowed parents to curtail their children's problematic interaction with 'natives' in the mission field. As one missionary stressed in 1911, 'the native girls, hired as servants in the house, taught the missionaries' children the nastiness current in their ordinary home-talk and thought no harm of it'.[36]

Administrators of both the boys' and the girls' school long considered freeing children from 'heathen' influences as one of the most important services they performed. However, they also stressed other means by which children who had been overseas 'recovered' from their early surroundings while in attendance. Annual reports claimed that staff worked hard to cultivate children's English accents, which, as Chapter 2 argued, served as a primary lens through which their racial as well as class identities were viewed. Walthamstow Hall's 1909 report highlighted school inspectors' praise for its progress in 'English subjects', noting that 'the girls speak out well and with a good accent. Considering the difficulties that arise from the arrival, at a tender age, of pupils from abroad who have had few advantages in hearing good English spoken, the elocution in the lower part of the School is quite creditable.'[37] With respect to their overall academic performance, initial difficulties were said to be surpassed once 'delicate' younger girls had begun to reap the physical benefits of the English climate. As the headmistress noted in 1915:

If their progress sometimes seems slow, they show later on that it has been thorough. In a school for children who come from foreign climates, the early years are often interrupted by ill-health, and great care has to be taken not to push delicate children beyond what they can do easily . . . the majority of the girls grow up strong and healthy, with few traces of early delicacy.[38]

Like many other school spokespersons over the years, this headmistress demonstrated considerable awareness of contemporary understandings

---

[35] WHSA, Newspaper Cuttings Book, 'One Who Loves Little Children', 'The Daughters of Missionaries: A Letter to Our Young Readers', *Christian World*, (March 1880).

[36] WHSA, *Report of the Institution*, 1911, 13–14.　　[37] WHSA, *Report of the Institution*, 1909, 20.

[38] WHSA, *Report of the Institution*, 1915, 17–18. References to girls' health were recurrent. See *Report of the Institution*, June 1864, 7; 1888, 15; 1908, 16.

concerning the bodily effects of childhood in 'the tropics', particularly on older girls, which have been explored in Chapter 1. A woman who attended Walthamstow Hall between 1908 and 1920 later recalled how the head had been careful to inform her of the physical changes adolescence would bring by the time she was 11: 'I was tall for my age', she remembered, 'and it was believed that we would come to puberty early as we had been brought up in the tropics'.[39] Children's sexual, and implicitly racial, development was linked to their geographical surroundings in many reports of both missionary schools, and boys as well as girls were long seen to require 'special attention' if they were to become 'robust and healthy' after the prolonged 'disadvantages' stemming from tropical residence.[40] A writer in the early 1920s considered their condition to be common knowledge, stating that 'all who have been in the tropical East will be aware that the adolescent school age is just that time of rapid growth when young people of European parentage require temperate climatic conditions to help them to a healthy and sturdy maturity'.[41]

While spokespersons from the Schools for the Sons and Daughters of Missionaries claimed to provide an atmosphere that cured children of the undesirable effects of early years overseas, they also stressed the one commendable aspect of childhood in 'tropical', 'heathen' lands that their pupils lost upon enrolment: the home and family arena they left behind in the mission field. Both schools foregrounded the family sacrifices missionary parents and their children endured for the sake of religious priorities, as a hymn Walthamstow Hall circulated among its supporters illustrates:

> Far from this favoured land of light
> Where English homes in beauty stand,
> In distant realms of darkest night
> God's heroes toil, a noble band.

> The happy sound of childhood's glee
> Is hushed within their silent home,
> While thoughts of loving memory
> To absent children fondly roam.[42]

---

[39] Joyce Wilkins, *A Child's Eye View, 1904–1920* (Sussex, 1992), 97.

[40] ECA, *Report*, 1886, 13; WHSA, Newspaper Cuttings Book, 'Missionaries' Children: Plea for a "Mothering" School', *Christian World* (21 May 1925).

[41] WHSA, Newspaper Cuttings Book, 'Children of Missionaries: Two Famous Schools in Danger', *The Christian* (6 Oct. 1921); see also 'The School Problem', *The Sunday at Home* (June 1937), xxviii.

[42] WHSA, 'Hymn', 'Institution for the Education of the Daughters of Missionaries: Programme on the Occasion of Laying the Foundation Stone of the New Building at Sevenoaks', June 26th, 1878'.

Family martyrdom featured prominently in the schools' fundraising propaganda, when its emotive potential was clearly deployed to solicit donations. A 1903 commentator echoed many other writers when he noted how 'missionaries' children appealed in a very special way to Christian sympathy . . . they were of necessity deprived of home-life which had often a most sacred influence'.[43] Lengthy family separations made their pupils 'grass orphans' for whom school staff acted as 'foster parents' as well as educators. As one writer put it in 1921, the schools endeavored to be 'Mother and Father and indeed home itself to their charges'.[44] That this rhetoric of institutional domesticity should appear prominently in writings about Walthamstow Hall is unsurprising, given the common tendency for many girls' schools to play up their home-like environments. In this instance, however, the School for the Sons of Missionaries invoked its role as the boys' 'English "Home"' replete with a 'home-atmosphere' just as often as did its counterpart for girls.[45] In portraying itself primarily as a domestic space, only secondarily as an educational facility, and placing little emphasis on sport, it set itself apart from the vast majority of British boys' boarding schools, some of which are examined below.

An additional means by which the Schools for the Sons and Daughters of Missionaries provided 'homes' for their pupils was by enabling children without relatives to visit to remain on the grounds during the holidays. While administrators sought to send children to stay with local evangelical families during holidays if they lacked nearby relations, this preferred means of 'introducing them to English family life' was not always possible in practice, and many children thus lived at the schools year-round.[46] These schools thus became environments where pupils experienced little other than a missionary-influenced lifestyle. Even after the entry of lay children in the late nineteenth century, missionaries' offspring continued to reside in settings where their parents' activities, although taking place far away, remained the central and

---

[43] WHSA, *Report of the Institution*, 1903, 12. Similar statements appear in Newspaper Cuttings Book, 'Children of Our Missionaries: Have We Any Responsibility?', *Christian World* (6 Oct. 1921); ECA, *Report*, 1879; 1887, 10.

[44] WHSA, Newspaper Cuttings Book, 'Children of Our Missionaries', *Christian World* (6 Oct. 1921); 'The Children of Venture', *Baptist Times* (10 Feb. 1922); 'The Missionary Schools', *Baptist Times* (27 Jan. 1922); 'Concerning Some "Grass Orphans"', *Outward Bound* (Jan. 1921), 299; 'Children of the Pioneers of the Kingdom of God', *British Weekly* (16 Feb. 1922). In addition to these 'symbolic orphans', the schools also enrolled children of deceased overseas missionaries, often free of charge.

[45] ECA, *Report*, 1879, 11; 1883, 7; 1888, 6.

[46] ECA, *Report*, 1889, 7; 1899, 12; Wilkins, *Child's Eye View*, 94.

defining feature of their lives. The cultural and religious atmosphere prevailing at both schools set great store by their parents' work as well as encouraged pupils to take up these vocations themselves once they completed their education. Boys at the School for the Sons of Missionaries/Eltham College and girls at Walthamstow Hall received periodic visits from missionaries in England on leave, who through their sermons, lectures, and musical programs reminded children of the value of foreign mission work and proposed that they pursue it as adults. At Eltham College, moreover, boys were encouraged to join the Student Volunteer Missionary Union or the Christian Union, whose meetings included lectures on regions of the world where their parents worked.[47] In addition, once the school had instituted a house system following its expansion along public-school lines, Livingstone House, Moffat House, Carey House, and Chalmers House served constantly to remind boys of their link to these famous men.[48]

Other aspects of school life further illustrate the institutions' expectation that many pupils would ultimately return to the mission field overseas. Music and scriptural attainment were central and intertwined components of both schools' curricula from the outset, the former being valued not only for 'tending to enliven domestic worship' but also because it acted as 'a most useful auxiliary to the missionary cause' in overseas stations.[49] Alongside music, Walthamstow Hall focused mainly on providing instruction in basic academic subjects as well as on teaching girls domestic skills such as cookery, dressmaking, and needlework. School administrators envisioned its pupils as future homemakers, stating in 1847 that they trained 'the beloved children committed to their care for the *private walks* of domestic life' and cultivated 'in them all that is calculated to make *home* happy,—whether that home be placed amid "the hearths of England", the wilds of Africa, the groves of India, or the Islands of the Seas'.[50] Most girls were not educated to pursue occupations aside from missionary work, although towards the late nineteenth century the school

[47] Wilkins, *Child's Eye View*, 68, 114–16; ECA, *Report*, 1899, 26. E. Rowlands, who followed in his father's footsteps as a missionary, recalled that 'many of our generation received the personal call from what was then named the Student Volunteer Missionary Union' in the 1890s; see his 'The Voyage Back', in Witting, *Glory of the Sons*, 153; also *Elthamian*, 3/5 (1938), 165.

[48] ECA, *Elthamian*, 1/2 (1924), 30–3; *Elthamian*, 3/11 (1941), 381–4.

[49] Pike and Curryer, *Story of Walthamstow Hall*, 20–3; ECA, *Report*, 1878, 11; 1899, 24–6; WHSA, Board of Education, 'Report of the Inspection of Walthamstow Hall School for the Daughters of Missionaries, Sevenoaks, Kent, held on 23rd, 24th, and 25th Jan., 1929', 12.

[50] WHSA, *Report of the Institution*, 1847, 8; 1886, 7.

encouraged them to acquire medical training after they left in order to qualify as medical missionaries. While most missionary families could not afford to provide this for their daughters, Walthamstow Hall reserved a special place of honor for its former pupils who succeeded in training to work as doctors or nurses overseas.[51] The School for the Sons of Missionaries resembled the girls' school in its praise for those who combined medical and missionary professions, alluding to its 'Edinburgh men' who had gone to Scotland to study medicine upon leaving school and who planned to work on behalf of the missions when they finished.[52] Although former pupils at the boys' school embarked upon a wide variety of careers in Britain as well as overseas following their education, administrators repeatedly declared themselves satisfied with the numbers who entered foreign missionary service. Throughout the nineteenth and early twentieth centuries, both institutions publicized their status as 'A Nursery of the Missionaries of the Future', claiming to have educated over 200 male and female missionaries by the early 1930s.[53]

Of Walthamstow Hall's school leavers, many more women re-established their ties to overseas mission life in an unofficial capacity than this total suggests, however. As will be considered further below, missionaries' daughters resembled those of men employed in other colonial occupations in that they appeared more likely than their brothers to live in the empire as adults because they typically returned to their parents' place of residence after school and later married men met in these surroundings. The school strongly urged girls to go back to their parents and engage in similar work; a 1852 report, for example, related how 'Miss Regel, who was for many years a pupil . . . has this spring returned to India, to engage in a [teaching] situation on the Neilgherry Hills, which offers a promising opportunity of promoting her future interests, and which fulfils her father's hope of welcoming her once more to her native shores'.[54] Although unspecified, Miss Regel's 'future interests' might plausibly have included not only missionary or lay teaching but also marriage prospects to men from within her parents' circle of colonial acquaintances. Regardless of the path she ultimately followed, she was one of many former Walthamstow Hall girls who, through both her school's and her parents' foreign affiliations,

---

[51] WHSA, *Report of the Institution*, 1891, 10; 1896, 11; 1899, 15–16; *Walthamstow Hall Old Girls' Association Annual News Sheet*, 1904, 7–8; 1911, 3, 6–9; 1925, 20–1; 1937, 14–16, 31–3. On India's importance as an arena where professional British medical women could play a role, see Antoinette Burton, 'Contesting the Zenana: The Mission to Make "Lady Doctors for India", 1874–1885', *Journal of British Studies*, 35/3 (1996), 368–97.

[52] ECA, *S. S. M. Magazine*, n.s., 4/4 (1892), 86; *Report*, 1899, 18; 1902, 11; *Elthamian*, 2/1 (1929), 2, 32–5.

[53] WHSA, *Report of the Institution*, 1904, 12; 1908, 11; 1913, 64; Newspaper Cuttings Book, 'A Reminder', *Baptist Missionary Society Herald* (June 1932), 79; ECA, *Report*, 1902, 11.

[54] WHSA, *Report of the Institution*, 1852, 9–10.

was encouraged to experience family and possibly professional life in the empire in adulthood. 'Many have returned to their parents, helping them in missionary work, many have married—some of them missionaries, thus carrying on the work abroad; while others as wives of civil servants in India have shed Christian light on many households', asserted a writer in 1879.[55] Annual reports of the Walthamstow Hall Old Girls' Association show a tradition of overseas adult life continuing through the interwar period, with news of former pupils engaged in teaching, secretarial employment, and mission work as well as marrying in India and other regions. In 1933, the association had branch secretaries as well as periodic reunions throughout the world, including in Calcutta, Shanghai, Bulawayo, and Alberta.[56]

Missionaries' sons were also likely to return to the empire to follow non-religious occupations. Letters and old boys' columns in *The S.S.M. Magazine* and later in *The Elthamian* continually updated pupils still at school about those working in India in the civil service, the police, as planters, and as businessmen in addition to publicizing news of missionaries, providing informal career guidance in the process.[57] The large number of Old Elthamians earning their living overseas in 1932 caused a contributor to wonder, 'Do we send a bigger percentage to foreign lands than any other school in Britain?'[58] Exact numbers of old boys working abroad at any given time were never compiled, but a comparison between the School for the Sons of Missionaries and other boys' boarding schools suggests that others catering to children with parents in the empire matched or exceeded its totals. While Walthamstow Hall occupies a unique position as a school with substantial documentation of girls born abroad who returned as adults, Eltham College was only one of many boys' schools long characterized by this tradition. In the following pages, its missionary constituency and inclinations are compared with boys' schools where different social and occupational backgrounds predominated, and which correspondingly oriented many pupils towards a variety of other colonial endeavors.

---

[55] WHSA, Newspaper Cuttings Book, 'Institution for the Education of the Daughters of Missionaries', 1879, 2.

[56] WHSA, *Walthamstow Hall Old Girls' Association Annual News Sheet*, 1911, 3, 7–9; 1921, 13–17, 22–3; 1922, 13–18, 23–5; 1931, 29–31; 1933, 1.

[57] ECA, *S.S.M. Magazine*, n.s., 3/3 (1891), 50–5; *Elthamian*, 2/1 (1929), 32–5; *Elthamian*, 3/5 (1939), 192–8. See *Elthamian*, 2/6 (1932), 268, on branches of the Old Elthamians' Association in Argentina, Australia, South Africa, India, China, Malaya, and Burma.

[58] ECA, *Elthamian*, 2/6 (1932), 270.

BRITISH BOYS' SCHOOLS AND IMPERIAL OPPORTUNITY

Other schools that British-Indian families outside missionary circles commonly chose for their sons include the United Services College (later known as the Imperial Services College) and Haileybury College; the boys' schools run by the Harpur Trust in Bedford, especially Bedford Grammar School but also Bedford Modern School to a lesser extent; and Cheltenham College. They resembled the School for the Sons of Missionaries not only because they long catered to families with imperial occupational histories but because they also sent many school-leavers back overseas to earn their livings.[59] Moreover, when compared with many other boys' private schools in Britain, they too offered middle-class parents a far more moderately priced education for their sons. Some of these institutions could be formally defined as 'public schools', particularly Cheltenham College and Haileybury. Bedford Grammar School and the United Services College, meanwhile, fell into the more nebulous category of minor public schools or grammar schools that aspired to public-school status. Their histories all directly correspond with the expansion of educational offerings for the disparate middle classes in the mid-nineteenth century. Many schools were either founded or reorganized during this period according to the priorities of families lacking the income to send sons to Eton, Harrow, or other elite public schools, using these along with Rugby School following its reform by Thomas Arnold as their models. As will be explored below, however, while the schools examined here tried to emulate some features of the best-known public schools' structure and ethos, in other key respects they deliberately distinguished themselves from them in order to satisfy their specific clientele.

Close analysis of these institutions sheds light on several neglected issues in the history of British education and imperialism. Most importantly, they illustrate not only the multi-generational patterns of Indian and other overseas service but just as centrally that the families most likely to find this appealing were often from the middle to lower reaches of the middle class who earned their living through a wide variety of occupations. Previous studies of Britain's representatives in India focus overwhelmingly on those entering the Indian Civil

---

[59] This group of schools' successes in professional examinations were publicized in the British-Indian press and were widely known among this community. The *Madras Mail* noted in 1902 that 'it cannot be denied that a group of the more modern Public Schools offer undeniable advantages, which embrace both the question of a cheap and, at the same time, a wide field of instruction'. In its discussion of the number of open scholarships gained at Oxford and Cambridge along with successes in the Woolwich and Sandhurst examinations, Cheltenham, Bedford, Clifton, Eton, Wellington, and Haileybury were at the top of the list. CCA, Cheltenham College Scrap Book, 1900–07, 'Public School Successes', *Madras Mail*, 24 Feb. 1902.

Service or other high-ranking officials and military personnel, a tendency exemplified by P. J. Cain's and A. G. Hopkins's work. They assert that 'from the 1850s, military and civil appointments in India became a large, vested interest of the educated *upper middle class*'.[60] Although they do admit that many recruits into British service employment came from families situated in the lower sectors of the middle classes and attended less prestigious public or grammar schools, their analysis remains largely restricted to the most elite public schools, the careers of colonial governors, and the 'gentlemanly' values associated with the ICS.[61] While Cain and Hopkins are correct when they allude to careers in India as 'vested interests', like most historians their work ultimately provides a very limited analysis of a very few 'upper middle class' Britons in India. Scholars by and large have failed to give due consideration to those in non-official branches of work including planting and commerce along with other state services such as the Public Works Department, the Indian Police, and the Indian Forest Service—to name but a few. Even army officers receive inadequate attention.

Such selectivity obscures the reasons why imperial employment traditions proved so resilient in certain families. Less high-ranking British-Indians outside (or even within) the 'heaven born' of the ICS or the army typically needed to weigh carefully the costs of education along with the tangible employment prospects British schools might offer their sons. For the large numbers who could provide their male children little in the way of private income and needed to minimize the overall costs of career preparation, the schools they chose were expected to accomplish a great deal at what were considered reasonable fees. As such, less famous and less expensive schools are a more promising starting-point for examining imperial family histories than the institutions that have dominated educational historians' attention to date.

Bedford Grammar School (now known as Bedford School) proved well suited to the needs and aspirations of many British-Indian parents. It grew

---

[60] P. J. Cain and A. G. Hopkins, *British Imperialism: Innovation and Expansion, 1688–1914* (London, 1993), 329; emphasis added.

[61] P. J. Cain and A. G. Hopkins, *British Imperialism: Crisis and Deconstruction, 1914–1990* (London, 1993), 24–6, 178–9. David C. Potter's *India's Political Administrators, 1919–1983* (Oxford, 1983) examines the educational background of men in the Indian Civil Service in greater depth. Although he does not explore their fathers' professional backgrounds, his work shows that Cheltenham, Haileybury, and Bedford were among the most popular schools attended by these men in the early twentieth century. See also Takehiko Honda, 'Indian Civil Servants, 1892–1937: An Age of Transition', D.Phil. thesis, University of Oxford (1996), 3, 12–13, 19, 47–57, on the numbers whose fathers had also been employed in India. Honda and Potter (pp. 68–9) both illustrate the wide variety of public schools ICS men had attended. The schools examined here thus illustrate educational paths common for those entering the ICS, but their uniqueness stems more from their history of preparing boys whose fathers pursued a much wider range of Indian careers to enter an equally varied set of colonial occupations.

from 100 boys in 1831 to 700 by 1887, prospering largely through the efforts of several public-school-oriented headmasters who implemented curricular changes, added boarding facilities and playing fields, and developed the house system.[62] Because its endowment by the Harpur Trust kept fees low during the decades when it increasingly resembled a public school, families coveting this style of education but unable to afford more expensive institutions either moved to Bedford or found their sons guardians there while they attended as day scholars, or boarded them at the school. In 1912, the school charged between £10 and £16 a year for each day boy's tuition (the exact amount depending upon his age), while boarders paid between £79 and £86 annually.[63] The influx of families into Bedford who sought to take advantage of the fees for day boys included considerable numbers supported by Indian and other colonial occupations or pensions, and they became a significant component of the town's middle-class population in the Victorian and Edwardian era and beyond.[64] Bedford Modern School also expanded during this period and counted many British-Indian boys on its rolls, but it remained characterized by its predominantly local constituency and never matched the Grammar School's overseas element.[65]

Cheltenham College was better known than Bedford Grammar School but enrolled similarly high numbers of British-Indians. Like Bedford, Cheltenham Spa was a renowned center for Britons connected with Indian work and included retirees, widows, and those on furlough along with the wives and children of men still overseas; these two colonial communities will receive further attention in the next chapter. Bedford Grammar School's expansion attracted many with colonial affiliations to the locality, but Cheltenham College both originated and prospered from the town's pre-established population of civil and military officers and their dependants. Retired army officers in

---

[62] John Sargeaunt and Ernest Hockliffe, *A History of Bedford School* (Bedford, 1925); F. A. M. Webster, *Our Great Public Schools: Their Traditions, Customs and Games* (London, 1937), 21–36; Joyce Godber, *The Harpur Trust, 1552–1973* (Luton, 1973), 58–82; BSA, *Ousel*, 3/64 (21 July 1887), 105.

[63] Beverley Ussher (ed.), *Public Schools at a Glance (Boarding Schools at £80 a year and over): A Guide for Parents and Guardians in Selecting a Public School for Their Boys* (London, 1912), 17.

[64] Many English towns with reputable boys' schools experienced a similar influx of families—often headed by widows—seeking to take advantage of a prestigious form of education while their sons lived at home and saved the expense of boarding. See T. W. Bamford, *The Rise of the Public Schools: A Study of Boys' Public Boarding Schools in England and Wales from 1837 to the Present Day* (London, 1967), 21; and J. R. de S. Honey, *Tom Brown's Universe: The Development of the Victorian Public School* (London, 1977), 125, on Bedford Grammar School's clientele.

[65] Andrew Underwood, *Bedford Modern School of the Black and Red* (Biggleswade, 1981); F. W. Kuhlick, 'Chronicles of Bedford Modern', published in 23 parts in the *Eagle*, 1947–1955; L. R. Conisbee, *Bedford Modern School: Its Origin and Growth* (Bedford, 1964).

Cheltenham dominated the school's list of founders in 1841, selling shares to support their 'proprietary college'.[66]

Early sources detailing Cheltenham College's origins stressed 'the difficulty experienced by gentlemen in the middle class of society, and even of a higher grade, in obtaining a superior education for their sons at reasonable rates'.[67] In accordance with this oft-stated economic priority, the cost of a boy's education was initially the price of one share (originally ranging from £20 to £40) in addition to £35 a year if he boarded at the school. Since many had parents living in the town and attended the college as day pupils, it provided a cheaper alternative to more famous public schools, particularly at the outset. Its popularity, however, caused the number of boys enrolled to increase from 200 to 600 in its first twenty years and the costs of shares to multiply. By 1889, annual fees amounted to £6 to rent a share and an additional £18 to £28 for day pupils and £51 to £57 for boarders; in 1912, the costs ranged between £84 and £103 for boarders. Although Cheltenham was considerably more expensive than Bedford Grammar School its fees remained well below those at elite schools such as Eton or Harrow, which at that time respectively charged a boarder £166 and £153 each year he attended.[68] Its cost, the ease with which it accommodated local day boys, and its academic offerings caused Cheltenham College to retain large numbers of British-Indian pupils until well into the twentieth century. Along with those whose parents lived in the town, many others came as boarders because of the school's high reputation among overseas British families irrespective of their place of residence while in the metropole.

Cheltenham College was one of many proprietary schools founded in the nineteenth century by middle-class families seeking a respectable but affordable education for their sons.[69] Another was the United Services College in Westward Ho! in Devon, which began in 1874 and recruited both its first headmaster and initial group of pupils from Haileybury College in Hertford. Haileybury itself had obvious connections with the empire, most notably through inhabiting the buildings and grounds of the former East India College, which had closed in 1857. When it opened as a public school in 1862, Haileybury drew

---

[66] M. C. Morgan, *Cheltenham College: The First Hundred Years* (Calfont St Giles, Bucks., 1968); Tim Pearce, *Then and Now: An Anniversary Celebration of Cheltenham College, 1841–1991* (Cheltenham, 1991).

[67] 'An Old Cheltonian', *Reminiscences of Cheltenham College* (London, 1868), 1; see also CCA, Cheltenham College Scrap Book, 1841–1867, 'Cheltenham College Prospectus, 1858', 2.

[68] Morgan, *Cheltenham College*, 8–10; CCA, Cheltenham College Scrap Book, 1868–1892, 'Note of Explanation' [1889] and 'Cheltenham College Prospectus, December 1889', 3; Ussher (ed.), *Public Schools*, 25, 33, 39.

[69] E. C. Mack, *Public Schools and British Opinion, 1780–1860* (London, 1938), 346–7.

upon the facility's former occupants for many of its pupils and traditions, although officially it had no connection with the first and now defunct institution. From the outset, however, it had in effect a pre-existing set of old boys, many of whom chose the new school for their sons. Haileybury long took pride in its associations with the East India College, exemplified in 1893 in the school magazine's delineation of both its institutional and its pupils' genealogies:

To the student at Haileybury the abiding subject of interest was the expansion and maintenance of British rule in India. If not himself son or grandson of men whose praises were in all men's mouths, or whose names were registered in the most stirring pages of Indian history, he was pretty sure to be closely akin to them . . . Many a Haileyburian had been dandled as a child in arms which had helped to bind a province to the empire or to bring savage tribes into subjection.[70]

The United Services College derived from such 'stock'. As its name suggested, its founders were military officers who typically had served overseas, and in this respect the school's constituency resembled both Haileybury's and Cheltenham's. Like at Bedford Grammar School and Cheltenham College, moreover, those patronizing the United Services College sought a socially acceptable education at lower cost than was possible at Haileybury, Wellington College (also founded for officers' sons), and many other boarding schools. Purchasing fifty shares at £1 each allowed one boy to be nominated at reduced fees, which in 1883 amounted to £60 a year for an officer's son who boarded; unnominated officers' and civilians' sons were charged £70 and £75 annually.[71] Economy remained a key source of attraction for parents throughout the school's history, even after it moved from Westward Ho!, merged with another institution, and was reconstituted as the Imperial Services College at Windsor in 1912. The ISC functioned for the benefit of less affluent overseas civil service as well as military families until, following a drop in enrolment, it amalgamated with Haileybury in 1942—in effect returning to its roots.[72]

[70] HCA, *Haileyburian*, 10/232 (1893), 357–8. Additional references to the familial links between students at the East India College and Haileybury College include *Haileyburian*, 8/307 (18 March 1901), 325; Imogen Thomas, *Haileybury 1806–1987* (Hertford, 1987), 43. On the East India College, see Bernard Cohn, 'The Recruitment and Training of British Civil Servants in India, 1600–1860', in *An Anthropologist Among the Historians and Other Essays* (New Delhi, 1987), 500–53. For Haileybury pupils' fathers' professions as well as their own future occupations, see L. S. Milford, *Haileybury Register, 1862–1910*, 4th edn. (London, 1910).

[71] HCA, leaflet, 'United Services Proprietary College, December 1883'. In 1880, annual fees for a boarder at Wellington were approximately £132, compared with £60 at the USC; HCA, leaflet, 'Wellington College and the United Services College, Westward Ho!', from *The Field* (30 Oct. 1880).

[72] At a meeting to discuss refounding the USC as the ISC, Field Marshall Lord Grenfell emphasized the anxiety many officers (particularly those forced to retire early) faced over funding their sons' education. 'As a rule', he argued, 'up to the rank of Colonel, the highest sum these officers can draw is a pension of £420 a year'. For a retired officer with several sons and little private income, the College was said to be both reliable and a bargain at £80 a year for each boy. HCA, leaflet, 'Report of Mansion House Meeting, 30 June 1909', 12.

Since these schools all had many India-connected families patronizing them, they allow for a detailed examination of how British-Indians with a variety of occupational backgrounds and incomes educated their sons. Data on British-Indian boys' schooling support W. D. Rubinstein's argument that a public-school style education was not restricted to elite circles but in fact became widely available throughout middle-class society.[73] Admissions registers illustrate the social profile of their colonial clientele most succinctly. At the United Services College, 27 per cent of its total enrolment between 1874 and 1912 was of British-Indian descent, and most of the remaining pupils came from families with connections elsewhere in the empire. Most boys' fathers were officers in the British or Indian Armies, but the school included pupils from other imperial occupational backgrounds as well, such as its most famous 'old boy', Rudyard Kipling, whose attendance between 1878 and 1882 is the only context in which most are familiar with the institution today.[74] Cheltenham College's registers provide less detail and fail to list many pupils' fathers' professions. As up to one-third attended as day boys while living with retired parents or other guardians in the town, Indian addresses alone do not fully indicate the school's British-Indian contingent.[75] None the less, 29 of the 146 entrants in 1841 listed their fathers as working in India, mainly in the Civil Service (18) or the army (8). In 1881, their proportion remained high with 20 of 186 fathers employed or previously employed in the subcontinent, including 8 in the ICS, 8 in the military, 1 as a civil engineer, 1 as an officer in the Indian Medical Service, 1 as a merchant, 1 as an indigo planter, and 1 whose profession was unspecified. Six more fathers were army officers who were likely to have spent a considerable portion of their careers stationed overseas, even though an Indian residence was not listed at the time the boys entered. In 1901, 23 of 167 fathers had similar Indian occupational backgrounds, as did 17 of 169 in 1921. Given these representative samplings, at least 10–20 per cent of the boys at Cheltenham at any given time were British-Indians, but their actual numbers may well have been significantly higher than the registers indicated.[76]

Bedford Grammar School's admissions information reveal similarly significant numbers of British-Indian boys between the late nineteenth and mid-twentieth centuries. They too, however, are likely to underestimate their totals due to a comparable lack of parental information for the day boys who made

---

[73] W. D. Rubinstein, 'Education and the Social Origins of British Elites, 1880–1970', *Past and Present*, 112 (1986), 163–207; *Capitalism, Culture, and Decline in Britain, 1750–1990* (London, 1993), 102–39.

[74] *O.U.S.C. Register, 1936* (Canterbury, 1936).

[75] Lawson, *At Home on Furlough*, 210.

[76] CCA, *Register of Entries*, information on entrants in 1841, 1881, 1901, and 1921.

up the vast majority of the school. As they stand, 10 per cent of boys entering the school in 1892, 1902, 1912, and 1922 demonstrate family connections with India through their fathers' occupations.[77] Since a much higher percentage was listed as residing with widowed mothers, retired parents, or guardians in the town, this figure is likely to be only a fraction of the total British-Indians in a school within a town known for attracting this group. Fathers with Indian occupations indicated in the registers ranged broadly from higher-ranking civil and military officers down through various types of commercial or other non-official work. In 1902, for example, of 19 British-Indian fathers 6 were military officers, 2 were in the Indian Civil Service, 1 worked in mining, 1 as an engineer, 1 in the mills, and 1 as a reverend; the remaining 7 had unspecified careers.[78] Since its fees were one of Bedford Grammar School's main attractions, many of these families presumably lacked private incomes beyond their salaries or pensions. Moreover, judging from the schools boys had previously attended, a number of the India-connected families choosing Bedford Grammar were situated well below the upper reaches of colonial society. In 1892, 6 of 22 boys whose fathers had worked in India had begun their education at schools in India, as did 7 of 19 in 1902.[79] As Chapter 2 showed, attending schools in India was a lower status option for families whose restricted budgets necessitated postponing education in Britain.

Perhaps unsurprisingly given their large imperial enrolment, daily life for boys at these schools was imbued with constant reminders of India. Even those lacking overseas connections became well versed in this pervasive subculture. Donald Johnson, the son of a Lancashire doctor, recalled India's predominance in school discourse during his time at Cheltenham during the First World War thus:

[The School] seemed less a part of England—or any England that I knew—than it did a transplanted section of Anglo-India . . . Within a week of the beginning of term it was easy to think of Simla and Poona, Allahabad and Srinagar, as being considerably nearer than Bury or Bolton or Rochdale were. I have never been to India . . . But . . . if [I] go, the real India will never quite replace in my mind the India-images which are based on the asphalt yard and the playing fields of the Cheltenham Junior School.[80]

Boys' early years in and ongoing family links with India surfaced repeatedly in school magazines. Pupils' compositions about family trips 'From Calcutta to

---

[77] BSA, *Bedford Grammar School Register, 1888–1906*, 59–76, 233–48; *Bedford Grammar School Register, 1906–1931*, entries no. 6611–742 and 8180–348.

[78] BSA, *Bedford Grammar School Register, 1888–1906*, 1912 entrants' fathers' professions, 59–76.

[79] Ibid., schools previously attended by British-Indian boys entering in 1892 (59–76) and 1902 (233–48).

[80] Donald McI. Johnson, *A Doctor Regrets* (London, 1949), 32–3.

the Himalayahs' or on 'The Excavated Temples of India' were common fare in these publications, and these most likely resembled unrecorded conversations touching upon shared memories of their time overseas.[81] 'Hobson-Jobson' vocabulary appeared to be part of everyday speech for boys at the United Services College, as this letter to its magazine's editor in 1882 suggests:

Dear Sir,

Is there no possibility of allowing study-fags to fellows who aren't Prefects? . . . I find it rather hard to be always washing or wiping up . . . There's such a lot of unemployed labour playing in the corridor . . . [signed] An Overworked Bheestie.[82]

'Bheestie' referred to an Indian servant who carried water; when invoked in this setting, familiar colonial terminology based upon racial and occupational distinctions became adapted to reinforce an age-based British boarding-school hierarchy.

Material as well as linguistic evidence of combined institutional and familial connections with the empire also abounded on school grounds. Pupils and their parents commonly donated objects like tiger skulls, stuffed 'foreign birds', and Indian butterflies to schools' natural history collections; school buildings themselves, moreover, bore the traces of empire in their names as well as through the objects and persons inhabiting them.[83] At Haileybury, the connection between boys living in boarding houses named after famed individuals linked with the 'old Haileybury' of the East India College—including Lawrence House, Colvin House, Thomason House, Edmonstone House, Trevelyan House, and Bartle Frere House—and these thus honored forefathers was reinforced through the school's long-standing tradition of calling recently arrived boys 'New Governors'.[84]

While more famous public schools provided inspiration for some features of these newer schools' culture—such as the system whereby boys were divided into boarding houses for whose sports teams they played—they were not emulated in other crucial respects. All these institutions developed curricula far more heavily weighted towards 'modern' subjects that diverged from the 'classical' emphasis that predominated at the 'great public schools'.[85] Indeed,

---

[81] BSA, *Ousel*, 3/71 (6 June 1888), 189–91; HCA, *United Services College Chronicle*, 16 (15 Oct. 1883), 199–200.

[82] HCA, *United Services College Chronicle*, 8 (20 March 1882), 88.

[83] HCA, *United Services College Chronicle*, 13 (12 March 1883), 161.

[84] HCA, *Haileyburian*, 7 (1 March 1869), 91–2; James McConnell, *English Public Schools* (London, 1985), 166.

[85] See, for example, CCA, 'Cheltenham College', *Hadley's Shilling Guide to Cheltenham* (Cheltenham, 1856), 51.

Cheltenham, Bedford Grammar, Haileybury, and the United Services College were all early examples of schools where older pupils could choose the 'Classical Side'—which emphasized Latin, Greek, and some mathematics—or alternatively opt for the 'Modern Side', where Greek was largely replaced with more mathematics, modern languages, and other subjects including sciences. The 'Modern Side' at all these schools surpassed the 'Classical' in numbers and importance, because the latter catered mainly to the smaller group of boys preparing for university entrance and Indian Civil Service examinations. On the 'Modern Side'—alternatively and indicatively known as the 'Army Side' at some schools—boys were tutored for qualifying examinations for military academies, engineering colleges, and a range of other professions.

An educational ethos heavily oriented towards providing specific career qualifications dominated the academic agenda at all the institutions considered here.[86] Their histories are inseparable from the contemporaneous advent of competitive entrance examinations for public services, many of which also dated from the middle of the nineteenth century. Open competition began with the Indian Civil Service in 1854 and extended to encompass the army and other home and colonial services over the following decades.[87] J. M. Bourne's study of patronage in nineteenth-century England connects the rise of the public schools (and particularly the establishment of new institutions) in this period to the decline of personal connections as a means of securing employment for the service middle classes and its replacement by open competition.[88] An early issue of the *Haileyburian* succinctly encapsulated the link between competition and the school's role in preparing its pupils for these new career criteria through its modern curriculum:

[86] At Haileybury and the USC, articles repeatedly appeared in their magazines on army examinations. Several include HCA, *Haileyburian*, 2/26 (7 Oct. 1871), 17–18; *United Services College Chronicle*, 2/41 (27 March 1889), 61–3, followed by three similar entries in 1890 and 1891.

[87] C. J. Dewey, 'The Education of a Ruling Caste: The Indian Civil Service in the Era of Competitive Examination', *English Historical Review*, 347 (1973), 262–85; J. M. Compton, 'Open Competition and the Indian Civil Service, 1854–1876', *English Historical Review*, 327 (1968), 265–84; R. J. Moore, 'The Abolition of Patronage in the Indian Civil Service and the Closure of Haileybury College', *Historical Journal*, 7/2 (1964), 246–57. The Indian Medical Service introduced competitive examinations in 1855; see Mark Harrison, *Public Health in British India: Anglo-Indian Preventive Medicine, 1859–1914* (Cambridge, 1994), 15. The Royal Indian Engineering College at Cooper's Hill opened in 1871 to train successful competitors for employment in the Indian Public Works Department. See Brendan Cuddy and Tony Mansell, 'Engineers for India: The Royal Indian Engineering College at Cooper's Hill', *History of Education*, 23/1 (1994), 115. On the abolition of the purchase system for army officers and the advent of competitive examinations to enter the military academies, see T. A. Heathcote, *The Indian Army: The Garrison of British Imperial India, 1822–1922* (Newton Abbot, 1974).

[88] J. M. Bourne, *Patronage and Society in Nineteenth-Century England* (London, 1986), 34, 104–5.

The age of jobbery is passing away; and though interest and family still have considerable weight, they are more than counterbalanced by ability and industry. Junior members of 'The Upper Ten' are thus deprived of the posts which, from long use, they have been led to consider their birthright; and they are thrown into the general arena, to jostle and contend with men of superior ability, equal refinement and education, but inferior lineage . . . the classics, and the earlier branches of mathematical science, are indispensable for success in any career; but in addition to this, some extra study should be devoted to those subjects which tell most in the peculiar line which is to be adopted.[89]

A historical overview of Cheltenham College written in 1890 made similar reference to how 'competitive examinations . . . struck a death-blow to nepotism, nominations, and old hereditary claims to lucrative posts'; as a result, subjects that had 'hitherto taken a subordinate position in the curriculum of the older schools, forced [their] way to the front', because knowledge of them determined whether a boy succeeded in jumping these new hurdles.[90]

Academic offerings at schools like these thus corresponded closely with the structure of the examinations pupils would ultimately try to pass.[91] Maths dominated their curricula, but the same pragmatism accounted for boys' instruction in other subjects. At Cheltenham, for example, teaching natural science was justified not only as 'an instrument of general mental education' but first and foremost because it was an examination subject.[92] Boys could learn Italian at the school for similar reasons, as a writer in its magazine summarized in 1870. Since they had already studied Latin, boys could acquire a rudimentary knowledge of Italian faster than French or German, and tangibly benefit therefrom:

not least of [Italian's] advantages, at any rate in the eyes of anxious parents with sons training for the competitive examinations, there is an equal number of marks given to Italian as to French or German, and I noticed (I refer especially to the India Civil Service examinations) a far higher average of marks gained in Italian by those who took it up than in French or German. It seems to me a standing disgrace to any institution that professes *to give an education of any refinement, not to mention, to take a lower ground, utility,* that it should be neglected.[93]

[89] HCA, *Haileyburian*, 6 (8 Dec. 1868), 74.

[90] Andrew Alexander Hunter (ed.), *Cheltenham College Register, 1841–1889* (London, 1890), 1.

[91] For a listing of public examination subjects and the marks allotted for them, see W. J. Chetwode Crawley, *Handbook of Competitive Examinations for Admission to Every Department of Her Majesty's Service* (London, 1880), and successive editions.

[92] CCA, Cheltenham College Scrap Book, 1868–1892, 'Report of the Committee on the Teaching of Natural Science', 12 Oct. 1880, 92. Views on science were similar at the USC; see HCA, *United Services College Chronicle*, 2/58 (17 Dec. 1894), 281.

[93] CCA, *Cheltenham College Magazine* I (April 1870), 118–19; emphasis added.

A curriculum focused upon 'modern' subjects and preparation for qualifying examinations for the Royal Military College at Sandhurst, the Royal Military Academy at Woolwich, the Indian Civil Service, and a host of other imperial services constituted a far more important part of school life at the institutions discussed here than at public schools catering to wealthier pupils. These boys' fathers may have been loosely described as 'gentlemen', but the same economic limitations that steered them towards more modestly priced schools also decisively influenced their educational priorities for their sons. As one man argued at Bedford Grammar School's speech day in 1901:

Every parent, unless he had a fortune, had to ask himself how he could provide an opening for his children . . . Many fathers of families therefore were now asking themselves what was the use of giving their sons a classical education. Would it obtain for them a good place in the general competition for appointments? Would it pay? Would it not be better to give up the time now devoted exclusively to Latin and Greek to the study of French, German, or natural sciences?[94]

More affluent boys at elite schools who had studied mainly Latin and Greek might rectify their shortcomings in 'modern' examination subjects by undergoing additional specialized instruction after leaving school from so-called 'crammers'—establishments that hastily prepared aspiring army, civil service, and other public service officers to fulfil entry requirements.[95] Schools that attracted families with more restricted budgets, however, continually stressed that they prepared boys to pass civil and military service examinations 'direct from the school' without further expensive tutelage.[96] A 1933 history of the United Services College listed this as the primary reason for opening the school, stating that 'the founding of the USC was an effort to eliminate "crammers", who at that time [1874] were charging the heavy fee of £250 to £300 per annum to coach a boy for the cadet colleges'.[97] Major-General Lionel Dunsterville—better known to Kipling's readers as the model for the character 'Stalky'—noted the intense competition for Sandhurst in the 1880s, recalling that 'the normal procedure was for a boy to finish his time at a public school and then go for six months, or a year, to a crammer, and then take the exam'. At

---

94 BSA, *Ousel*, n.s., 5/174 (29 July 1901), 100.

95 The common practice of sending boys to crammers upon leaving public school is briefly noted in W. J. Reader, *Professional Men: The Rise of the Professional Classes in Nineteenth-Century England* (London, 1966), 100–2, 109–11; Edward C. Mack, *Public Schools and British Opinion Since 1860* (New York, 1941), 154–5, 212; Jonathan Gathorne-Hardy, *The Public Schools Phenomenon* (Harmondsworth, 1979), 156; John Roach, *Public Examinations in England, 1850–1900* (Cambridge, 1971), 198–9, 217–22.

96 On parents' desire to avoid the expense of crammers, see 'An Old Cheltonian', *Reminiscences*, 2; HCA, *United Services College Chronicle*, 2/57 (24 July 1894), 269.

97 Major H. A. Tapp, *United Services College, 1874–1911* (Aldershot, 1933), 1.

the United Services College, however, the headmaster 'passed us all into Woolwich and Sandhurst direct from the school without the delay and expense of cramming'.[98] This school and its successor as well as Cheltenham College and Bedford Grammar School all boasted similar feats, in effect sparing families the added costs of preparing sons for examinations by becoming 'crammers' themselves.[99] Thus, a man who attended Cheltenham in the late nineteenth century summarized his education largely as a combination of 'cramming and cricket'. 'We were made specialists almost as soon as we started', he recalled. 'For those hoping to reach Sandhurst or Woolwich, the two gates to commission in the Army, as many Cheltonians did, it was a matter of maths, maths and still more maths'.[100]

A closer look at institutions commonly patronized by British-Indian families reveals aspects of public-school-style boys' education between the mid-Victorian and interwar period that scholars largely have ignored. Schools imperial families chose for their sons exemplify the expansion of educational provisions for middle-class boys who needed formal credentials acquired at a reasonable price to embark upon well-paid professions, since most lacked substantial family resources either for their education or to augment their salaries later. Such boys required more than a public-school ethos which inculcated 'manliness' and other class-based cultural attributes such as *esprit de corps*, exposure to the classics, and an appreciation for hierarchy, stoicism, and athleticism—the features of public-school life that dominate most work on the subject.[101] While the public, minor public, and grammar schools explored here certainly valued these cultural elements of boys' education as well, they offered 'refinement' in combination with 'utility'. As Charles Lawson, the author of *At Home on*

---

[98] Major-General L. C. Dunsterville, *Stalky's Reminiscences* (London, 1928), 57. See Rudyard Kipling, 'An English School', in Thomas Pinney (ed.), *Rudyard Kipling: Something of Myself and Other Autobiographical Writings* (Cambridge, 1990), for his recollections of boys 'grinding' for army examinations at the USC.

[99] CCA, Cheltenham College Scrap Book, 1868–1892, 'Cheltenham College India Civil Service Classes', 1889, 176; Hunter (ed.), *Cheltenham College Register, 1841–1889*, 7, 35, 41, 43; Johnson, *A Doctor Regrets*, 40. For Bedford Grammar School's many pupils who passed Sandhurst, Woolwich, the Indian Civil Service, Indian Woods and Forest Department, and other examinations direct from the school, see BSA, *Ousel*, n.s. 20 (13 July 1896), 90–3; *Supplement to the Ousel*, n.s., 5/174 (20 July 1901). On the USC and ISC, see HCA, *United Services College Chronicle*, 14 (31 May 1883), 182; *Imperial Services College Chronicle*, 1/8 (August 1914), 160.

[100] Ivor Brown, *The Way of My World* (London, 1954), 17.

[101] These include Honey, *Tom Brown's Universe*, 126–37; David Newsome, *Godliness and Good Learning: Four Studies on a Victorian Ideal* (London, 1961); J. A. Mangan, *Athleticism in the Victorian and Edwardian Public School* (Cambridge, 1981); *The Games Ethic and Imperialism: Aspects of the Diffusion of an Ideal* (Harmondsworth, 1986); J. A. Mangan (ed.), *'Benefits Bestowed?': Education and British Imperialism* (Manchester, 1988); John Tosh, *A Man's Place: Masculinity and the Middle-Class Home in Victorian England* (New Haven, CT, 1999), 104–5, 117–19.

Furlough, fulminated to his British-Indian readership in the 1870s, middle-class families like themselves needed to steer clear of schools charging high fees for a largely 'ornamental' education that, at best, rendered their sons 'good cricketers' and 'indifferent classicists'. 'The "elegant imbecility" engendered by a devotion to classical studies to the exclusion of the subjects of daily use', he concluded, only created a 'gentleman' who 'runs a good chance of starving'.[102] Christine Heward's study of Ellesmere College—a minor public school—during the 1930s and 1940s is one of the few works to stress this wider range of qualities that middle-class families had long expected boys to develop at such institutions. Parents who sent boys to minor public schools because they could not afford the most prestigious made a considerable financial sacrifice, and expected results that surpassed attainments that would make their sons 'gentlemen' in a narrowly defined cultural sense alone. For them, as Heward summarizes, 'manliness was first and foremost about being a good breadwinner'.[103]

Making up the less exalted side of middle-class boys' education, then, pragmatic career preparation, parental economy, and stress upon 'modern' subjects were none the less omnipresent at many schools, whether formally 'public' or not.[104] Schools that prioritized training boys to pass competitive examinations 'direct from the school' may well have had this significant dimension of their histories neglected for the same reason that time with a 'crammer' has received so little (and indeed often no) analysis in the historiography on middle- and upper-middle-class male education. As W. J. Reader once observed, six months at a crammer's became 'an accepted if not very dignified episode in the education of a Victorian gentleman'.[105] Such deviations from the classics-and-cricket image of gentlemanly education that prevailed both at the time and in the priorities of subsequent writers conceivably did much to render them largely invisible in scholarly analyses. These very features, however, are integral to explaining why these schools' long-standing imperial identities both emerged and became perpetuated.

Institutional traditions of preparing boys for imperial careers thus derived from a combination of school culture along with the backgrounds, needs, and inclinations of the families patronizing them. The strong tendency for sons to

---

[102] Lawson, *At Home*, 347–54.

[103] Christine Heward, *Making a Man of Him: Parents and Their Sons' Education at an English Public School, 1929–50* (London, 1988), 1, 8, 13.

[104] Rubinstein has suggested that 'modern' alongside classical learning did not emerge at public schools until the twentieth century, but this argument appears questionable if less elite and expensive schools are taken into account. 'Education and the Social Origins', 206.

[105] Reader, *Professional Men*, 109. As John Tosh notes, 'the literature on the other kinds of school [other than well-known public schools] patronized by middle-class families is frustratingly inadequate', perhaps in part for the same reasons. *A Man's Place*, 216.

enter either the same or similar occupations as their fathers was marked in most social sectors in nineteenth- and twentieth-century Britain.[106] Boys from families supported by Indian work often later found themselves employed overseas as well because firmly rooted knowledge and experience of such opportunities could make this an obvious and desirable choice. Family imperial traditions, however, were greatly enhanced by, and indeed inseparable from, the environment sons encountered at school. Whether they attended as day scholars or as boarders, boys at schools containing a substantial British-Indian and wider colonial clientele experienced a peer group, academic preparation, and extracurricular daily life imbued with references to empire and particularly to India, and received constant reminders of career opportunities overseas that influenced their choices upon leaving school.

British-Indian families' common economic limitations, moreover, did much to persuade sons to opt for imperial life in adulthood. Just as schools that specialized in preparing boys to pass examinations without additional expensive 'cramming' were attractive to families lacking substantial private incomes, so too were Indian occupations because they typically offered higher pay than metropolitan equivalents as compensation for living overseas. Sons who could expect little if any private financial support when they embarked upon their careers received constant reminders of the benefits imperial work offered, both from their parents as well as through school channels. School magazines published numerous articles throughout this period that specifically stressed the attractive rates of pay obtainable for work in India, whether it be military or in other branches of state or private employment. Readers of the *Haileyburian* in 1871, for instance, not only learned how best to prepare to enter the Indian Civil Engineering College at Cooper's Hill but also that upon completing their training their salary in the Indian Public Works Department would commence at £420 a year and could subsequently rise to as much as £3,000.[107] In a similar vein, boys at the United Services College were told in 1882 about the rewards of a career in the Indian Staff Corps, where officers received higher pay and had fewer living expenses than in British Army regiments stationed in India. As a member of the Staff Corps wrote, their family finances made this form of military service a strong possibility:

It is a recognized fact that only those unfortunates, who are not blessed with much superfluous money, enter the Staff-Corps, for what well-to-do man would deliver him-

---

[106] Jose Harris, *Private Lives, Public Spirit: Britain 1870–1914* (Harmondsworth, 1994), 68.
[107] HCA, *Haileyburian*, 22 (24 Feb. 1871), 317–19.

self up voluntarily to 'grill' all his service in this caustic region? Listen therefore, O ye U. S. C. boys, whose chances of an 'allowance' are small. The above lot was mine . . . Here I am going merely to state facts about English Regiments stationed in India . . . The pay of a Subaltern in these regiments is 202 Rupees a month, out of which he has to pay a heavy mess-bill, house rent, and servants. My experience is that, unless a young officer has an 'allowance', he cannot meet all these expenses with his pittance . . . this drove me into the Staff Corps . . . [receiving at least 425 Rupees a month].[108]

This writer was far from the only USC, Bedford Grammar, Cheltenham, or Haileybury old boy to enter the Staff Corps following their customary probationary year with a British Army regiment in India.[109] Many without private incomes to supplement their salaries chose the Indian Army in favor of the British Army, and the former was long known for accommodating many officers of comparatively lower social and economic origins.[110] Indian careers of many descriptions came highly recommended for financial reasons through the interwar era. At Haileybury, the Indian Medical Service was promoted in the mid-1930s for offering an annual starting salary that was considerably more than a young physician could typically hope to earn in Britain.[111] Boys at Bedford Grammar School in 1929, meanwhile, learned about Indian Police careers in a lecture by an Old Bedfordian visiting on furlough, who not only offered advice about competing to enter but also praised the service because 'the young policeman could live on his pay and obtain many opportunities for displaying his prowess in sport'.[112]

Reports like this suggest key reasons why Indian careers were pursued by many families across the generations and also illustrate how extra-familial influences could help to steer boys towards overseas futures. Encouragement to work in India might come both from fathers as well as old boys who made periodic visits to the schools and told of their experiences while on leave.[113] School magazines, moreover, frequently published letters from former pupils who had entered occupations as diverse as the Indian Civil Service, Indian Police, Indian Political Service, Indian Army, planting, railway work, and mining.[114] Alongside promoting the economic incentives such

---

108 HCA, *United Services College Chronicle*, 12 (11 Dec. 1882), 144.

109 HCA, *United Services College Chronicle*, 26 (2 Nov. 1885), 333–4.

110 P. E. Razzell, 'Social Origins of Officers in the Indian and British Home Army: 1758–1962', *British Journal of Sociology*, 14/3 (1963), 248–60; Heathcote, *Indian Army*, 116, 122–9, 140–1.

111 HCA, *Haileyburian* 26/609 (2 April 1935), 826–8.

112 BSA, *Ousel*, 33/638 (25 May 1929), 80.

113 HCA, *Haileyburian*, 13/296 (25 May 1900), 126; Kipling, 'An English School', 184.

114 BSA, *Ousel*, 4/104 (22 Oct. 1892), 251–2; HCA, *Haileyburian*, 9/209 (6 April 1892), 341–3; *Haileyburian*, 12/281 (8 March 1899), 301–2.

careers offered, these reports emphasized that boys opting for India could enjoy ample sport, particularly hunting, and suggested that they might even partake of such pleasures in the company of old acquaintances.[115] One former Bedford Grammar School pupil managing his uncle's coffee estates in Coorg wrote back in 1888 that 'there are several fellows out here, old Bedford boys . . . We are rather thick on the spot here for the jungle . . . I cannot forget my old school, as it is so well known out here. Everybody knows Bedford.'[116] Twenty years later little had changed when another Old Bedfordian described entering the Indian Police in Burma to find that three of his ten fellow trainees had attended his school. He in turn played his own part in attempting to perpetuate this school tradition by encouraging younger readers to 'continue to enter for this appointment'.[117]

Taken together, school records illustrate that these multiple forms of encouragement succeeded in convincing many pupils to pursue imperial occupations. The casual remark from an Old Bedfordian in interwar Ceylon [Sri Lanka] that 'the East is almost entirely populated by O.B.s!' was one which might have appeared in any of Cheltenham's, Haileybury's, or the United Services College/Imperial Services College's magazines between the late-nineteenth and mid-twentieth centuries.[118] Countless notices of Old Boys' Club dinners, marriages, and promotions occurring throughout the Indian subcontinent show the wide variety of public and private occupations former pupils pursued, often as army officers but also in the Indian Civil Service, Police, Public Works Department, Forest Service, railways, planting, and commercial employment.[119] Plentiful anecdotal evidence of Indian careers in school magazines add color to available statistics on the professional futures of their pupils. By 1889, Cheltenham College claimed to have educated 1,771 army officers and 65 Indian Civil Servants in under fifty years, a tradition which continued unabated for decades afterwards. Meanwhile, between 1874 and 1922, USC old boys included 666 officers in the British and Indian Armies and an additional 308 who worked overseas in other colonial services or in non-official capacities, leaving only about 400 who found employment in Britain. Approximately one-fifth of its school-leavers made their careers in India alone.[120] Kipling's 1883 poem 'The Song of the Exiles' further

[115] HCA, *Haileyburian*, 5/119 (11 April 1883), 544–5; *Haileyburian*, 22/480 (14 March 1919), 308.

[116] BSA, *Ousel*, 3/74 (12 Nov. 1888), 233.

[117] BSA, *Ousel*, 12/344 (6 June 1908), 73.

[118] BSA, *Ousel*, 33/640 (27 July 1929), 142.

[119] BSA, *Ousel*, 13/361 (25 Feb. 1909), 18; *Ousel*, 31/617 (12 Feb. 1927), 5; *Ousel*, 37/667 (1 April 1933), 62; CCA, *Cheltonian*, (Jan. 1882), 22–7; *Cheltonian*, (Nov. 1919), 391–3; HCA, *Haileyburian*, 26/587 (23 June 1932), 197; *United Services College Chronicle*, 2/50 (11 April 1892), 171–2.

[120] Hunter (ed.), *Cheltenham College Register, 1841–1889*, 7; Col. H. A. Tapp and Lt.-Gen. W. G. H. Vickers, *United Services College, 1874–1911* (Cheshunt, Herts., 1959), 24, 29, 30, 34.

1 Home leave, March 1912, on 'S. S. Macedonia'.

2 Frances with Ayah, 1922.

3 Child in a dandy with five servants, c.1908.

4 Christmas 1925.

5 'Mum, Dad, Me and Three Office Staff, probably in a NWFP Station, c.1920'. Maisie and Donald Scott with their daughter Dorothy, surrounded by three of Donald's Indian co-workers.

6 Wedding of Iris Butler and Gervas Portal, Central Provinces, January 1927. Montagu Butler is seated to the left of the bride; Ann Butler is seated in the second row, fourth from the right; Rab Butler stands in the back row, second from the right; his wife Sydney is seated in the second row, farthest to the right.

7 Family of Benjamin L. Rice and Mary Sophia Rice, Naini Tal (?), 1901.

8 'Granny Rice' [Mary Sophia Rice], 1869.

9 Children's Picnic at Fairy Falls, Kodai, May 1911.

10 Laetitia, Herman, William, and Jeannette Beveridge with two of the family's servants, *c*.1888.

11 Gravestones of Laetitia
Beveridge and Herman
Beveridge, Eastbourne
Cemetery.

12 Port Said, April 1938.
Donald Scott en route to
retirement years in Britain,
pictured here with his
daughter Dorothy on a
stopover during their last
voyage from India.

alluded to the diverse forms of work his schoolmates ultimately pursued while chasing 'Her Majesty's rupee', making their careers on tea estates, in forestry, engineering, the police, the civil service, or the military—to name but a few.[121]

In sum, these boys' schools known for catering to families supported by work in India and other imperial arenas resembled the Schools for the Sons and Daughters of Missionaries in important respects. School culture revealed pupils' overseas links at every turn, and documentation illustrates how the same institutions noted for their substantial British-Indian intake also sent many school-leavers back into the empire. Alongside personal narratives, these schools' histories offer further evidence that imperial life alternating between Britain and India was often a long-term family condition aided considerably by institutional traditions, and due in large part to the higher incomes that work overseas offered for men. For many British-Indian families, sending children to 'respectable' British schools and preparing sons for careers was accomplished with considerable difficulty. The sacrifices families made to provide this coveted form of British education could be great, but with respect to boys they were mainly viewed in financial, as opposed to emotional, terms. These costs, however, yielded higher cultural status and incomes that worked together to bolster white racial standing that cheaper forms of education—such as at 'European' schools in India—were unlikely to provide for future imperial breadwinners.

Historical records of Cheltenham College, Haileybury, the United Services College/Imperial Services College, and Bedford Grammar School make no mention of these children's British school years as a time of family sacrifice. Whereas the two missionary schools and some private accounts alluded to family emotional traumas when boys and girls were sent home to school, other boys' boarding schools were well known for promoting values in opposition to those of the sentimentalized family and domestic sphere.[122] School authorities (and presumably most pupils) understood parent–child separations as a term-time fact of life shared by all boarders regardless of whether their parents lived relatively nearby or thousands of miles away, and as such their condition seldom provoked comment, at least publicly. Morose pupils, for obvious reasons, never featured in in-house publications meant to promote a favorable impression of the school. In all-male environments dominated by stoicism, pragmatic academic preparation, and sport, boys undoubtedly dwelled on emotional

[121] HCA, *United Services College Chronicle*, 16 (15 Oct. 1883), 198–9.

[122] Honey, *Tom Brown's Universe*, 204–6; John Tosh, 'Imperial Masculinity and the Flight from Domesticity in Britain, 1880–1914', in Timothy P. Foley (ed.), *Gender and Colonialism* (Galway, 1995), 76–7.

responses to imperial family circumstances at their peril. One of the few references to this in school documentation appeared in the form of a humorous student essay on 'The Ways of Aunts' in the *Haileyburian* that ridiculed those with whom the author and others like him spent their holidays:

> The genus aunt may be divided into three main species—the maiden aunt, the married aunt, and the adopted aunt . . . Having no motherly affection for one she will mete out chastisement with a heavy hand and decide to 'be firm with the child' . . . She takes charge of one when one's parents go abroad, and decides that one has hitherto been treated too fondly.[123]

By thus both downplaying and making light of family separations, these boys' schools highlight only the opportunities they offered their pupils. While largely sidelined in institutional sources, however, family did as much as school traditions to bring school-leavers back to the empire. As the concluding pages of this chapter argue, young men and especially young women headed to India may well not have left British shores had earlier generations not paved the way.

THE PULL OF FAMILY TIES

After what were often many years characterized largely by separation, young people returning to India could experience what was tantamount to a family reunion as well as a reimmersion in childhood surroundings. Kipling claimed that after leaving the United Services College he sailed for India and 'found myself at Bombay where I was born, moving among sights and smells that made me deliver in the vernacular sentences whose meaning I knew not'. He moved on to Lahore, 'where my people lived', and 'a joyous home-coming':

> I had returned to a Father and Mother of whom I had seen but little since my sixth year . . . the Mother proved more delightful than all my imaginings or memories. My father was not only a mine of knowledge and help, but a humorous, tolerant, and expert fellow-craftsman . . . I do not remember the smallest friction in any detail of our lives. We delighted more in each other's society than in that of strangers; and when my sister came out, a little later, our cup was filled to the brim.[124]

Looking back on re-establishing relations with his parents, Kipling paints an idyllic picture devoid of any hint of ongoing estrangement, let alone resentment stemming from his unhappy early childhood experiences in England

---

[123] HCA, *Haileyburian*, 22/482 (4 June 1919), 375–6.
[124] Rudyard Kipling, *Something of Myself*, in Pinney (ed.), *Rudyard Kipling*, 25–6.

recounted in the previous chapter. Other authors were less sanguine about the extent to which grown children and their parents could recultivate attachment after years spent apart; Sara Jeannette Duncan's short story 'A Mother in India', for example, delineates a mother–daughter relationship characterized by a complete lack of common interests and ongoing emotional indifference after the daughter rejoined her parents.[125] However strong or weak the emotional dimension of return to a family arena overseas may have been, parents were none the less fully responsible for their grown children's resumption of imperial life in both cases. For Kipling, moreover, going back was directly related to practical career considerations assisted by family networking on his behalf, since his first appointment on a newspaper staff in Lahore was secured with his father's help. Although he was to stay in India only through his mid-twenties, many other British-Indian children returning as adults remained part of the colonial community for much of their lives.

How common, then, was it for young men whose fathers had careers in India to embark on similar paths? Records of the schools explored above provide a partial indication of the extent of this, and studies of the background of officers in several of the civil and military branches of service support these findings. While the tendency for sons to pursue their fathers' professions unsurprisingly declined after open competition replaced earlier methods of recruitment by patronage in the mid to late nineteenth century, the extent to which family traditions of official employment persisted despite this impediment remains striking. In addition, throughout the late imperial era sons of British-Indians appeared just as likely to return to India to embark on careers distinct from those of their fathers as they were to enter the same branch of employment.[126] It is impossible to know whether families, schools, or other factors did most to encourage sons to make their careers in the empire, but most likely it was some combination of these influences. Several individuals' accounts attribute their returns almost exclusively to lineage, with knowledge about career openings playing a secondary role. Sir John Cotton became the sixth generation of his family to work in India, joining the Indian Political Service in the 1930s following several years in the Indian Army, whereas his

---

[125] Sara Jeannette Duncan, 'A Mother in India' (1903), in Saros Cowasjee (ed.), *Stories from the Raj from Kipling to Independence* (London, 1982), 74–118.

[126] Of the 348 recruits into the Indian Medical Service between 1885 and 1896, 100 Europeans were born in India; Harrison, *Public Health*, 29–31. In the Indian Civil Service, between 1870 and 1874 23.7 per cent of successful applicants were either born in India or had fathers who had served there; Compton, 'Open Competition', 281–3. Of the Indian Staff Corps officers entering between 1890 and 1895, 40 had fathers employed in India and 89 in the United Kingdom. Of the 40 in India, 29 were army officers (ISC), 9 were in the Indian Civil Service, and 2 worked in other capacities; Heathcote, *Indian Army*, 141.

father had been in the Indian Civil Service. 'It wasn't my decision to go back to India', he claimed; rather, 'it was always the hope of my father that one of us would follow perpetually this family connection'.[127] John Rivett-Carnac similarly became a fifth-generation British-Indian seemingly by default, opting for the Indian Police as his father had done because 'I really didn't know of any other place where I could earn a living'. 'Rose tinted' childhood memories of the subcontinent accomplished the rest, making his return attributable not only to a failure of the imagination but to a positive inclination as well.[128]

Data concerning the backgrounds of men in non-official work are lacking, but it is highly plausible that the numbers of young men who found employment as planters, businessmen, or in other sectors through their fathers', uncles', or brothers' connections in India were even greater than was the case for occupations into which entry was controlled by the state through formal examination procedures. Just as Kipling's first newspaper job came as a result of his father's endeavors, other men similarly recount the importance of family connections in finding work. For John Erskine, for example, beginning a career in tea planting in the 1940s was a logical step; his family's links with many estates in Ceylon and India made finding positions in both places a relatively straightforward and indeed expected procedure.[129]

For other men, overseas careers might take a very different course from those of their fathers yet remain fully inspired by their imperial background. Theon Wilkinson's father was a member of the Cawnpore business community, and had he chosen to seek similar employment he undoubtedly would have benefited from well-established commercial contacts throughout the region. However, he recalled how he had long pinned his hopes on an Indian Civil Service career because he saw it as the best way to do his duty to what he considered his 'mother country'. 'From a sort of young idealistic point of view', he explained, 'I was always talking about one's service to India . . . that having been brought up there and having all the privileges there . . . that one had a duty to serve.'[130] Wilkinson's account of his aspirations suggests how sons with prior family and childhood links with India might be drawn back by a strong identification with a white imperial service ethos that could take precedence over socio-economic inducements, a straightforward familiarity with Indian career possibilities following long exposure, or direct assistance from relatives. As it emerged, he was thwarted in his ICS ambitions since India achieved its independence before he

---

127 OIOC, MSS Eur T18, Sir John Cotton, transcribed interview, n.d. [*c.*1973], 3.
128 OIOC, MSS Eur T55, John Rivett-Carnac, transcribed interview, n.d. [early 1970s], 8–9.
129 John Erskine, interview by author, tape recording, 17 April 1995.
130 Theon Wilkinson, interview by author, tape recording, 12 July 1995.

completed his education, but he none the less managed to '[fulfil] that objective in another place', in the Colonial Service in Kenya, 'until that got independence'. In thus shifting his overseas emphasis to a different part of the empire, Wilkinson exemplifies how younger British-Indians also might prolong family ties with the empire by going to other colonies, both before and after 1947. As documentation from the schools considered above illustrates, boys born in India could just as readily choose to pursue opportunities throughout the rest of Britain's formal (and informal) empire as decide to return to India or stay at home.

Young women appeared just as likely as their brothers—and in some families, more likely—to make their adult lives in India. Many returned to their parents' homes after finishing their education as a matter of course, just as they would have done in Britain had their families lacked overseas ties. Once back in India, many had the option of marrying a man employed there if they chose, given the surplus of males in the British-Indian community. Maud Diver estimated during the Edwardian period that 'more than half the Englishwomen in India today have spent their girlhood and early childhood in the country itself, which, in most cases, means that they have been sent "Home" at the age of seven or thereabouts, returning at seventeen'.[131] Parents as well as brothers and other relatives working in India facilitated young women's marriages to other British-Indian men by providing them with ready access to a pool of eligible partners from their own circle of friends and colleagues.[132] Interviews with Janet Erskine and Enid Boon revealed how both stayed overseas long after their parents' departure by marrying their brothers' friends.[133] Enid's recollections in particular suggest common means by which multi-generational histories in India emerged as well as the diverse range of careers male relatives pursued. Returning to India in the early 1930s after completing school, she chose to stay after her father retired from the ICS a year later. Lucknow society proved too appealing to give up, it seemed; 'there were dances, there were balls . . . oh, we had a great time, all the girls did . . . a lot of young men would come in from outside [Lucknow], either army or planters or such people, and so many girls

---

[131] Diver, *Englishwoman in India*, 11.

[132] As Leonore Davidoff has begun to explore, the importance of family relationships extending beyond those between parents and children remains an under-researched aspect of family history. See her 'Where the Stranger Begins: The Question of Siblings in Historical Analysis', in *Worlds Between: Historical Perspectives on Gender and Class* (New York, 1995), 206–26, as well as Isabelle Bertaux-Wiame, 'The Pull of Family Ties: Intergenerational Relationships and Life Paths', in *International Yearbook of Oral History and Life Stories*, ii. 39–50.

[133] Janet de Vries (née Erskine), interview by author, 17 April 1995; Enid Boon, interview by author, 23 April 1995.

had a good time, tennis, riding . . .' She found work as a governess once her parents left but soon married a man who worked with her brother in the Indian Police. Enid's husband had also spent part of his childhood in India while his father, a British Army officer, was stationed there. Enid's maternal grandfather, moreover, had been an indigo planter in Bihar, making all the principal characters in her story second- or third-generation British-Indians supported by work across many state and private employment sectors.

While Enid Boon's account shows men and women both perpetuating family ties to India through their choice of career or spouse respectively, other British-Indian families like the Butlers became multi-generational mainly in the female line. Ann's parents were no longer in India when she went out in the 1890s for a protracted visit with one of several older brothers who had opted for careers there, meeting and marrying Montagu as a result; nearly thirty years later their daughter Iris married an army officer on Montagu's staff during his time as Governor of the Central Provinces.[134] (Illustration 6) Iris thus was a third-generation British-Indian on her mother's side and went on to add the fourth in the 1920s and 1930s, but the imperial tradition lasted only one generation for the men on her father's side. Montagu (an Old Haileyburian) and his brother Harcourt, who also rose to become a provincial Governor, neither came from British-Indian lineage nor had sons who followed in their footsteps. Although Montagu had entertained the notion that his son Rab 'might consider the bar here . . . our connection wd help [him] with a start', Rab had other ideas; as is well known, he embarked on a life in politics at home instead.[135] None the less, India seemingly remained part of his career fantasy, as he admitted in his memoir that the impossibility of fulfilling his dream of becoming Viceroy in the wake of India's independence 'can still give me the sharpest of pangs'. Thus thwarted in his own lofty imperial ambitions, he undoubtedly failed to reflect upon the extent to which so many members of his family had long both enjoyed and benefited from their time in India when, as Conservative Home Secretary in 1962, he stood squarely behind the Commonwealth Immigrants Act that severely circumscribed the opportunities for former colonial subjects to try their luck in Britain.[136]

As a well-educated man enjoying considerable financial support from his family (as well as his Courtauld in-laws) when embarking on professional life in the 1920s, Rab Butler could pick and choose from a wide range of professions

---

[134] OIOC, MSS Eur F225/18, letters from Ann Smith (Butler) to Montagu Butler, 1897–1901; MSS Eur F225/5, Montagu Butler to his mother, 6 Aug. 1926.

[135] OIOC, MSS Eur F225/11, Montagu Butler to Ann Butler, 27 July 1919.

[136] R. A. Butler, *The Art of the Possible: The Memoirs of Lord Butler* (London, 1971), 1; 205–6.

in either the metropole or the empire, and opted for the former. No one, however, imagined any future for his sister Iris other than marriage, and given that
her parents were still in India when she left school at 17 it comes as no surprise
that she soon became a wife and mother there rather than in Britain.[137] As
both Enid Boon's and Iris's stories suggest, while career decisions determined
whether sons of British-Indians spent their adult lives in India this was seldom
the case for daughters, even in the last decades of British rule. Some women like
Enid may have briefly worked as governesses or teachers prior to marriage, but
it was rare for British-Indian parents to encourage their daughters either to
train for or engage in paid work beyond a limited range of domestic or quasi-
domestic forms of temporary employment. India did provide a fertile field for
some British women wanting to pursue careers—particularly in medicine,
teaching, and through missionary endeavors—some of which long remained
closed to them in the metropole.[138] However, women seizing these opportunities may well have come from families without prior links to India given the
long-standing social and racial stigmas attached to many types of women's
employment within British-Indian society. As Chapter 2 argued, earning a living could easily connote both economic necessity and possible mixed-race
status for women, and would have counteracted the white genteel attributes
they were meant to have gained as a result of schooling in Britain. As Ann
Stoler has suggested, while European men could commonly view colonial life
as a realm of enhanced opportunity, European women might encounter far
more rigid restrictions on their domestic, economic, and political choices.[139]
Still, to judge from the women Mary Procida analyzes, many derived considerable satisfaction and empowerment as memsahibs, viewing themselves as their
husbands' active partners in the work of empire—even if they personally
received no remuneration for their contributions.[140]

---

[137] CSAA, MT20, Mrs Iris Portal, transcribed interview with Mary Thatcher, 15 Oct. 1974, 8.

[138] Burton, 'Contesting the Zenana', 369; Janaki Nair, 'Uncovering the Zenana: Visions of Indian
Womanhood in Englishwomen's Writings, 1813–1940', in Catherine Hall (ed.), *Cultures of Empire: A Reader: Colonizers in Britain and the Empire in the Nineteenth and Twentieth Centuries* (Manchester, 2000),
224–45; Kumari Jayawardena, *The White Woman's Other Burden: Western Women and South Asia During
British Colonial Rule* (New York, 1995), Parts I and II; Jane Haggis, 'White Women and Colonialism:
Towards a Non-Recuperative History', in Clare Midgley (ed.), *Gender and Imperialism* (Manchester, 1998),
45–75. On British women's work opportunities throughout the empire more generally, see many essays in
Nupur Chaudhuri and Margaret Strobel (eds.), *Western Women and Imperialism: Complicity and Resistance*
(Bloomington, IN, 1992).

[139] Ann Laura Stoler, *Carnal Knowledge and Imperial Power: Race and the Intimate in Colonial Rule*
(Berkeley, CA, 2002), 34, 42, 60–1.

[140] Mary A. Procida, *Married to the Empire: Gender, Politics and Imperialism in India, 1883–1947*
(Manchester, 2002).

Between returning to India and marrying, then, most young women focused mainly on leisure activities or perhaps unpaid voluntary work. In Iris Butler Portal's recollection, the two summers she spent in India before her marriage 'were completely given up to riotous living' in Simla.[141] It took a strong family culture that valued both intellectual pursuits and women's education for daughters of comfortably well-off parents to evade dominant female trends. Janet and Day Bannerman, for instance, successively rejoined their parents after leaving school in Edinburgh prior to the First World War. Having come several years before her sister, Janet wrote her letters describing an endless round of golf, tennis, and dances in Madras and the hill station of Kodaikanal, yet she soon became thoroughly bored with a repetitive and mindless social scene. 'I wish you could come out here for a bit and see all the lovely places about though you wouldn't think much of the club nor of lots of the people who look a most shoddy lot', she reported.[142] Upon arrival, Day opted to bide her time during the year prior to their father's retirement by enrolling in the Madras Medical College; she subsequently completed her studies in Edinburgh and practiced medicine there. Janet also left India when her parents retired and entered the University of Edinburgh, but ultimately returned to Madras at the age of 29. Long influenced by her parents' religious commitments, she trained as a missionary of the Church of Scotland and taught science at a school for Indian girls. She continued her work after her marriage to another missionary teacher in 1930, staying with her husband in India until they retired in 1961.[143] As the records detailing the future lives of the missionary daughters who attended Walthamstow Hall also suggest, women who entered mission work often remained actively employed after marriage, but throughout the imperial era far more British-Indian daughters maintained a multi-generational presence in the subcontinent through marriage alone.

Children of British-Indian parents thus often chose to add another chapter to their family's imperial history for many reasons. Young men returned because they were convinced that the empire offered them appealing career prospects, a belief fostered both by their families and their schools. Young women occasionally focused on work opportunities in India, but they were rare when compared with the far greater number who spent much of their adult lives overseas as wives and mothers without paid employment. For them,

[141] CSAA, MT20, Iris Portal interview, 8.

[142] NLS, Dep. 325/XII, Janet Bannerman to Day Bannerman, 25 Mar. 1913.

[143] Elizabeth Hay, *Sambo Sahib: The Story of Little Black Sambo and Helen Bannerman* (Edinburgh, 1981), 138, 145, 147.

returning to India after their school years in Britain and then staying may have been what they had long dreamed of once sent away as children, or largely a result of treading familiar and well-laid paths for women of their background. Regardless of the reasons behind individual decisions to continue British-Indian family traditions, however, periods spent in the metropole were crucial in enabling young men and women to re-enter colonial society at far more exalted levels than had they not had a British education. Alongside enabling socio-economic, cultural, and racial elevation in India, moreover, time in Britain also made imperial life more alluring because it revealed, often starkly, how status in the empire commonly failed to translate into status in the metropole. This was just as much the case during returns in adulthood as it was for children at school. As the next chapter argues, while few British-Indians ceased to claim Britain as 'home', sojourns there on furlough or after retiring made many identify even more strongly with imperial culture and the privileges they had enjoyed in India, creating yet another incentive for the next generation to maintain family ties with the empire.

5

From Somebodies to Nobodies: Returning Home to Britain and Perpetuating Overseas Connections

[Mr. and Mrs. Turton] reached their bungalow, low and enormous . . . Their withdrawal from the Club had broken up the evening, which, like all gatherings, had an official tinge. A community that bows the knee to a Viceroy and believes that the divinity that hedges a king can be transplanted, must feel some reverence for any viceregal substitute. At Chandrapore the Turtons were little gods; soon they would retire to some suburban villa, and die exiled from glory.

E. M. Forster, *A Passage to India* (1924)[1]

For thousands of Britons who lived and worked in India in the nineteenth and twentieth centuries, thoughts of home were never far away. Home meant their national homeland, Britain, or often more specifically England, Scotland, Ireland, or Wales. Attenuated though ties with Britain may have been after long periods spent overseas, a strong sense of personal connection commonly remained central to their lives and imaginations. This was true not only for transient British-Indians who periodically revisited Britain for schooling or on furlough, and planned ultimately to retire there; it also defined the identity of domiciled Europeans and Anglo-Indians who may never have seen the land their ancestors left.[2] Even if they lacked emotional attachments deriving from personal experiences, the British nation remained home by virtue of ancestral links with the colonizing power that provided these groups (to varying degrees) with cultural capital and a privileged position above the colonized

[1] E. M. Forster, *A Passage to India* (1924; repr. Harmondsworth, 1986), 49–50.
[2] Alison Blunt, ' "Land of our Mothers": Home, Identity, and Nationality for Anglo-Indians in British India, 1919–1947', *History Workshop Journal*, 54 (2002), 49–72.

in India.[3] For many of British descent in India, Britain was indeed an 'imagined community' of which they simultaneously claimed to be a part yet of which they had limited or no direct knowledge.[4] For British-Indians who did remain in intermittent contact with the metropole, however, home often contained, and stood for, much of what they longed for but lacked in India: British landscapes and a temperate climate, along with a culture to which these expatriates felt they belonged, and believed they understood. Absence from home, in short, commonly produced nostalgic sentiments that kept them mentally anchored within Britain even while living far away. In analyzing the connections between the experience of cultural (and physical) displacement and the construction of identity, Angelika Bammer stresses the 'vital double move between marking and recording absence and loss and inscribing presence'—an assessment that suggestively conveys how British-Indians' ideas about home were structured by migration and expatriate status.[5]

Home also had a second, and often much more potent, connotation for British-Indians: as a domestic space or place of residence in which daily life and family relations were conducted. For Britons connected with India, a home signifying a fixed household where a family came together could prove just as elusive as the national homeland. As Chapter 3 examined, family separations were a ubiquitous feature of colonial culture, with adults in India divided from children and other family members residing in Britain. The sanctity of the domestic sphere and the importance of family intimacy that symbolized the idealized middle-class household in Britain were not common features of daily life for those supported by Indian careers, and as a result many families anticipated the postponed attainment of these conditions upon their eventual return to the metropole.

Along with the prospect of reuniting with loved ones, parents also looked forward to going home in order to establish a stable domestic environment. Many occupations supporting British men and their dependants in India involved frequent transfers between one district, office, or cantonment and the next. Memoirs and letters contain countless stories of repeatedly packing and moving from one place to another, with each new accommodation filled with its own set of included or cheaply purchased furnishings. Given this continual

---

[3] See Angela Woollacott, *To Try Her Fortune in London: Australian Women, Colonialism, and Modernity* (Oxford, 2001), 3–4, 19, for an analysis of how white Australian women also imagined Britain as 'home' despite a lack of personal contact with the metropole.

[4] Benedict Anderson, *Imagined Communities: Reflections on the Origins and Spread of Nationalism*, rev. edn. (London, 1991).

[5] Angelika Bammer, 'Introduction', in Angelika Bammer (ed.), *Displacements: Cultural Identities in Question* (Bloomington, IN, 1994), p. xiv.

mobility, British-Indian families accumulated relatively few pieces of furniture and kept only a small quantity of portable decorative objects. Donald Scott, employed in the Posts and Telegraphs Department, described a familiar scenario in letters to his brother in the early 1930s:

As for keeping up a home, a government servant in India doesn't attempt it on account of the frequent transfers. It is no use buying good furniture if you have got to sell it at a sacrifice in a couple of years' time and clear off to a place a thousand miles away. Our principle in buying furniture is that if we only pay £2. for a thing, we can't possibly lose more than £2. on it when we sell off.

In consequence, he later summarized, 'our nomadic life prevents our making heirlooms of our furniture'.[6]

Returning to Britain upon retirement promised to end this impermanent, provisional, and increasingly wearying lifestyle, and men and women alike eagerly anticipated settling in a stable, long-term 'home at home'. Dream homes in Britain were filled not only with seldom-seen children long since sent back for their education, but also with newly acquired material manifestations of middle-class domesticity. Meanings of home for British-Indians thus united what were often highly idealized understandings of the nation, family intimacy, and domesticity.[7] The private spaces and artefacts in and around which these personal interactions were staged all constituted aspects of middle-class British life that were constantly challenged in India, yet which a return to their land of origins promised to provide.

Life in Britain, however, often fell far short of returned expatriates' high expectations in fundamental ways. Taking up themes briefly considered by B. J. Moore-Gilbert and Benita Parry, this chapter argues that years of residence in colonial communities created outlooks and provided material conditions that frequently made coming home both on furlough as well as in retirement

---

[6] OIOC, MSS Eur D1232/6, Donald Scott to Bert Scott, 15 Oct. 1930; D1232/9, Donald Scott to Bert Scott, 6 May 1931. For a similar account of buying and selling household goods, see Agatha Florence James, 'Housekeeping and House Management in India', in *The Lady At Home and Abroad* (London, 1898), 370–1.

[7] The multiple meanings of the highly evocative term 'home' have been explored by a number of scholars, such as those contributing to a special issue of *New Formations*, 17 (1992), 'The Question of "Home"'. Far fewer have examined understandings of 'home' as one's country of origin as well as a domestic milieu in an interconnected way; see however Eric Hobsbawm, 'Introduction', in Arlen Mack (ed.), *Home: A Place in the World* (New York, 1993), 61–4; Antoinette Burton, *Dwelling in the Archive: Women Writing House, Home, and History in Late Colonial India* (New York, 2003). Within the field of British history, two studies stand out for their perceptive linking of gendered domesticity with conceptions of national culture. See Wendy Webster, *Imagining Home: Gender, 'Race' and National Identity, 1945–64* (London, 1998); Alison Light, *Forever England: Femininity, Literature, and Conservatism Between the Wars* (London, 1991). Also see Rosemary Marangoly George, *The Politics of Home: Postcolonial Relocations and Twentieth-Century Fiction* (Cambridge, 1996).

culturally as well as economically unsatisfying.[8] Some misgivings applied equally to men and women, while others were gender-specific. British-Indians' often contentious relationship with the metropole had much to do with the impossibility of maintaining lifestyles and the level of status to which they had grown accustomed in India. India acted as the site of 'family fortunes', creating a durable and multi-faceted imperial identity dependent upon culture and livelihoods attained from a combination of British lineage and colonial careers and residence.[9] The ways many middle-class families' aspirations were both sustained and compromised by an uneasy balancing of two geographical and cultural arenas—the imperial and the metropolitan—appear in numerous accounts written both during and after years spent in India.

After examining British-Indian fantasies about their future lives in Britain, then, this chapter explores how many navigated what often proved to be turbulent waters when they tried to make themselves at home in their homeland, in large part by staying in contact with other returned colonials. Case studies of British-Indian communities in the metropole illustrate one way in which the nation's imperial dynamics had local as well as global impacts. It concludes by discussing how their metropolitan experiences and circumstances frequently became another reason why family involvement in India (that could also extend to other parts of the empire) commonly was perpetuated when children later followed in their parents' footsteps. Once established, the pattern of imperial migrations resulting in empowerment was likely to remain part of family life, even if this also meant rootlessness. A deeply ensconced lack of permanence due to continual movement between Britain and India and also within India may well have played its own part in encouraging a spirit of *Wanderlust* that led to disillusionment with a settled life at home as well as the next generation's desire to return overseas. Recalling his early years in the Indian Civil Service in a letter to his mother in 1911, Montagu Butler described this as a common disposition: 'during my seven years of settlement I was seldom more than fourteen days in any one place and this grows into one', he proposed. 'Whence the restlessness you observe in us'.[10] Multi-generational transience meant feeling at home in both Britain and India, yet at the same time in neither. British-Indians led—to use Homi Bhabha's terms—'interstitial' lives

---

[8] B. G. Moore-Gilbert considers their difficulties adjusting to British life in the 1840s to the 1880s in *Kipling and 'Orientalism'* (London, 1986), 42–7, as does Benita Parry for a later era in *Delusions and Discoveries: India in the British Imagination, 1880–1930*, 2nd edn. (London, 1998), 50–3.

[9] Leonore Davidoff and Catherine Hall, *Family Fortunes: Men and Women of the English Middle Class, 1780–1850* (Chicago, 1987).

[10] OIOC, MSS Eur F225/2, Montagu Butler to 'My dear Mother', 30 July 1911.

'in-between', and developed identities to match.[11] As Mrinalini Sinha puts it, they were part of an 'imperial social formation', a transnational domain formed by interaction between these multiple metropolitan and colonial arenas.[12]

CASTLES IN THE AIR: DOMESTIC FANTASIES

Correspondence between parents and children in the Talbot family during the 1880s and 1890s, introduced in Chapter 3, illustrates many dilemmas a father's Indian occupation could pose with respect to family relationships, domestic life, and social standing. Their letters highlight fantasies that centered on multiple conceptions of home as their land of origin that would simultaneously provide the setting in which families reunited within one household. Born in 1845, Adelbert Talbot began his career as an Indian Army officer and then moved into the Indian Political Service, in which he served between 1873 and 1900. Letters he and his wife, Agnes, wrote to their four children once the latter successively returned to England document their resentments stemming from family separations as well as their lack of a home they could call their own in either India or Britain. Although Agnes generally returned to England for several months every two years, Adelbert's travels were restricted by the periods of furlough he received, which often meant five-year intervals between visits with his children. In several letters written in 1883 to his 10-year-old daughter, Guendolen—whom he had not seen since she left India five years earlier—he told her how 'it is sad to me to think that I have been away from you now half your life but I hope to see you some time this year and to have my little girls to myself again for a few short weeks'.[13] He feared that 'you must have forgotten Papa quite by this time and will not know me if I walk into the house some fine day not very many months hence I hope'.[14] Happily, he was able to visit his children in England that year, but afterwards again had to wait years before their next reunion. In 1884 he answered Guendolen's question 'can't you come home this year?' by writing, 'I must follow my profession in order to get money to bring you up and all the others'.[15] However, his reassurance that 'we are not

---

[11] Homi K. Bhabha, 'Frontlines/Borderposts', in Bammer (ed.), *Displacements*, 269; see also his *The Location of Culture* (New York, 1993).

[12] Mrinalini Sinha, 'Britishness, Clubbability, and the Colonial Public Sphere: The Genealogy of an Imperial Institution in Colonial India', *Journal of British Studies*, 40/4 (2001), 491, 521.

[13] OIOC, MSS Eur E410/6, Adelbert Talbot to Guendolen Talbot, 20 Jan. 1883.

[14] Ibid., Adelbert Talbot to Guendolen Talbot, 9 Jan. 1883.

[15] Ibid., Adelbert Talbot to Guendolen Talbot, 17 Feb. 1884.

much more than three weeks post apart are we?' most likely consoled neither his daughter nor himself.[16]

These periods of prolonged separation caused both Agnes and Adelbert to comfort themselves as well as their children in letters by making plans for their future happiness when all would be together in England. Writing to Guendolen in 1889, Agnes told her that 'I used to be so fond of building castles in the air when I was a girl and I have the same inclination now in a way, but what I think of is how to furnish comfortably and prettily a small house in which Papa and I can spend the rest of our lives [with] you all I hope for some years and years.'[17] As an 11-year-old writing from her boarding school, Guendolen helped her parents to envision a future in which their 'coming home' to England would mean, first temporarily and then permanently, a house where they would all live together. 'This night last year was Mama's last night with us, I remember it well, but you will both be coming home in a year or less now won't you?', she wrote to her father. 'How delightful it will be for us to be all together again; Mama and I used to make castles in the air about it often, of how we should like our house to be.'[18] For many years, however, the Talbots' visions of home remained both imaginary and unrealized, a 'castle in the air'.

As Adelbert embarked upon his final years in the Indian Political Service in the 1890s, the family gradually made more concrete plans for his retirement. The Talbots' correspondence illuminates the extent to which a man's domestic fantasies might match, or possibly exceed, those of his wife and daughter, despite cultural emphases that cast home life as a predominantly feminine realm and preoccupation. While John Tosh convincingly suggests that many young men initially may have found colonial life attractive as a 'flight from domesticity' into a masculine imperial world, this assessment may have been less true for somewhat older men for whom the glamor of empire could be replaced by longings for a quiet family life in Britain.[19] After frequent transfers between different Indian princely states throughout his career, Adelbert Talbot looked forward to an English garden he and Agnes could call their own, in 'a place we could occupy for good'; similarly, he thoroughly enjoyed the notion of owning a full complement of household furnishings for the first time. As he reflected in amusement to Guendolen at the age of 47:

[16] Ibid., Adelbert Talbot to Guendolen Talbot, 30 May 1884.

[17] OIOC, MSS Eur E410/27, Agnes Talbot to Guendolen Talbot, 22 Aug. 1889.

[18] OIOC, MSS Eur E410/33, Guendolen Talbot to Adelbert Talbot, 23 Nov. [*c.*1884].

[19] John Tosh, 'Imperial Masculinity and the Flight from Domesticity in Britain, 1880–1914', in Timothy P. Foley et al. (eds.), *Gender and Colonialism* (Galway, 1995), 72–85. See also his book *A Man's Place: Masculinity and the Middle-Class Home in Victorian England* (New Haven, CT, 1999), 170–94.

Our only property consists at present of some [Persian] carpets and a few brass pots and pans! The furnishing of a house from top to bottom is an expensive affair, but must be managed somehow or other. It is curious beginning at our time of life to do that [which] young couples starting in it busy themselves about. However, that is the accident of our position as exiles.[20]

Before selecting furniture, however, the family needed a house for it to fill. Prior to Adelbert's retirement, Agnes left India to settle in England permanently once their two eldest daughters, Guendolen and Muriel, had finished school; Adelbert, meanwhile, eagerly awaited the chance to complete the family when his career ended. While he remained in India, however, he, Agnes, and Guendolen exchanged views through the post about how best to turn their visions of home into reality. Because they were on location the Talbot women embarked upon the search for a home, but they relied on Adelbert's advice and followed his orders from afar given their lack of experience with househunting and evaluating localities considered suitable for their social class in Britain. He adamantly steered his wife and daughter away from places that failed to match their status aspirations and financial resources. Barnet (outside London), for instance, was proposed and rejected, since it 'is not a nice neighbourhood, having no county society about it of any sort and mainly composed of cockney villas I fear. No, if we want something cheap it must be in a midland county, away from London', since the desirable areas of London itself were dismissed as too costly.[21] The gulf between their social 'needs' and their projected available income in retirement proved difficult to bridge, for the Talbots sought a home in a neighborhood which was simultaneously 'cheap' by their standards but did not sacrifice their respectability. Adelbert nevertheless remained confident that 'the best of castlets will be chosen eventually', within 'our means'.[22] They finally selected a home which fitted their exacting price and status specifications in Frant, outside Tunbridge Wells. Their long-cherished hopes for English domesticity, permanency, and family unity soon were shattered, however, by Agnes's untimely death after a brief illness in 1894. This misfortune disrupted all their carefully laid plans for their future together in England, as will be discussed further below.

The Talbots may be numbered among the many families supported by Indian occupations whose high hopes for retirement years at home never materialized. Even had Agnes Talbot lived, it appears likely that British residence

---

[20] OIOC, MSS Eur E410/6, Adelbert Talbot to Guendolen Talbot, 19 Sept. 1892.

[21] Ibid., Adelbert Talbot to Guendolen Talbot, 20 Jan. 1893.

[22] Ibid., Adelbert Talbot to Guendolen Talbot, 8 July 1892, 24 July 1892.

may well have fallen short of their seemingly unrealistic expectations. As the following pages argue, the Talbots' concerns about money and social standing were widely shared among returned British-Indians, yet at the same time their relative affluence cannot be over-emphasized. Adelbert's position in the colonial hierarchy, his income, and the family's educational background elevated them well above the vast majority of colonial families. Adelbert had attended Eton and then Woolwich, entering the Indian Army and later the Indian Political Service; he ended his career in 1900 as the Political Resident of Kashmir, and was knighted. In an era when the middle class was broadly defined as including families having incomes between £300 and £1,000 a year, Adelbert claimed to earn just over £2,000 in 1894; his salary later nearly doubled upon becoming Resident.[23] His son followed him to Eton at a cost of approximately £120 a year in school fees, and subsequently attended Oxford.[24] Following their education, his daughters spent time with their mother in Germany and Switzerland to enhance their knowledge of German and French; later, they were presented at Court, thanks to the influence exerted on their behalf by the family's wealthy distant relations.[25] Before Adelbert's retirement, then, their finances as well as their cultural practices placed the Talbots well above the upper limits of the ordinary middle class. Although their income decreased when Adelbert's career ended and he claimed to lack substantial savings or a private income beyond his salary or pension, they none the less remained comfortably situated within the upper reaches of the British bourgeoisie.[26]

Most retired families fell far below the Talbots in terms of income since few men reached comparable high-ranking positions within the more prestigious branches of government service. British-Indian incomes varied drastically according to occupation, conditions of recruitment, and seniority, while pensions correspondingly took account of the total years of work and the position a man ultimately attained within his profession.[27] While most retirees still qualified as middle class, they had considerably less income at their disposal

---

[23] For middle-class incomes, see Dudley Baxter, *The National Income* (London, 1868), 15, adjusted to conform with Sir Josiah Stamp's estimates in *British Incomes and Property* (London, 1916), 449, cited in Harold Perkin, *The Rise of Professional Society: England since 1880* (London, 1989), 29. In 1906 one commentator defined British families with annual incomes of between £160 and £700 as living in 'comfort', those with more than £700 as having 'riches', and those with under £160 as subsisting in 'poverty'. See L. G. Chiozza Money, *Riches and Poverty*, 3rd edn. (London, 1906), 42.

[24] OIOC, MSS Eur E410/7, Adelbert Talbot to Guendolen Talbot, 29 Sept. 1894, 9 Nov. 1894.

[25] OIOC, MSS Eur E410/5, Adelbert Talbot to Guendolen Talbot, 12 April 1891; MSS Eur E410/8, Adelbert Talbot to Guendolen Talbot, 11 May 1895.

[26] OIOC, MSS Eur E410/7, Adelbert Talbot to Guendolen Talbot, 13 July 1894.

[27] On the wide range of salaries and pensions within particular sectors of government service, see for example *The India List and India Office List for 1900* (London, 1900), 161–72, along with other editions.

than they enjoyed during the breadwinner's working years. The most striking examples of this were widows whose husbands had died before retirement age, along with families in which the father was forced to retire prematurely due to physical incapacity. Widows or invalided men often had young or adolescent children still in school to support on limited resources, and family pensions could be quite low if a man had failed to make additional contributions while still employed. In the Indian Medical Service in the early twentieth century, for instance, the basic allowance for widows ranged between £40 and £160 a year according to the deceased medical officer's professional grade; his orphaned children each received between £10 and £45 annually.[28] These rates could be substantially higher, but because middle-class families during and after the Victorian period were commonly underinsured in case of death many widows were left with incomes of £100 to £300 a year or even less and reduced to lower middle-class status.[29] Even when husbands and wives survived to return to Britain together with some level of middle-class financial means, however, the transition remained fraught with distressing economic as well as cultural readjustments. British-Indians' homecomings could appear anything but welcoming, and being solidly middle class often fell disappointingly short of the status they had enjoyed in the empire.

EXILED FROM GLORY: DOMESTIC DISAPPOINTMENTS

Accounts describing returns home contained many common features between the mid-nineteenth century and the era of decolonization. Edward Waring's 1866 guidebook for the long-absent 'native', *The Tropical Resident at Home*, highlighted issues that became endlessly reiterated by later writers. Waring's intended audience included those beginning permanent reacclimation to the metropole upon retiring from work not only in India but also other colonies, particularly in the West Indies as he himself had done. The advice he and other authors offered to the newly repatriated indicates how home could become unfamiliar and unknowable without counsel to those long based overseas, who

---

[28] Major B. G. Seton and Major J. Gould, *The Indian Medical Service: Being a Synopsis of the Rules and Regulations Regarding Pay, Pensions, Leave, Examination, Etc.* (Calcutta, 1912), 91–134.

[29] Cynthia Curran, 'Private Women, Public Needs: Middle-Class Widows in Victorian England', *Albion*, 25/2 (1993), 217–36. For definitions of lower middle-class status and incomes, see Geoffrey Crossick, 'The Emergence of the Lower Middle Class in Britain: A Discussion', in Geoffrey Crossick (ed.), *The Lower Middle Class in Britain, 1870–1914* (London, 1977), 34. On the general provision of pensions in Britain, see Pat Thane, *Old Age in English History: Past Experiences, Present Issues* (Oxford, 2000); Leslie Hannah, *Inventing Retirement: The Development of Occupational Pensions in Britain* (Cambridge, 1986).

were felt likely to benefit from assistance in relearning its intricacies. Waring began by seeking to temper the high expectations and idealizations of Britain many had built from afar. For those who longed for its temperate climate during years on the hot and dusty Indian plains, Waring cautioned that 'you have forgotten or ignored the cold . . . cheerless days of October and November . . . those dense, pea-soup-like fogs which render gas at mid-day a necessity; the thick, drizzling rain . . . the long, dreary winter evenings'.[30]

Readjusting to the weather proved considerably easier than accepting their loss of status upon return, he argued:

Another source of disappointment arises from a feeling, which is more or less experienced by all, but especially by those who have held high and important positions in India and other portions of our colonial empire, of their comparative insignificance as individuals in the busy world of England, and of London in particular. For years, perhaps, in their distant homes, they have been held in high and deserved respect, have exercised a wide and powerful influence, have been leaders in the society in which their lot has been cast . . . They come to London, and find that they are nobodies . . . they are speedily lost in the crowd.[31]

A fictional representation of the stark contrast between British-Indian lives before and after retirement by Alice Perrin—the daughter of a general in the Bengal Cavalry and the wife of a Public Works Department officer—supports Waring's account. Perrin's 1912 novel *The Anglo-Indians* provides an in-depth depiction of the return to Britain by juxtaposing the Indian lives of John Fleetwood, a 'mightily senior civilian' in the Indian Civil Service, his wife, Emily, and their three daughters, with their metropolitan aftermath. At their large bungalow encircled by verandas, an orange grove, and 'a small village of stables and servants' quarters' for the thirty Indian domestics they employed, 'the Fleetwoods were people of consequence and could live luxuriously and entertain with lavish generosity'. John relished hunting, fishing, and riding along with the prestige and responsibility his occupation brought, but all came to an end when he reached the compulsory retirement age of 55: 'a difficult time lay ahead for the Fleetwood family when they should find themselves in England, pensioned, unimportant . . . with nothing considerable in the way of savings, and no realization of the cost of living at home'.[32]

---

[30] Edward J. Waring, *The Tropical Resident at Home: Letters Addressed to Europeans Returning from India and the Colonies on Subjects Connected with their Health and General Welfare* (London, 1866), 5–6.

[31] Ibid., 14–15.

[32] Alice Perrin, *The Anglo-Indians* (London, 1912), 18–19. On Perrin's writing and life, see Parry, *Delusions*, 78–102, 266.

Their new circumstances became apparent immediately upon arriving home. On his first day back in London, John Fleetwood's walk through the city proved jarring, not only physically but also culturally:

the crowd irritated him—hurrying, heedless people who jostled and pushed . . . [and] who blocked the pavements without consideration . . . an omnibus passed him packed with people . . . He recognized the profile of a fellow-civilian, rather senior to himself, who had retired two or three years ago after holding a very high appointment . . . Logan was on a state elephant last time he saw him, going to open some show or other—now here he was in a 'bus, squeezed up in a row of very ordinary people, looking very ordinary himself; paying a penny for his fare![33]

Although written nearly fifty years apart, Waring's and Perrin's accounts suggest that returnees' complaints took on familiar and durable contours. Earlier renditions of their contrasting lives in India and Britain in fact may have directly influenced later authors. Perrin's Edwardian story detailing the descent from elephant to omnibus bears suspicious resemblance to an anecdote in the novelist M. M. Kaye's memoir published in 1990. Recounting her parents' chance meeting in London with an old friend from India—a former Governor of Assam—once they had all retired in the 1920s, Kaye described how he

recalled wistfully that on the last occasion that they had met was on an official visit to the Viceroy and had arrived in Calcutta in the Governor's private yacht, to travel up to Simla in a special train complete with platoons of ADCs, assorted hangers-on and acres of red carpet. And now here he was, fighting for a strap on the Underground![34]

Such comparable renditions of changed standing upon returning to the metropole suggest the interplay between fictionalized and 'real' stories, both of which relied upon their authors' understandings of a familiar social milieu and its discontents. Whatever their veracity, Waring's, Perrin's, and Kaye's accounts contribute to a wider paradigm of British-Indian experiences which, if not shared by all, became at least a common resilient trope among this community.

Expressions of displeasure at the prospect of being merely 'ordinary', insignificant 'nobodies' in Britain who were 'lost in the crowd' and treated 'without consideration' derived largely from two interrelated ways that those returning from India saw their status decline. The first pertains to their white racial identity and its differential value in Britain and India, although this is rarely acknowledged directly in memoirs or other renditions of colonial retirement. This is perhaps unsurprising; as Catherine Hall and other scholars have

---

[33] Perrin, *Anglo-Indians*, 148–9.
[34] M. M. Kaye, *The Sun in the Morning: My Early Years in India and England* (New York, 1990), 413–14.

explored, whiteness has traditionally been a neglected racial category.[35] Urging the inclusion as opposed to the 'active silencing' of race in analyses of white English identity, Hall stresses that 'white men and women experience their gender, their class, their sexual identities through the lens of race just as black men and women do. The difference is that while black has been a signifier of subjection, white has been a signifier of domination, and the dominant rarely reflect on their dominance in the ways that the subjected reflect on their subjection'.[36] Britons with direct experiences in imperial arenas such as India, however, were perfectly poised to reflect on the privileges that whiteness brought in the empire, even if few chose to write about it explicitly. While residing in an arena where white Britons were a small minority amidst a large colonized population, whiteness was one of the most symbolic attributes which identified them as rulers rather than ruled. Even those situated beneath the higher echelons of British-Indian society enjoyed greatly enhanced prestige and opportunities because of their racial status and national affiliation to the imperial power. Upon returning to the metropole, however, they shared this symbol of imperial privilege with nearly everyone. One of the few accounts to address the different ways whiteness was experienced at home and in India is George Roche's memoir detailing his return to Britain as a child after the First World War. Roche recalled his confusion when encountering the crowds on Oxford Street, where 'everyone was white'; at Harrods, his family were attended by 'white assistants', while in India the women working in the department stores they visited were typically Anglo-Indian; and, at his grandfather's house, 'it seemed strange that . . . the servants were white. I had never seen white ladies in that role before.'[37] In Britain unlike in India, whiteness was no longer a symbol of empowerment and failed to separate British-Indians from mass society and, more specifically, from the working classes. Rather, they merged with the crowds in the street and joined the throngs of passengers on buses or the Underground, with not an elephant in sight to elevate them.

---

[35] Within a growing scholarship across a range of national contexts, several key examinations of whiteness include Ruth Frankenberg (ed.), *Displacing Whiteness: Essays in Social and Cultural Criticism* (Durham, NC, 1997); Woollacott, *To Try Her Fortune*; Ann Laura Stoler, *Race and the Education of Desire: Foucault's History of Sexuality and the Colonial Order of Things* (Durham, NC, 1995); David Roediger, *The Wages of Whiteness: Race and the Making of the American Working Class* (London, 1991); Grace Elizabeth Hale, *Making Whiteness: The Culture of Segregation in the South, 1890–1940* (New York, 1998); Vron Ware, *Beyond the Pale: White Women, Racism, and History* (London, 1992); Richard Dyer, *White* (London, 1997).

[36] Catherine Hall, *White, Male, and Middle Class: Explorations in Feminism and History* (New York, 1992), 206, 21.

[37] George Roche, *Childhood in India: Tales from Sholapur*, ed. by Richard Terrell (London, 1994), 10–13, 20–1.

If most British-Indians wrote little about their racial identity, they made up for this by focusing relentlessly on the interconnected issue of class. In India race combined with class to enable them to constitute what Francis Hutchins described as a 'middle-class aristocracy', living 'in a manner well above the station from which they had sprung in England'.[38] David Cannadine reiterates this argument, stressing that many 'sought to replicate Britain's social hierarchy overseas, on account of their *enhanced position within it*'.[39] For those belonging to Britain's 'second eleven' and falling below the highest levels of metropolitan society, time in India could provide career opportunities and salaries far more difficult to obtain at home, along with other trappings of power including numerous servants, honor, and prestige.[40] In his book *At Home on Furlough* published in 1875, Charles Lawson summarized the different status men who chose Indian careers might have expected had they remained in Britain:

There is no small temptation for a man who has discovered that he is somebody in India, to think that had he remained at home, he would have been recognised as a somebody in England, and been rewarded in proportion to his present estimate of his merits. But it is pretty certain that a very small proportion even of the highest officials in India could, had they remained at home, have found the means of earning a comfortable livelihood . . . Had the average Anglo-Indian for example, never gone abroad, he might have become Lord Chancellor, Prime Minister, Field Marshall, Admiral of the Fleet, Speaker, or something of that sort; but . . . the chances were in favour of his lapsing into lifelong genteel poverty.[41]

Incomes and occupations that enabled exalted lifestyles in a colonial arena, then, were not sufficient to make British-Indians part of the upper classes—or 'a somebody', as defined here—when they returned to the metropole on furlough, nor were the reduced pensions which replaced full salaries upon retirement. Attitudes about the minimum amount considered 'necessary' in retirement illustrate status ideals that appear fairly widespread. In the 1860s Waring believed that at least £500 a year was essential, for 'no married man, who in the tropics has held the position of "an officer and a gentleman", can secure the comforts of home life . . . with an income of less amount than this';

---

[38] Francis G. Hutchins, *The Illusion of Permanence: British Imperialism in India* (Princeton, NJ, 1967), 107–8.

[39] David Cannadine, *Ornamentalism: How the British Saw Their Empire* (London, 2001), 130, 126, 128; see also Joseph A. Schumpeter's suggestions in *Imperialism and Social Classes* (New York, 1951).

[40] On India-connected Britons being part of the 'second eleven' at home, see J. M. Bourne, *Patronage and Society in Nineteenth-Century England* (London, 1986), 181; see also P. J. Marshall's discussion of their social origins in 'British Immigration into India in the Nineteenth Century', in P. C. Emmer and M. Moerner (eds.), *European Expansion and Migration: Essays on the Intercontinental Migration from Africa, Asia, and Europe* (Oxford, 1992), 188–90.

[41] Charles A. Lawson, *At Home on Furlough*, 2nd ser. (Madras, 1875), 465–6.

by the 1930s, 'Mauser'—the author of *How to Live in England on a Pension*—assumed he was writing for civil and military officers who would have at least £800 a year, and ideally more.[42]

Despite such assertions as to how much income was deemed vital in Britain, many retiring from India had considerably less at their disposal. Donald Scott in the Posts and Telegraphs Department wrote home to his brother in 1932 and expressed his reaction to reading 'Mauser's' book in no uncertain terms:

The johnny who wrote the book assumed that it was not possible to have any comfort in England on less than about £1000 or £1500 a year, so his views did not carry so much weight with me . . . I felt that I could have given him a tip or two on how to live in England on £300 a year. I am pretty sure I shall not have a thousand to live on after retirement. The Irish sweep has let me down again.[43]

He continued his rant in a later letter, repeating, 'yes, the ass who wrote about how to live on a thousand a year made me sick. I dare swear there is not one in a thousand of the people in England who gets a thousand a year, even in his dreams, and yet this fool wrote as if even a thousand a year would be a pretty tight pinch and take some managing.'[44] Scott, whose brother worked as a commercial traveller, came from a lower middle-class background, and retiring on £300 a year meant that in later life he would maintain this status once he returned to Britain. Although he frequently alluded to limited finances in his letters, he reflected upon his status *vis-à-vis* social superiors in a tone more joking than angry, conveying no resentment about his exclusion from richer and more powerful company in India. As Peter Bailey suggests, 'self-depreciating humor is one of the significant yet unacknowledged markers of the [lower middle] class', illustrating 'an acute sensitivity to social difference and the nuances of status that could be turned outward to puncture pretensions in the larger world'.[45]

Donald Scott's attitudes provide a useful reminder that many renditions of British-Indian life are overly dependent upon examining the more elite and wealthy sectors and largely exclude any consideration of the many who fell outside them. Just as importantly, his views underscore how readjustment to Britain may have been more fraught for colonial elites than for those in less elevated occupational sectors, since the former contrasted their domestic standing

---

[42] Waring, *Tropical Resident*, 233; 'Mauser' (pseud.), *How to Live in England on a Pension: A Guide for Public Servants Abroad and at Home* (London, 1930).

[43] OIOC, MSS Eur D1232/10, Donald Scott to Bert Scott, 11 Oct. 1932.

[44] Ibid., Donald Scott to Bert Scott, 24 Nov. 1932.

[45] Peter Bailey, 'White Collars, Gray Lives? The Lower Middle Class Revisited', *Journal of British Studies*, 38/3 (1999), 288–9.

with that of Britain's upper classes. ' "Old Indians" of the present day, in comparison with the upper ten thousand of English society, are a poor class',
Waring asserted.[46] Similarly, when M. M. Kaye recalled that after her father
retired in the 1920s her family's annual income amounted to £700—placing
them financially between general practitioners and dentists, who in the late
1920s earned an average of £756 and £601 a year respectively—she stressed 'how
little we had to live on'; socially, her frames of reference were the 'Débutante
Set' and the London Season, despite her family's distance from these circles.[47]
While their standard of living far exceeded that of the vast majority of the
British population, frequent reference was made to their 'comparative poverty
at home', as 'Mauser' phrased it in 1930.[48] 'Poverty' could mean resorting to
crowded buses or the London Underground, or simply their exclusion from
the best circles of metropolitan society after they had once been members of
their equivalents in India.

As these statements indicate, on some levels the complaints voiced by mid-
Victorian repatriates had much in common with the grievances of their interwar successors. Accounts written about the interwar years and their aftermath,
however, indicate that the increased costs of living and taxes in Britain which
reduced the real value of pensions made the transition from working life in
India to retirement years at home more difficult than before. A letter to the
editor of the Indian newspaper *The Pioneer* from a newly retired Indian Army
colonel in 1919 described how higher prices for clothing, food, rents, and
houses made it 'a safe estimate to add at least a third to the general cost of living
in England compared with pre-war costs'. He advised others about to retire to
bring back as many household goods and clothes as possible in order to
decrease the costs of resettlement. Yet there was a limit to the comforts enjoyed
in India that might be imported. 'Be prepared to pay high wages for servants',
he stressed, 'they are very difficult to get. My wife and I find it absolutely necessary to do most of the housework ourselves. We have a small house and are
lucky to get one servant.'[49]

The 'servant problem' in Britain provides one of the best illustrations of both
the continuities of British-Indian lifestyles and discontents across this period as

---

[46] Waring, *Tropical Resident*, 62; see also Lawson, *At Home*, 465.
[47] Kaye, *Sun in the Morning*, 434–5, 430; Alan A. Jackson, *The Middle Classes, 1900–1950* (Nairn, 1991), 336.
Even the high-ranking 'Heaven Born' of the Indian Civil Service were said to experience financial 'difficulties' after retirement, and few entrants to this service were of upper-class origin. See Bradford Spangenberg,
British Bureaucracy in India: Status, Policy and the I.C.S. in the Late 19th Century (Columbia, MO, 1976), 51,
19.
[48] 'Mauser', *How to Live*, 1930 edn., p. x.
[49] 'Indian Army Colonel', 'Living in England: To The Editor', *The Pioneer*, 9 June 1919.

well as the changed circumstances after the First World War. Complaints about British domestic servants were common well before then; as one returned memsahib noted in 1898, 'from long experiences at home and abroad I have learned to look on fault-finding with servants as a national failing of the English', both when in Britain and in India.[50] Alice Perrin's rendition of the Fleetwoods' dissatisfaction with both the number and quality of those they employed further exemplifies this long-standing tendency. After having thirty servants in India, the four they could afford at home seemed insufficient. Furthermore, 'when servants stayed they were usually incompetent; when they knew their work and did it they either had illnesses, or did not like something connected with the situation and gave notice. They came and went, principally went.' Emily Fleetwood summed up her attitude towards her English maids and cooks by sighing, 'no one knows what I suffer with these people!'[51] The sharp decline of domestic service as an institution during the interwar years, however, meant that many middle-class families could only afford one maid, who was increasingly likely to work as a 'daily help' as opposed to 'living in'.[52]

Stories of the relationship between retired British-Indians and their 'maids of all work' in the 1920s and 1930s offer some of the most detailed depictions of their attitude towards reduced circumstances after leaving India. In his book first published in 1930, 'Mauser'—also a retired Indian Army officer—channeled many grievances into repeated diatribes against 'the modern maid'. While discussing ways to reduce fuel bills, for example, he portrayed those employing servants but needing to economize as at the mercy of inherently wasteful members of the 'lower orders':

A gas-cooker is very good, and if you use it yourself it will be effectual and economical; but if a domestic uses it you are helpless to control it. The extravagance of a burning jet never seems to strike the lower orders unless they are paying for it themselves . . . The modern maid will leave a gas fire burning in one room while she sits in another, without batting an eyelash. She doesn't have to pay.[53]

Given the increased availability of alternative occupations for working-class women, finding and retaining capable maids necessitated sacrifices by their employers, for 'in these days one must bow before the domestic help'.[54] The

---

[50] James, 'Housekeeping', 372.

[51] Perrin, *Anglo-Indians*, 165, 193, 211.

[52] Miriam Glucksmann, *Women Assemble: Women Workers and the New Industries in Inter-War Britain* (London, 1990), 37–8, 50–4, 244–52; Judy Giles, *Women, Identity and Private Life in Britain, 1900–1950* (London, 1995), 84, 133–8.

[53] 'Mauser', *How to Live*, 1930 edn., 18.

[54] Ibid., 58.

contrast between servant-keeping in India and Britain could not have been stronger, for along with being much more numerous, 'Indian menials' were, as 'Mauser' put it, 'maddening but biddable'—a succinct illustration of how drastically the ability both to hire servants as well as dictate their conditions of work and attain status through the ability to do so was thought to have faded once British-Indians came home.[55]

Such interwar conditions described by male writers do not refer to gender-specific ways retired couples experienced them. In several crucial respects, however, the loss of status upon coming home discussed thus far had very different manifestations for men and women. When a man's working life in India ended, his wife's responsibilities typically became more of a burden once they resettled in Britain. Women had long borne the brunt of the household economies that British domesticity necessitated, but with fewer domestic servants after the war women were forced to play a more active role in undertaking the physical aspects of housework than before, when their primary responsibilities were more likely to involve managing other women's labor than doing manual work themselves. M. M. Kaye recalled how in the 1920s her mother had to do many household chores herself for the first time, given the scarcity both of servants and money to pay them. One anecdote described the day her mother 'answered the doorbell wearing a duster tied round her head, a vast and rather grubby cooking apron over her dress, and with her hands blackened and her face liberally adorned by the dark smudges that an amateur at the job is apt to acquire when first trying her hand at cleaning either silver or brass'—to find neighbors paying a welcome visit:

Confronted by two elderly, grey-haired ladies dressed in their best . . . armed with calling cards and inquiring in impeccable upper-class accents if her mistress was at home, Mother said baldly: 'Yes.' And, having ushered them into the drawing-room, fled upstairs . . . and returned after a few minutes looking as serene as any lady of leisure, apologizing for keeping them waiting. Believe it or not, they never realized that the 'maid' and the 'mistress' were one and the same.[56]

Kaye's rendition of her mother's transition from privileged memsahib in India to a woman of indeterminate status somewhere between domestic servant and 'lady of leisure' in Britain suggests how women might find their domestic role reversed once they left colonial life behind. As one woman wrote in the journal *Overseas* in 1931, 'many a wife whose husband is due for retire-

[55] 'Mauser' (pseud.), *How to Live in England on a Pension: A Guide to Public Servants Abroad and at Home,* new and enlarged edn. (London, 1934), 152.
[56] Kaye, *Sun in the Morning,* 411–12.

ment looks forward only with dread to the tussle she knows awaits her' while living on a pension that amounted to half their former income. Necessary economies included drastically reducing the scale of entertaining and largely curtailing other leisure activities, but the biggest savings, she felt, came when 'all but the minimum of paid services [were] dispensed with'. New electrical household technology was widely advocated as a cheaper substitute for servants. 'It is always the wisest plan to spend every possible penny on labour-saving devices', this writer added; 'electric cookers, irons, kettles, ideal boilers, vacuum cleaners . . . so that where possible the work of the house can be done by the lady of the house herself'.[57] 'Mauser' wrote in the same vein, recommending modern houses that enabled 'all the cleverly-designed electric labour-savers' to be 'a boon to the housewife in these days of servant difficulty', and also suggested forgoing servants altogether as a result.[58] Despite the advantages of new appliances to those able to afford them, however, it is debatable if they were truly labor-saving if used by women who formerly had most of their housework done by others. As Ruth Schwartz Cowan has noted of developments in household technology, 'the labor saved by labor-saving devices was not that of the housewife but of her helpers'.[59] With domestic service in decline, middle-class women spent more time doing housework regardless of how many appliances they might own.[60]

Men's experiences after leaving India often stood in complete contrast to that of their wives. While ex-memsahibs were portrayed as having far greater domestic responsibilities once their husbands retired, men were repeatedly said to find themselves at a loss to fill the empty hours. Alongside her description of a woman's new domestic burdens, the woman writing in *Overseas* depicted the typical husband as 'a busy man suddenly turned idle. He has a good chance of at least twenty years of life before him. What is he going to do?'[61] Yet another army officer writing in the 1950s encapsulated the difference between men's and women's experiences in ways that illustrate their longevity:

Your wife *never* retires. If you retire from work at home it merely means that she goes from a large sink to a small one. If you retire from work overseas it's considerably worse

[57] Ella F. M. Leakey, 'On Retiring', *Overseas*, 16/190 (1931), 58–60.

[58] 'Mauser' (pseud.), *How to Live in England on a Pension*, 3rd edn. (London, 1938), 41; 'Mauser', *How to Live*, 1934 edn., 155.

[59] Ruth Schwartz Cowan, *More Work for Mother: The Ironies of Household Technology from the Open Hearth to the Microwave* (New York, 1983), 178.

[60] Adrian Forty, *Objects of Desire: Design and Society Since 1750* (London, 1995), 210; Sue Bowden and Avner Offer, 'The Technological Revolution that Never Was: Gender, Class, and the Diffusion of Household Appliances in Interwar England', in Victoria de Grazia with Ellen Furlough (eds.), *The Sex of Things: Gender and Consumption in Historical Perspective* (Berkeley, CA, 1996), 268.

[61] Leakey, 'On Retiring', 58.

for her as, bereft of her native cook, she'll find herself for the first time regarding the baleful glare of a very dead cod on a plate and wondering how on earth to turn it into lunch.

That's another point. Lunch. For years and years she's seen you off to the office, barracks, or factory, knowing that you'll have lunch there. And now, not only are you cluttering up the place all morning, but you'll be wandering in at 1 p. m. demanding a hearty meal.[62]

Indeed, authors ranging chronologically from Waring to this mid-twentieth-century writer rarely failed to highlight boredom as a central aspect of colonial men's retirement years in Britain. Because the retirement age in Indian state services was 55, men had long faced the dilemma of what Charles Lawson had called 'compulsory idleness' when they were still energetic.[63] Writers suggested a number of ways to combat forced inactivity and a general lack of purpose once 'the guillotine of completed service' had been reached.[64] Waring optimistically described the mental stimulation men could find by taking up new hobbies including 'entomology, conchology, and geology', while 'Mauser' suggested gardening, hiking, carpentry, or becoming a boy scout master.[65] Low cost was the key factor recommending these new amusements, since many forms of sport men had enjoyed in India proved unaffordable in Britain on a pension. In *The Anglo-Indians*, for example, John Fleetwood's riding, shooting, and fishing became 'a dream of the past' in England, and the only recreational expense he allowed himself was his club membership, where he 'talked with men he had known in India, smoked and read the papers, and found he looked forward to seeing *The Pioneer Mail*'.[66] Should men wish either to retire early or supplement their pensions (as well as fill their time) by finding a paying occupation, moreover, they were repeatedly told that they would have limited success because they were middle aged and lacked experience that was marketable outside colonial settings.[67] According to 'Mauser', it was only possible to earn substantial additional income by working independently, and he recommended starting a small fruit farm by purchasing a house with additional

[62] W. P. A. Robinson, *How to Live Well on Your Pension* (London, 1955), 72–3.

[63] Lawson, *At Home*, 464.

[64] Perrin, *Anglo-Indians*, 204–5.

[65] Waring, *Tropical Resident*, 23–39; 'Mauser', *How to Live*, 1930 edn., 167–77.

[66] Perrin, *Anglo-Indians*, 187, 164; see also 179, 218, 225, 227.

[67] Lawson, *At Home*, 462–4; Perrin, *Anglo-Indians*, 183–4; 'Mauser', *How to Live*, 1930 edn., 113–16, 145–55. Despite these commentators' pessimism, however, some retirees did manage to embark on second careers after leaving India; see Takehiko Honda, 'Indian Civil Servants, 1892–1937: An Age of Transition', D.Phil thesis, Oxford University (1996).

acres adjacent to it. In this way, men might earn several hundred extra pounds annually as long as they remained physically active.[68]

Thus, although men's difficulties readjusting to British life were distinct from women's in many ways, both sexes underwent a substantial transition from one laboring role to another less empowered one. Women often undertook more domestic work formerly done by servants after their husbands retired while men searched for new activities once their years as salaried professionals ended, but reduced financial circumstances underlay their experiences irrespective of gender. Of course, these conditions also characterized the later part of the life cycle of many middle-class retired men and their wives who had no overseas connections, but returned British-Indians' response to them reflected their specific imperial background. Their new socio-economic status worked in tandem with shared cultural understandings developed during their years in India to influence how many sought ways to ease the transition between their old and new lives.

As the next pages examine, many men and women returning from overseas attempted to mitigate feelings of dissatisfaction and alienation at home by maintaining contact with a colonial social network. In Perrin's novel *The Anglo-Indians*, John Fleetwood's frequent visits to his London club to meet other men who had worked in India illustrate this phenomenon, as did his family's place of residence. After living temporarily in South Kensington, the Fleetwoods had greatly exceeded their income and economized by moving into a house appropriately named 'Combe Down' in 'Norbleton', a thinly disguised depiction of Norbiton. This suburb had two features recommending it: lower costs of living than in 'respectable' neighborhoods in central London, and proximity to friends from India who had previously settled there upon retiring.[69] Although fictional, this enclave of returned colonials described by Perrin in the early twentieth century had many counterparts in reality. In the 1860s, Waring described the already common tendency of 'old Indians' to 'fix their tents in close proximity to each other' for cultural as well as economic reasons. 'When brought into immediate contact with the richer classes, they feel their poverty, and this leads them to enter into a common cause, and they form these small communities, colonies you may almost call them, where something like an equality of means exists amongst the members', he wrote. Furthermore, they came together because of shared experiences:

---

[68] 'Mauser', *How to Live*, 1930 edn., 114–44, 154; 1934 edn., 113.
[69] Perrin, *Anglo-Indians*, 184–92.

Though they may never have met before, they have topics of conversation which have special interest to each; they have resided, perhaps at different periods, in the same localities; they have hosts of mutual acquaintances . . . and they understand each other's language; they require no aid from a dictionary to understand the meaning of '*Durzee*' or *Ghorawallah*, and they do not want an explanation if you should happen to speak of a *pucka* house! In fact, their past lives and present ideas cannot do otherwise than form a strong bond of union.[70]

Common imperial backgrounds thus created outlooks that set them apart from others sharing their socio-economic status in Britain, enhancing the appeal of living in a 'colony' of similar individuals upon returning home.

Despite the diversity in their incomes while on leave or in retirement, then, returned British-Indians often shared similar priorities and inclinations. Many of course did not actively seek out the company of other repatriates while in Britain and could be found scattered randomly throughout the country. None the less, a substantial number did settle where others like themselves had become a noticeable presence. Profiles of characteristic enclaves—areas of London and particularly Bayswater, Cheltenham Spa, Eastbourne and other towns on England's south coast, and Bedford—show how 'colonies' of British-Indians in Britain, regardless of their specific socio-economic contours, provided cultural comfort and met daily social needs for all age groups.[71] Women were often more visible than men in these communities, given that many spent time in Britain with their children during their husbands' working years. 'Grass widows' were joined by actual widows who also remained defined by their

---

[70] Waring, *Tropical Resident*, 59, 62–3. *Durzee* translates as 'tailor', *Ghorawallah* as 'white man', and *pucka* as 'genuine', or 'proper'.

[71] This chapter covers only some of the better known and more fully documented enclaves of returned colonials in Britain. Waring, *Tropical Resident*, 64, 228, notes communities in Brighton, Leamington Spa, Bath, Tunbridge Wells, and Clifton; Lawson, *At Home on Furlough*, 202, 317–31, mentions similar towns but also includes Matlock and Buxton. Little contemporary attention and subsequent historical work has focused on British-Indian enclaves in Scotland, but brief reference has been made to neighborhoods in Edinburgh in 'An Anglo-Indian', *Our Parish, All About It; or, Rural Scotland at the Present Day* (Edinburgh, 1875), 6–7; and to St Andrews in Douglas Young, *St Andrews: Town and Gown, Royal and Ancient* (London, 1969), 209–10. Work on returned colonials living in Dundee is much needed, given the city's domination by the Bengal-connected jute industry. Studies of jute in Dundee and Bengal have focused on the Scottish and Indian working classes, while far less is known about the mill managers, overseers, and trained technicians working in India who were largely recruited from the Dundee area. However, see Gordon T. Stewart, *Jute and Empire: The Calcutta Jute Wallahs and the Landscapes of Empire* (Manchester, 1998); Dipesh Chakrabarty, *Rethinking Working-Class History: Bengal, 1890–1940* (Princeton, NJ, 1989), 52, 155; James G. Parker, 'Scottish Enterprise in India, 1750–1914', in R. A. Cage (ed.), *The Scots Abroad: Labour, Capital, Enterprise, 1750–1914* (London, 1985), 210; Eugenie Fraser, *A Home by the Hooghly: A Jute Wallah's Wife* (London, 1993), 202, 227. Relevant records at the Department of Archives and Manuscripts, University Library Dundee, include the Bengal Project Interviews. For perspectives on Scots returning from Jamaica in an earlier era, see Douglas J. Hamilton, 'Patronage and Profit: Scottish Networks in the British West Indies, c.1763–1807', D.Phil. thesis, University of Aberdeen (1999), ch. 8.

connections with the subcontinent. These localities illustrate British-Indians' ongoing transience in spatial terms. Not only did they take their character from those who already had traversed and blurred the boundaries between 'home' and 'away', but their very existence created additional circumstances that worked to perpetuate impermanent lifestyles among British-Indians across the generations.

TRANSPLANTED EMPIRE FRAGMENTS:
COLONIAL COMMUNITIES IN BRITAIN

Of all the places British-Indians might temporarily visit or live in for extended periods after coming home, London unsurprisingly reigned supreme. Britain's capital was often the first destination after those travelling from the empire disembarked from their ships docking at nearby ports, and thereby formed part of many British-Indians' metropolitan sojourns almost by default. In London, Britons returning from India or other colonies joined a steady stream of colonizers and colonized who flowed into and out of the imperial metropolis, staying for varying amounts of time.[72] Colonial peoples of all races, classes, and geographical origins were present at the heart of the empire, as studies ranging from Laura Tabili's research on colored seamen within the working classes in port cities and Angela Woollacott's work on white Australian women in London illuminate.[73] Those travelling from India were especially prominent within this global city and included not only British-Indians but also Indians of many class and gender backgrounds, as Antoinette Burton and Rozina Visram have examined.[74] London was home, at least temporarily, to persons as diverse as ayahs, lascars, and princes along with Indian students and

---

[72] Jonathan Schneer, *London 1900: The Imperial Metropolis* (New Haven, CT, 1999); Felix Driver and David Gilbert (eds.), *Imperial Cities: Landscape, Display and Identity* (Manchester, 1999).

[73] Laura Tabili, 'Women "of a Very Low Type": Crossing Racial Boundaries in Imperial Britain', in Laura L. Frader and Sonya O. Rose (eds.), *Gender and Class in Modern Europe* (Ithaca, NY, 1996), 165–90; and *'We Ask for British Justice': Workers and Racial Difference in Late Imperial Britain* (Ithaca, NY, 1994); Woollacott, *To Try Her Fortune*.

[74] Antoinette Burton, *At the Heart of the Empire: Indians and the Colonial Encounter in Late-Victorian Britain* (Berkeley, CA, 1998); Antoinette Burton, 'Tongues Untied: Lord Salisbury's "Black Man" and the Boundaries of Imperial Democracy', *Comparative Studies in Society and History*, 43/2 (2000), 632–61; Burton, *Dwelling in the Archive;* Janaki Agnes Penelope Majumdar (née Bonnerjee), *Family History*, ed. and intro. by Antoinette Burton (New Delhi, 2003); Rozina Visram, *Ayahs, Lascars and Princes: The Story of Indians in Britain, 1700–1947* (London, 1986). Nor were Anglo-Indians absent from the metropole. See Judith R. Walkowitz's discussion of Olive Christian Malvery in 'The Indian Woman, the Flower Girl, and the Jew: Photojournalism in Edwardian London', *Victorian Studies*, 42/1 (1998/1999), 3–46.

merchants, to name but a few groups. All sectors made their mark upon London's culture, British-Indians included.

While few areas of the capital remained completely untouched by this immense range of peoples and cultures from overseas, some districts witnessed more visible manifestations than others. In keeping with their social status, better-off British-Indians and Indians frequented the fashionable West End and neighborhoods adjacent to it in particular. For army or Indian Civil Service officers who were retired or on leave, gentlemen's clubs—among which the Army and Navy in Pall Mall, the East India United Service in St James's, or the Oriental Club in Hanover Square predominated—were among the key venues offering social opportunities, as well as accommodation for bachelors.[75] Similarly, many joined organizations focused on imperial issues such as the East India Association, the Northbrook Society, and the National Indian Association, which involved varying degrees of interaction with Indian elites also resident in London.[76] By the interwar period, moreover, those wanting Indian cuisine could dine at one of London's first Indian restaurants, Veeraswamy's, opened on Regent Street in 1926 by Edward Palmer after debuting at the British Empire Exhibition at Wembley two years earlier. By the 1930s there were a handful run by Indians as well.[77]

Shoppers, meanwhile, found the Army and Navy Stores near Victoria Station, other department stores, and countless colonial outfitters throughout central London ready to re-equip them with goods not only for their time in Britain but also for return journeys to India.[78] Excursions to West End shops

---

[75] Waring, *Tropical Resident*, 61; George James Ivey, *Clubs of the World: A General Guide or Index to the London and County Clubs* (London, 1880), 2–4, 34, 69; Ralph Nevill, *London Clubs: Their History and Treasures* (1911; repr. London, 1969), 211, 244–5, 251–3; 254–5; Anthony Lejeune and Malcolm Lewis, *The Gentlemen's Clubs of London* (London, 1979), 27, 109–10, 175–9; Sinha, 'Britishness', 493–500.

[76] On these organizations' activities, see Lala Baijnath, *England and India: Being Impressions of Persons and Things, English and Indian, and Brief Notes of Visits to France, Switzerland, Italy, and Ceylon* (Bombay, 1893), 96, 159–60; T. N. Mukharji, *A Visit to Europe* (Calcutta, 1889), 193; Vizram, *Ayahs, Lascars and Princes*, 77–8, 178–80; Burton, *Heart of the Empire*, 55–62, 120–2.

[77] 'London News: India Restaurant Opens', *Englishman*, (17 May 1926), 29; see also Caroline Adams (comp. and ed.), *Across Seven Seas and Thirteen Rivers: Life Stories of Pioneer Sylhetti Settlers in Britain* (London, 1987), 50. These restaurants, however, had a short-lived predecessor a century earlier, as Michael Fisher's study of Dean Mahomed demonstrates. Between 1810 and 1812, Mahomed ran his 'Hindostanee Coffee House' for a largely India-connected male British clientele, who came for Indian cuisine, décor, and hookahs. His establishment was located on George Street near Portman Square, then home to prominent returned 'Nabobs'. See Michael H. Fisher, *The First Indian Author in English: Dean Mahomed (1759–1851) in India, Ireland, and England* (Delhi, 1996), 251–61.

[78] Alison Adburgham (ed.), *Yesterday's Shopping: The Army and Navy Stores Catalogue 1907*, facsimile (Newton Abbott, 1969); Christopher Breward, 'Sartorial Spectacle: Clothing and Masculine Identities in the Imperial City, 1860–1914', in Driver and Gilbert (eds.), *Imperial Cities*, 250–2.

and department stores were often among the first activities British-Indians, especially women, undertook upon returning from overseas, using dress as a means to combat a compromised sense of belonging.[79] George Roche later recalled his mother's hasty trip to Harrods in 1918 to update her wardrobe after coming back following a five-year absence, when she feared her friends would think 'I've got old-fashioned since I've been in India'.[80] A 1930 advertisement for Austen Reed's on Regent Street bargained that men might prove equally anxious to fit in with fashionable society:

Is it possible, in London, to get really good clothes quickly? To the man, just home on leave, sadly aware of the anachronisms in his wardrobe, this is always a burning problem. Let a man take a taxi straight from Victoria. Within two hours he can leave Austin Reed's possessed of all the kit he will need while he is in England.[81]

Whether only passing through or staying in London for more extended periods, then, British-Indians had many venues throughout respectable parts of the city in which to acquire or replace colonial commodities and easily make contact with their own set. Although South Kensington was also said to be popular, Bayswater facilitated these diverse activities more than any other neighborhood and as such became especially well known for its India-connected residents.[82] As a part of the Paddington district which developed rapidly after the 1830s as a predominantly upper- and middle-class area, Bayswater derived its social character from its favorable location just west of the West End and north of Hyde Park. While Tyburnia north of Marble Arch was referred to as 'the pensioned Indian's undisturbed resort' in 1866, Bayswater to its west attracted more attention for its colonial inhabitants and their culture from the mid-nineteenth century onward.[83] As Waring put it, 'the wealthier

---

[79] Erika Diane Rappaport, *Shopping for Pleasure: Women in the Making of London's West End* (Princeton, NJ, 2000). Narratives of return stressing the importance of London shopping trips upon arrival include Ann Butler's letters from the early twentieth century, for example OIOC, MSS Eur F225/23, Ann Butler to Montagu Butler, 22 Mar. 1907, 12 April 1907, 23 April 1907. Also see Perrin, *Anglo-Indians*, 146.

[80] Roche, *Childhood*, 14.

[81] *Overseas*, 15/168 (1930), p. v.

[82] Waring, *Tropical Resident*, 88.

[83] 'The Ladies in Parliament', *Macmillan's Magazine*, 15 (Nov. 1866), 4. Works on Bayswater's development making brief reference to its British-Indian population include D. A. Reeder, 'A Theatre of Suburbs: Some Patterns of Development in West London, 1811–1911', in H. J. Dyos (ed.), *The Study of Urban History* (London, 1968), 253–71; T. F. T. Baker (ed.), *A History of the County of Middlesex*, IX: *Hampstead and Paddington Parishes* (Oxford, 1989), 190–217; Patricia L. Garside, 'West End, East End: London, 1890–1940', in Anthony Sutcliffe (ed.), *Metropolis, 1890–1940* (London, 1984), 230; Donald J. Olsen, *The Growth of Victorian London* (London, 1976), 162–8; P. J. Atkins, 'The Spatial Configuration of Class Solidarity in London's West End 1792–1939', *Urban History Yearbook*, 17 (1990), 36–65; Roy Porter, *London: A Social History* (London, 1994), 212; Rappaport, *Shopping for Pleasure*, 9, 18–25. Special thanks to Erika Rappaport for suggesting some of these readings as well as providing me with portions of her book prior to publication.

generally affect Tyburnia . . . whilst those of more restricted means go a little further west, and are content with Bayswater or its vicinity. . . . I feel assured that there are more old Indians within three miles of Hyde Park Corner in a north-westerly direction, than would be found in the whole of the rest of London put together; the district is indeed often nicknamed Asia Minor!'[84]

By 1885 'Asia Minor' had developed such an entrenched colonial profile that the *Bayswater Annual* could describe its residents and their lifestyle in intricate detail. 'Since the Mutiny', it reported, 'Bayswater has been more notably the English home of Anglo-Indian families'. Along with the Havelocks and the Outrams, other 'companions in arms of the heroes of Lucknow and Delhi are yet with us, and may be found in almost every street of "Asia Minor"'. Aware-ness of this local dimension of imperial history surely inspired Virginia Woolf's portrayal of Colonel Abel Pargiter, living in Bayswater in 1880, in her 1937 novel *The Years*.[85] Bayswater was likely to be part of men's Indian career cycle long before retirement, and in many instances even preceded it. Young men hoping to become army officers or 'the future administrators of our Indian empire' also formed part of 'Asia Minor's' community of temporary settlers when preparing for Indian service entrance examinations, studying with 'tutors and coaches'—better and more accurately known as 'crammers'—based in the vicinity.[86] British-Indians in the making and pensioners were joined by civil and military officers in mid-career who visited Bayswater on furlough. More numerous still were their female relatives who, like their fathers and hus-bands, remained in continual transit:

here, too, in the meantime, wives and daughters await their husbands' and sires' return, or not less readily the summons to join them and share their Oriental life. Between Bayswater and India there is a constant interchange. From the Ghats of Kensington-gardens Square to the Ghats of Calcutta, the storied boarding-houses of Bayswater to those on the banks of the Hugli, the change is but little thought of by the wives and children of an imperial race, to whom the Suez Canal becomes even more familiar than the Canal of Paddington.[87]

Small wonder, then, that women like Annette Beveridge arrived in London in the 1880s and 1890s carrying the addresses of many friends to visit whom they

[84] Waring, *Tropical Resident*, 59.

[85] City of Westminster Archives Centre, London, 'Bayswater: The "Asia Minor" of Anglo-Indians', *The Bayswater Annual* (London, 1885), 5; Virginia Woolf, *The Years* (London, 1937).

[86] 'Bayswater: The "Asia Minor"', 5; Advertisement for Wren and Gurney, 3, Powis Square, Westbourne Park, *The Paddington, Kensington, and Bayswater Chronicle*, 20 Sept. 1879.

[87] 'Bayswater: The "Asia Minor"', 5.

had known in India and now lived in this area, as did Ann Butler several decades later.[88]

British-Indians of both sexes gravitated to London's 'Asia Minor' both for its fashionability and conveniences especially suited to people like themselves. Along with exclusive homes to buy for £2,000 or let from £120 annually, Bayswater had a ready supply of more modestly priced terraced houses and flats which could be rented, furnished or unfurnished, on a short-term basis— offerings which appealed greatly to those either visiting temporarily or returning for longer periods without substantial household goods.[89] From the later nineteenth century until the interwar era numerous estate agents in Westbourne Grove and other main thoroughfares publicized their 'special service to overseas visitors'.[90] One of London's largest concentrations of hotels and boarding houses emerged to increase the area's transient population still further.[91] Many depended heavily upon overseas guests for their clientele, advertising in both local directories as well as Indian newspapers such as the *Englishman* how they were 'patronized by American and Colonial Visitors' or offered 'a home-like hotel which caters particularly for English people from India'.[92]

Alongside accommodations, commercial and leisure facilities reflected returned colonials' wants and needs in London. Many of the neighborhood's retailers purveyed goods that enabled Westbourne Grove to be described as 'the Chowringhee of Bayswater'. For decades, specialized shops provided 'an Indian outfit complete at a day's notice', trunks, and other goods for those requiring 'tropical' apparel; a number of local grocers, meanwhile, sold fruits, vegetables, and other foods commonly eaten in the

---

[88] OIOC, MSS Eur C176/59, Annette Beveridge's Diary, 1883, front pages; OIOC, MSS Eur C176/68, Annette Beveridge's Diary, 1892, front pages; OIOC, MSS Eur F225/23, Ann Butler to Montagu Butler, 17 April 1907; OIOC, MSS Eur F225/32, Ann Butler to Montagu Butler, 5 June 1919; OIOC, MSS Eur F225/36, Ann Butler to Montagu Butler, 5 June 1925.

[89] 'Bayswater', *The Builder*, 13 Sept. 1862; Reeder, 'Theatre of Suburbs', 257, 264.

[90] *Paddington Past and Present*, 6th edn. (London, 1936), 18–25, 108; see also *The Paddington and Bayswater Directory for 1875* (London, 1875), 249, 258; Frederick Bingham, *The Metropolitan Borough of Paddington: Official Guide* (London, 1925), 32, 58, 112.

[91] Reeder, 'Theatre of Suburbs', 255–6, 263–4; Baker (ed.), *History of the County of Middlesex*, IX, 238–9.

[92] Frederick Bingham, *The Official Guide to the Metropolitan Borough of Paddington* (London, 1917), 103; 'Where to Stay in England', *Englishman* (6 May 1926), 3; 'Bayswater: The "Asia Minor"', 5; advertisements in *Overseas*, 12/192 (1927), pp. xlii–xliii, and *Overseas*, 13/144 (1928), p. xxxix. Annabel Huth Jackson, for instance, described passing through Bayswater upon returning to England with her mother in the 1880s, en route to Cheltenham Ladies' College, because her brothers had taken lodgings there. See *A Victorian Childhood* (London, 1932), 125, 129.

subcontinent.[93] As Bayswater's largest and best-known shopping establishment, moreover, Whiteley's department store fulfilled not only their material desires but also doubled as a social arena. Its morning lounge known as the 'Menagerie' was popular among the India-connected wanting to 'exchange greetings' who found 'common ground' among the 'birds, beasts, and fishes that remind them of home life in India: the green parrots, the mynas, the crow-pheasants, the köel-cuckoo, and . . . now and then a stray mungoose . . . remind them of past days'.[94] Many visitors to Whiteley's in search of social interaction alongside refreshments were undoubtedly women shoppers; men were more likely to frequent the Bayswater Club, established in 1879 for a membership largely consisting of retired military and civil service officers who sought 'the comforts of a good West End Club without the inconveniences of a long journey'.[95] Other local associations open both to men and women enhanced Bayswater's links with India in religious, spiritual, and social terms, including 'zenana missions', the London headquarters of the Theosophical Society, and the congregation of Christ Church at Lancaster Gate—known as 'The Empire Church' since it served as 'a religious centre for visitors from overseas'.[96]

The facility with which Bayswater catered to transients en route to or from the subcontinent added another dimension to its 'Asia Minor' status, since Indians as well as British-Indians often stayed in the neighborhood while in London. At least some elite Indians stayed in Bayswater as a result of pre-existing personal connections with British-Indians living there. Lady Login, for example, described residing in Bayswater after her husband retired as a court surgeon in the 1860s, when their acquaintance Duleep Singh wrote asking them 'to secure a house for his mother in London, close to where we were then living, at Lancaster Gate'. They found 'a large house, next door but one to our own' for the 'Maharanee', who came with a full entourage of servants. Cooking areas arranged for 'the natives' behind the house proved 'a source of perpetual attraction to the street urchins, who clung in hordes to the railings, looking down upon a scene which they regarded as superior in interest to any bear-pit in Regent's Park'.[97] Bayswater's mixed colonial population grew

[93] 'Bayswater: The "Asia Minor"', 5; *The Paddington and Bayswater Directory for 1872* (London, 1872), p. iii; Bingham, *Metropolitan Borough of Paddington* (1925), 154, 273. Also see Nupur Chaudhuri, 'Shawls, Jewelry, Curry, and Rice in Victorian Britain', in Nupur Chaudhuri and Margaret Strobel (eds.), *Western Women and Imperialism: Complicity and Resistance* (Bloomington, IN, 1992), 245, which notes that the 20 April 1876 issue of *Queen* told readers that 'soojee for Bombay pudding can be procured from a grocer at Talbot Road at Bayswater'.

[94] 'Bayswater: The "Asia Minor"', 5.

[95] 'Local Gossip', *The Paddington, Kensington, and Bayswater Chronicle*, 18 Oct. 1879; see also 'The Clubs of Bayswater', *The Bayswater Annual* (1885), 15; Ivey, *Clubs of the World*, 13.

[96] *Paddington Past and Present* (1936), 31, 44; 'Bayswater: The "Asia Minor"', 5.

[97] E. Dalhousie Login, *Lady Login's Recollections: Court Life and Camp Life, 1820–1904* (London, 1916), 209–10.

increasingly entrenched in tandem with the neighborhood's expansion in later decades. When *The Bayswater Annual* wrote that 'we are largely an Oriental people', its description encompassed 'the Mohammedans and Hindoos in Bayswater, numerous and wealthy as they are', alongside Britons having connections to the subcontinent.[98] As the author of a London guide book wrote in 1902, 'here live the rich and cultured Orientals, those who have come over for pleasure, business, trade, or education'.[99]

Many of Bayswater's empire-oriented places and social circles correspondingly served both Indians and British-Indians. Living on the same streets, their children might attend the same schools, as a solicitor's son's recollections of his 1860s and 1870s childhood suggest. His neighbors included a retired major who had fought in the Indian 'Mutiny' and his son who later embarked upon his own overseas military career, while his schoolmates at a local 'Academy for Young Gentlemen' included two Indian boys.[100] Similarly, Indians and British-Indians were both said to frequent Whiteley's Menagerie and feel equally at home among its 'exotic' flora and fauna, while British-Indian shoppers visiting smaller colonial outfitters in the area might do business with Indian proprietors.[101] Bayswater's hotels and boarding houses advertising their services for British families returning from overseas also attracted Indian guests, providing additional settings in which these two sectors of middle-class and elite colonial society came together during time spent in London.[102]

It was thus highly likely that the British-Indian and Indian communities in London, whether living in Bayswater or other parts of the city, would cross paths; moreover, contacts occurred not simply by accident or through geographical proximity but also because many British-Indians encouraged them. Lala Baijnath, a judge who visited London in the 1890s, found the enthusiasm with which some sought contact with Indians both striking and puzzling. He described being frequently approached in the street by 'those who had been in India [and] seemed to take a pleasure in speaking to me in broken or half-forgotten Hindustani'. But their friendliness and interest in 'keeping up their knowledge of India' also had its ironic side:

---

[98] 'Bayswater: The "Asia Minor" ', 5; also see 'Rambler', 'A Strange Critic in Asia Minor', *The Paddington, Kensington, and Bayswater Chronicle*, 14 June 1879.

[99] Mrs E. T. Cook, *Highways and Byways in London* (London, 1902), 295.

[100] Sir William Bull, M.P., 'Some Recollections of Bayswater Fifty Years Ago', *The Paddington, Kensington, and Bayswater Chronicle*, 25 Aug. 1923.

[101] 'Bayswater: The "Asia Minor" ', 5; Bingham, *Metropolitan Borough of Paddington* (1925), 273.

[102] The Coburg Hotel on Bayswater Road, for instance, promoted itself to British-Indians in advertisements in *The Englishman*, 6 May 1926, but was also where Indian friends of the Butler family stayed while in London. See OIOC, MSS Eur F225/33, Ann Butler to Montagu Butler, 22 July 1921.

Another thing which I often noticed about many of them, was the extraordinary fondness for India and its people which their retirement had created in their minds. To some of them, the country and its inhabitants seemed to possess attributes which they would probably never have given them credit for in India. Others seemed to pine for it more keenly than they did for England when in India. The value of water is felt when the well is dry![103]

British-Indians' seeming willingness to mix with Indians, however newly developed it may have been, also might manifest itself within the domestic sphere. Baijnath noted how Indians visiting London not only typically found lodgings in Bayswater but also that a number of students rented rooms in the homes of retired British-Indian families.[104] While living in London to study law between 1888 and 1891 Mohandas Gandhi did both, initially lodging in 'an Anglo-Indian's house in West Kensington' and later living in other accommodations in Bayswater.[105] Some British-Indians may have sought lodgers to provide additional income; Ann Butler, for instance, contemplated 'taking Indian boys' to supplement her husband's pension when he discussed the possibility of early retirement in the 1920s, although this never came to pass.[106]

Indians who visited British-Indian homes, however, were more likely to have been invited for non-economic reasons. Ann Butler's letters reveal how her London friends and relatives asked her to tea parties attended by visiting rajas and ranis, and her son Rab later recalled dining with Indian princes at his uncle's table over his school holidays during the First World War.[107] One of Montagu Butler's letters home to Ann in 1930 illustrates how ties forged in India became extended onto metropolitan soil. 'Md. Amir of Shamsabad came to see me at Simla', he wrote; 'Md. Akram, his eldest son, is in England . . . you might send for him for tea or something . . . I'm glad you saw Bahadur. They do so appreciate any kindness to their sons in England.'[108] Ann served in this capacity on countless occasions during her extended stays in Britain prior to her husband's retirement. Her time was spent overseeing not only her own children's education but also that of Montagu's 'ward', Sirdar Muhammad Nawaz

---

[103] Baijnath, *England and India*, 29, 159.

[104] Ibid., 38–9.

[105] Mohandas K. Gandhi, *Autobiography: The Story of My Experiments with Truth*, trans. by Mahadev Desai (New York, 1983), 42, 52. Also see Stephen Hay, 'The Making of a Late-Victorian Hindu: M. K. Gandhi in London, 1888–1891', *Victorian Studies*, 33/1 (1989), 90.

[106] OIOC, MSS Eur F225/33, Ann Butler to Montagu Butler, 26 May 1921.

[107] OIOC, MSS Eur F225/36, Ann Butler to Montagu Butler, 1 April 1925; Richard Austen Butler, *The Art of the Possible: The Memoirs of Lord Butler* (London, 1971), 8–9. His uncle—Ann's brother James Dunlop Smith—had taken up an appointment as Political ADC at the India Office after retiring, and had distinguished Indian visitors to his home as a result.

[108] OIOC, MSS Eur F225/16, Montagu Butler to Ann Butler, 25 July 1930.

Khan, while he attended Sandhurst. 'Nawaz' was a frequent guest at the Butler home during his holidays and often came accompanied by Indian friends. Although this hospitality may have originated as a favor to families with whom Montagu had political interactions overseas, it was undertaken voluntarily and enthusiastically by the Butlers as well as other returned British-Indians.[109] Still, although Ann clearly enjoyed Nawaz's visits, her behavior towards him belied a deep-seated sense of superiority, stemming perhaps from their age difference but suggestive of other mindsets as well. 'We talked religion and race busily last night', she told Montagu; 'He's a different boy if you treat him as man to man, it cramps him utterly to talk up to a guardian. I've had no difficulty at all since I discovered this.'[110]

One can only speculate as to Nawaz's reaction to Ann's seemingly ill-disguised condescension regardless of her good intentions, but the views of an earlier Indian visitor to Britain suggest one possibility. As T. N. Mukharji had noted of his encounters with British-Indians in late-Victorian London, he met some who 'pompously displayed their acquaintance with the Hindi language, however slight it might be, and their power and superiority over us'. Despite this, however, 'a fellow-feeling existed between the Anglo-Indians and ourselves as if they were our countrymen in that strange land', and 'at the end, ten to one, it would end in an invitation'.[111] For those outside Britain's 'best circles'—like the Butlers and most other returned British-Indians to an even greater degree—interacting with and maintaining a sense of superiority over India's upper classes at home may have served as a comforting reminder of their elevated status in the empire which counted for considerably less upon reaching the metropole. Alice Perrin's novel describes similar circumstances when the Fleetwoods gloried in re-establishing contact with Indian princely acquaintances in London, a visit that provided a longed-for glamorous contrast to the dreary and humble realities at 'Combe Down' in 'Norbleton'.[112] Like living in neighborhoods such as Bayswater and maintaining a largely British-Indian social circle, socializing with Indians can be counted among the ways

[109] A letter to the wife of a retired Indian Police officer in the early 1920s shows how affectionate, quasi-familial relationships could develop between British-Indian guardians and young Indian men in Britain. Upon returning to India after several years at Sandhurst, Sarwar Ali Khan, Nawab of Kurwar, wrote to thank 'My dear Mummy' in the following terms: 'I have always looked forward for the term to end so as to come and stay with you . . . Daddy really has been more than a father to me and I am sure that even if my father were alive he wouldn't have treated me so well as he has . . . In return, I hope I have been a good son to you and Daddy and a good brother to Janey and William and Buddy.' OIOC, MSS Eur Photo Eur 291/2, Sarwar Ali Khan, Nawab of Kurwar, to Mrs W. S. Davis, 3 June 1921.

[110] OIOC, MSS Eur F225/33, Ann Butler to Montagu Butler, 22 Jan. 1922.

[111] Mukharji, *Visit to Europe*, 106–7. See also Burton, *Heart of the Empire*, 176–7, on Mukharji's and Baijnath's discussions of Bayswater.

[112] Perrin, *Anglo-Indians*, 172–3, 229–30, 238–68.

British-Indians formed 'colonies' that helped them to perpetuate a form of colonial culture in the 'strange land' that Britain had become.

In sum, because London was a hub for imperial travellers, it contained many public and private sites where British-Indians could meet with each other as well as with Indians if they chose. Bayswater was the geographical focus for these interactions beginning in the 1860s, but by the *fin de siècle* the British-Indian population was no longer as concentrated in this neighborhood as before. Although evidence suggests their ongoing presence there throughout the interwar period, during the twentieth century it became far more muted in tandem with London's inexorable spread outwards to encompass ever-widening swathes of suburbia. Returnees living around London were increasingly likely to be found on its outskirts, possibly in middle-class suburbs which, like the fictional 'Norbleton', had other British-Indian residents. Writing his guide to living in England on a pension in 1930, for instance, 'Mauser' counted Camberley and Farnham—both in Surrey—among the 'agglomerations of transplanted Empire fragments'.[113] Regardless of their place of residence, however, those in the vicinity of London easily remained in touch with a colonial community by converging in the city center on day trips to visit clubs, shops, restaurants, and friends. Ann Butler, for instance, lived in various locations throughout the home counties during her stays in England in the 1920s, but having a car enabled frequent contact with family members and countless acquaintances from India in and around London.[114]

London's growing range of suburban alternatives partly explain why many returning from India chose to live outside Bayswater or other central areas after the late-Victorian period. Both during as well as after Bayswater's heyday as 'Asia Minor', however, many shunned London because of the expense that keeping up appearances there entailed. Adelbert Talbot, it will be recalled, refused to contemplate London as a place of retirement in the 1890s on these grounds. Because he was hesitant to live in a cheaper and lower-status London suburb potentially 'full of cockney villas' like Barnet, he opted out altogether and settled his family outside Tunbridge Wells.[115] 'Mauser' predictably ranted about London's expense in the interwar years, bemoaning his experiences renting a 'poky' flat for £160 a year in what had previously been the servants' quarters of a large house, paying for public transport whenever he went out, and needing fashionable new clothes in order to hold his head up within a cosmopolitan society. He ultimately fled to Surrey, from which he could comfort-

---

[113] 'Mauser', *How to Live*, 1930 edn., 171.
[114] OIOC, MSS Eur F225/37, Ann Butler to Montagu Butler, Feb.–Sept. 1927.
[115] OIOC, MSS Eur E410/6, Adelbert Talbot to Guendolen Talbot, 20 Jan. 1893.

ably visit London by rail but avoid the everyday costs of living there.[116] For those wanting a less costly albeit still respectable lifestyle, almost anywhere in Britain was preferable to London. This chapter now turns to other British-Indian communities outside the metropolis, all of which similarly provided the comforts of familiar society. They did so, however, at less expense and with added bonuses ranging from perceived health benefits to schooling opportunities for children that appealed specifically to returned colonials.

Cheltenham Spa's history as the best-known British-Indian enclave in the metropole spanned well over a century, beginning not long after the Gloucestershire town established its reputation as a fashionable health resort. Although it never achieved Bath's social prominence, following George III's trips there in the 1780s Cheltenham joined the ranks of other English towns popular among the middle and upper classes for their purported physical benefits through 'taking the waters' combined with recreational opportunities.[117] Most visitors stayed only briefly or for a season, but others made the town a more permanent place of residence or retirement. Britons returning from India (and to a lesser extent from the Caribbean colonies) soon became a key segment of both the transient and longer term sectors of the spa's population. Rural areas near Cheltenham also contained recognizably India-connected persons as well as buildings. Two notable local country estates were built by men who had achieved varying degrees of fame—or infamy—in the Indian subcontinent: Warren Hastings's Daylesford House, dating from the 1780s; and Sezincote House, built in the early 1800s for Sir Charles Cockerell, a retired East India Company official, were both replete with Indian architectural influences. Coupled with the British-Indian community in the town, these stately homes caused a later local historian to refer to Cheltenham and environs as 'Calcutta in the Cotswolds'.[118]

The town's popularity as a health spa peaked between the 1790s and the 1840s, and British-Indians initially were attracted because the spa's waters were

---

[116] 'Mauser', *How to Live*, 1930 edn., 4–5, 8.

[117] For a comparative account of European spa culture, see David Blackbourn, '"Taking the Waters": Meeting Places of the Fashionable World', in Martin H. Geyer and Johannes Paulmann (eds.), *The Mechanics of Internationalism: Culture, Society, and Politics from the 1840s to the First World War* (Oxford, 2001), 435–57; for Cheltenham's history in the context of British spas, see Phyllis Hembry, *The English Spa, 1560–1815: A Social History* (London, 1990); *British Spas from 1815 to the Present*, ed. by Leonard W. Cowie and Evelyn E. Cowie (London, 1997).

[118] Bryan Little, 'Calcutta in the Cotswolds', *Bristol and Gloucestershire Archaeological Society Transactions* 98 (1980), 5–7; see also CPLRD, 'Indian Summer: An Exhibition Highlighting Cheltenham's Anglo-Indian Connections in the Nineteenth Century', exhibition leaflet, 28 June–15 Sept. 1985, Pittville Pumproom Museum.

widely claimed to help cure a variety of ailments thought to result from prolonged residence in hot climates.[119] Throughout the Regency era, however, the
town developed leisure facilities that targeted the healthy along with the invalid
members of fashionable society. Pump rooms, assembly rooms, promenades,
gardens, and places for concerts, theater, golf, riding, racing, and hunting all
made Cheltenham much more than a watering place for the sickly. Catherine
Sinclair's account of a visit to Cheltenham in the early 1830s summarized the
town as a 'Castle of Indolence', full of 'resolute idlers . . . determined to see and
be seen'.[120] During these decades coinciding with East India Company rule
over the subcontinent, commentators like Sinclair drew explicit connections
between the well-off colonial community patronizing the spa, its illnesses, and
its search for amusement in ways that echoed disparaging views of so-called
'nabobs' and others whose wealth and status flowed from overseas.[121] Although
she had never visited India, Sinclair discussed Cheltenham's social atmosphere
and urban landscape through reference to familiar images of the subcontinent
she knew from paintings and popular stereotypes:

This is indeed a brilliant city; in many places so much resembling Daniel's [*sic*] Views
of Madras, that, the day being hot, I began to fancy myself there, and very nearly
ordered a currie for dinner. The wide open verandahs and porches want nothing but a
pagoda tree to be occasionally shaken, and a nabob might forget he had returned
home.[122]

While Sinclair's assessment of Cheltenham enveloped critique with humor, her
contemporary William Cobbett responded with a scathing indictment, seeing
in the town a facet of the corrupt society he rallied against. For Cobbett, the
town and its colonial patrons in 1826 epitomized an immorality redolent of ill-
gotten gains and which manifested itself through physical disorders:

Cheltenham . . . is what they call a '*watering place*'; that is to say, a place, to which East
India plunderers, West India floggers, English tax-gorgers, together with gluttons,
drunkards, and debauchees of all descriptions, *female* as well as male, resort, at the suggestion of silently laughing quacks, in the hope of getting rid of the bodily consequences of their manifold sins and iniquities.[123]

---

[119] A. B. Granville, *Spas of England and Principal Sea-Bathing Places*, II: *The Midlands and South* (1841;
repr. Bath, 1971), 301–24; Steven Blake and Roger Beacham, *The Book of Cheltenham* (Buckingham, 1982),
35; Bryan Little, *Cheltenham* (London, 1952).

[120] Catherine Sinclair, *Hill and Valley; or, Hours in England and Wales* (Edinburgh, 1838), 359–60.

[121] The term 'nabob' evolved from the Persian *nawab*, which originally meant a governor serving the
Mughal emperor, and was used to describe servants of the East India Company.

[122] Sinclair, *Hill and Valley*, 361.

[123] William Cobbett, *Rural Rides* (1830; repr. London, 2001), 370–1.

The 'bodily consequences' of colonial life that Cheltenham's waters became well known for treating were wide-ranging. Between the early nineteenth and early twentieth centuries, physicians and writers of promotional material repeatedly recommended the town to those suffering from specific problems believed common among British-Indians, such as liver and spleen ailments, malaria, anaemia, and 'disorders of young females'. Most commonly, however, they randomly targeted 'those whose health has been impaired by a protracted sojourn in unhealthy climates', namely, 'the tropics'.[124] Depending on the writer, these illnesses stemming from tropical life were said to result from the climate alone or in combination with a debauched lifestyle. The latter accusation was most prevalent in the earlier nineteenth century, when writers like Sinclair and Cobbett invoked entrenched metropolitan understandings of 'nabobs' who immorally enriched themselves in India and lived to excess both overseas and upon returning home, where they had long been criticized and lampooned as vulgar upstarts with inappropriate social and political aims. As E. M. Collingham's research suggests, perceptions of their bodily health and morality were closely intertwined, and perhaps were best exemplified by the liver diseases supposedly common among returned British-Indians following long-term over-indulgence in alcohol, spicy food, and a host of other unstated forms of physical self-abuse and moral lassitude.[125] In short, the afflictions bringing them to Cheltenham were easily portrayed as the just desserts of a dissipated Indian lifestyle.

As examined in Chapter 1, anxieties about the dangers posed by tropical climates to European bodies and morals persisted for decades, albeit in a less condemnatory form, after nabob imagery had faded by the mid-1800s. Long after English spa towns lost their earlier prominence as health resorts and relied more heavily upon leisure and other facilities to draw visitors and residents, Cheltenham continued to be promoted as medically beneficial for those suffering from tropical afflictions but owed its ongoing popularity more to other factors.[126] After the 1840s and the onset of the spa's decline, the town's

---

[124] Granville, *Spas of England*, 302–3, 324; Edwin Lee, *Cheltenham and its Resources: Mineral Waters, Climate, Etc. Considered Chiefly in a Sanitary Point of View* (London, 1851), 94; W. J. Moore, *Health Resorts for Tropical Invalids in India, at Home, and Abroad* (London, 1881), 161; *Cheltenham: The Garden Town of England*, 3rd edn. (Cheltenham, 1893), 33; Thomas Davy Luke, *Spas and Health Resorts of the British Isles: Their Mineral Waters, Climate, and the Treatment to be Obtained* (London, 1919), 132.

[125] On cultural representations of the nabob in Britain, see E. M. Collingham, *Imperial Bodies: The Physical Experience of the Raj, c.1800–1947* (Cambridge, 2001), 13–49; Philip Lawson and Jim Phillips, ' "Our Execrable Banditti": Perceptions of Nabobs in Mid-Eighteenth Century Britain', *Albion*, 16/3 (1984), 225–41; James M. Holzman, *Nabobs in England: A Study of the Returned Anglo-Indian, 1760–1785* (New York, 1926).

[126] Continental Europe offered additional spas, most notably Plombières, that specialized in 'colonial diseases'. Blackbourn, ' "Taking the Waters" ', 456.

reputation increasingly veered towards that of sedate respectability inflected with a strong evangelical tone locally personified by Francis Close, the future Dean of Carlisle.[127] As Cheltenham became less chic among the wealthy, its appeal to British-Indians increased still further. House rents and social amenities cost less as a result, making the town affordable to a wider range of returned colonials than during its heyday as a watering place.[128] Although it remained a genteel community with its British-Indian element consisting mainly of civil servants, army officers, and their families, it attracted those with more moderate incomes to a larger extent than in earlier decades and thus enhanced its existing reputation as another 'Asia Minor' within Britain.[129] In tandem with the shift from Company to Crown rule in India, Cheltenham's tamer reputation as relatively 'poor, proud, and pretty' by the later nineteenth century was a far cry from its earlier nabob-dominated image. Its greater accessibility, however, made it a haven for a more prosaic variety of British-Indians throughout the remainder of the imperial era.[130]

As was the case with Bayswater, British-Indians came to Cheltenham on furlough or in retirement in large part because they sought to retain contact with the social circles in which they felt most at ease. Catherine Sinclair's observation that a man back from India 'might forget he had returned home' was echoed in nearly every mention of this enclave of returned colonials throughout the next hundred years. As Charles Lawson commented of his visit to Cheltenham in the 1870s:

Only this moment I chanced to take up from a table in the coffee-room of the 'Plough', the Cheltenham Free Press . . . and the first thing that caught my eye was a long extract from the Madras Mail, with reference to the late Moplah outbreak in Malabar, with a local editorial note stating that a 'Cheltonian well known to many of our readers', had been chiefly instrumental in suppressing it. And five minutes ago, there was a knot of officers standing on the hearth-rug yonder, discussing India from the standpoint of personal experience.[131]

Men could thus easily find comrades with whom to pass the time and talk about current Indian events as well as past experiences virtually everywhere

---

[127] Little, *Cheltenham*, 87.

[128] Lee, *Cheltenham*, 33–5; Alan Hollingsworth, *Cheltenham* (London, 1983), 15.

[129] W. E. Adams, *Memoirs of a Social Atom* (London, 1903), 3. See also *Who's Who in Cheltenham* (Newport, 1911), 31–73, for a profile of the town's more important inhabitants. In comparison with British-Indians earning their livelihoods from civil and military service, non-official sectors were poorly represented.

[130] CPLRD, Manuscript Collection, Alfred Miles, 'History of Cheltenham and District Vol. X', autograph manuscript (n.d., c.1920s), 295–7; Gwen Hart, *A History of Cheltenham* (Gloucester, 1981), 208–10.

[131] Lawson, *At Home on Furlough*, 203.

they went. Army officers, moreover, were particularly well represented; as a writer joked in 1903, 'you couldn't fire a shot gun in any direction without hitting a colonel . . . Half-pay officers abounded there. The place, so to say, was redolent of Eastern battles.'[132] Another *fin de siècle* observer called Cheltenham the place where 'all—or, at any rate, very many—good Anglo-Indians go before they die'.[133] An article appearing in the *Times of India* in 1900 provided perhaps the most complete description of Cheltenham's attractions, extolling its plentiful opportunities for familiar companionship and reasonable costs of living, while still briefly referring to its possible health benefits:

> not only is the Spa of the very greatest efficacy in ameliorating and curing many tropical diseases, but the town itself and Cheltenham society . . . must appeal with peculiar force to the Englishman whose social ideals have been modified by the long-continued environment of the East . . . it is here he will be able to find a society congenial to his taste, a standard of living well suited to his resources, and last, but not least, many an old friend and colleague of the days gone by.[134]

These many observations of Cheltenham's British-Indian community indicate its long-standing cultural visibility and prominence within the town's respectable circles, yet they provide only a partial illustration of its diversity. Highlighting the presence of older men who had retired from India, they reveal less about those who visited in mid-career while on leave and nothing about the many British-Indian women, young and old, as well children and adolescents of both sexes living in the town. The entire community was defined not only by its Indian past but just as importantly by its ongoing connection with those still overseas. Unsevered links with the subcontinent, as well as a broader picture of the community's composition, were perhaps best delineated in a poem entitled 'Cheltenham and India' published in the *Cheltenham Examiner* after news of the 1857 'Mutiny' reached Britain. As reports of the Indian revolt and British deaths spread, the public exhibitions of shock, grief, and anger far surpassed the patriotic outrage expressed throughout the country as a whole. So many Cheltenham residents had close relations or friends still in India who were killed during the uprising that it took on added layers of personal and communal significance. Printed in the wake of the deaths at Cawnpore, the poem referred to one of many large public meetings at which townspeople mourned

[132] Adams, *Memoirs*, 3.

[133] Henry Branch, 'The Anglo-Indian's Paradise', in *Cotswold and Vale; or, Glimpses of Past and Present in Gloucestershire* (Cheltenham, 1904), 177.

[134] 'Garden Town', 5.

their losses in both religious and civic memorial contexts.[135] As well as illustrating Cheltenham's imperial society and its lifestyle, it tellingly portrayed the 'Mutiny' deaths in familial terms, referring to the town's 'sons' and 'sweet, darling girls' who were killed, wounded, or still missing. Retired officers were linked to their descendants who had perpetuated family ties with India, in this instance through outpourings of grief that punctured a British-Indian idyll:

> What loyal English town
> More whelm'd with anguish? Where the happy hearths
> More robb'd than ours?—
> O, 'tis a pleasant place
> This Cheltenham! the good old officer,
> All bronz'd and bruis'd with manifold campaigns
> Beneath the skies of Hindoostan, returns
> To nestle here . . .
>
> .   .   .
>
> What meetings then with comrades! morn and eve
> Hear the old fights re-fought, and how they slew
> The monarch of the jungle—Merry days!
> Merrier than this!—to-day the laugh is dumb
> Grief in the face, and crape upon the hat,
> Bad news to-day![136]

The poem then depicted Cheltenham as both a symptom of and site for the replication of family links with India. Older men and also women watched the next generation leave for the subcontinent, either for work or marriage, on this occasion to find expectations uncharacteristically dashed:

> It is a drawing-room
> The walls stand thick with portraits, manly son
> And valiant nephew, each in uniform,
> Ta'en ere they left for India, there they hang!
> Fine lordly features all! and all are gone,
> Full of high hope and enterprise, to fight
> Hereditary foes, perchance to vie
> With their stout father's fame. Where are they now?
> 'God knows!' a lady's bursting sobs replied,
>
> .   .   .
>
> Sad, yet not saddest,—you remember well

---

[135] See newspaper coverage of local prayer meetings, assemblies, and reports of events in India in *Supplement to the Cheltenham Examiner*, 19 Aug. 1857, 26 Aug. 1857, 8 Oct. 1857; see also *Cheltenham Examiner*, 23 Sept. 1857; CPLRD, Manuscript Collection, Alfred Miles, 'History of Cheltenham and District Vol. III', autograph manuscript (n.d., *c*.1920s), 129.

[136] J. D. M., 'Cheltenham and India', *Cheltenham Examiner*, 23 Sept. 1857.

Sweet Emmeline the beautiful?—'twas she
The belle of belles that scarce two years ago
All eyes so worshipp'd—on the Promenade,
Or in the dance, who like her? Merry girl!
And good as merry!—well, the wedding came,

.   .   .

All joys—and in the nuptial toast 'twas said
How she should go to India and grow rich
And live so long and happily!—and so
They sail'd.—anon, the blessed mails arriv'd
Bearing glad news of both—anon they spake
Of Emmeline's sweet infant—and anon   ·
Of neither babe nor parent![137]

Thoroughly imbued with emotions specific to 1857, this depiction neatly illustrated some of the ways Cheltenham worked to perpetuate India as part of both
family heritage and local tradition. Sons and nephews in the military vying
'with their stout father's fame' also spent time with retired family members in
the town either before beginning their own Indian careers or while home on
leave. While there, local social provisions such as promenades, assembly rooms,
and indeed the drawing rooms of their parents, their colonial acquaintances,
and other neighbors provided countless opportunities to court the daughters
of similar families.[138] As census reports from later in the century reveal in
detail, middle- to high-ranking military and Indian Civil Service pensioners
often lived in Cheltenham with their wives and unmarried daughters; similarly,
the widows and offspring of such men also formed part of the local community,
as did wives and children of men still working overseas who then visited on
furlough.[139] Cheltenham thus facilitated intermarriage among the next
generation of British-Indians, with daughters readily meeting potential spous-
es among their families' local circle of acquaintances and, like 'sweet Emmeline
the beautiful' of the 1857 poem, subsequently returning to India with their
husbands.

Census returns along with profiles of local schools also reveal the extent to
which British-Indian children as well as grown-up sons and daughters were
well represented among Cheltenham's colonial community. During the same
period when its spa dimension was in decline, a number of schools were
opened that can be largely credited with maintaining the town's prosperity

[137] Ibid.
[138] Jackson, *Victorian Childhood,* 129, 185.
[139] See, for example, CPLRD, *Census of England and Wales, 1891.* Cheltenham, Enumeration District No.
14, Ecclesiastical Parish or District of St Paul's, 3, 6, 14; Enumeration District No. 31, Christ Church, 24, 58.

when fewer visitors came on health grounds.[140] Starting in the mid-1800s many families appear to have come to the town not simply so that adults could enjoy its social amenities in the company of fellow returned colonials, but first and foremost for their children's education. Parents still overseas also visited on furlough and often sent their children from India to live with aunts, grandparents, or other guardians in the town.[141] Hugh Gaitskell's family's connection with Cheltenham illustrates all these tendencies. He recalled spending over a year there as a small child in the early twentieth century when his parents came home from Burma on leave; they stayed with his grandfather, a retired army officer who had once sent Hugh's father to school locally as well.[142] As examined in the last chapter, Cheltenham College became particularly well known for catering to British-Indians. Founded in 1841 by a group of army officers, it educated many day boys whose retired parents came to Cheltenham following years in India; other boys lived with their mothers who stayed behind in England, and others still boarded until their parents came to the town while on leave. As the College became known for training boys for colonial civil and military careers, it played a key role in maintaining the town's history of overseas service traditions within families. British-Indian parents patronized other local schools as well, including Cheltenham Ladies' College, the Dean Close School, and a host of boys' preparatory and private girls' schools, but none so consistently as Cheltenham College.[143]

Far from serving merely as a resting-place for those retired from Indian service, then, Cheltenham 'abound[ed] with past, present, and future Anglo-Indians'.[144] It was a community where many families were split, their members continually coming from or going to India: children arrived for school and parents for furloughs or more extended mid-career visits; young adults returned overseas for work or married life; and parents ultimately returned upon retirement. Cheltenham was to maintain its reputation as a British-Indian enclave until India became independent. In the 1930s, a Gloucestershire travel writer still considered it 'an ideal residential town, where the Army, Navy and Indian Civil Service can retire, educate their children and find for themselves a comfortable way of living'.[145] Cheltenham appeared to have a visible British-

---

[140] Branch, *Cotswold and Vale*, 172; Luke, *Spas and Health Resorts*, 128; Little, *Cheltenham*, 87, 107; Blake and Beacham, *Book of Cheltenham*, 35, 93.

[141] CPLRD, *Census of England and Wales, 1891*. Cheltenham, Enumeration District No. 14, St Paul's, 13; Enumeration District No. 31, Christ Church, 24, 28, 35, 37, 40, 48, 58.

[142] Philip M. Williams, *Hugh Gaitskell: A Political Biography* (London, 1979), 3–5.

[143] See CPLRD, *Census of England and Wales, 1891*. Cheltenham, Enumeration District No. 31, Christ Church, 14–15, 17–20, 26–7, 32, 38–40, 44–5, showing entries for pupils born in India boarding at a number of smaller schools in the town.   [144] Lawson, *At Home on Furlough*, 203.

[145] Edward Hutton, *Highways and Byways of Gloucestershire* (London, 1932), 191.

Indian contingent even in the early 1950s, when a local historian referred to them as a 'now diminishing band'.[146] So well known was this transplanted colonial community, however, that twenty years after the raj ended a journalist could still allude to its traces, at least metaphorically, by referring to 'mem-sahibs still pining ruefully away in Cheltenham'.[147]

Although nowhere else in Britain was as well known for its density of returned colonials as Cheltenham, other towns outside London also attracted British-Indians in disproportionate numbers. Seaside resorts along England's south coast emerged as likely destinations for those coming back from overseas for reasons similar to those that made Cheltenham attractive. After the mid-nineteenth century, many coastal resorts, chiefly those in Sussex, took on estab-lished functions of the inland spa towns and provided new venues for the middle and upper classes seeking health and amusement. Initially, sea-bathing was recommended as a restorative treatment for many physical disorders, but later the sea air and coastal climate more generally drew those in search of improved health. Some towns such as Brighton had a far longer history as watering places for the fashionable, while most others like Eastbourne devel-oped this role mainly for the middle classes only after the 1850s, when parks, piers, pavilions, hotels, clubs, theaters, and golf courses gradually appeared on the scene. Inland spas like Bath and Cheltenham lost their prominence as health and recreational centers in part precisely because of seaside competition for their clientele. British-Indians became a growing presence spread out across the south coast because, like Cheltenham, it served many of their needs well. Alongside boasting health, leisure, and residential provisions, the region became home to countless private schools and a substantial retired popula-tion.[148] In time, British-Indians living in the metropole on either a short- or a long-term basis were just as likely to find familiar company there as in Bayswater or Cheltenham, but scattered in smaller pockets rather than con-centrated in a single location.

Eastbourne epitomized the reasons British-Indians opted for this region.[149] Since at least the 1870s and increasingly thereafter, popular medical manuals,

---

[146] Little, *Cheltenham*, 123.

[147] James Cameron, 'The Land of Chota-Pegs and Tiffin and the Bheestie and Ooty and—Most Impor-tant of All—the Memsahib', *Daily Telegraph Magazine*, 18 Aug. 1967, 23.

[148] James Walvin, *Beside the Seaside: A Social History of the Popular Seaside Holiday* (London, 1978); John K. Walton, *The English Seaside Resort: A Social History, 1750–1914* (Leicester, 1983), and *The British Seaside: Holidays and Resorts in the Twentieth Century* (Manchester, 2000).

[149] On Eastbourne's development as a seaside resort, see David Cannadine, *Lords and Landlords: The Aristocracy and the Towns, 1774–1967* (Leicester, 1980), chs. 3 and 15–25.

promotional literature, and travel guides recommended its 'bracing sea air' as ideal for children and the elderly, particularly for those considered to be 'delicate' if not outright invalids.[150] The exclusive schools which quite literally mushroomed in Eastbourne during this same era undoubtedly owed at least some of their popularity to these purported health benefits for children. When Annette Beveridge left India with her four children in 1890 because of her anxieties about India's physical dangers, she chose to settle the family in Eastbourne after considering Clifton, Ilfracombe, and other towns. 'No place promises so well', she told her husband, as Eastbourne had a strong educational reputation coupled with the climate she felt was 'best for Anglo-Indians'.[151] Common fears about India's detrimental effects upon British children's health discussed in Chapter 1 clearly influenced at least some parents' choice of school and often place of residence. Furthermore, as noted in the previous chapter, schools in Eastbourne and across the south coast region recognized this appeal and actively recruited colonial families, playing up how they offered what was 'considered by medical authorities the best possible climate for children from the tropics' as much as they promoted academic and social offerings when advertising in Indian newspapers.[152] Boys' public schools like Eastbourne College were available there and in similar coastal towns, but the region remained best known for its small preparatory schools for younger boys in addition to socially (if not often academically) prestigious girls' schools. South coast educational specialities thus catered first and foremost to the same groups— younger boys, but girls of all ages—who dominated colonial medical literature due to the belief that their physical condition was the most fragile.

The Beveridges were only one among many British-Indian families choosing schools in this locality. As a turn-of-the-century medical writer summarized, 'many children whose health does not permit them to be sent to inland schools are provided for . . . and the children of Indian Civil Servants and military men are largely represented on the school lists of Eastbourne'.[153] As such, British-Indian pupils formed a noticeable element within what commentators identified as a key segment of the locality, namely its 'floating school popula-

---

[150] George Moseley, *Eastbourne as a Residence for Invalids and Winter Resort* (London, 1882), 27, 38; R. N. Wilson, *Leafy Eastbourne* (Eastbourne, 1906), 29, 46, 49; *Eastbourne and Neighbourhood* (London, 1919), 15; Lawrence Stevens, *A Short History of Eastbourne*, comp. by Marie Lewis and Owen Daish (Eastbourne, 1987), 20, 22.

[151] OIOC, MSS Eur C176/27, Annette Beveridge to Henry Beveridge, 9 Jan. 1890, 12 Jan. 1890, 4 May 1890, 14 July 1890. On the Beveridges in Eastbourne, see also Lord Beveridge, *India Called Them* (London, 1947), 323–31, 349; Jose Harris, *William Beveridge: A Biography* (Oxford, 1977), 18–19; Cannadine, *Lords and Landlords*, 361–2.

[152] *Times of India, Overland Weekly Edition*, 7 April 1900, 19.

[153] Charles Roberts, *Eastbourne as a Health Resort* (Eastbourne, 1899), 26–7.

tion' estimated at 5,000 children attending nearly a hundred different institutions within a community numbering 45,000 in the early twentieth century.[154] 'The existence of these boarding schools was responsible in no small measure for the large number of visitors frequenting Eastbourne in its early days, because of their desire to be near to their children attending the schools', an interwar writer noted.[155] Alongside those boarding at the schools were still more who attended as day pupils and lived with their parents who had moved to the town for reasons that resembled Annette Beveridge's, thereby swelling Eastbourne's residential as well as its visiting population. Not all newcomers attracted by Eastbourne's schools, climate, and leisure provisions were British-Indians, but they were well represented among those who either lived there with or periodically visited their children.

So far, so Cheltenham. Eastbourne and other nearby seaside resorts thus similarly became home for mothers staying in England with their children as well as for parents stopping over on furlough or living there after retiring from Indian careers. Within its population of middle-class and occasionally more wealthy residents, British-Indian adults could also enjoy ongoing relationships with friends they had made overseas. Annette Beveridge's letters to her husband told how 'constantly we are with Anglo-Indians'; indeed, alongside Eastbourne's schools and sea air, she was attracted to the town because 'it is nice too to be in a place where one is so apt to meet friends'.[156]

Eastbourne's British-Indian contingent survived long after the late-Victorian era Annette Beveridge's letters describe, as did that in other seaside communities. The Butler family correspondence tells similar stories of Brighton and its neighboring Hove just before the First World War, when Ann briefly rented a house there while her son Rab was attending a local preparatory school. She learned of the school by word of mouth, and although only about fifty boys were enrolled she knew a number of their parents and subsequently met other British-Indians who sent their sons there.[157] While her letters to Montagu said nothing about the climate as a reason to be in Hove, she was drawn there largely by colonial connections as well as educational provisions.

---

154 Wilson, *Leafy Eastbourne*, 70; Roberts, *Eastbourne*, 26–7; A. R. Hope Moncrieff (ed.), *Black's Guide to Hastings and Eastbourne, St Leonards, Bexhill, Rye, Winchelsea, Etc.* (London, 1899), 65, 67.

155 Harold Clunn, *Famous South Coast Pleasure Resorts Past and Present* (London, 1929), 236.

156 OIOC, MSS Eur C176/27, Annette Beveridge to Henry Beveridge, 23 Oct. 1890, 24 Aug. 1890, 10 Dec. 1890, 18–19 Feb. 1891, 3 Sept. 1890; MSS Eur C176/67, Annette Beveridge's diary, 1891, entries for 31 Dec. 1890, 16 Jan. 1891.

157 OIOC, MSS Eur F225/27, Ann Butler to Montagu Butler, 24 Sept. 1911; 'Sunday'; MSS Eur F225/28, Ann Butler to Montagu Butler, 31 Dec. 1912, 22 Jan. 1913.

Ann's response to Hove's British-Indian community differed drastically from Annette Beveridge's enthusiasm about Eastbourne, however. She reported endless social engagements with people from India, but often found them more depressing than fulfilling. Her rendition of one gathering provides a succinct profile of the group that simultaneously pulled her in yet left her both bored and apprehensive:

I went to tea with the Canon Walkers on Monday, and by the way their son Geoff returned to India . . . I found Lady C. W. seated on the floor playing hunt the slipper with a few kids while old George sadly strayed round and their youngest daughter a very handsome flapper with gorgeous red hair—who's at a day school here . . . Two of the children turned out to be those of Col. Coates, who also lives in Hove with his handsome wife whom I once met in Murree. The others were guests—offspring of some other Anglo-Indian called Grant—also rather sad and weary. He turned up to fetch [the] kids home, I suppose a pleasant job allotted him to pass the time. I don't think you'll retire in seven years, lovey, not if you meet these ghosts of better things now shadowing Hove.[158]

Insular colonial circles in Britain might thus prove dissatisfying and stifling for some, perhaps particularly so for younger women like Ann whose husbands had not yet retired. Mixing with former colonials at home might signal a dull and depressing old age in store far more than it provided a friendly and familiar community welcome to those who had grown estranged from metropolitan society during time in India. Accounts like Ann's provide an essential alternative view of these enclaves not found among the glowing reports of Cheltenham, where 'all good Anglo-Indians go before they die'. They also point towards a range of other factors that could mar the pleasures of living in many such communities with a British-Indian contingent that ultimately caused some families to move away, as both the Beveridges and the Butlers did from Eastbourne and Hove.

Despite Annette Beveridge's liking for the British-Indians around whom she focused her social interactions, in other respects Eastbourne failed to fulfil the high expectations which had originally attracted her. Most tragically, her belief that the town provided the healthiest setting in England for her children after they had survived India's hazards did not prevent the deaths of two of her four offspring. Herman, the youngest, died at age 5 within months of their arrival, and two years later Letty, the eldest, was struck down by influenza when she was 15[159] (Illustration 11). These experiences undoubtedly did much to cloud

[158] OIOC, MSS Eur F225/28, Ann Butler to Montagu Butler, 10 Dec. 1912, 31 Dec. 1912.
[159] OIOC, MSS Eur C176/66, Annette Beveridge's diary, 1890, entry for 12 Sept.; MSS Eur C176/69, Annette Beveridge's diary, 1893, entry for 14 April.

the Beveridge family's outlook about the town, which had so quickly become a place of unhappy experiences. Still, even if the children's deaths had failed to render Eastbourne unappealing as a permanent residence, the financial costs of living there had made it clear it would be a temporary home from the start. Annette initially felt the high rents in Eastbourne worth paying given the town's climatic and educational advantages, and took out a four-year lease on a house costing £150 a year. Henry's letters from India, however, informed her that 'when your lease . . . is out we must go to some cheaper place', thereby portending their departure in 1894.[160] Herman's and Letty's deaths, William's transfer from his Eastbourne preparatory school to Charterhouse, and Henry's retirement and correspondingly reduced income came together to make their move desirable on many levels.

Ann Butler's reservations about Hove, meanwhile, suggested that long-term residence there was unlikely from the start. Unlike Annette Beveridge, she found the company of other British-Indians living nearby no inducement to stay; moreover, she quickly expressed her unwillingness to continue to pay to live there. The town house she rented and its upkeep amounted to £5.5.0 a week, and was 'too expensive to go on'; given the high school fees they paid (over £100 a year for each of their four children) she 'determine[d] never again to take a house in a town at this rent, requiring 3½ servants and a char'.[161] She returned to India after several months in Hove, and in all her subsequent lengthy stays in Britain prior to her husband's retirement she never lived there again. Despite having all four of her children at nearby boarding schools, she only passed through for brief visits and opted to live in more modestly priced places. If the Beveridges and the Butlers—both supported by the high salaries of Indian Civil Servants—felt unable to remain in upmarket seaside towns because of their expense, for British-Indians lower down the socio-economic ladder Eastbourne, Hove, Brighton, or indeed Cheltenham were never options at all. If they sought some of the same qualities at less expense, however, they might instead opt to live in Bedford.

Bedford had attracted Britons connected with India and other parts of the empire since the mid-nineteenth century. This trend peaked between the 1860s and the First World War, and although levelling off thereafter it survived to a considerable degree through the 1940s. The town did not boast health or leisure amenities that made Cheltenham and the south coast appealing, but in other respects British-Indians came for the same reasons they chose the

---

160 OIOC, MSS Eur C176/28, Henry Beveridge to Annette Beveridge, 18 Feb. 1892.
161 OIOC, MSS Eur F225/28, Ann Butler to Montagu Butler, 9 Feb. 1913.

localities discussed above. Bedford provided desirable educational opportunities and a colonial-oriented sector of local middle-class society such that
British-Indians could feel at home there. Crucially, Bedford fulfilled these twin
aspirations at much lower cost: as a local observer later recalled of the town's
late-Victorian imperial contingent, 'the wealthier service people retired to
Cheltenham, the poorer to Bedford'.[162]

To a far greater extent than Cheltenham depended upon Cheltenham College to attract residents, Bedford's British-Indian community was inextricably
connected with the offerings of the two Harpur Trust-run boys' schools,
Bedford Grammar School and Bedford Modern School.[163] As considered in
the previous chapter, the impressive record of boys from both schools, but particularly those from the Grammar School, in gaining entrance to Woolwich,
Sandhurst, and a wide range of official and unofficial Indian employment sectors made these institutions attractive to families seeking overseas posts for
their sons. In comparison with other schools boasting similar achievements,
Bedford's charged relatively low fees—only £13 annually for upper-school day
boys at the Grammar School in 1903—and catered more for day pupils.
Middle-class families with restricted finances who none the less wanted to give
their sons a public school-style education enabling future careers overseas
found Bedford well suited to their needs, and many moved to the town specifically to take advantage of the schools and save the costs of boarding their
children.[164] Local community leaders recognized and actively promoted the
town's appeal to the less affluent among both the imperial and metropolitan
middle classes, singling out widows as among those who might most covet
Bedford's reasonably-priced schools and housing. As a letter appearing in *The
Bedfordshire Times* in 1869 elaborated, Bedford Grammar School

is the one school in the whole country which is open to those cases which no other educational establishment meets—I mean the widows of the clergy, naval and military officers, and civil servants, often left almost destitute, with the refined tastes, feelings and
aspirations which belong to their order . . . The advantages are not sufficient to attract
the well to do . . . but it is a haven of hope and rest to many a poor widow, destitute of
friends and means, and who would otherwise look almost with despair in the faces of
her young children, craving the educational armour and weapons which would enable
them to enter on the battle of life with good hope of maintaining the social position of
their fathers. Again, to meet the necessities of the case, a class of houses has sprung up

---

[162] C. D. Linnell, 'Late-Victorian Bedford', *Bedfordshire Magazine*, 7/51 (1959–60), 80.

[163] Patricia Bell, 'Aspects of Anglo-Indian Bedford', *Publications of the Bedfordshire Historical Record Society*, 57 (1978), 181.

[164] Waring noted this source of Bedford's appeal as early as the 1860s; *Tropical Resident*, 48–9.

suited to their narrow means, and those used to refined society know that they will find it there among their equals in rank and fortune.[165]

While they epitomized those who came to the town in straitened circumstances, widows constituted only one element of Bedford's British-Indian population who had chosen the community for these reasons. A clearer picture of the town's British-Indian sector emerges in late-nineteenth-century census returns for recently developed streets populated by middle-class newcomers, revealing the overwhelming extent to which residents had Indian or other colonial affiliations. In Grove Place, for instance, most houses had at least one occupant and often many born in India, and nearly as many listed as head of household a man employed in India or a military officer serving elsewhere overseas (presumably either on furlough or absent), a man retired from these occupations, or his widow. A sampling of the Grove Place entries reveals houses occupied by a returned missionary, his wife, and two sons (one born in India); an army major's widow with five sons (born in Nova Scotia, Brunswick, Price Edward's Island, Africa, and Kent); the wife of a captain presently in India, and their three children; a widow pensioner with six children, five of whom were born in Bengal; and a widowed teacher, her mother, cousin, and three children, all born in Bengal. Most of the sons in these households were listed as attending either Bedford Grammar School or Bedford Modern School.[166] Other examples illustrate how widows and grass widows needing to economize did so by cohabiting; as one local observer later recalled, 'it was not unusual for two ladies whose husbands were abroad or dead to take a house between them where their children, for the time being, formed one family'.[167]

Retired couples who still had school-age children but had to provide for them on pensions were also well represented in Bedford. Some men had been invalided out of colonial service before the standard retirement age, and, like the widows, consequently had pensions far lower than those able to serve out their full career. While some had been in the Indian Civil Service, many others worked in occupations which paid less or had not reached the higher levels of their branch of employment. Whatever their status, most appeared to lack private resources to supplement incomes or pensions, while others simply had too many children to choose more expensive schools in more fashionable localities.

An indication of family income levels among India-connected Bedford residents can be extrapolated from Edwardian-era commentary about house rents

[165] Revd E. W. Fenwick, 'Letter to the Editor of the *Times*', reprinted in *Bedfordshire Times*, 2 Mar. 1869.
[166] BLARS, CRT 130 BED 188, 'Extracts from the 1871 Census for Bedford for Certain Streets and Houses', 6, 8.
[167] Ibid., 11–12; Linnell, 'Late-Victorian Bedford', 81.

typically paid by this segment of local society. In 1910 reporters for *The Bedfordshire Times* interviewed house agents about the demand for middle-class accommodation and found that requests came from retired army officers and other professionals, 'largely from India, and there are a few from Canada, Ceylon, and other parts of the world'. Such clients sought houses with rents between £25 and £50 a year.[168] Since families during this era commonly spent one-tenth of their annual income on housing and often more if lower middle class, the average annual resources of Bedford's returned colonials plausibly ranged between £200 and £500.[169] Often having far less than the £500 a year Waring recommended in the 1860s as the bare minimum needed to maintain a 'comfortable' lifestyle in the metropole, Bedford's British-Indian families counted among the bottom sectors of the middle class or within the lower middle class in terms of income. All told, Bedford's colonial contingent was a world away from the Beveridges and the Butlers on the south coast in terms of how much its members could afford to spend on both education and rent.

Economic factors correspondingly did much to influence the social and cultural milieu created among repatriates in Bedford, as did experiences and understandings developed while in India. Their lives in and expectations of the town were also age- as well as gender-specific. A different image from that of widows or wives living on their own with their children emerges in C. J. Maltby's depiction of 'Bedford as Seen by the Anglo-Indian'—in this instance, by man in his late fifties. Writing in a town promotional booklet in 1913, Maltby attributed his decision to retire there to its schools and reasonable costs of living: 'I am not writing for the returned wanderer who has made a large fortune, and can pick and choose *ad lib.*, but for him who, like myself, has to consider ways and means.' He praised the Harpur Trust boys' schools for placing day pupils at no social disadvantage, and welcomed having his sons at home not only because it reduced expenses but also since 'having been perforce separated from one's children for years, one is glad to see what one can of them all the year round, and not only during their holidays'. Bedford's schools thus might claim to offer dual advantages to retired colonials, namely family unity in the aftermath of parent–child separations in addition to good value. Maltby also alluded to the existence of a community of fellow British-Indians as another source of the town's appeal. 'The society in Bedford is just what the Anglo-Indians have been accustomed to', he asserted. Unlike other towns within

---

[168] 'House-Letting in Bedford and District', *Bedfordshire Times*, 23 Sept. 1910.

[169] W. D. Rubinstein, *Men of Property: The Very Wealthy in Britain Since the Industrial Revolution* (London, 1981), 49; Jackson, *Middle Classes*, 338–9; Perkin, *Rise of Professional Society*, 29; S. Martin Gaskell, 'Housing and the Lower Middle Class, 1870–1914', in Crossick (ed.), *Lower Middle Class*, 166–7, 176–7.

commuting distance to London, where 'the unfortunate retired officer finds himself with no companionship to his taste during the greater part of the day; the men go off to their business in town, and only return in the evening', in Bedford 'birds of this feather have flocked together. Paterfamilias has no difficulty about finding kindred spirits to play golf, bridge, or row, and do whatever he has a mind to.'[170]

Members of Bedford's British-Indian community participated in many local clubs and other organizations, but appeared to spend much of their time in one another's company. Relationships forged via common colonial experiences remained central in the daily lives of those opting to live on the same streets and attend the same churches. Many went to St Andrew's church in the early 1900s where the congregation was headed by the former Archdeacon of Calcutta, whose sons attended Bedford Grammar School and whose wife hosted Christmas 'Tamashas' at their home.[171] Active reminders of their past lives abroad pervaded the public as well as the private interactions of Bedford's ex-colonials. Beryl Irving, who grew up in the town at the turn of the century after her father was invalided out of the Indian Army and subsisted on his pension, recalled her childhood years among streets where 'Anglo-Indians were trying to make ends meet with dignity'. She attended a nearby girls' school run by a widow from India where her fellow pupils were as likely to be from colonial families as their brothers at the Harpur Trust schools. Domestic life was similarly permeated by vestiges of India. 'Our houses were crammed with Benares tables, strings of little carved elephants, placid Buddhas and malevolent gods', she remembered, and 'our mothers made good curries'.[172]

Ruby Spankie, one of Irving's schoolmates, provided additional insights into such homes by depicting their economic constraints. Her family lived in the neighborhood between 1900 and 1916 after her father died shortly before retiring from the Indian Army, after which 'inexpensive education, and rents, and living generally, became all the more important'. Like Irving, she recalled typical household furnishings but stressed that in the wake of long-term transience their homes were spartan regardless of the curios brought back from overseas. 'The Anglo-Indians, and indeed, the Army wives and widows, *brought* no furniture to the town . . . they had been moving from place to place with their husbands and had never settled anywhere, but I think they acquired sufficient

---

170 C. J. Maltby, 'Bedford as Seen by the Anglo-Indian', in Bedford Trade Protection Society, *Bedford Town and Bedford Schools* (Bedford, 1913), 15.

171 Bell, 'Aspects of Anglo-Indian Bedford', 189–90, 196.

172 Beryl Irving, 'Our Road', *Bedfordshire Magazine*, 6/46 (1958), 225; Beryl Irving, 'Edwardian Schooldays', *Bedfordshire Magazine*, 9/67 (1963–4), 95.

furniture—probably cheap and nasty!'[173] Bedford's British-Indians may have resembled the Talbots discussed above in needing to establish a residence and enhance a new-found domestic space later in life, but they seemingly did so with considerably less income.

Recollections of late-Victorian and early twentieth-century Bedford strongly suggest that their financial condition coupled with a common colonial occupational background created a highly insular British-Indian community in the town. One resident later described how the 'large colony of retired soldiers, sailors, planters and officials who had spent their working lives in India and settled in Bedford' were collectively called 'Squatters' by native Bedfordians. Despite—and most likely because of—their precarious finances along with class and cultural anxieties upon returning to Britain, British-Indians were said to place themselves socially above most local circles, yet were in turn shunned by the more elite:

The 'Squatters' so called, constituted Society, which was very exclusive, not to say snobbish. Besides the officers at the Barracks, only a few of the leading doctors, clergymen and lawyers were admitted, and hardly any of the business community . . . Though many of them had connections with noble families, they had little intercourse with the 'county' families, who looked down on them as poor and proud.[174]

Their social interactions thus largely limited to themselves, Bedford's British-Indians' 'poverty' and pride worked together both to bar those deemed less 'respectable' from their company as well as to place them outside the acquaintance of the more established and well-to-do in the vicinity. Some Bedfordians of longer standing unsurprisingly exhibited hostility towards newcomers with airs, exemplified by disparaging commentary which appeared in a local newspaper in 1891 concerning the supposed living conditions of the servants working in British-Indian homes:

A correspondent states that there are tales about of 'kitchen hunger' in some houses in Bedford, where the servants have not enough to eat and that costly article, bread, is kept locked up. He says that this is what happens with some of the rulers of our 'great dependency', their ideas of what is necessary to keep up the strength and physique of an English servant being derived from their experience with natives who live on rice and wear scanty raiment.[175]

While this anecdote is of questionable truth, its wittily phrased charges of stinginess and imperious behavior clearly provided critical townspeople with a

---

[173] BLARS, CRT 130 BED 191, letter from Miss R. M. Spankie to Patricia Bell, 18 Mar. 1980.
[174] Linnell, 'Late-Victorian Bedford', 80–1.
[175] *Bedfordshire Times*, 24 Jan. 1891.

means of evening the score against a group deemed unjustly arrogant and exclusive. Accusing British-Indians of treating their English servants improperly as though they were 'natives' suggests that at least some Bedford residents resented being 'colonized' by self-important new arrivals.

Local dislike of 'Squatters' from the empire derived from the view that British-Indians came to Bedford only to benefit from its educational offerings and reasonable rents, and lacked concern for its long-term condition. Not only did they often restrict their social interactions largely to their own circles but many never became permanent residents. While obituaries printed in local newspapers indicate that a significant number of those who had retired from India did remain in Bedford for decades until they died, countless others left the area after only a few years.[176] Younger people from India-connected families often returned to India, taking up where their parents left off. The Harpur Trust boys' schools facilitated this by placing their pupils in overseas careers, but other factors account for the perpetuation of Indian connections as well. Living in a community within a community created a cultural atmosphere that strongly encouraged the next generation to resume overseas life. As will be examined further below, dissatisfaction with their marginal standing and comparative 'poverty' in Britain may have led the offspring of repatriates to look back to the empire once they reached adulthood, since life there was seen to have benefited the family's fortunes in the past. As long as India or other colonial settings offered career opportunities, young men easily found reasons to perpetuate family links with these areas and, moreover, lived and studied in settings which made doing so a matter of course. Although relatively few young British-Indian women went back for a career, many more returned as wives after meeting men from similar backgrounds in Bedford just as others did in Cheltenham. This was true in Ruby Spankie's family, with several brothers following their father into the Indian Army and several sisters marrying either army officers or engineers based in the subcontinent who had once attended Bedford schools. Similarly, Beryl Irving and her sister both married naval officers they met in Bedford, while their brothers later pursued careers in India or Malaya.[177] Evelyn and Captain William Chaldecott (formerly a Grammar School pupil), whose later childrearing concerns in India were discussed in Chapter 2, also married after a Bedford courtship facilitated by two families with prior histories overseas or in the military.[178] Once back in India, such

---

[176] 'Obituary: C. J. Maltby', *Bedfordshire Standard*, 23 April 1937.

[177] BLARS, CRT 180 BED 191, letter from Miss R. M. Spankie to Patricia Bell, 18 Mar. 1980; BLARS, CRT 180/300, letter from Carol Irving to Patricia Bell, 6 Mar. 1980.

[178] 'Marriage of Capt. Chaldecott and Miss Edwards', *Bedfordshire Mercury*, 9 Aug. 1907.

families helped to perpetuate the presence of British-Indians in Bedford by spreading word of the town's attractions to others. As one of the house agents interviewed in 1910 noted, 'applications for houses frequently come on the recommendation of old Bedfordians and customers who have settled in various parts of the globe'.[179] Despite the failure of many of its members to settle there permanently, then, word of mouth helped to make Bedford's 'Squatter' community self-replicating.

British-Indian families in Bedford were considered temporary 'Squatters' not only because the next generation commonly returned to the empire after passing through the town's schools or marriage market, however. In many cases, married women, widows, or retired parents who came for their children's schooling also moved away once they had completed their education, regardless of desirable housing costs or the social pleasures to be found within a community of fellow colonial families. The reasons why these 'birds of a feather' did not always flock together permanently in retirement and simply spend the rest of their days in Bedford are not clear, but this tendency fits the wider pattern of ongoing transience among many British-Indians, as was seen earlier with the Beveridges and the Butlers. Rather than basing themselves in one particular locality when back on furlough or in retirement, British-Indians in all the enclaves considered here often remained unsettled within the metropole. Indeed, these same communities known for their substantial population of returned colonials were also those where many residents were impermanent by definition. Bayswater's countless hotels and boarding houses, and Cheltenham's and the seaside resorts' role as temporary holiday, health, and boarding-school destinations simultaneously attracted this migratory population and, moreover, encouraged it to remain so. Having grown accustomed to frequent mobility while overseas and in the course of multiple journeys to and from Britain, British-Indians might well remain rootless within the metropole, regardless of previous talk about making a 'home at home' while they were away. Whether stemming from an entrenched spirit of restlessness, unsatisfying experiences, or attenuated ties to specific places, many British-Indians remained birds of passage in Britain. Cultural and geographical estrangement after long periods away in combination with an unwillingness to adapt to 'reduced circumstances' after retirement, moreover, made others decide not to return at all and opt to remain abroad even after careers in India had come to an end.

[179] 'House-Letting in Bedford'.

RETIRING OVERSEAS

British-Indians unwilling to return to the metropole after retiring could choose from a number of alternative locales with fewer perceived drawbacks. Continental Europe provided some with a warmer climate and better living conditions on fixed incomes than they could find at home, and a number of destinations counted a significant proportion of colonial retirees among their British expatriate communities. Beginning in the early 1800s, Brittany's coastal resorts—especially Dinan, Dinard, St Malo, and St Servan—became popular among middle-class Britons seeking to retrench and, as John Pemble has put it, 'making do with cut-price gentility'.[180] As one *fin-de-siècle* writer enthused, 'there is no pleasanter place to economise than in Brittany. Comparisons are always odious, and here amongst the English there are none. It is pleasanter to live simply where others are doing likewise, and it takes less courage to wear last season's fashions when your next door neighbour is wearing the season's before.'[181] He singled out retired army officers as typical of those who benefited from the lower costs of living in the region, stating:

The man—say a retired colonel with a wife and a moderate family—who has £500 a year can live in comfort in a great many places, though he may not be able to send his sons to expensive public schools, or to Oxford. But to the same man with £300 a year life is a problem, and that problem can be solved by living in a place like St Servan, where he has no position to keep up . . . rents are cheaper, and high-class servants are much cheaper . . . you can do with one where you would need two in England.[182]

Switzerland served a similar purpose for other British-Indians. Writing in 1910, J. H. Rivett-Carnac—the scion of a family well known for Indian connections spanning many generations—attributed his decision to spend most of the year there to the cheaper lifestyle; 'amusements cost less', he summarized, and there was no need 'to keep up appearances, as one would have to do if one were to settle down in one's own country amongst one's peers'.[183]

By the early twentieth century and particularly during the interwar period, however, British-Indians in search of these conditions increasingly opted for Mediterranean resorts, including not only French or Italian Riviera towns such

[180] John Pemble, *The Mediterranean Passion: Victorians and Edwardians in the South* (Oxford, 1987), 106.

[181] Douglas Sladen, *Brittany for Britons* (London, 1896), 101. On Britons at continental European seaside resorts more generally, see John K. Walton, 'The Seaside Resorts of Western Europe, 1750–1939', in Stephen Fisher (ed.), *Recreation and the Sea* (Exeter, 1997), 40, 44–6, 49, 51.

[182] Sladen, *Brittany*, 6; see also 5, 77, 100.

[183] J. H. Rivett-Carnac, *Many Memories of Life in India, at Home, and Abroad* (Edinburgh, 1910), 397.

as Alassio, Rapallo, Nice, and Monte Carlo, but also Majorca and Corsica.[184] All were recommended by their climate, favorable exchange rates, and British expatriate communities in which both retirees and colonials were well represented. Not all places were considered conducive to saving; one writer warned against retiring to Monte Carlo, for instance, since 'most Anglo-Indians haven't any money to spare, and would prefer not to be always exposed to this temptation [of the casino]'.[185] None the less, as one historian noted, 'through most of the inter-war period it was not difficult for British expatriates to live a comfortable but unspectacular life in a Riviera villa with perhaps two servants on £300 a year', and receive income tax relief as well through living abroad.[186]

Regardless of continental Europe's attractions for some colonials, writers focusing on Britain's drawbacks more commonly advocated other retirement venues, specifically those within the empire. Discussions about retiring from India to other imperial settings became particularly widespread during the 1920s and 1930s. In part, this stemmed from the economic and social conditions examined above that caused many pensioners to feel that middle-class standards of living in Britain had declined since the war, particularly for those on a fixed income. Some choosing not to return to Britain combined a Mediterranean lifestyle with ongoing imperial residence by retiring in Cyprus, but organizations such as the Overseas League that actively promoted imperial settlement far more commonly recommended areas specifically designated as white settler colonies. Targeting the dominions, especially Canada, was meant to expand their English-speaking population and thereby help to strengthen the bonds of loyalty between Britain and regions that were increasingly charting their own course politically and economically. Advocates of dominion settlement also hoped that emigration would help to defuse the social tensions Britain experienced during a period of mass demobilization and high unemployment after the war. Soldier settlement and other schemes that facilitated emigration throughout the interwar years focused on ex-officers as well as rank-and-file servicemen, attracting men forced to retire early as a result of military retrenchment along with those leaving work at more standard ages.[187] Those retiring from India or other colonial arenas, whether from the military, civil service, or non-official professions, appear among the most

[184] Leakey, 'On Retiring', 60; 'Mauser', *How to Live*, 1930 edn., 156.

[185] C. du Pré Thornton, 'The Advantage of Retiring to the Riviera for Anglo-Indians', *The Cooper's Hill Magazine*, 12/5 (1925), 70–2.

[186] Patrick Howarth, *When the Riviera Was Ours* (London, 1977), 152–3.

[187] Kent Fedorowich, *Unfit for Heroes: Reconstruction and Soldier Settlement in the Empire Between the Wars* (Manchester, 1995); Stephen Constantine (ed.), *Emigrants and Empire: British Settlement in the Dominions Between the Wars* (Manchester, 1990).

likely to contemplate settling overseas because living outside Britain had become normal and, at least for some, was seen as increasingly desirable.

Whether those leaving India chose Cyprus, Nova Scotia, British Columbia, or a number of other imperial destinations, they were drawn by their similar reputations for allowing a better standard of living on their income than Britain. The Overseas League's journal praised Cyprus as an escape from inflation and higher taxes, allowing a family to 'live well' on £300 a year.[188] Articles extolling various parts of the dominions repeatedly spelled out their advantages for families with annual incomes ranging from £200 to £500, and who as such teetered at the lower end of middle-class British society—in short, those whose economic status resembled that of many who selected Bedford or the Riviera. Moreover, writers promoting emigration for officer-class families typically devoted attention to the opportunities they might have to increase their incomes from pensions, assuming limited private resources at best. Those who could raise the start-up capital to acquire land and embark upon small-scale, part-time agricultural endeavors—growing oranges in Cyprus and apples in Nova Scotia were two examples—were said to be able to increase their incomes by several hundred pounds a year.[189] Although some commentators also attempted to encourage retirees to enter into small-scale farming in Britain as well in the wake of the First World War, their chances of success (which were always limited, regardless of location) were seen as greater overseas.[190] In this manner, as several satisfied émigrés in Nova Scotia and British Columbia reported, life outside Britain offered retirees from Indian service the prospect of living 'comfortably' on between £200 and £400 a year and be considered rich with an income of £1,000, along with ample sporting opportunities at little cost, low taxes, and affordable, socially acceptable state education for children.[191] These advantages led one former engineer from India to describe Nova Scotia as a 'real white man's country', for it enabled a lifestyle that returning to the metropole largely foreclosed for middle-class retirees.[192] A white racial identity that had become defined as inseparable from a privileged

---

[188] S. H. C. Hawtrey, 'Orange Growing in Cyprus', *Overseas*, 17/200 (1932), 33–5.

[189] 'The Over-Seas League Migration Committee', *Overseas*, 12/137 (1927), 31–2; 'British Columbia from the Interior, by a Member in B. C.', *Overseas*, 13/144 (1928), 53–4; Lt.-Col. D. G. Robinson, 'A Suggestion for Would-be Emigrants of the Middle Classes', *Overseas*, 13/153 (1928), 47–8; 'The O.-S. League Migration Bureau: The Charm of British Columbia', *Overseas*, 15/169 (1930), 41–2.

[190] See n. 68.

[191] 'British Columbia from the Interior', 54; 'The O.-S. Migration Bureau', 41–2; 'The Over-seas League', 31; Robinson, 'A Suggestion', 47–8.

[192] 'Mente Manuque', 'Nova Scotia for Proportional Pensioners', *The Cooper's Hill Magazine*, 12/5 (1925), 70.

socio-economic status in British-Indian eyes, therefore, might well be seen as better preserved through the higher standards of living obtainable overseas than by returning to the 'old country'.

Attitudes concerning racial privilege developed after time in India, moreover, played a role in leading others to choose retirement in settler colonies in Africa, most commonly in Kenya, but also in Southern Rhodesia and, to a lesser degree, South Africa.[193] There as in India they could remain part of a small and empowered community within a predominantly non-white population, whereas in Canada or other 'white' dominions they merged with the majority of the inhabitants in racial terms just as they did in Britain. As Dane Kennedy's research reveals, newcomers to Kenya and Southern Rhodesia in the interwar era included a visible contingent of Indian Army officers as well as other India-connected men and their families who came in search of many of the same qualities that drew others to Canada or other dominions. Like those heading to other imperial destinations outside the metropole, they typically shared derogatory views of a changing Britain and fled 'the rising rate and progressive bent of income taxes and death duties, the declining number and increasing expense of servants, the spreading influence of technocratic and meritocratic values, [and] the growing power of the working class' that worked together 'to the detriment of the social standing and living standards of the traditional gentleman'. As Kennedy aptly summarizes of Kenya, 'here indeed was a haven for those whose social self-perceptions were not matched by their economic resources'.[194]

The appeal of settler colonies in East and Central Africa was so widely recognized in Indian civil and military circles that by the 1930s an Indian Army officer was sent on a special tour to gather more detailed information on retirement possibilities there for officers. His 1936 report highlights factors that clearly influenced some to spend their old age there as opposed to Britain, Canada, or other possible settings. While living expenses in Kenya, Southern Rhodesia, or other nearby British colonies were higher than in the dominions or popular continental venues noted above, the report nevertheless favored Africa over Britain in countless respects. Incomes could be supplemented through agricultural pursuits; sport and social activities resembling those to

---

[193] C. J. Duder, ' "Men of the Officer Class": The Participants in the 1919 Soldier Settlement Scheme in Kenya', *African Affairs*, 92/366 (1993), 69–87; and 'The Settler Response to the Indian Crisis of 1922 in Kenya: Brigadier General Philip Wheatley and "Direct Action" ', *Journal of Imperial and Commonwealth History*, 17/3 (1989), 349–73.

[194] Dane Kennedy, *Islands of White: Settler Society and Culture in Kenya and Southern Rhodesia, 1890–1939* (Durham, NC, 1987), 71–2; 60, 83–6.

which families had grown accustomed in India were readily available in another colonial setting; and the climate was said to 'suit those who have spent long years in the East and who wish to escape the rigours of the European winter'.[195] African settler colonies also offered specific advantages to women. Even the most glowing accounts of Canadian life warned about the hardships it entailed for most women because of the difficulties of getting domestic servants, who, if found at all, worked for wages considered high even by British standards. If written by men, they merely alluded in passing to the shortage of domestic labor as a minor inconvenience for those who 'like a simple life and do not mind doing most of their own housework'.[196] But, as one woman's account of British Columbia in 1927 stressed, 'the uncertainty of getting any sort of domestic help' made retirement there far more labor-intensive for women than anything they had experienced previously. 'Few women', she believed, 'lead more strenuous lives than those who make their home on a ranch in the far west of Canada . . . [they] take on the combined duties of cook, housemaid, charwoman and children's nurse, to which we must add a certain amount of laundry work'.[197] In Kenya or Southern Rhodesia, on the other hand, labor shortages were said to be nonexistent. 'Plenty of native labour, both agricultural and domestic, is forthcoming at very cheap rates', the 1936 report enthused. The African, furthermore, 'makes a cheerful and willing servant'—in other words, providing a stark contrast with the countless grievances expressed concerning both the lack of servants in Britain or Canada and their supposed failure to be diligent workers.[198] As a result, 'Kenya houses are a revelation in comfort, appearance and cheapness . . . compared with what one could hope to do in this respect in England, one can indulge in a rich man's tastes for the same money'—and, it might be added, a rich woman's tastes as well.[199]

Families with children were also said to benefit from relocating to Africa. Chapters 1 and 2 considered parental reservations about keeping children in India because of concerns about the climate, interactions with Indians in the home, and the social and racial implications of sending them to schools in the company of mixed-race or poorer British children. White children's and adolescents' health was not widely believed to suffer if they remained in Kenya or Rhodesia, nor was reference made to any dangers stemming from their proximity to Africans. Unlike in India, moreover, educating children locally

[195] OIOC, V/27/820/19, Government of India, *A Report on Southern Rhodesia, Northern Rhodesia, Nyasaland and Kenya* (Simla, 1936), 1, 16, 12, 20.
[196] 'British Columbia from the Interior', 54.
[197] 'Ruth', 'A Rancher's Wife in British Columbia', *Overseas*, 12/133 (1927), 39–40.
[198] OIOC, V/27/820/19, *Report on Southern Rhodesia*, 3, 11, 121.   [199] Ibid., 17, 121

did not suggest a lower socio-economic standing that implied possible mixed-race heritage largely because far fewer persons of these descriptions were said to live there; in fact, mixed-race persons rarely entered discussions at all. Like many other depictions of East and Central Africa, the 1936 report stressed the relative social uniformity of their white populations: 'the artisan and labouring classes are relatively small in number, and tend to be superior socially to their counterparts at home, largely on account of the presence of the native population who provide most of the actual manual labour. This is an important point to remember when considering the suitability of the Government schools from the social point of view.' Despite their being inexpensive and occasionally free, there was 'nothing derogatory' about attending them, since children 'would meet there many [others] of the same social status'.[200]

Ideas about their appropriateness for British middle-class children do much to explain why certain East and Central African colonies became constructed as appropriate for permanent European settlement while India decidedly did not; uninterrupted residence and schooling in Africa was not perceived as a social or racial setback, even for boys needing good career prospects. Periodic trips to and education in Britain, while they undoubtedly reflected and enhanced status, were not as essential to respectability nor as much of a defining characteristic of whiteness. Thus, families formerly based in India but who did not count themselves among its 'domiciled' community might contemplate settling in parts of Africa and the likelihood that their children would remain there permanently without the fear that this would connote declining racial status. Instead, they could look to Africa to provide aspects of a colonial lifestyle—including plentiful domestic help, leisure opportunities, and an empowering racial status—they had long enjoyed and which Britain commonly failed to provide.

If many families were hesitant about returning to Britain and sought to perpetuate many of the advantages they had enjoyed in India by settling in East or Central Africa, then, did others simply opt to remain where they were after retiring? Paul Scott's post-colonial fiction has popularized the notion that Britons might 'stay on' in India upon retirement, typically at one of the hill stations in the Himalayas or the Nilgiris, rather than go back to a homeland from which they had become estranged. They might thus remain in the subcontinent until they died and even, as in Scott's novel, long outlive the raj itself.[201] The extent to which this image had a significant counterpart in reality either

---

[200] OIOC, V/27/820/19, 10, 114. Kennedy, however, rightly notes that depictions of a homogeneous society were often a myth, albeit an extremely potent and long-lasting one. *Islands of White*, 182–3, 186.

[201] Paul Scott, *Staying On* (1977; repr. London, 1978).

before or after 1947, however, is doubtful. Some indeed did 'stay on'; a 1926 account, for instance, described Ootacamund's appeal for 'those who fly from the taxes, rents, servants, and labour troubles of England', where they 'passed contentedly the evening of their days in the sweet half-English Nilgiri air'.[202] Nevertheless, given the cultural and racial threats that acquiring a domiciled European identity entailed, parents with children still at school would have been unlikely to settle in India unless they could afford a metropolitan education for them. In this scenario, 'staying on' in India only perpetuated the need to pay for journeys home and family separations. Considered from this perspective, it is significant that Scott chose to make Tusker and Lucy Smalley, his elderly characters living in a hill station in the 1960s and 1970s, a childless couple. 'Staying on' with children, given the long-standing reservations about the meanings of 'domiciled' status for subsequent generations, was not actively contemplated by most parents, even those who decided to forsake the metropole for an old age in Africa, Canada, or Europe.

Crucially, however, many families 'stayed on' in India even though it was uncommon to remain after retirement. Parents might go home or settle elsewhere, but children often returned to perpetuate family traditions without acquiring the status of permanent residents. This chapter concludes by briefly considering how a family's presence in India came to be transferred from one generation to the next. This occurred in part due to educational patterns, as the previous chapter outlined, but also because family culture and experiences facilitated an ongoing Indian connection for young men and women who were born, and ended up remaining, transient British-Indians.

RETURNS TO INDIA

Despite the drawbacks to living away from home, many Britons maintained their ties to the subcontinent for decades and often for generations. Some who had known India in early childhood had nostalgic memories of it and made efforts to return, while many also embarked on a second period of life in India as young adults because of career openings or marriage possibilities there. In many cases, children's and adolescents' lives in Britain had been marked by the conditions described above, and going back to India offered a means of sidestepping these social, economic, and cultural dilemmas. For Rumer Godden and her sisters as well as for M. M. Kaye, all of these factors contributed to

---

[202] J. Chartres Molony, *A Book of South India* (London, 1926), 47.

their return. For Godden, adolescence in England meant separation from her father and living with her mother and sisters in rented houses, which 'had to be cheap and . . . were small with shabby furniture'; middle class 'was the height of aspiration'. For her and her three sisters, rejoining their father in India and ultimately marrying there brought comparative luxury.[203] For Kaye, her longing for India during childhood years in England only grew stronger after her parents retired. The prospect of an adult life devoid of glamor was reinforced upon witnessing both her mother's domestic drudgery and reminiscences about 'the gaiety of India; all the parties and dances and shooting-camps, "the folly and the fun" '. Their rescue from social obscurity and economic limitations came when her father accepted a special assignment in India and took his family back with him, allowing Kaye to return to long-missed childhood haunts, enjoy romance with a surplus of young single officers, and ultimately marry one and embark upon the lifestyle her mother had cherished.[204] For other families like the Talbots, meanwhile, the next generation may have returned to India partly because of opportunities there and partly because pre-existing connections facilitated going back even when this had not been planned originally.

After Agnes Talbot's death, the family dreams for a future when, as Adelbert had said, 'we should all be together for good' in England were destroyed.[205] Adelbert left all four children in England and planned to rejoin them once he retired six years later. Since his eldest daughters Guendolen and Muriel had finished school, however, they contemplated spending the time with him in India—a possibility that never would have arisen had their mother survived to supervise them in England. Living with their father saved the cost of maintaining their home near Tunbridge Wells, but Muriel pressured their father to agree for less practical reasons. Adelbert wrote to Guendolen from his post with the Foreign Office at Simla that Muriel 'constantly writes extolling Simla, and if I stay here would no doubt insist on coming out, for nothing I could say I fear would dissuade her from the belief that Simla in an Earthly Paradise'.[206] From Muriel's perspective, the choice between quiet domesticity and social anonymity at Frant and life as the daughter of a prominent official in one of British India's foremost social arenas was simple, but her father proved harder to convince. Adelbert assumed that if his daughters joined him they would

---

[203] Rumer Godden, *A Time to Dance, No Time to Weep* (New York, 1987), 25, 52.
[204] Kaye, *Sun in the Morning*, 432, 435–48.
[205] OIOC, MSS Eur E410/7, Adelbert Talbot to Guendolen Talbot, 8 Sept. 1894.
[206] Ibid., Adelbert Talbot to Guendolen Talbot, 25 Aug. 1894.

marry and replicate the family's pattern of residence away from home, which he had come to regret. He wrote to Guendolen,

My own preference would be that you should stay at Frant in our own little home, secure from the many risks of Indian life. These are not the creations of my brain believe me: at the present time there is an epidemic of typhoid fever going on at Mhow . . . Indian life is hard at the best of times, with the separations it means and the frequent loss of health. If a girl married a poor man in a Native Infantry Regiment in these days of the fallen rupee there would be a miserable life before her, poverty of the most depressing kind would be her lot.[207]

Gradually realizing his efforts were futile, he later continued,

Your mother and I hoped that you would none of you come out to India, but if you wish to do so I will not stand in the way. Remember that an Indian life is a hard one for women in many ways. You know what it has meant in our case, and how we have been practically exiles, with many separations from those we love, and in these days of bad exchange but poor prospect of comfort at the end of it all. You must weigh against this prospect a quiet life at Frant in our own little home, in your own country with Addy and Esmé.[208]

Adelbert's half-hearted campaign to convince his daughters to stay home ultimately proved ineffectual, and Guendolen and Muriel left England to join him in 1894. Once Muriel sent back glowing reports of their activities and described the beauties of Kashmir where their father had become Resident, Esmé became equally eager to go. 'Kashmir sounds a perfect Paradise . . . I wonder if Papa will let me come out there . . . ?', she wondered.[209] Adelbert conceded, and she arrived in short order. Despite many qualms about life in India, Adelbert's guidance to his children about making their future there was always contradictory as he alternated between emphasizing its disadvantages and promoting its opportunities. On the one hand, in response to an English friend's request for advice in getting a son a place in the Indian Police, he mused to Guendolen, 'I wonder why India has such an attraction for people: in these days of bad pay [due to the fallen rupee] it seems to me to be a very second-rate place in which to earn a living, and a young fellow with health and energy ought to do better in the old country.'[210] Nevertheless, while his son Addy was

---

[207] Ibid., Adelbert Talbot to Guendolen Talbot, 12 Aug. 1894.

[208] Ibid., Adelbert Talbot to Guendolen Talbot, 18 Oct. 1894. In the late nineteenth century, Britons in India paid in rupees experienced a decline in real income due to the rupee's depreciation. See Arnold Kaminsky, '"Lombard Street" and India: Currency Problems in the Late Nineteenth Century', *Indian Economic and Social History Review*, 17/3 (1980), 307–27; D. K. Malhotra, *History and Problems of Indian Currency, 1835–1959: An Introductory Study*, 6th edn. (Simla, 1960), I, 5–11.

[209] OIOC, MSS Eur E 354/36, Esmé Talbot to Muriel Talbot, 19 Feb. [n.d.; 1896].

[210] OIOC, MSS Eur E 410/7, Adelbert Talbot to Guendolen Talbot, 3 Nov. 1894.

at Oxford he repeatedly reminded him of the age limits for beginning an Indian Civil Service career 'should he hereafter develop a taste for coming out here', and sent him information about the entrance examination.[211] Regardless of his and his deceased wife's longing to return to their homeland and establish a domestic environment within it that they hoped to enjoy in old age with their children nearby, he failed to achieve this in part because of the messages he passed on to his son and daughters that led all four to pursue adult lives in India when he returned to England.

Adelbert retired in November 1900; in the same month Addy arrived in the subcontinent as a newly appointed Indian Civil Service officer.[212] Although Addy entered a different branch of employment than his father, their paths none the less mark a passing of the imperial service baton from one generation to the next. All three of Adelbert's daughters also embarked upon the course followed by many young British-Indian women by returning to their father after they finished school and then marrying and remaining in India past their father's eventual departure. Of their husbands, two of the three resembled Adelbert professionally. Guendolen, true to his prediction, married less than two years after her arrival. Her husband, Stuart Godfrey, was also in the Indian Political Service, and their meeting occurred as a result of his posting as Political Agent at Gilgit in Kashmir during Adelbert's period as Resident of the state. Periods of leave in England aside, she remained in India until Stuart retired in 1916. Esmé married another Indian Political Service officer, Armine Dew, with whom she had ' "clicked" at once' upon meeting at the Residency in Kashmir; Muriel, meanwhile, married Percy Brown of the Indian Educational Service, who was Principal of the Mayo School of Art in Lahore.[213] Correspondence between Muriel, Percy, and their daughter while she was at boarding school in Britain the 1920s showed the same family difficulties in coping with parent–child separations as had existed between the Talbot children and their parents.[214] Adelbert's children's decisions to choose paths that largely mirrored his and his wife's expatriate lives were a result of India's career and social opportunities as well as a consequence of earlier generations having paved

---

[211] OIOC, MSS Eur E 410/7, Adelbert Talbot to Guendolen Talbot, 25 Nov. 1894, 2 Dec. 1894.

[212] For the particulars of Adelbert Talbot's and his son's careers, see *The India Office List for 1907* (London, 1907), 643.

[213] OIOC, Sir Armine Dew Papers, MSS Eur D1222/1, 'Our Affairs' by Esmé Mary Dew (née Talbot), n.d. [c. 1943], photocopy of typescript; Part II, 19–20; OIOC, MSS Eur E354/98, card, 'Marriages: Brown: Talbot'. Excerpt from *The Times* (London), 3 Nov. 1908.

[214] OIOC, MSS Eur E354/28, letters to Muriel Brown from Barbara Brown, c.1924–31; MSS Eur E354/29, letters to Muriel and Percy Brown from Barbara Brown, 1922–3.

the way for them to return and continue the family's tradition of imperial service, despite the resulting family problems they all resented.

Adelbert's dreams of family domesticity in England were therefore largely limited to seeing his children during their brief visits on furlough and to looking after his grandchildren during many of their holidays once they had left India for boarding school. Guendolen's son Jack Godfrey, born in 1897 and sent to England in 1904, later described spending his holidays alone with 'Bapa', a seemingly melancholy and reclusive old man. According to Jack, Adelbert was 'wrapped up in memories of his long-dead wife, and was not given to much talk. But within his powers he was very good to me, and undoubtedly very fond of me also: and I grew to love him.'[215] When Adelbert died in 1920, Guendolen and Addy were back in England permanently, but Muriel and Esmé still lived in India. Writing to Muriel, Esmé described her sadness along with her reflections on the tenuousness of the family's ties with both England and India as a result of leading lives divided between the two places. 'He was such a loving father and gave us all such warm welcomes home—indeed, High Barn was the only place we could look on as home in England . . . How cut off one feels out here, where there are few left who knew him—and no one really cares.'[216] Ironically Adelbert, whose own ties with home had been renewed late in life and were done alone rather than as a family endeavor, came to represent home to his children based overseas. For Esmé, three interconnected meanings of home—as family, a stable household, and England—were lost or diminished upon her father's death.

Later writings, however, also suggest that Esmé's feelings about home grew more ambivalent the longer she remained defined by ongoing imperial migration. While India had come to lose its allure for Adelbert and his wife who longed for home near the end of his career, for Esmé its attractiveness seemingly never waned. In her memoir written in the 1940s long after her husband retired, she described how the transient British-Indian lifestyle that she had experienced since birth had made home seem a threat as well as a promise:

We never had a settled home and moved about to furnished rooms or houses, when Mother and sometimes my Father too, came home. This has had a distinct influence on one's character I feel sure, and though there is a side of me that has longed for an ancestral home, steeped in centuries of thoughts, aspirations and traditions of one

---

[215] OIOC, MSS Eur E410/108, Brigadier J. T. Godfrey, photocopy of typewritten extract from 'Personal Tale', n.d., 12–13.
[216] OIOC, MSS Eur E354/36, Esmé Dew to Muriel Brown, 31 Dec. [1920].

family, and the rooted feeling that must give, there is another side which would be suffocated by so much sameness, and as strongly longs to roam the world.[217]

Looking back while in her sixties, Esmé recounted her and her husband's lives during his Indian Political Service years with relish. Often moving to a new posting every six months and making frequent journeys back to Britain, they acquired few possessions and broke many others in transit, but Esmé recalled living in remote Himalayan regions as offering freedom from domestic constraints. When her husband retired in 1921, she remembered:

It was with a terrible constriction of the heart I realised that from now on the care-free life of the past years, speaking from a domestic point of view, with its freedom from the heavy pressure of urban restrictions and conventions, a life lived in the exquisite purity of light-filled air among well-loved mountains and wide spaces, was gone forever along with our youth. The poetry of life with its unforgettable starlit nights . . . the silent music of the great mountains . . . seemed quenched by the prose of daily life on a pension.[218]

Although imbued with considerable nostalgia, this retrospective account suggests that Esmé never idealized domesticity as her parents had, just as her homeland lacked the same appeal. She and her husband tellingly managed to circumvent 'the prose of daily life on a pension' in Britain by spending the first ten years of his retirement in Switzerland, which offered not only further opportunities for travel and proximity to the mountains both had grown to love, but also a cheaper lifestyle.[219] While they ultimately returned to Britain, Esmé and Armine Dew did so only after considerably prolonging their absence from home and living in further makeshift accommodation, preferring to stay on the move and indulge in activities that otherwise were beyond their means on a pension.

As these many accounts suggest, therefore, misgivings about some aspects of British-Indian life were frequently offset by a strong appreciation of its many advantages. Awareness of India's benefits derived in part from experiences in the subcontinent, but acknowledgement of them often came during periods of time spent at home. Central to British-Indians' reservations about metropolitan life was their reduced class standing. In India, a white British and middle-class status succeeded in elevating many into the higher echelons of colonial society and enabled them to enjoy its countless privileges, while in Britain race

---

[217] OIOC, MSS Eur D1222/1, 'Our Affairs' by Esmé Mary Dew, Part I, 8.
[218] Ibid., Part III, 5–8; 78–9; 81.
[219] Ibid., 81.

lost its ability to set them as far above the majority as many would have liked. Although reduced circumstances at home came in part when their incomes declined in retirement, even their full salaries were insufficient to allow them to live in any manner resembling Britain's upper classes, with whom they commonly compared themselves. Retirement in Europe, the dominions, or African settler colonies was therefore an appealing alternative for some families, while for others the solution came when the next generation returned to India.

Maintaining a foothold in Britain allowed families to evade the lower status attached to the 'domiciled' community in India at the same time as it reminded them how much they benefited from ongoing involvement overseas, where they were far more likely to be part of the colonial equivalent of Britain's 'upper ten thousand' than was possible in the metropole. Imperial transience, indeed, quite literally allowed British-Indians both to define and partake of what constituted 'posh'. 'Port outward, starboard home' was how the more affluent British-Indians travelled on ocean liners between metropole and empire, but while epitomizing 'posh' on board ship they rarely merited this distinction upon arriving home.[220] Interstitial identities created by outsider status as colonizers both when Britain and in India, yet simultaneously by connections with both arenas, perhaps caused them to be most fully 'at home' on the ships travelling between the two.

Many families maintained this pattern of migration until Indian independence in 1947, and indeed have continued to embark on figurative returns to India in the post-colonial era. *Empire Families* concludes by considering how nostalgic memories of long-term family and personal engagement with India have continued to remain part of many Britons' sense of self long after the end of empire. Moreover, their written and spoken renditions of the raj have become an important facet of British public culture in recent decades, perhaps ironically making those long situated on the margins of metropolitan society far more central to its self-definition in the aftermath of empire than during their period of direct involvement overseas.

---

[220] Although these origins of the term 'posh' have been disputed by some, in *The Oxford English Dictionary*, 2nd edn., vol. XII (Oxford, 1989), 164, there are no proposed alternatives.

Conclusion

Plain Tales and Family Romances: Remembering the Raj in Post-Colonial Britain

Over the decades spanning the end of empire in the Indian subcontinent until the present day, how have the British assessed national and individual endeavors in South Asia? Writing in 1997, Charles Allen argued that common conceptions had changed radically, in part as a result of efforts by persons like himself to 'resuscitate the Raj':

It is hard to believe now in the mid-1990s how hostile the British media and British academia were to all notions of Empire a quarter of a century ago. This hostility wasn't limited to the concept of imperialism but extended to all those who in one way or another had been involved in running the empire . . . Yet it seemed that my own father was one of these oppressors. All those first years of my childhood in India when I'd so often seen him receiving deputations of the local tribespeople on the front verandah, listening and talking to them in their own dialects, or when he'd gone away for months long tours in the hills—was that what he'd been doing? Oppressing them? Somehow it didn't quite seem to fit the bill.[1]

Allen's desire to defend 'good decent people . . . [who] were being vilified simply for being part of an historical process over which they had no control' applies to many men and women who made personal and family stories of British India public after decolonization. Yet Allen occupies a paramount position in the spate of rememberings and retellings; indeed, his oral history project and its multi-media dissemination in the mid-1970s provided much of the initial momentum behind the proliferation of raj memories more than thirty years after independence. *Plain Tales from the Raj* began as a series of programs for BBC Radio 4 in 1974 and was followed by a second series the following year. Accompanying these was a book which reached the number two position in the

---

[1] Charles Allen, 'Resuscitating the Raj', in Rosie Llewellyn-Jones (ed.), *Chowkidar, 1977–1997* (London, 1997), 4.

non-fiction bestseller lists and has since sold over 400,000 copies. The book remains in print today; moreover, in British bookstores whose stock related to Indian history often amounts to less than one shelf of display space, *Plain Tales* is one of titles most certain to appear. Its success led Allen to compile other broadcasts and books treating British experiences in colonial Africa and Southeast Asia, suggesting that a substantial audience had been established for stories of Britain's overseas history.[2]

Throughout the previous chapters, *Empire Families* has examined the family lives of Britons whose livelihoods came from Indian careers, often for more than one generation. Many participants stressed the downsides to their links with the subcontinent: risks to health and character, especially for vulnerable children; risks to racial and class identity if children stayed in India 'too long' and failed to receive a British education; family separations once the coveted school experiences in the metropole began; and lengthy absences from home. Weighed against these disadvantages, however, were happy childhood memories of India; measures taken to minimize threats posed by India's geography and peoples and often extol rather than condemn colonial social contacts; and a keen awareness of the superior professional and socio-economic status members of white society enjoyed in India that dwindled upon return to a homeland from which absences had produced alienation. These do much to explain multi-generational family presences in the Indian subcontinent without participants being seen as domiciled 'country borns' who had lost contact with the metropole. By the time of Indian and Pakistani independence in 1947, many middle-class Britons who had derived pleasure and power from South Asia had family histories long inseparable from the raj's. Most supported by official occupations left upon decolonization. Those who were part of the commercial, missionary, or planting communities may have stayed longer, but they too ultimately terminated their involvement, usually by the late 1960s.

When Charles Allen set out to record memories of imperial India on British soil, then, he encountered many individuals like himself with strong vested interests in the raj, both personal and ancestral, that were far from forgotten after the end of empire. Like its former colonies and dependencies overseas Britain is a post-colonial nation, defined after the Second World War as much

---

[2] Ibid., 6; Charles Allen in association with Michael Mason, *Plain Tales from the Raj* (London, 1975). Cassettes based upon the broadcasts were also widely available for purchase. Subsequent publications and radio series included Charles Allen, *Raj: A Scrapbook of British India, 1877–1947* (London, 1977); Charles Allen in association with Helen Fry, *Tales from the Dark Continent* (London, 1979), and *Tales from the South China Seas* (London, 1983).

by the loss of its empire as it once was characterized as its possessor. As Stuart Hall suggests, the post-colonial concerns a 'general process of decolonisation which, like colonisation itself, has marked the colonising societies as powerfully as it has the colonised'.[3] Considering how citizens of South Asian nations have critiqued, rejected, accepted, or adapted aspects of the raj's ideological, institutional, and material remains to their own ends is beyond the scope of this book.[4] Yet unlike former British territories such as South Africa and Zimbabwe that had substantial white settler communities, South Asians grappling with their imperial history have not done so in the midst of more than a negligible number of whites who 'stayed on'. One of the most salient features of *Britain's* post-coloniality, however, involves ongoing re-evaluations and debates about the imperial legacy both by former colonizers who returned home as well as by a wider public. Late twentieth- and early twenty-first-century renditions of British India certainly constitute the post-colonial, but they reflect a specific juncture when the colonial era itself remains a living memory for many people. Albeit a dwindling group, raj survivors are at least partly responsible for the tenor that interpretations of colonial South Asia have taken to date. Later generations exploring these issues once the wider 'process' of decolonization has moved further along will, of necessity, reach their own conclusions about Britain's imperial history and its legacy.

This book concludes with a brief examination of former British-Indians' contributions to understandings of empire in the aftermath of widescale decolonization in the 1950s and 1960s. As the previous chapter argued, many who returned to the metropole prior to 1947 considered themselves cultural outsiders following long periods and countless life experiences far from Britain's shores. In the late twentieth century, however, their stories became highly influential in shaping wider conceptions of the nation's imperial heritage. As a recent collection of essays edited by Stuart Ward attests, the long-standing contention that Britons at home remained largely unaffected by, and unconcerned about, the end of empire is now under heavy scholarly fire. Arthur Marwick's view that 'the most notable consequences were felt by members of the upper and upper-middle classes who no longer had the raj as a territory in which to

---

[3] Stuart Hall, 'When was "the Post-Colonial"? Thinking at the limit', in Iain Chambers and Lidia Curti (eds.), *The Post-colonial Question: Common Skies, Divided Horizons* (London, 1996), 246. Valuable insights on 'the post-colonial' are also provided by Anne McClintock, *Imperial Leather: Race, Gender, and Sexuality in the Colonial Contest* (New York, 1995), 9–17.

[4] Suggestive works on these issues include Tapan Raychaudhuri, 'British Rule in India: An Assessment', in P. J. Marshall (ed.), *The Cambridge Illustrated History of the British Empire* (Cambridge, 1996), 357–69; Zareer Masani, *Indian Tales of the Raj* (London, 1987); Ramachandra Guha, *A Corner of a Foreign Field: The Indian History of a British Sport* (London, 2002); Ian Baucom, *Out of Place: Englishness, Empire, and the Locations of Identity* (Princeton, NJ, 1999).

exploit their natural gifts of leadership' is challenged by many researchers engaged in charting far wider repercussions of decolonization within British society and culture.[5] Former participants certainly were not the only Britons upon whom the end of empire had a impact, but they did play disproportionate roles in shaping broader national understandings of the raj through generating and disseminating a rich seam of recollection. Public forms of 'knowledge' about the past and its meanings are often generated outside universities, and in this instance contributions by repatriated British-Indians have proved extremely influential.[6] What were the contents of their stories, and which types of imperial experiences predominate in raj memories? What accounts for the timing of their emergence in the post-colonial metropole? Moreover, how do personal narratives interact with media and academic portrayals of British India—some of which are inflected by nostalgia, while others are influenced by post-colonial criticism even stronger than the hostility Charles Allen identified yet claimed had receded into the background?

Allen's encapsulation of his own impulse for raj resuscitation resembles countless other late twentieth-century accounts by Britons once involved in India. His childhood memories and assessment of his father's career appeared at odds with metropolitan social perceptions, driving him to solicit the views of others who wanted their experiences to go on record. Narratives by the middle classes make up the vast majority of such accounts. Class bias characterizes not only Allen's documentaries but also most other media and archival projects that encouraged raj participants to commit their memories to paper or tape (a theme discussed further below), as well as those who did so of their own accord. While working-class Britons also went to India in large numbers (often during the course of military service), they left behind far fewer detailed descriptions of their time overseas. Whether this stems from the fact that many spent only a limited tour of duty rather than a considerable part of their lives in the subcontinent, is attributable to a more limited enthusiasm for looking back upon a time that was not deemed worthy of their positive recollection, or reflects their being less frequently approached by persons responsible for compiling raj experiences for posterity is unclear.[7] Within the corpus of recollections by the better-off, however, men and women writing or talking about their time in South Asia appraise their own earlier lives and the roles played by family

---

[5] Arthur Marwick, *British Society Since 1945*, 3rd edn. (London, 1996), 103, cited in Stuart Ward, 'Introduction', in Stuart Ward (ed.), *British Culture and the End of Empire* (Manchester, 2001), 4.

[6] Raphael Samuel, *Theatres of Memory*, Vol. I: *Past and Present in Contemporary Culture* (London, 1994); Patrick Wright, *On Living in an Old Country: The National Past in Contemporary Britain* (London, 1985).

[7] For an excellent discussion of how '*all* archives are provisional, interested, and calcified in both deliberate and unintentional ways', see Antoinette Burton, *Dwelling in the Archive: Women Writing House, Home, and History in Late Colonial India* (New York, 2003), 26.

members in comparable ways. While some aspects of their stories differ by virtue of the gendered nature of their imperial experiences, several examples share remarkable similarites with respect to their nostalgia, their pride concerning the roles they and/or their families played in the empire, and their reasons (whether implicit or explicit) for recording their accounts for other audiences. Their texts range from those that became disseminated fairly widely upon publication to those intended for a much more limited circle of readers, but their contents as well as their tone none the less take on broadly identifiable contours.

Raleigh Trevelyan's 1987 book *The Golden Oriole: A 200-Year History of an English Family in India* exemplifies the intersection of personal, family, and colonial India's histories. As its title indicates, his text documents the Trevelyan family's lengthy association with the subcontinent dating from the late 1700s to the 1930s. Trevelyan's imperial lineage was a formidable one, including most notably Charles Trevelyan, Governor of Madras in the 1830s; the eminent historian and commentator Thomas Babington Macaulay; persons killed during the 1857 uprising; G. O. Trevelyan, who authored *The Competition Wallah* in 1864; and his own father, an Indian Army officer during the first third of the twentieth century.[8] In *The Golden Oriole*, he recounts his multiple visits back to South Asia in the 1970s and 1980s which originated from genealogical curiosity and an anxiousness to rediscover his nearly forgotten early childhood in Kashmir. He describes his subsequent time in English boarding schools starting at the age of 8 as 'years of blankness', when separation from his parents created long-standing emotional estrangement from them.[9] Claiming, moreover, always to have felt out of place in Britain following his first years overseas, Trevelyan journeyed to India and Pakistan after his father's death in an attempt to rediscover the colonial background they shared through returning to what had been familial terrain. Family photograph albums of his childhood years sparked his desire to return. 'When I saw again those wonderful pictures of the country around Gilgit I knew that some day I must return there', he recalled. 'Could any place have been so beautiful? Could I ever have been so happy? . . . Nostalgic fool that I was, and am, I nearly wept.'[10]

 The Golden Oriole became the product of Trevelyan's search for roots: 'the book that I vaguely had in my mind to write was a nostalgic one about going

---

 [8] Another relative, Humphrey Trevelyan, contributed *The India We Left* (London, 1972) to the family canon.

 [9] Raleigh Trevelyan, *The Golden Oriole: A 200-Year History of an English Family in India* (New York, 1987), 9.

 [10] Ibid., 10–11.

back and what it was like to have lived in such remote places. Gradually this also developed into a kind of quest, not for identity, but proof of existence.'[11] Trevelyan's reassessment of his own past became linked with documenting ancestral links with South Asia, the two strands converging in his reflections about his childhood and simultaneously the implications of belonging to the last generation to witness British rule firsthand. 'I often feel that I belong to a tribe that is becoming extinct', he states at the outset.[12] Like many others who have contributed personal accounts of the raj since the 1970s, he seeks to enhance the historical record of empire as a member of an ageing cohort —and, crucially, to do so before it becomes 'too late' and the 'tribe' vanishes completely.

Childhood occupies a pivotal position in Trevelyan's work, as it does in countless other post-colonial raj recollections. In his study of autobiographies that emphasize this time of life, Richard Coe notes that 'the need to establish an identity, in one way or another, is one of the most compelling motives for writing a childhood'.[13] Carolyn Steedman similarly charts the ways that the child-figure has long had a privileged role within Western cultural understandings of adults' 'interiority', or selfhood.[14] For Trevelyan, the very title of his book illustrates the extent to which his 'quest' to revisit and comprehend his own past and family history is propelled by recollections of his early life prior to separation from his parents and the land of his birth: the golden oriole was the bird he remembered seeing the day he left Gilgit en route to school, and alienation, in England.[15]

Born in 1923 and looking back in the late 1980s at a childhood only two decades prior the raj's demise, Trevelyan is able to relish these early memories in part by standing one step removed from adults whom critics of empire might ask to shoulder the blame for it, given that his own personal involvement ended when he was 8. Anthropologist Renato Rosaldo has provided an apt analysis of the manner in which sentimental notions of childhoods past can act as a justification for imperial domination. 'Much of imperialist nostalgia's force resides in its association with (indeed, disguise as) more genuinely innocent tender recollections of what is at once an earlier epoch and a previous stage of life', he argues, 'transform[ing] the responsible colonial agent into an innocent

---

[11] Ibid., 13.

[12] Ibid., 1.

[13] Richard Coe, *When the Grass Was Taller: Autobiography and the Experience of Childhood* (New Haven, CT, 1984), 61–2.

[14] Carolyn Steedman, *Strange Dislocations: Childhood and the Idea of Human Interiority, 1780–1930* (London, 1995).

[15] Trevelyan, *Golden Oriole*, 37–8.

bystander'.[16] 'As a child [I] had little sense of colonial guilt', Trevelyan reflected.[17] His age thus enabling him to evade the full brunt of active participation, he remains able both to retain his happy childhood memories as well as to extol his ancestors' (and his nation's) heroism, accomplishments, and good intentions in the subcontinent at the same time as he displays an uneasy awareness that there were, and remain, many who disagree with such an assessment of imperialism. Unabashed praise for Charles Trevelyan, who helped to 'lay the foundations of India's democracy' in the post-colonial era, exemplifies his pride in Britain's imperial legacy and his ability to claim a blood relationship with a prominent imperial figure. Similarly, he takes pleasure in recounting the views of Indians he met decades after independence who conveyed their own admiration for aspects of British rule with which he felt so intimately connected.[18]

Ronald Rice also counts among the post-colonial authors who chart their lengthy family histories in the subcontinent through the prism of their own returns after the end of empire. In his unpublished manuscript 'Mysore Revisited, 1973', Rice describes revisiting what was not only his birthplace but also the setting where three earlier generations of his forebears spent much of their lives and made their careers. He chronicles what he called 'four weeks of holiday and pilgrimage to the places linked with our family', the term 'pilgrimage' suggesting the quasi-sacred role India occupied within his personal and ancestral past.[19] His journey encompassed the sites of his great-grandfather's missionary endeavors, museums holding his grandfather's archaeological and scholarly works, and bridges his father, an engineer, helped to construct. Throughout his travelogue, Rice stresses the strong commitment to India by both individual Britons and the nation as a whole within the framework of his ancestors' wide-ranging professional activities. Of his trip to see the Maddarhalla Aqueduct, completed in 1911 under his father's technical supervision, he writes, 'the length of this aqueduct with its 77 spans . . . made me realise what a vast amount of capital and trouble the British put into India during their occupation. *I always feel sure that my father and the others felt it was their service to India rather than their exploitation of it.*'[20]

Like both Raleigh Trevelyan and Charles Allen, Rice invokes the specter of exploitation in a manner strongly suggesting nagging uncertainties (regardless

[16] Renato Rosaldo, 'Imperialist Nostalgia', in *Culture and Truth: The Remaking of Social Analysis* (Boston, MA, 1989), 70.
[17] Trevelyan, *Golden Oriole*, 401.
[18] Ibid., 490, 156.
[19] CSAA, Rice Papers, Ronald Rice, 'Mysore Revisited, 1973: Also Ootacamund and Colombo', typewritten manuscript (1973), 1.
[20] Ibid., 16; emphasis added.

of 'always feeling sure') about whether he should acquiesce to a guilty conscience about an indissociably imperial family history in the post-colonial period. Yet like the other two raj descendants, he ends by rejecting this unpalatable possibility in favor of highlighting his ancestors' hard work and selflessness on India's behalf; moreover, he enlists Indian opinions to support his own assessment. Describing his visit to the Government Museum in Mysore, which housed many of his grandfather's archaeological discoveries and studies, he emphasizes the curator's warm welcome:

When he heard who I was he practically embraced me, and said that my grandfather was the greatest character in the historical investigations of Mysore State. He showed me a series of about 20 volumes . . . [of] inscriptions in the Canarese or Kannada language. He said that my grandfather must have worked 18 hours a day to get through the research needed for this series.[21]

Scholarly and technological remains thus serve as means of defending the history of empire as well as direct ancestral participation in it; asserting that Indians continue to value these as well allows personal anxiety about possible 'exploitation' to be assuaged. Other descendants of British-Indian families long involved in the subcontinent assert similar positive balance sheets of raj endeavors, crediting the British for providing independent South Asian nations with, among other things, a developed tea industry, postal service, railway system, civil service, and indeed (as Trevelyan put it) democracy itself. Such assertions resemble arguments long deployed by advocates of empire during the era of high imperialism itself when, as Nicholas Dirks has summarized, 'colonial rulers align[ed] themselves with the inexorable and universal forces of science, progress, rationality, and modernity'. In this way, colonialism was— and remains—able to transform 'domination into a variety of effects that masked both conquest and rule'.[22]

Proclamations of Indian respect and gratitude both for individual Britons and the results of British rule feature prominently in much post-colonial British travel writing, a theme Hsu-Ming Teo explores in her analysis of the genre.[23] This trope also asserts itself more generally within memoirs of personal and family life in the subcontinent when authors turn to the subject of the Indian independence movement. Betsy Macdonald's 1988 autobiography

---

[21] Ibid., 17.

[22] Nicholas B. Dirks, 'Introduction: Colonialism and Culture', in Nicholas B. Dirks (ed.), *Colonialism and Culture* (Ann Arbor, MI, 1992), 7.

[23] Hsu-Ming Teo, 'Wandering in the Wake of Empire: British Travel and Tourism in the Post-Imperial World', in Ward (ed.), *British Culture*, 168–70.

records her memories of her own childhood, her father's work in the Indian Political Service, and her husband's family's sugar factory in Bihar, illustrating how defenses of British endeavors are commonly mounted. Recalling her encounter with an Indian nationalist in the 1940s, her response to him was that 'many of us, ourselves included, loved India and our parents and grandparents and others had worked truly and earnestly for the good of his country, with no thought of gain and had left with scant remuneration and, at times, ill health'.[24] An Indian's reproach to British imperialism rests uncomfortably alongside her desire to present a favorable image of British activities and personnel in India to the post-colonial (and largely British) readers of her book. She positions Indian dissatisfaction as the exception proving the rule she wishes to have existed, wherein most Indians supported British institutions and their representatives in the subcontinent. Far more numerous are anecdotes concerning the respect and admiration her in-laws' and husband's sugar plantation laborers and her own household servants demonstrated for the family. Their domestic servants, she writes, 'were very faithful and became almost like our children, looking upon us as their parents and calling us "Ma", "Bap" (Mother and Father), bringing their troubles and trusting us implicitly'.[25] Similarly, her husband's family, thanks to the fair treatment of their employees over three generations and charitable acts such as founding a school for village children, 'were invariably so popular with the local people and left behind a name to be cherished'.[26]

A final example illuminating—and indeed epitomizing—the convergence of childhood memories, the celebration of family histories in British India, and modes of defending the raj in its aftermath appears in the autobiographical work of the novelist M. M. Kaye. All three volumes of her memoirs published in the course of the 1990s have titles that immediately suggest their nostalgic content: *The Sun in the Morning, Golden Afternoon,* and *Enchanted Evening*.[27] Chronicling in minute detail her happy childhood as the daughter of an Indian Army officer in the early twentieth century followed by boarding school in England, her memoirs then describe her return to India as a young woman and culminate with marriage to an army officer. Like many other late twentieth-century authors including Betsy Macdonald, Kaye

---

[24] Betsy Macdonald, *India . . . Sunshine and Shadows* (London, 1988), 135.

[25] Ibid., 63.

[26] Ibid., 57.

[27] M. M. Kaye, *The Sun in the Morning: My Early Years in India and England* (New York, 1990); *Golden Afternoon* (London, 1997); *Enchanted Evening* (London, 1999).

deploys the 'evidence of experience'—both her own as well as her father's—to illustrate Britain's good works in India, and, just as importantly, the 'fact' that Indians were grateful for their endeavors and repaid the British with loyalty and affection.[28] Benita Parry argues that invoking 'their years of residence as giving them access to the real India' was a conceit such Britons displayed during the imperial era, and it clearly remained common to do so thereafter as well.[29] Stories of love and gratitude still prevail. Indian domestic servants, for instance, were Kaye's family's 'firm friends and allies', and as a child 'there was little we didn't know' about their lives and attitudes, given the ability 'to chatter non-stop' with them in their own language. Subalterns who worked under her father's supervision, meanwhile, 'worshipped him' and 'loved and revered him and would be forever grateful for the encouragement he had given them'.[30] These feelings were said to be mutual, but came at a price:

men of my race who spent their lives in Indian service were not overpaid and pampered 'Burra-Sahibs' lording it over 'the natives', but were really people like [my father] who worked themselves to the bone to serve, to the best of their ability, a country and a people whom they had come to love so much.[31]

Both Kaye's and Macdonald's texts make recurrent reference to the strong personal relationships between Indians and Britons, even though the era they describe was characterized by rising nationalism that terminated British rule not long after. Emphasis on friendship was common, but familial rhetoric and references to love even more so. Exalting the previous generations of British-Indians from which these writers are directly descended is one form family myths take in their texts,[32] but their use of familial terminology extends far beyond the realm of actual blood relations to encompass those between colonizers and colonized. Framing the links between Britons and Indians as comparable to those between parents and children (or, less commonly, to those

[28] One of the most influential critiques of this tendency is Joan Wallach Scott, '"Experience"', in Judith Butler and Joan W. Scott (eds.), *Feminists Theorize the Political* (New York, 1992), 22–40.

[29] Benita Parry, *Delusions and Discoveries: India in the British Imagination, 1880–1930*, 2nd edn. (London, 1998), 34.

[30] Kaye, *Sun in the Morning*, 91, 383.

[31] Ibid., 303.

[32] Oral historians have explored how family stories and myths are transmitted to, and interpreted by, subsequent generations in ways that are also relevant for understanding written genres. See especially Luisa Passerini, 'Mythbiography in Oral History', and John Byng-Hall, interviewed by Paul Thompson, 'The Power of Family Myths', in Raphael Samuel and Paul Thompson (eds.), *The Myths We Live By* (London, 1990), 49–60, 216–24; Daniel Bertaux and Paul Thompson (eds.), *International Yearbook of Oral History and Life Stories*, vol. II: *Between Generations: Family Models, Myths, and Memories* (Oxford, 1993).

between men and women[33]) constitutes a variation on what Lynn Hunt calls 'family romances'. In her reading of the discourse of the French Revolution, Hunt asserts that distinctive family models became 'metaphors for political life', reflecting how 'people collectively imagine—that is, think unconsciously about—the operation of power, and the ways in which this imagination shapes and is in turn shaped by political and social processes'.[34]

Familial understandings of British India took many forms: references to Britain as the 'mother country'; to colonies as well as individual 'natives' as 'children' whom benevolent, assiduous colonizers would train to become self-dependent 'when the time was right'; to the concept of 'Ma–Bap' that Macdonald highlights in her portrayals both of plantation workers and her household staff.[35] Love, trust, worship, reverence, gratitude: all were recurring terms for depicting colonizer/colonized interactions as at once harmonious and hierarchical. As Piya Chatterjee notes, 'the mai–baap was more than the personhood of the planter' and came to signify power relations more generally —whether the arenas in question were the tea plantations she studied or other spheres of British activity. 'The deployment of the mai–baap was the planter's attempt to create a legitimating aura around his governance', she continues, yet this aura 'contained the threads of both consent and coercion, acts of paternal benevolence and absolute power'.[36] As Betsy Macdonald's story shows, mem-sahibs could also lay claim to this form of 'paternalism' in ways that failed to acknowledge underlying political and social inequalities and the possibility that acquiescence by the colonized might not reflect free will. Writing about colonial discourse in a different context, Catherine Hall cogently stresses that familial language emanating from male and female colonizers' tongues

---

[33] Jenny Sharpe considers how literary representations of the 'imperial embrace' could encompass both metaphors of 'marriage and romantic love' as well as their corrupt and fallen form, those of rape and sexual violence. *Allegories of Empire: The Figure of Woman in the Colonial Text* (Minneapolis, MN, 1993), 141. Mrinalini Sinha, meanwhile, explores constructions of masculinity and femininity that became applied to British and Indian men in *Colonial Masculinity: The 'Manly Englishman' and the 'Effeminate Bengali' in the Late Nineteenth Century* (Manchester, 1995).

[34] Lynn Hunt, *The Family Romance of the French Revolution* (Berkeley, CA, 1992), 199, 8. It will be clear that my delineation of 'family romances' differs from Freud's; see Sigmund Freud, 'Family Romances', in *The Pelican Freud Library Vol. 7: On Sexuality: Three Essays on the Theory of Sexuality and Other Works*, trans. by James Strachey, ed. by Angela Richards (Harmondsworth, 1977), 221–5.

[35] On these themes, see Zohreh T. Sullivan, *Narratives of Empire: The Fictions of Rudyard Kipling* (Cambridge, 1993), 3; McClintock, *Imperial Leather*, 45; Joanna de Groot, ' "Sex" and "Race": The Construction of Language and Image in the Nineteenth Century', in Catherine Hall (ed.), *Cultures of Empire: A Reader: Colonizers in Britain and the Empire in the Nineteenth and Twentieth Centuries* (Manchester, 2000), 44, 50. On 'Ma-Bap' as an ideal and an ideology of paternalist rule that declined in the late imperial era, see Clive Dewey, *Anglo-Indian Attitudes: The Mind of the Indian Civil Service* (London, 1993), 55–9.

[36] Piya Chatterjee, *A Time for Tea: Women, Labor, and Postcolonial Politics on an Indian Plantation* (Durham, NC, 2001), 120–1.

commonly 'mark[ed] both kinship and a gap' between individuals and groups with vastly unequal access to power.[37] Family photographs provide ample suggestions of distance as well as inequality. Some show Indian servants seemingly resigned to their labors and give no evidence of warmth towards the families employing them (Illustration 3), while others show pet dogs within the family circle while Indians are either altogether absent or stand apart to one side (Illustrations 6 and 4).

Closely linked to assertions of family-style intimacy between many Britons and Indians is the emphasis on widespread Indian collaboration within post-colonial British accounts. Ranajit Guha's work outlines how an emphasis on collaboration has long been prominent within much historiography, which by focusing on the British and their supporters enabled colonialism to emerge 'with a hegemony which was denied to it by history'.[38] This mode of analysis is equally apparent within many post-colonial personal narratives by those once affiliated with the raj. Conflict and contestation become subsumed by stories of affection and gratitude meant to connote overall consent to British rule. The deferential 'real India', exemplified by stereotypical peasants and princes, constituted the loyal majority, while the Indian middle classes and others wanting more were condemned as unrepresentative and misguided.[39] Such views are present in all four of the texts discussed above to varying degrees, but M. M. Kaye is perhaps the most insistent on this point: 'only later were many of the unthinking [turned] into anti-British revolutionaries and rioters', she asserts.[40]

Despite downplaying the extent as well as the nature of Indian nationalism, however, post-colonial writers seeking to provide positive assessments of the raj cannot entirely obliterate it from their accounts given the fact of the independence movement's resounding success. John Darwin notes that British policy-makers needed to 'make myths as fast as they unmade colonies', portraying 'their demission of empire as the actions of an enlightened father, wisely conferring responsibility on his boisterous, but essentially good-natured,

---

[37] Catherine Hall, *Civilising Subjects: Metropole and Colony in the English Imagination, 1830–1867* (Cambridge, 2002), 19.

[38] Ranajit Guha, 'Dominance without Hegemony and its Historiography', in Ranajit Guha (ed.), *Subaltern Studies* Vol. VI (Delhi, 1989), 305. A key piece outlining the role of collaboration is Ronald Robinson, 'Non-European Foundations of European Imperialism: Sketch for a Theory of Collaboration', in Roger Owen and Bob Sutcliffe (eds.), *Studies in the Theory of Imperialism* (London, 1972), 117–42. John Darwin places this approach among other predominant modes of assessing imperialism and decolonization in *The End of the British Empire: The Historical Debate* (Oxford, 1991), 94–5.

[39] Parry, *Delusions and Discoveries*, 42. See also Parry's 'The Content and Discontents of Kipling's Imperialism', *New Formations*, 6 (1988), 49–63.

[40] Kaye, *Sun in the Morning*, 363.

offspring'.[41] British-Indians long implicated in India, whether in an official or an unofficial capacity, partook of this tendency, although many relied upon older myths rather than inventing new ones. Hard work, selflessness, and family sacrifice on India's behalf 'with no thought of gain' remain prominent features, although references to the array of socio-economic and cultural benefits many of Britain's 'second eleven' relished overseas and lost back at home are often toned down. Benevolent British parental figures guiding appreciative colonized children towards maturity, or alternatively a marriage that ended with an amicable and consensual separation: such were the positive readings of what ultimately proved a case of family breakdown. More unseemly inversions of power in which thankless children declared their parents illegitimate and ejected them from what was rightfully their own house, or in which unequal partners ended their relationship through an acrimonious divorce, on the other hand, tell tales of a family romance that failed miserably. Given the unwillingness of such unappealing renditions of the end of British rule in South Asia to recede from the historical record, it seems plausible to advance another reason why the last generations of British-Indians have proved so eager to defend their own, and previous generations', lives and actions in the subcontinent. Despite frequent assertions to the contrary, most Indians singularly failed to live up to the roles of grateful child-figures in which they unwillingly were cast, thereby leaving the task of extolling British imperial protagonists to their *literal* offspring—the ageing remnants of a 'tribe' increasingly verging on extinction.

Verging on extinction, perhaps—but in the late twentieth and early twenty-first centuries not yet gone. Many born between the early 1900s and the interwar period attribute their decision to tell their stories to a sense of responsibility as part of the last generation of Britons to have experienced colonial life first-hand; by the later 1970s and 1980s, many realized that the time left for them to 'set the record straight' was limited. Giving voice to memories of empire depended equally upon a substantial group of people willing to discuss them and audiences willing to listen to their interpretations, with the links between producers and consumers of raj stories provided by archivists, publishers, and those working in radio, television, and the film industry.

The four individuals examined above suggest the diverse forms of distribution that participants' stories can take. Ronald Rice's was typed and deposited along with other family papers at the Cambridge South Asian Archive, while

---

[41] John Darwin, 'British Decolonization since 1945: A Pattern or a Puzzle?', *Journal of Imperial and Commonwealth History*, 12 (1984), 188, 206.

Betsy Macdonald's memoir was published by a small press whose titles appeal mainly to raj aficionados.[42] The significance of such accounts, however, stems not from any unique perspectives they might contain, nor from their number of readers. Indeed, taken individually many published or unpublished personal narratives and family biographies, along with novels and popular histories by former British-Indians, reach a fairly limited audience of fellow travellers or scholars. But they represent only the tip of the iceberg of British-Indian memories that have made the journey from the realm of private recollection to wider publics, the sheer volume of which is impressive. At the Cambridge South Asian Archive, donations of private papers, ciné films, and photographs rest alongside tapes, transcribed interviews, and questionnaires generated through archivists' initiatives; since its inception in the late 1990s the Empire and Commonwealth Museum in Bristol has initiated its own oral history project and solicited similar contributions. The British Library's Oriental and India Office Collections houses the largest collection of papers and also has worked to record additional interviews that now join the tapes and transcriptions of interviews made in the course of Charles Allen's *Plain Tales from the Raj* project (the latter are also contained within the collections of the School of Oriental and African Studies).

These accumulations of raj stories, whether in print, unpublished, or on tape, suggest why most are heavily imbued with nostalgia for imperial India and assertions of its positive qualities and contain only limited critiques of empire. Few people who wanted to forget either their own, or their families', experiences in India seemingly agreed to spend the time writing or speaking about them, leaving the task of recollection largely to those who wanted to recall them and tell their versions of the raj to others. Moreover, archivists may well have prioritized approaching those able, not to mention willing, to provide positive narratives and done less to gather the accounts by the less privileged, who, in retrospect, could not look back on their contacts with India with the same fondness. Accounts by Indian Civil Servants, army officers, and better-off businessmen and planters, along with their wives and children, predominate while those by men and women of working-class origins are a distinct minority (albeit not completely absent).

Additionally, these collections illustrate the considerable crossover potential characterizing material found and used in academic archives and by the media. Persons working on popular histories of British India that take multi-media

---

[42] Her work, and much other autobiographical material by members of families once affiliated with British India, has been published by the British Association for Cemeteries in South Asia, an organization founded in London in the 1970s.

forms are able to draw upon the same materials academic researchers use, while scholars also take advantage of written and recorded reminiscences that originally were produced for radio or television productions, with the *Plain Tales* collections exemplifying this. Although most of these written, spoken, and visual accounts have remained obscure, they share much in common with those that have reached wider audiences. As noted above, Raleigh Trevelyan's *The Golden Oriole* and M. M. Kaye's autobiographies contained similar messages as Rice's and Macdonald's stories, but both were published by Viking Penguin in Britain as well as issued in the United States by Simon and Schuster's Touchstone imprint and St Martin's Press respectively.

M. M. Kaye provides perhaps the best illustration of someone who had a large personal stake in empire and subsequently has worked hard to influence public perceptions of this history through her writing. Denouncing those who 'make a mint of money out of denigrating the Raj and all its works on the basis of second-, third-, or fourth-hand information', she clearly considers profiting from firsthand—and hence 'authentic'—versions of raj history to be acceptable, given her own successes.[43] Prior to her autobiographies, Kaye's mystery-romance fiction set in India and elsewhere overseas had reached a substantial audience, but her best-known work remains the bestselling historical epic *The Far Pavilions*. This first appeared as a novel in 1978 and was later filmed as a popular television mini-series that aired in the mid-1980s. In addition to writing novels and autobiographies, she has also edited and illustrated both new and standard works of British-in-India fiction, poetry, and memoirs for publishers seeking to capitalize on the popularity of raj nostalgia.[44] 'A time may come', Kaye hopes, 'when the world will look back on the era of the Pax Britannica as a golden age, and not, as the present tendency seems to be, a dark, disgraceful period of brutal colonial repression'.[45] Should this fail to occur it will certainly not reflect a lack of effort on her account; however, thanks in part to persons like herself, in some eyes at least this time may already have arrived.

A number of factors encouraged the proliferation of raj stories to the extent that they became an established feature of Britain's cultural landscape in the

---

[43] Kaye, *Sun in the Morning*, 87.

[44] These include Mrs Eliza Fay, *Original Letters from India (1779–1815)*, new intro. by M. M. Kaye (London, 1986); M. M. Kaye (ed.), *The Golden Calm: An English Lady's Life in Moghul Delhi* (Exeter, 1980); M. M. Kaye (ed.), *Picking Up Gold and Silver: A Selection of Kipling's Short Stories* (London, 1989); *Moon of Other Days: M. M. Kaye's Kipling: A Selection of Favourite Verses*, notes and sketches by M. M. Kaye, paintings by George Sharp (London, 1988).

[45] Kaye, *Sun in the Morning*, 419.

1980s. What Stuart Hall identified as historical amnesia about imperial history within cultural and political discourses before the late 1970s has been balanced with, and arguably become superseded by, imperial glorification thereafter.[46] At this time, Britain's period of widescale decolonization had finally come to an end after decades of wrangling with anti-colonial nationalists and hammering out arrangements for the transfer of power in one colonial arena after the next. The British thus might begin to recall empire without immediately thinking of tedious and protracted pullouts, some of which had become national embarrassments (such as Rhodesia, an imbroglio from which Britain finally extracted itself in 1980). That imperial heritage might actually be reinscribed as a positive feature of national identity became even more likely after Britain emerged victorious from the Falklands War in 1982. Although the islands were of negligible practical importance, symbolically they briefly took center stage and played a key role in enabling the nation's imperial connections—past and present—to be depicted as a legitimate source of pride and patriotism. For Margaret Thatcher and many others, remnants of empire in the South Atlantic might be taken as symbols of Britain's revival, helping narratives of the empire now lost to be reinterpreted as something other than a symptom of weakness and decline.[47]

Imperial nostalgia also gained ground as British India became subjected to thorough treatment by what has become broadly construed as the heritage industry by the mid-1980s. Alongside becoming the theme of documentaries and museum displays,[48] the raj proved a scenic and entertaining backdrop for costume dramas on television and in the cinema, including *The Jewel in the Crown, A Passage to India, Heat and Dust,* and *The Far Pavilions.* Their popularity both reflected and helped to enhance a favorable climate of opinion for those seeking to recount their experiences in the subcontinent before 1947. Despite negative messages contained within these films, they also worked to highlight India's possibilities for romance, glamor, and adventure in tandem

---

[46] Stuart Hall, 'Racism and Reaction', in John Rex et al., *Five Views of Multi-Racial Britain* (London: Commission for Racial Equality, 1978), 25. Also relevant are Bill Schwarz, ' "The Only White Man in There": The Re-racialisation of England, 1956–1968', *Race and Class,* 38/1 (1996), 65–78; Anna Marie Smith, *New Right Discourse on Race and Sexuality: Britain 1968–1990* (Cambridge, 1994), 25, 129–32, 174.

[47] On the Falklands/Malvinas War, see Eric Hobsbawm, 'Falklands Fallout'; Robert Gray, 'The Falklands Factor'; and Tom Nairn, 'Britain's Living Legacy', in Stuart Hall and Martin Jacques (eds.), *The Politics of Thatcherism* (London, 1983), 257–88.

[48] Prominent among the latter was the National Portrait Gallery's exhibition shown in 1990–1, the catalogue for which was C. A. Bayly (ed.), *The Raj: India and the British, 1600–1947* (London, 1990); on the postcolonial complexities informing its staging, see Christopher Bayly, 'Exhibiting the Imperial Image', *History Today,* 40 (Oct. 1990), 12–18.

with the good works, or at least the good intentions, of Britons most directly involved there—and, by extension, of the nation as a whole.[49]

Such public attention was at its high point in the 1980s and diminished somewhat thereafter. While Antoinette Burton accurately assesses raj nostalgia as a hackneyed genre by the 1990s, it has yet to disappear from the media landscape.[50] When a documentary entitled 'Echoes of the Raj' put together by Raleigh Trevelyan appeared in 2000, some of the participants had long since become established fixtures in such projects. Alongside M. M. Kaye were others who had contributed to *Plain Tales from the Raj* over twenty-five years before, including Iris Butler Portal, a familiar figure from previous chapters. The usual suspects had been rounded up once again.[51] As interview footage remains available to be drawn upon at later dates, Trevelyan's documentary suggests that those once involved in the raj may well continue to have a voice even once they are indeed a fully extinct tribe.

As long as there remains a public willing to receive positive messages about the imperial dimensions of the nation's history, individuals who had strong vested interests in portraying British endeavors in India to advantage will continue to provide them. Their version of events has become a deeply ingrained mode of interpretation in post-colonial Britain, and appears likely to survive their passing—due to the effective role they already have played in publicizing their views in multi-media forms and in filling a range of archives with their accounts. In this respect Britain appears distinct as a post-colonizing nation. A collection edited by Andrea Smith comparing the returns of Indonesian Dutch, Angolan Portuguese, and Algerian French to their respective European 'homelands' following the brutal end of settler colonialisms suggests that no one wanted to remember them but themselves. As Frederick Cooper summarizes, such colonial repatriates were 'living embodiments of a history repudiated' and of national overseas embarrassments who refused 'to disappear when they no longer served a purpose'.[52] Former British-Indians in post-

49 John McBratney, 'The Raj Is All the Rage: Paul Scott's *The Raj Quartet* and Colonial Nostalgia', *North Dakota Quarterly*, 55/3 (1987), 204–9; Tara Wollen, 'Over Our Shoulders: Nostalgic Screen Fictions for the 1980s', in John Corner and Sylvia Harvey (eds.), *Enterprise and Heritage: Crosscurrents of National Culture* (London, 1991), 178–93; Andrew Higson, 'Re-presenting the National Past: Nostalgia and Pastiche in the Heritage Film', in Lester Friedman (ed.), *British Cinema and Thatcherism: Fires Were Started* (London, 1993), 109–29; Sharpe, *Allegories of Empire*, 142–4; Richard Dyer, 'There's Nothing I Can Do! Nothing!', in *White* (London, 1997), 184–206; Vron Ware, 'Moments of Danger: Race, Gender, and Memories of Empire', *History and Theory*, 31/4 (1992), 116–37.

50 Antoinette Burton, 'India, Inc.? Nostalgia, Memory, and the Empire of Things', in Ward (ed.), *British Culture*, 226.

51 'Echoes of the Raj', broadcast on BBC2, 21 May 2000.

52 Frederick Cooper, 'Postcolonial Peoples: A Commentary', in Andrea L. Smith (ed.), *Europe's Invisible Migrants* (Amsterdam, 2003), 172, 183.

colonial Britain also refused to disappear, but largely because they were given the limelight in which to bask.

In analyzing the media's portrayal of imperial India in the 1980s and targetting the televised version of M. M. Kaye's *The Far Pavilions* in particular, Salman Rushdie warned of nostalgia's power to propagate the false notion that 'the British and Indians actually understood each other jolly well . . . that . . . the British weren't as bad as people make out . . . and, above all, the fantasy that the British Empire represented something "noble" or "great" about Britain; that it was, in spite of all its flaws and meannesses and bigotries, fundamentally glamorous'.[53] Biased as many versions of Britain's imperial past are, there might be good reason to hope that their popularity might recede and that one-sided interpretations might become extinct along with the 'tribe' of former colonizers. Nostalgic renditions of what the empire might have meant demand to be challenged, but they do at least provide an essential reminder of how Britain's identity has long been connected with its status as a imperial power—and also with the loss of that status. This should remain on the agenda not merely to be either glamorized and whitewashed or silenced with a reversion to historical amnesia, but to be a subject for analysis and debate.

Ongoing reassessments of raj history will, inevitably, continue to take place both within South Asia as well as within Britain and beyond. In Britain, moreover, such debates have and will continue to take their tone within the context of 'the empire striking back', initially via the immigration of many Asians, Afro-Caribbeans, and Africans during the imperial era and increasing in its wake, and continuing as second- and third-generation descendants help to reshape what 'Britishness' means.[54] Isaac Julien and Kobena Mercer suggested in the late 1980s that imperial nostalgia works symbiotically with narratives of, and debates about, post-war British multi-culturalism. Comparing these views with those expressed in contemporary black British cinema, they assert that

---

[53] Salman Rushdie, 'Outside the Whale', *Granta*, 11 (1984), 138.

[54] Within a burgeoning field of scholarship, some key titles remain: Centre for Contemporary Cultural Studies (ed.), *The Empire Strikes Back: Race and Racism in 70s Britain* (London, 1983); Paul Gilroy, *'There Ain't No Black in the Union Jack': The Cultural Politics of Race and Nation* (Chicago, 1987); Simon Gikandi, *Maps of Englishness: Writing Identity in the Culture of Colonialism* (New York, 1996); Talal Asad, 'Multiculturalism and British Identity in the Wake of the Rushdie Affair', *Politics and Society*, 18/4 (1990), 455–80; Stuart Hall, 'Ethnicity: Identity and Difference', *Radical America*, 23/4 (1991), 9–20; Antoinette Burton, 'Who Needs the Nation? Interrogating "British" History', in Hall (ed.), *Cultures of Empire*, 137–53; Shula Marks, 'History, the Nation and Empire: Sniping from the Periphery', *History Workshop Journal*, 29 (1990), 111–19.

the wave of popular films set in imperial India or Africa also acknowledge, in their own way, Britain's postcolonial condition in so far as they speak to contemporary concerns. The competing versions of narrative, memory and history in this conjuncture might be read symptomatically as a state of affairs that speaks of—articulates—conflicting identities within the 'imagined community' of the nation.[55]

Historians of India, especially those supportive of the Subaltern Studies project, ask us to consider 'who speaks for Indian pasts', and with what ideological motives and powers of being heard.[56] Telling anything that becomes fully accepted as 'Plain Tales of the Raj' in multi-cultural, post-colonial Britain is clearly an impossible task—yet when has that ever stopped many from trying?

---

[55] Isaac Julien and Kobena Mercer, 'De Margin and De Center', in David Morley and Kuan-Hsing Chen (eds.), *Stuart Hall: Critical Dialogues in Cultural Studies* (London, 1996), 450. See also John Hill, *British Cinema in the 1980s* (Oxford, 1999), chs. 5, 10, and 11.

[56] Dipesh Chakrabarty, 'Postcoloniality and the Artifice of History: Who Speaks for "Indian" Pasts?', *Representations*, 37 (1992), 1–26; Gyan Prakash, 'Writing Post-Orientalist Histories of the Third World: Perspectives from Indian Historiography', *Comparative Studies in Society and History*, 32/2 (1990), 383–408.

BIBLIOGRAPHY

ARCHIVAL COLLECTIONS

Bedford High School Archives, Bedford, UK (BHSA)
The Aquila.
Bedford High School, Second Admissions Register, 1894–1917.
Bedford High School, Third Admissions Register, 1917–1935.

Bedford School Archives, Bedford, UK (BSA)
Bedford Grammar School Register, 1888–1906.
Bedford Grammar School Register, 1906–1931.
The Ousel.

Bedfordshire and Luton Archives and Records Service, Bedford, UK (BLARS)
Bedford Trade Protection Society, *Bedford Town and Bedford Schools* (Bedford, 1913).
'Extracts from the 1871 Census for Bedford for Certain Streets and Houses', CRT 130 BED 188.
Letter from Carol Irving to Patricia Bell, 6 Mar. 1980, CRT 180/300.
Letter from Miss R. M. Spankie to Patricia Bell, 18 Mar. 1980, CRT 180 BED 191.
Letters from Evelyn Chaldecott in India to her mother, Mrs Cochrane Forster, in Bedford, 1914–19, Z186.

Bishop Cotton School, Shimla, India (BCSS)
Admissions Register, 1879–.
Board of Governors Minute Book, Bishop Cotton School, Simla, 1863–c.1900.
Board of Governors Second Minute Book, Bishop Cotton School, Simla, 1901–29.
Board of Governors Third Minute Book, Bishop Cotton School, Simla, 1930–58.
The Cottonian.

Cambridge South Asian Archive, Cambridge, UK (CSAA)
Mrs Veronica Bamfield, transcribed interview with Mary Thatcher, 10 Sept. 1981, MT46.
Clough Papers, Mrs M. F. Clough, 'A Childhood in Travancore, 1922–1931', typewritten manuscript (1983).
Mrs Joan Davis, transcribed interview with Mary Thatcher, 24 Aug. 1981, MT45.
Dench Papers, Mrs M. O. Dench, 'Memsahib', typewritten manuscript (1979).
Donaldson Papers, Barbara Donaldson, 'India Remembered', typewritten manuscript (1983).
Grove Papers, typewritten copy of the untitled autobiography of Major-General Henry Leslie Grove, n.d. [c.1890s].

Mosse Papers (1983), Kay Mosse, 'Home', typewritten manuscript, n.d.

Portal Papers, Mrs Iris Portal, 'Song at Seventy', typescript manuscript, n.d. [*c.*1975].

Mrs Iris Portal, transcribed interview with Mary Thatcher, 15 Oct. 1974, MT20.

Rice Papers, Mary Sophia Rice, 'My Memoirs' (privately published, n.d. [*c.*1920s]).

Rice Papers, Ronald Rice, 'Mysore Revisited, 1973: Also Ootacamund and Colombo', typewritten manuscript (1973).

Mrs A. G. Shoosmith, 'Poems of Childhood in India', autograph manuscript, No. 25, 'The Topi', n.d.

'Women in India: Replies to Questionnaire'.

'Women in India: Replies to Questionnaire on Childhood'.

Cheltenham College Archives, Cheltenham, UK (CCA)

Cheltenham College Scrap Books, 1841–1867; 1868–1892; 1893–1899; 1900–1907.

The Cheltenham College Magazine.

The Cheltonian.

Cheltenham Ladies' College Archive, Cheltenham, UK

Cheltenham Ladies' College Admissions Registers.

The Cheltenham Ladies' College Magazine.

Cheltenham Public Library Reference Department, Cheltenham, UK (CPLRD)

Census of England and Wales, 1891. Cheltenham: Enumeration District No. 14, St Paul's; Enumeration District No. 31, Christ Church.

'Indian Summer: An Exhibition Highlighting Cheltenham's Anglo-Indian Connections in the Nineteenth Century', exhibition leaflet, 28 June–15 Sept. 1985, Pittville Pumproom Museum.

Manuscript Collection, Alfred Miles, 'History of Cheltenham and District', Vols. III, V, X, autograph manuscript (n.d., *c.*1920s).

City of Westminster Archives Centre, London, UK

The Bayswater Annual (London, 1885).

Eltham College Archives, Eltham, UK (ECA)

The Elthamian.

The Home and School for the Sons and Orphans of Missionaries, Blackheath: Report and List of Subscribers, 1878, 1879, 1881, 1883, 1886, 1887, 1888, 1889, 1899, 1902.

Kentish, Owen, 'The Past History of Eltham College and Its Present Position: An Address Delivered to the Members of the Eltham College Parents' Association on 8th March, 1932'.

The S.S.M. Magazine.

Haileybury College Archives, Hertford, UK (HCA)

The Haileyburian.

The Imperial Services College Chronicle.

'Report of Mansion House Meeting, 30 June 1909'.

The United Services College Chronicle.
'United Services Proprietary College, December 1883'.
'Wellington College and the United Services College, Westward Ho!', from *The Field* (30 Oct. 1880).

Library of the London School of Economics, London, UK (LSE)
Beveridge Papers, BP.

Mount Hermon School Archives, Darjeeling, India (MHSA)
Admissions Register, 1895–1933.
Admissions Register, 1934–1947.
The Blue and Gold.

National Library of Scotland, Edinburgh, UK (NLS)
Major-General William Bannerman, Indian Medical Service, and his wife (Helen), letters written to their children from India, 1902–17, Dep. 325.

Oriental and India Office Collections, British Library, London, UK (OIOC)
Beveridge Collection, MSS Eur C176.
Brown Collection, MSS Eur E354.
Butler Papers, MSS Eur F225.
Sir John Cotton, transcribed interview, n.d. [*c.*1973], MSS Eur T18.
Walter Stuart Davis Papers, MSS Eur Photo Eur 291.
Dawkins Collection, MSS Eur D931.
Sir Armine Dew Papers, MSS Eur D1222.
Godfrey Collection, MSS Eur E410.
Revd R. C. Llewelyn, interview by Mrs E. D. Cornish, tape recording, 27 Sept. 1982, MSS Eur R214/37.
John Rivett-Carnac, transcribed interview, n.d. [*c.* early 1970s], MSS Eur T55.
Donald Langham Scott Papers, MSS Eur D1232.
Watson Collection, MSS Eur F244.
The Lawrence Military Asylum (Sanawur, 1858).
P/T 592, A. N. Gordon (ed.), *About the Domiciled Community* (Madras, 1914).
P/T 722, the Revd O. Younghusband, *The Domiciled Community in India* (n.p., n.d.).
P/T 724, *Historical Retrospect of Conditions of Service in the Indian Public Works Department* (All-Indian Service of Engineers), n.d. [*c.*1925].
V/24/4429, Sir Alfred Croft, *Review of Education in India, 1886* (Calcutta, 1888).
V/24/4432, R. Littlehailes, *Progress of Education in India, 1922–27: Ninth Quinquennial Review*, Vol. 1 (Calcutta, 1929).
V/24/4432, J. A. Richey, *Progress of Education in India, 1917–1922: Eighth Quinquennial Review*, Vol. I (Calcutta, 1923).
V/26/861/1, *Committee Upon the Condition of Hill Schools for Europeans In Northern India*, Vol. I: *Report* (Calcutta, 1904).
V/26/861/2, *Committee upon the Financial Condition of Hill Schools for Europeans in North India*, Vol. II: *Evidence and Appendices* (Calcutta, 1905).

V/27/820/19, Government of India, *A Report on Southern Rhodesia, Northern Rhodesia, Nyasaland and Kenya* (Simla, 1936).

V/27/861/1, A. J. Lawrence, *Report on the Existing Schools for Europeans and Eurasians Throughout India* (Calcutta, 1873).

V/27/861/3, *Code of Regulations for European Schools in Bengal for the Year 1884–85* (Calcutta, 1884).

Perth and Kinross Council Archive, A. K. Bell Library, Perth, UK (PKCA)
Martin Family Papers, MS 72.

St George's College, Mussoorie, India (SGCM)
The Manorite.
Right Reverend Dr Delany and the Brothers of St Patrick (Wellington [Nilgiris], 1955).
'St George's College, Log Book', autograph manuscript, n.d.

Trinity College, Cambridge
R. A. Butler Papers, RAB.

University Library Dundee, UK, Department of Archives and Manuscripts
Bengal Project Interviews.

Walthamstow Hall School Archives, Sevenoaks, UK (WHSA)
Board of Education, Kent, 'Report of Inspection of the School for the Daughters of Missionaries, Walthamstow Hall, Sevenoaks, held on 18th, 19th and 20th October 1922'.

Board of Education, 'Report of the Inspection of Walthamstow Hall School for the Daughters of Missionaries, Sevenoaks, Kent, held on 23rd, 24th, and 25th Jan., 1929'.

'Hymn', 'Institution for the Education of the Daughters of Missionaries: Programme on the Occasion of Laying the Foundation Stone of the New Building at Sevenoaks', June 26th, 1878'.

'Institution for the Education of the Daughters of Missionaries', 1879.

Newspaper Cuttings Book.

Report of the Institution for the Education of the Daughters of Missionaries, Walthamstow Hall, Sevenoaks, 1847, 1852, 1858, 1864, 1865, 1886, 1888, 1891, 1896, 1899, 1903, 1904, 1908, 1909, 1911, 1912, 1913, 1915, 1916.

A Ship's Log (Sevenoaks, 1988).

Walthamstow Hall Old Girls' Association Annual News Sheet.

Wynberg Allen School, Mussoorie, India (WASM)
A Brief Historical Sketch: Centenary Magazine, 1888–1988, Wynberg Allen School, Mussoorie.
The Excelsior.

Author's interviews and questionnaires

Enid Boon, interview by author, 23 April 1995.

John Erskine, Janet de Vries (née Erskine), and Jane Turner (née Erskine), interview by author, 17 April 1995.

Basil La Bouchardière, interview by author, 20 April 1995.

Margaret Ramsay-Brown, interview by author, 23 May 1995.

Theon Wilkinson, interview by author, 12 July 1995.

'Questionnaire on British Children and Family Life in India Before 1947', compiled by author, completed by Jack Sewell, Peter Cashmore, Mrs Geraldine Hobson, Rachel Taylor, and Peter Clark, 1995.

Peter A. Clark, letters to author, 18 June 1995, 17 July 1995.

NEWSPAPERS AND PERIODICALS

The Aquila
The Baptist Missionary Society Herald
The Baptist Times
The Bedfordshire Mercury
The Bedfordshire Standard
The Bedfordshire Times
The Blue and Gold
The British Weekly
The Builder
The Calcutta Review
The Cheltenham College Magazine
The Cheltenham Examiner
The Cheltenham Ladies' College Magazine
The Cheltonian
The Christian
The Christian World
The Cooper's Hill Magazine
The Cottonian
Daily Telegraph Magazine
The Elthamian
The Englishman
The Excelsior
Fraser's Magazine
The Guardian
The Haileyburian
The Huddersfield Examiner
The Imperial Services College Chronicle
Macmillan's Magazine
The Madras Mail

The Manorite
The Ousel
Outward Bound
Overseas (The Monthly Journal of the Over-seas League)
The Paddington, Kensington, and Bayswater Chronicle
The Parents' Review
The P.C.K.'s Own
The Pioneer
The S.S.M. Magazine
St Andrew's Colonial Homes Magazine
The Sunday at Home
The Times (London)
The Times of India, Overland Weekly Edition
The United Services College Chronicle

PRIMARY SOURCES

Adams, W. E., *Memoirs of a Social Atom* (London, 1903).

Adburgham, Alison (ed.), *Yesterday's Shopping: The Army and Navy Stores Catalogue 1907*, facsimile (Newton Abbott, 1969).

Allen, Charles, in association with Michael Mason, *Plain Tales from the Raj* (London, 1975).

—— *Raj: A Scrapbook of British India, 1877–1947* (London, 1977).

—— in association with Helen Fry, *Tales from the Dark Continent* (London, 1979).

—— in association with Helen Fry, *Tales from the South China Seas* (London, 1983).

—— 'Resuscitating the Raj', in Rosie Llewellyn-Jones (ed.), *Chowkidar, 1977–1997* (London, 1997), 4–7.

'An Anglo-Indian', *Our Parish, All About It; or, Rural Scotland at the Present Day* (Edinburgh, 1875).

'An Old Cheltonian', *Reminiscences of Cheltenham College* (London, 1868).

Baijnath, Lala, *England and India: Being Impressions of Persons and Things, English and Indian, and Brief Notes of Visits to France, Switzerland, Italy, and Ceylon* (Bombay, 1893).

Baines, J. A., *Census of India, 1891. General Report* (London, 1893).

Balfour, Andrew, 'Personal Hygiene in the Tropics and Minor Tropical Sanitation', in W. Byam and R. G. Archibald (eds.), *The Practice of Medicine in the Tropics by Many Authorities* (London, 1921), i. 1–238.

Baxter, Dudley, *The National Income* (London, 1868).

Bevan, Sheila, *The Parting Years: A British Family and the End of Empire* (London, 2001).

Beveridge, Lord, *India Called Them* (London, 1947).

Bingham, Frederick, *The Official Guide to the Metropolitan Borough of Paddington* (London, 1917).

—— *The Metropolitan Borough of Paddington: Official Guide* (London, 1925).

Blaker, Richard, *Scabby Dichson* (London, n.d. [*c*.1920s]).

Bowlby, John, *Child Care and the Growth of Love* (Harmondsworth, 1953).

——*Attachment and Loss*, Vol. II: *Separation Anxiety and Anger* (Harmondsworth, 1975).

Branch, Henry, 'The Anglo-Indian's Paradise', in *Cotswold and Vale; or, Glimpses of Past and Present in Gloucestershire* (Cheltenham, 1904), 172–8.

Brittain, Vera, *Testament of Youth: An Autobiographical Study of the Years 1900–1925* (1933; repr. London, 1988).

Brown, Hilton (ed.), *The Sahibs: The Life and Ways of the British in India as Recorded by Themselves* (London, 1948).

Brown, Ivor, *The Way of My World* (London, 1954).

Burnett, Frances Hodgson, *A Little Princess* (1905; repr. Ware, Hertfordshire, 1994).

—— *The Secret Garden* (1911; repr. Ware, Hertfordshire, 1993).

Butler, R. A., *The Art of the Possible: The Memoirs of Lord Butler* (London, 1971).

Castellani, Sir Aldo, *Climate and Acclimatization: Some Notes and Observations* (London, 1931).

'Cheltenham College', *Hadley's Shilling Guide to Cheltenham* (Cheltenham, 1856).

Cheltenham: The Garden Town of England, 3rd edn. (Cheltenham, 1893).

Clunn, Harold, *Famous South Coast Pleasure Resorts Past and Present* (London, 1929).

Cobbett, William, *Rural Rides* (1830; repr. London, 2001).

Cook, Mrs E. T., *Highways and Byways in London* (London, 1902).

Craig, Hazel Innes, *Under the Old School Topee* (London, 1990).

Crawley, W. J. Chetwode, *Handbook of Competitive Examinations for Admission to Every Department of Her Majesty's Service* (London, 1880).

Diver, Maud, *The Englishwoman in India* (Edinburgh, 1909).

Duncan, Sara Jeannette, 'A Mother in India' (1903), in Saros Cowasjee (ed.), *Stories from the Raj from Kipling to Independence* (London, 1982), 74–118.

Dunsterville, Major-General L. C., *Stalky's Reminiscences* (London, 1928).

Eastbourne and Neighbourhood (London, 1919).

'Echoes of the Raj', broadcast on BBC2, 21 May 2000.

Ewart, Joseph, *Goodeve's Hints for the General Management of Children in India in the Absence of Professional Advice*, 6th edn. (Calcutta, 1872).

—— 'On the Colonisation of the Sub-Himalayahs and Neilgherries. With Remarks on the Management of European Children in India', *Transactions of the Epidemiological Society of London*, 3 (1883–84), 96–117.

Fay, Mrs Eliza, *Original Letters from India (1779–1815)*, new intro. by M. M. Kaye (London, 1986).

Fayrer, Sir Joseph, *European Child-Life in Bengal* (London, 1873).

Fleming, Mrs A. M., 'Some Childhood Memories of Rudyard Kipling, by His Sister', *Chambers's Journal* (March 1939), 168–73.

—— 'My Brother, Rudyard Kipling (I)', in Harold Orel (ed.), *Kipling: Interviews and Recollections* (London, 1983), i. 9–12; originally published in *Kipling Journal*, 14 (Dec. 1947), 3–5.

Forster, E. M., *A Passage to India* (1924; repr. Harmondsworth, 1986).

Fraser, Eugenie, *A Home by the Hooghly: A Jute Wallah's Wife* (London, 1993).

Freud, Anna, and Burlingham, Dorothy, *Infants Without Families* and *Reports on the Hampstead Nurseries 1939–1945* (London, 1974).

Freud, Sigmund, 'Family Romances', in *The Pelican Freud Library Vol. 7: On Sexuality: Three Essays on the Theory of Sexuality and Other Works*, trans. by James Strachey, ed. by Angela Richards (Harmondsworth, 1977), 221–5.

Gait, E. A., *Census of India, 1911*, Vol. I: *India*. Part I: *Report* (Calcutta, 1913).

Gandhi, Mohandas K., *Autobiography: The Story of My Experiments with Truth*, trans. by Mahadev Desai (New York, 1983).

Gidney, Lieut.-Col. H., 'The Status of the Anglo-Indian Community Under the Reforms Scheme in India', *Asiatic Review*, 21/68 (1925), 657–62.

Gidney, Sir Henry, 'The Future of the Anglo-Indian Community', *Asiatic Review* 30/101 (1934), 27–42.

Glimpses of Anglo-Indian Life Here and At Home (Madras, 1901).

Godden, Jon, and Godden, Rumer, *Two Under the Indian Sun* (1966; repr. New York, 1987).

Godden, Rumer, *The River* (1946; repr. Calcutta, 1991).

—— *The Peacock Spring* (1975; repr. Harmondsworth, 1987).

—— *A Time to Dance, No Time to Weep* (New York, 1987).

Graham, the Very Revd J. A., 'The Education of the Anglo-Indian Child', *Journal of the Royal Society of Arts*, 83 (23 Nov. 1934), 21–46.

Granville, A. B., *Spas of England and Principal Sea-Bathing Places*, Vol. II: *The Midlands and South* (1841; repr. Bath, 1971).

Green, C. R. M., and Green-Armytage, V. B., *Birch's Management and Medical Treatment of Children in India*, 5th edn. (Calcutta, 1913).

Hall, G. Stanley, *Adolescence: Its Psychology and Its Relation to Physiology, Anthropology, Sociology, Sex, Crime, Religion and Education*, 2 vols. (New York: D. Appleton, 1904).

Harston, G. Montagu, *The Care and Treatment of European Children in the Tropics* (London, 1912).

Hull, Edmund C. P., *The European in India; or, Anglo-India's Vade Mecum* (London, 1871).

Hunter, Andrew Alexander (ed.), *Cheltenham College Register, 1841–1889* (London, 1890).

Hutton, Edward, *Highways and Byways of Gloucestershire* (London, 1932).

Hutton, J. H., *Census of India, 1931*, Vol. I: *India*. Part I: *Report* (Delhi, 1933).

The India List and India Office List for 1900 (London, 1900).

The India Office List for 1907 (London, 1907).

Irving, Beryl, 'Our Road', *Bedfordshire Magazine*, 6/46 (1958), 225–9.

—— 'Edwardian Schooldays', *Bedfordshire Magazine*, 9/67 (1963–4), 95–8.

Ivey, George James, *Clubs of the World: A General Guide or Index to the London and County Clubs* (London, 1880).

'J. P.', *The Care of Infants in India*, 6th edn. (London, 1907).

Jackson, Annabel Huth, *A Victorian Childhood* (London, 1932).

James, Agatha Florence, 'Housekeeping and House Management in India', in *The Lady At Home and Abroad* (London, 1898), 364–80.

Johnson, Donald McI., *A Doctor Regrets* (London, 1949).

Kaye, M. M. (ed.), *The Golden Calm: An English Lady's Life in Moghul Delhi* (Exeter, 1980).

—— *Moon of Other Days: M. M. Kaye's Kipling: A Selection of Favourite Verses*, notes and sketches by M. M. Kaye, paintings by George Sharp (London, 1988).

—— (ed.), *Picking Up Gold and Silver: A Selection of Kipling's Short Stories* (London, 1989).

—— *The Sun in the Morning: My Early Years in India and England* (New York, 1990).

—— *Golden Afternoon* (London, 1997).

—— *Enchanted Evening* (London, 1999).

Kipling, Rudyard, 'Kidnapped', in *Plain Tales from the Hills* (1888; repr. Oxford, 1987), 97–101.

—— *The Light That Failed* (1891; repr. London, 1909).

—— 'The Tomb of His Ancestors', in *The Day's Work* (1898; repr. London, 1988), 102–33.

—— *The Complete Stalky & Co.* (1899; repr. Oxford, 1991).

—— 'The Exiles' Line', in *Rudyard Kipling: Complete Verse: Definitive Edition* (New York, 1989), 161–3.

—— 'Baa Baa, Black Sheep', in Thomas Pinney (ed.), *Rudyard Kipling: Something of Myself and Other Autobiographical Writings* (Cambridge, 1990), 135–70.

—— 'An English School', in Thomas Pinney (ed.), *Rudyard Kipling: Something of Myself and Other Autobiographical Writings* (Cambridge, 1990), 179–93.

—— *Something of Myself*, in Thomas Pinney (ed.), *Rudyard Kipling: Something of Myself and Other Autobiographical Writings* (Cambridge, 1990), 3–134.

Lawson, Charles A., *At Home on Furlough*, 2nd ser. (Madras, 1875).

Lee, Edwin, *Cheltenham and Its Resources: Mineral Waters, Climate, Etc. Considered Chiefly in a Sanitary Point of View* (London, 1851).

Linnell, C. D., 'Late-Victorian Bedford', *Bedfordshire Magazine*, 7/51 (1959–60), 80–93.

Login, E. Dalhousie, *Lady Login's Recollections: Court Life and Camp Life, 1820–1904* (London, 1916).

Luke, Thomas Davy, *Spas and Health Resorts of the British Isles: Their Mineral Waters, Climate, and the Treatment to be Obtained* (London, 1919).

Macdonald, Betsy, *India . . . Sunshine and Shadows* (London, 1988).

MacKinnon, Grace, 'Diseases of Women in the Tropics', in W. Byam and R. G. Archibald (eds.), *The Practice of Medicine in the Tropics by Many Authorities* (London, 1921), iii. 2471–98.

Mair, R. S., *Medical Guide for Anglo-Indians* (London, 1874).

Majumdar, Janaki Agnes Penelope (née Bonnerjee), *Family History*, ed. and intro. by Antoinette Burton (New Delhi, 2003).

Martyn, Margaret, *Married to the Raj* (London, 1992).

Masani, Zareer, *Indian Tales of the Raj* (London, 1987).

'Mauser' [pseud.], *How to Live in England on a Pension: A Guide for Public Servants Abroad and at Home* (London, 1930); new and enlarged edn. (London, 1934); 3rd edn. (London, 1938).

Milford, L. S., *Haileybury Register, 1862–1910*, 4th edn. (London, 1910).

Molony, J. Chartres, *A Book of South India* (London, 1926).

Moncrieff, A. R. Hope (ed.), *Black's Guide to Hastings and Eastbourne, St Leonards, Bexhill, Rye, Winchelsea, Etc.* (London, 1899).

Money, L. G. Chiozza, *Riches and Poverty*, 3rd edn. (London, 1906).

Moore, W. J., *Health Resorts for Tropical Invalids in India, at Home, and Abroad* (London, 1881).

Moore, Sir William, 'Is the Colonisation of Tropical Africa by Europeans Possible?', *Transactions of the Epidemiological Society of London*, 10 (1890–1), 27–45.

Moseley, George, *Eastbourne as a Residence for Invalids and Winter Resort* (London, 1882).

Mukharji, T. N., *A Visit to Europe* (Calcutta, 1889).

Murray, John (ed.), *A Handbook for Travellers in India and Ceylon* (London, 1891).

Neligan, Dr A. R. *et al.*, 'Discussion on the Adaptation of European Women and Children to Tropical Climates', *Proceedings of the Royal Society of Medicine*, 24, Part 2 (1931), 1315–33.

Nevill, Ralph, *London Clubs: Their History and Treasures* (1911; repr. London, 1969).

Newman's Guide to Darjeeling and Neighbourhood (Calcutta, 1922).

'One of the Community', *'The Euro-Asian' or 'Anglo-Indian': A Burma Brochure* (Rangoon, 1910).

Orwell, George, *Coming Up for Air* (1939; repr. London, 2000).

O.U.S.C. Register, 1936 (Canterbury, 1936).

The Oxford English Dictionary, 2nd edn. (Oxford, 1989).

The Paddington and Bayswater Directory for 1872 (London, 1872).

The Paddington and Bayswater Directory for 1875 (London, 1875).

Paddington Past and Present, 6th edn. (London, 1936).

Perrin, Alice, *The Anglo-Indians* (London, 1912).

Platt, Kate, *The Home and Health in India and the Tropical Colonies* (London, 1923).

Rhodes James, Richard, *The Years Between: A Tale of the Nineteen Thirties* (Bishop Wilton, York, 1993).

Risley, H. H., and Gait, E. A., *Census of India, 1901*, Vol. I: *India*. Part I: *Report* (Calcutta, 1903).

Rivett-Carnac, J. H., *Many Memories of Life in India, at Home, and Abroad* (Edinburgh, 1910).

Roberts, Charles, *Eastbourne as a Health Resort* (Eastbourne, 1899).

Robinson, W. P. A., *How to Live Well on Your Pension* (London, 1955).

Roche, George, *Childhood in India: Tales from Sholapur*, ed. by Richard Terrell (London, 1994).

Ross, Alan, *Blindfold Games* (London, 1986).

Rushdie, Salman, 'Outside the Whale', *Granta*, 11 (1984), 125–38.

Scott, Paul, *Staying On* (1977; repr. London, 1978).

Seton, Major B. G., and Gould, Major J., *The Indian Medical Service: Being a Synopsis of the Rules and Regulations Regarding Pay, Pensions, Leave, Examination, Etc.* (Calcutta, 1912).

Sinclair, Catherine, *Hill and Valley; or, Hours in England and Wales* (Edinburgh, 1838).

Sladen, Douglas, *Brittany for Britons* (London, 1896).

Sprawson, Cuthbert Allan, *Moore's Manual of Family Medicine and Hygiene for India* (London, 1921).

Staines, James Richard, *Country Born: One Man's Life in India, 1909–1947* (London, 1986).

Stamp, Sir Josiah, *British Incomes and Property* (London, 1916).

Steel, F. A., and Gardiner, G., *The Complete Indian Housekeeper and Cook* (1888; repr. London, 1917).

Tapp, Major H. A., *United Services College, 1874–1911* (Aldershot, 1933).

Tapp, Col. H. A., and Vickers, Lt.-Gen. W. G. H., *United Services College, 1874–1911* (Cheshunt, Herts., 1959).

Tilt, Edward John, *Health in India for British Women, and On the Prevention of Disease in Tropical Climates*, 4th edn. (London, 1875).

Trevelyan, Sir George, *The Competition Wallah* (1864; repr. London, 1907).

Trevelyan, Humphrey, *The India We Left* (London, 1972).

Trevelyan, Raleigh, *The Golden Oriole: A 200-Year History of an English Family in India* (New York, 1987).

Ussher, Beverley (ed.), *Public Schools at a Glance (Boarding Schools at £80 a year and over): A Guide for Parents and Guardians in Selecting a Public School for Their Boys* (London, 1912).

Waring, Edward J., *The Tropical Resident at Home: Letters Addressed to Europeans Returning from India and the Colonies on Subjects Connected with their Health and General Welfare* (London, 1866).

Watkins, Revd O. D., 'The Education of European and Eurasian Children in India', in *Pan-Anglican Papers, Being Problems for Consideration at the Pan-Anglican Congress, 1908: Church Work among those Temporarily Residing in Distant Lands* (London, 1908), 1–8.

Who's Who in Cheltenham (Newport, 1911).

Wilkins, Joyce, *A Child's Eye View, 1904–1920* (Sussex, 1992).

Wilson, R. N., *Leafy Eastbourne* (Eastbourne, 1906).

Woolf, Leonard, *Growing: An Autobiography of the Years 1904–1911* (New York, 1961).

Woolf, Virginia, *The Years* (London, 1937).

—— *Three Guineas* (1938; repr. London, 1977).

Willoughby, Maurice, *Echo of a Distant Drum: The Last Generation of Empire* (Sussex, 2001).

Yule, Col. Henry, and Burnell, A. C., *Hobson-Jobson: A Glossary of Colloquial Anglo-Indian Words and Phrases*, ed. by William Crooke (New Delhi, 1968, repr. of 2nd 1903 edn.).

SECONDARY SOURCES

Abel, Evelyn, *The Anglo-Indian Community: Survival in India* (New Delhi, 1988).

Abrams, Lynn, *The Orphan Country: Children of Scotland's Broken Homes from 1845 to the Present Day* (Edinburgh, 1998).

—— ' "There was Nobody like my Daddy": Fathers, the Family and the Marginalisation of Men in Modern Scotland', *Scottish Historical Review*, 78/2, No. 206 (Oct. 1999), 219–42.

Adams, Caroline (comp. and ed.), *Across Seven Seas and Thirteen Rivers: Life Stories of Pioneer Sylhetti Settlers in Britain* (London, 1987).

Anderson, Benedict, *Imagined Communities: Reflections on the Origin and Spread of Nationalism*, rev. edn. (London, 1991).

Armstrong, Nancy, *Desire and Domestic Fiction: A Political History of the Novel* (Oxford, 1987).

Armstrong, Nancy, 'The Rise of the Domestic Woman', in Nancy Armstrong and Leonard Tennenhouse (eds.), *The Ideology of Conduct: Essays on Literature and the History of Sexuality* (New York, 1987), 96–141.

Arnold, David, 'European Orphans and Vagrants in India in the Nineteenth Century', *Journal of Imperial and Commonwealth History*, 7/2 (1979), 104–27.

—— 'White Colonization and Labour in Nineteenth-Century India', *Journal of Imperial and Commonwealth History*, 12/2 (1983), 133–58.

—— (ed.), *Imperial Medicine and Indigenous Societies* (Manchester, 1988).

—— *Colonizing the Body: State Medicine and Epidemic Diseases in Nineteenth-Century India* (Berkeley, CA, 1993).

Asad, Talal, 'Multiculturalism and British Identity in the Wake of the Rushdie Affair', *Politics and Society*, 18/4 (1990), 455–80.

Atkins, P. J., 'The Spatial Configuration of Class Solidarity in London's West End 1792–1939', *Urban History Yearbook*, 17 (1990), 36–65.

Bailey, Peter, 'White Collars, Gray Lives? The Lower Middle Class Revisited', *Journal of British Studies*, 38/3 (1999), 273–90.

Baker, T. F. T. (ed.), *A History of the County of Middlesex*, Vol. IX: *Hampstead and Paddington Parishes* (Oxford, 1989).

Ballhatchet, Kenneth, *Race, Sex and Class under the Raj: Imperial Attitudes and Policies and their Critics, 1793–1905* (London, 1980).

Bamford, T. W., *The Rise of the Public Schools: A Study of Boys' Public Boarding Schools in England and Wales from 1837 to the Present Day* (London, 1967).

Bammer, Angelika, 'Introduction', in Angelika Bammer (ed.), *Displacements: Cultural Identities in Question* (Bloomington, IN, 1994), pp. xi–xx.

Baucom, Ian, *Out of Place: Englishness, Empire, and the Locations of Identity* (Princeton, NJ, 1999).

Bayly, C. A., *Imperial Meridian: The British Empire and the World* (London, 1989).

—— 'Exhibiting the Imperial Image', *History Today*, 40 (Oct. 1990), 12–18.

—— (ed.), *The Raj: India and the British, 1600–1947* (London, 1990).

Bear, Laura Charlotte, 'Traveling Modernity: Capitalism, Community and Nation in the Colonial Governance of the Indian Railways', Ph.D. diss. (University of Michigan, 1998).

Bear, Laura Gbah, 'Miscegenations of Modernity: Constructing European Respectability and Race in the Indian Railway Colony, 1857–1931', *Women's History Review*, 3/4 (1994), 531–48.

Beddoe, Deirdre, *Back to Home and Duty: Women Between the Wars, 1918–1939* (London, 1989).

Behlmer, George K., *Friends of the Family: The English Home and Its Guardians, 1850–1940* (Stanford, CA, 1998).

Bell, Patricia, 'Aspects of Anglo-Indian Bedford', *Publications of the Bedfordshire Historical Record Society*, 57 (1978), 181–203.

Bell, Vikki, 'Show and Tell: Passing and Narrative in Toni Morrison's *Jazz*', *Social Identities*, 2/2 (1996), 221–36.

Bertaux, Daniel, and Thompson, Paul (eds.), *International Yearbook of Oral History and Life Stories*, vol. ii: *Between Generations: Family Models, Myths, and Memories* (Oxford, 1993).

Bertaux-Wiame, Isabelle, 'The Pull of Family Ties: Intergenerational Relationships and Life Paths', in Daniel Bertaux and Paul Thompson (eds.), *International Yearbook of Oral History and Life Stories*, Vol. II: *Between Generations: Family Models, Myths, and Memories* (Oxford, 1993), 39–50.

Bhabha, Homi K., *The Location of Culture* (New York, 1993).

—— 'Frontlines/Borderposts', in Angelika Bammer (ed.), *Displacements: Cultural Identities in Question* (Bloomington, IN, 1994), 269–72.

Bickers, Robert, *Britain in China: Community, Culture, and Colonialism, 1900–49* (Manchester, 1999).

Bickford-Smith, Vivian, *Ethnic Pride and Racial Prejudice in Victorian Cape Town: Group Identity and Social Practice, 1875–1902* (Cambridge, 1995).

Blackbourn, David, '"Taking the Waters": Meeting Places of the Fashionable World', in Martin H. Geyer and Johannes Paulmann (eds.), *The Mechanics of Internationalism: Culture, Society, and Politics from the 1840s to the First World War* (Oxford, 2001), 435–57.

Blake, Steven, and Beacham, Roger, *The Book of Cheltenham* (Buckingham, 1982).

Blunt, Alison, 'Imperial Geographies of Home: British Domesticity in India, 1886–1925', *Transactions of the Institute of British Geographers*, n.s. 24 (1999), 421–40.

—— '"Land of our Mothers": Home, Identity, and Nationality for Anglo-Indians in British India, 1919–1947', *History Workshop Journal*, 54 (2002), 49–72.

Bond, Ruskin, *A History of Wynberg Allen, Mussoorie* (Mussoorie, 1988).

Bourne, J. M., *Patronage and Society in Nineteenth-Century England* (London, 1986).

Bowden, Sue, and Offer, Avner, 'The Technological Revolution That Never Was: Gender, Class, and the Diffusion of Household Appliances in Interwar England', in Victoria de Grazia with Ellen Furlough (eds.), *The Sex of Things: Gender and Consumption in Historical Perspective* (Berkeley, CA, 1996), 244–74.

Bowler, Peter J., *Evolution: The History of an Idea*, rev. edn. (Berkeley, CA, 1983, 1989).

Breward, Christopher, 'Sartorial Spectacle: Clothing and Masculine Identities in the Imperial City, 1860–1914', in Felix Driver and David Gilbert (eds.), *Imperial Cities: Landscape, Display and Identity* (Manchester, 1999), 238–53.

Brown, Judith M., 'India', in Judith M. Brown and Wm. Roger Louis (eds.), *The Oxford History of the British Empire: The Twentieth Century* (Oxford, 1999), iv. 421–46.

Buettner, Elizabeth, 'Haggis in the Raj: Private and Public Celebrations of Scottishness in Late Imperial India', *Scottish Historical Review*, 81/2, no. 212 (2002), 212–39.

Burman, Sandra (ed.), *Fit Work for Women* (London, 1979).

Burstyn, Joan N., *Victorian Education and the Ideal of Womanhood* (London, 1980).

Burton, Antoinette, *Burdens of History: British Feminists, Indian Women and Imperial Culture, 1865–1915* (Chapel Hill, NC, 1994).

—— 'Contesting the Zenana: The Mission to Make "Lady Doctors for India", 1874–1885', *Journal of British Studies*, 35 (1996), 368–97.

—— *At the Heart of the Empire: Indians and the Colonial Encounter in Late-Victorian Britain* (Berkeley, CA, 1998).

—— 'Tongues Untied: Lord Salisbury's "Black Man" and the Boundaries of Imperial Democracy', *Comparative Studies in Society and History*, 43/2 (2000), 632–61.

—— 'Who Needs the Nation?: Interrogating "British" History', in Catherine Hall (ed.), *Cultures of Empire: A Reader: Colonizers in Britain and the Empire in the Nineteenth and Twentieth Centuries* (Manchester, 2000), 137–53.

—— 'India, Inc.? Nostalgia, Memory, and the Empire of Things', in Stuart Ward (ed.), *British Culture and the End of Empire* (Manchester, 2001), 217–32.

—— *Dwelling in the Archive: Women Writing House, Home, and History in Late Colonial India* (New York, 2003).

Bush, Julia, 'Moving On–And Looking Back', *History Workshop Journal*, 36 (1993), 183–94.

Byng-Hall, John, interviewed by Paul Thompson, 'The Power of Family Myths', in Raphael Samuel and Paul Thompson (eds.), *The Myths We Live By* (London, 1990), 216–24.

Cage, R. A. (ed.), *The Scots Abroad: Labour, Capital, Enterprise, 1750–1914* (London, 1985).

Cain, P. J., and Hopkins, A. G., *British Imperialism: Innovation and Expansion, 1688–1914* (London, 1993).

—— *British Imperialism: Crisis and Deconstruction, 1914–1990* (London, 1993).

Caine, Barbara, *Destined to be Wives: The Sisters of Beatrice Webb* (Oxford, 1986).

Callan, Hillary, and Ardener, Shirley (eds.), *The Incorporated Wife* (London, 1984).

Callaway, Helen, *Gender, Culture and Empire: European Women in Colonial Nigeria* (London, 1987).

Cannadine, David, *Lords and Landlords: The Aristocracy and the Towns, 1774–1967* (Leicester, 1980).

—— *Ornamentalism: How the British Saw Their Empire* (London, 2001).

Caplan, Lionel, 'Cupid in Colonial and Post-Colonial South India: Changing "Marriage" Practices Among Anglo-Indians in Madras', *South Asia*, 21/2 (1998), 1–27.

—— 'Iconographies of Anglo-Indian Women: Gender Constructs and Contrasts in a Changing Society', *Modern Asian Studies*, 34/4 (2000), 863–92.

—— *Children of Colonialism: Anglo-Indians in a Post-Colonial World* (Oxford, 2001).

Carrington, C. E., ' "Baa Baa, Black Sheep": Fact or Fiction?', *Kipling Journal*, (June 1972), 7–14.

Cell, John W., 'Anglo-Indian Medical Theory and the Origins of Segregation in West Africa', *American Historical Review*, 91/2 (1986), 307–35.

Centre for Contemporary Cultural Studies (ed.), *The Empire Strikes Back: Race and Racism in 70s Britain* (London, 1983).

Chakrabarty, Dipesh, *Rethinking Working-Class History: Bengal, 1890–1940* (Princeton, NJ, 1989).

—— 'Postcoloniality and the Artifice of History: Who Speaks for "Indian" Pasts?', *Representations*, 37 (1992), 1–26.

Chartier, Roger, 'Intellectual History or Sociocultural History?: The French Trajectories', in Dominick LaCapra and Steven L. Kaplan (eds.), *Modern European Intellectual History: Reappraisals and New Perspectives* (Ithaca, NY, 1982), 13–46.

Chatterjee, Partha, *The Nation and Its Fragments: Colonial and Post-Colonial Histories* (Princeton, NJ, 1993).

Chatterjee, Piya, *A Time for Tea: Women, Labor, and Post/colonial Politics on an Indian Plantation* (Durham, NC, 2001).

Chaudhuri, Nupur, 'Memsahibs and Motherhood in Nineteenth-Century India', *Victorian Studies*, 31 (1988), 517–35.

—— 'Shawls, Jewelry, Curry, and Rice in Victorian Britain', in Nupur Chaudhuri and Margaret Strobel (eds.), *Western Women and Imperialism: Complicity and Resistance* (Bloomington, IN, 1992), 231–46.

—— 'Memsahibs and Their Servants in Nineteenth-Century India', *Women's History Review*, 3/4 (1994), 549–62.

—— and Strobel, Margaret (eds.), *Western Women and Imperialism: Complicity and Resistance* (Bloomington, IN, 1992).

Clancy-Smith, Julia, and Gouda, Frances (eds.), *Domesticating the Empire: Race, Gender, and Family Life in French and Dutch Colonialism* (Charlottesville, VA, 1998).

Coe, Richard, *When the Grass Was Taller: Autobiography and the Experience of Childhood* (New Haven, CT, 1984).

Coetzee, J. M., *White Writing: On the Culture of Letters in South Africa* (New Haven, CT, 1988).

Cohn, Bernard S., 'Representing Authority in Victorian India', in Eric Hobsbawm and Terence Ranger (eds.), *The Invention of Tradition* (Cambridge, 1983), 165–209.

—— 'The British in Benares: A Nineteenth Century Colonial Society', in *An Anthropologist Among the Historians and Other Essays* (New Delhi, 1987), 422–62.

—— 'The Census, Social Structure, and Objectification in South Asia', in *An Anthropologist Among the Historians and Other Essays* (New Delhi, 1987), 224–54.

—— 'The Recruitment and Training of British Civil Servants in India, 1600–1860', in *An Anthropologist Among the Historians and Other Essays* (New Delhi, 1987), 500–53.

—— 'Cloth, Clothes, and Colonialism: India in the Nineteenth Century', in *Colonialism and Its Forms of Knowledge: The British in India* (Princeton, NJ, 1996), 106–62.

Colley, Linda, 'Britishness and Otherness: An Argument', *Journal of British Studies*, 31 (1992), 309–29.

Collingham, E. M., *Imperial Bodies: The Physical Experience of the Raj, c.1800–1947* (Cambridge, 2001).

Colls, Robert, *Identity of England* (Oxford, 2002).

Colmcille, Mother Mary, *First the Blade: History of the I.B.V.M. (Loreto) in India, 1841–1962* (Calcutta, 1968).

Compton, J. M., 'Open Competition and the Indian Civil Service, 1854–1876', *English Historical Review*, 327 (1968), 265–84.

Conisbee, L. R., *Bedford Modern School: Its Origin and Growth* (Bedford, 1964).

Constantine, Stephen (ed.), *Emigrants and Empire: British Settlement in the Dominions Between the Wars* (Manchester, 1990).

Cook, Scott B., 'The Irish Raj: Social Origins and Careers of Irishmen in the Indian Civil Service, 1855–1914', *Journal of Social History*, 20 (1987), 507–29.

Cooper, Frederick, 'Postcolonial Peoples: A Commentary', in Andrea L. Smith (ed.), *Europe's Invisible Migrants* (Amsterdam, 2003), 169–83.

Coveney, Peter, *The Image of Childhood, the Individual and Society: A Study of the Theme in English Literature*, rev. edn. (Harmondsworth, 1967).

Cowan, Ruth Schwartz, *More Work for Mother: The Ironies of Household Technology from the Open Hearth to the Microwave* (New York, 1983).

Crick, Bernard, *George Orwell: A Life* (London, 1980).

Crossick, Geoffrey, 'The Emergence of the Lower Middle Class in Britain: A Discussion', in Geoffrey Crossick (ed.), *The Lower Middle Class in Britain, 1870–1914* (London, 1977), 1–60.

Cuddy, Brendan, and Mansell, Tony, 'Engineers for India: The Royal Engineering College at Cooper's Hill', *History of Education*, 23/1 (1994), 107–23.

Cunningham, Hugh, *Children and Childhood in Western Society Since 1500* (London, 1995).

Curran, Cynthia, 'Private Women, Public Needs: Middle-Class Widows in Victorian England', *Albion*, 25/2 (1993), 217–36.

Curtin, Philip D., 'Medical Knowledge and Urban Planning in Tropical Africa', *American Historical Review*, 90/3 (1985), 594–613.

—— *Death by Migration: Europe's Encounter with the Tropical World in the Nineteenth Century* (Cambridge, 1989).

Darwin, John, 'British Decolonization since 1945: A Pattern or a Puzzle?', *Journal of Imperial and Commonwealth History*, 12 (1984), 187–209.

—— *The End of the British Empire: The Historical Debate* (Oxford, 1991).

Davidoff, Leonore, 'Class and Gender in Victorian England: The Diaries of Hannah Cullwick and A. J. Munby', in *Worlds Between: Historical Perspectives on Gender and Class* (New York, 1995), 103–50.

—— 'Where the Stranger Begins: The Question of Siblings in Historical Analysis', in

Worlds Between: Historical Perspectives on Gender and Class (New York, 1995), 206–26.

——and Hall, Catherine, *Family Fortunes: Men and Women of the English Middle Class, 1780–1850* (Chicago, 1987).

——Doolittle, Megan, Fink, Janet, and Holden, Katherine, *The Family Story: Blood, Contract and Intimacy, 1830–1960* (London, 1999).

Davin, Anna, 'Imperialism and Motherhood', *History Workshop Journal*, 5 (1978), 9–65.

Davis, Fred, *Yearning for Yesterday: A Sociology of Nostalgia* (New York, 1979).

Dawson, Graham, *Soldier Heroes: British Adventure, Empire and the Imagining of Masculinities* (London, 1994).

D'Cruz, Glenn, 'Representing Anglo-Indians: A Genealogical Study', Ph.D. diss. (University of Melbourne, 1999).

De Caro, Francis A., and Jordan, Rosan A., 'The Wrong *Topi*: Personal Narratives, Ritual, and the Sun Helmet as Symbol', *Western Folklore*, 43/4 (1984), 233–48.

De Groot, Joanna, ' "Sex" and "Race": The Construction of Language and Image in the Nineteenth Century', in Catherine Hall (ed.), *Cultures of Empire: A Reader: Colonizers in Britain and the Empire in the Nineteenth and Twentieth Centuries* (Manchester, 2000), 37–60.

Delamont, Sara, *Knowledgeable Women* (London, 1989).

——'Distant Dangers and Forgotten Standards: Pollution Control Strategies in the British Girls' School, 1860–1920', *Women's History Review*, 2/2 (1993), 233–51.

Dewan, Dick B., *Education in the Darjeeling Hills: An Historical Survey: 1835–1985* (New Delhi, 1991).

Dewey, C. J., 'The Education of a Ruling Caste: The Indian Civil Service in the Era of Competitive Examination', *English Historical Review*, 347 (1973), 262–85.

Dewey, Clive, *Anglo-Indian Attitudes: The Mind of the Indian Civil Service* (London, 1993).

Di Leonardo, Micaela, 'The Female World of Cards and Holidays: Women, Families, and the Work of Kinship', *Signs: A Journal of Women in Culture and Society*, 12/3 (1987), 440–53.

Dirks, Nicholas B., 'Introduction: Colonialism and Culture', in Nicholas B. Dirks (ed.), *Colonialism and Culture* (Ann Arbor, MI, 1992), 1–25.

——*Castes of Mind: Colonialism and the Making of Modern India* (Princeton, NJ, 2001).

Doolittle, Megan, 'Missing Fathers: Assembling a History of Fatherhood in Mid-Nineteenth-Century England', Ph.D. thesis (University of Essex, 1996).

Doran, Christine, ' "Oddly Hybrid": Childbearing and Childrearing Practices in Colonial Penang, 1850–1875', *Women's History Review*, 6/1 (1997), 29–46.

Doyle, Brian, *English and Englishness* (London, 1989).

Driver, Felix, and Gilbert, David (eds.), *Imperial Cities: Landscape, Display and Identity* (Manchester, 1999).

D'Souza, Austin A., *Anglo-Indian Education: A Study of its Origins and Growth in Bengal up to 1960* (Delhi, 1976).

Duder, C. J., 'The Settler Response to the Indian Crisis of 1922 in Kenya: Brigadier General Philip Wheatley and "Direct Action"', *Journal of Imperial and Commonwealth History*, 17/3 (1989), 349–73.

—— '"Men of the Officer Class": The Participants in the 1919 Soldier Settlement Scheme in Kenya', *African Affairs*, 92/366 (1993), 69–87.

Dyer, Richard, *White* (London, 1997).

Dyhouse, Carol, *Girls Growing Up in Late Victorian and Edwardian England* (London, 1981).

Earle, Rebecca (ed.), *Epistolary Selves: Letters and Letter-Writers, 1600–1945* (Aldershot, 1999).

Edwards, Elizabeth, 'Photographs as Objects of Memory', in Marius Kwint, Christopher Breward, and Jeremy Aynsley (eds.), *Material Memories* (Oxford, 1999), 221–36.

Fedorowich, Kent, *Unfit for Heroes: Reconstruction and Soldier Settlement in the Empire Between the Wars* (Manchester, 1995).

Fisher, Michael H., *The First Indian Author in English: Dean Mahomed (1759–1851) in India, Ireland, and England* (Delhi, 1996).

Formes, Malia B., 'Beyond Complicity Versus Resistance: Recent Work on Gender and European Imperialism', *Journal of Social History*, 28 (1995), 629–41.

—— 'Post-imperial Domesticity Amid Diaspora, 1959–79: A Comparative Biography of Two English Sisters from India', paper presented at 'Post-Imperial Britain': 16th Annual Conference of the Institute of Contemporary British History, London, 8–10 July 2002.

Forty, Adrian, *Objects of Desire: Design and Society Since 1750* (London, 1995).

Francis, Martin, 'Tears, Tantrums, and Bared Teeth: The Emotional Economy of Three Conservative Prime Ministers, 1951–1963', *Journal of British Studies*, 41 (2002), 354–87.

Frankenberg, Ruth, *White Women, Race Matters: The Social Construction of Whiteness* (Minneapolis, MN, 1993).

—— 'Introduction: Local Whitenesses, Localizing Whiteness', in Ruth Frankenberg (ed.), *Displacing Whiteness: Essays in Social and Cultural Criticism* (Durham, NC, 1997), 1–33.

Frykman, Jonas, and Löfgren, Orvar, *Culture Builders: A Historical Anthropology of Middle-Class Life*, trans. by Alan Crozier (New Brunswick, NJ, 1987).

Gagnier, Regenia, *Subjectivities: A History of Self-Representation in Britain, 1832–1920* (New York, 1991).

Garside, Patricia L., 'West End, East End: London, 1890–1940', in Anthony Sutcliffe (ed.), *Metropolis, 1890–1940* (London, 1984), 221–58.

Gaskell, S. Martin, 'Housing and the Lower Middle Class, 1870–1914', in Geoffrey Crossick (ed.), *The Lower Middle Class in Britain, 1870–1914* (London, 1977), 159–83.

Gathorne-Hardy, Jonathan, *The Public Schools Phenomenon* (Harmondsworth, 1979).

George, Rosemary Marangoly, 'Homes in the Empire, Empires in the Home', *Cultural Critique*, (winter 1993–4), 95–127.

—— *The Politics of Home: Postcolonial Relocations and Twentieth-Century Fiction* (Cambridge, 1996).

Ghosh, Durba, 'Colonial Companions: Bibis, Begums, and Concubines of the British in North India, 1760–1830', Ph.D. diss. (University of California, Berkeley, 2000).

—— 'Making and Un-making Loyal Subjects: Pensioning Widows and Educating Orphans in Early Colonial India', *Journal of Imperial and Commonwealth History*, 31/1 (2003), 1–28.

Ghosh, Suresh Chandra, *The Social Condition of the British Community in Bengal, 1757–1800* (Leiden, 1970).

Gikandi, Simon, *Maps of Englishness: Writing Identity in the Culture of Colonialism* (New York, 1996).

Giles, Judy, *Women, Identity and Private Life in Britain, 1900–1950* (London, 1995).

Gillis, John R., 'Ritualization of Middle-Class Family Life in Nineteenth Century Britain', *International Journal of Politics, Culture and Society*, 3/2 (1989), 213–35.

—— 'Making Time for Family: The Invention of Family Time(s) and the Reinvention of Family History', *Journal of Family History*, 21/1 (1996), 4–21.

—— *A World of Their Own Making: Myth, Ritual, and the Quest for Family Values* (New York, 1996).

Gilman, Sander L., *Difference and Pathology: Stereotypes of Sexuality, Race, and Madness* (Ithaca, NY, 1985).

Gilroy, Paul, *'There Ain't No Black in the Union Jack': The Cultural Politics of Race and Nation* (Chicago, 1987).

—— *The Black Atlantic: Modernity and Double Consciousness* (Cambridge, MA, 1993).

Ginzburg, Carlo, 'Clues: Roots of an Evidential Paradigm', in *Clues, Myth, and the Historical Method*, trans. by John and Anne C. Tedeschi (Baltimore, MD, 1989), 96–125.

Gist, Noel P., and Wright, Roy Dean, *Marginality and Identity: Anglo-Indians as a Racially-Mixed Minority in India* (Leiden, 1973).

Glucksmann, Miriam, *Women Assemble: Women Workers and the New Industries in Inter-War Britain* (London, 1990).

Godber, Joyce, *The Harpur Trust, 1552–1973* (Luton, 1973).

—— and Hutchins, Isabel (eds.), *A Century of Challenge: Bedford High School, 1882–1982* (Biggleswade, 1982).

Gorham, Deborah, *The Victorian Girl and the Feminine Ideal* (Bloomington, IN, 1982).

Gouda, Frances, *Dutch Culture Overseas: Colonial Practice in the Netherlands Indies, 1900–1942* (Amsterdam, 1995).

Gould, Stephen J., *Ontogeny and Phylogeny* (Cambridge, MA, 1977).

—— *The Mismeasure of Man* (New York, 1981).

Gowans, Georgina, 'A Passage from India: British Women Travelling Home, 1915–1947', D.Phil. thesis (University of Southampton, 1999).

Gray, Robert, 'The Falklands Factor', in Stuart Hall and Martin Jacques (eds.), *The Politics of Thatcherism* (London, 1983), 271–80.

Guha, Ramachandra, *A Corner of a Foreign Field: The Indian History of a British Sport* (London, 2002).

Guha, Ranajit, 'Dominance Without Hegemony and Its Historiography', in Ranajit Guha (ed.), *Subaltern Studies* (Delhi, 1989), vi. 210–309.

Haggis, Jane, 'White Women and Colonialism: Towards a Non-Recuperative History', in Clare Midgley (ed.), *Gender and Imperialism* (Manchester, 1998), 45–75.

Hale, Grace Elizabeth, *Making Whiteness: The Culture of Segregation in the South, 1890–1940* (New York, 1998).

Hall, Catherine, *White, Male and Middle Class: Explorations in Feminism and History* (New York, 1992).

—— 'Introduction: Thinking the Post-Colonial, Thinking the Empire', in Catherine Hall (ed.), *Cultures of Empire: A Reader: Colonizers in Britain and the Empire in the Nineteenth and Twentieth Centuries* (Manchester, 2000), 1–33.

—— *Civilising Subjects: Metropole and Colony in the English Imagination, 1830–1867* (Cambridge, 2002).

Hall, Stuart, 'Racism and Reaction', in John Rex et al., *Five Views of Multi-Racial Britain* (London: Commission for Racial Equality, 1978), 23–35.

—— 'Ethnicity: Identity and Difference', *Radical America*, 23/4 (1991), 9–20.

—— 'When was "the Post-Colonial"? Thinking at the limit', in Iain Chambers and Lidia Curti (eds.), *The Post-Colonial Question: Common Skies, Divided Horizons* (London, 1996), 242–60.

Hamilton, Douglas J., 'Patronage and Profit: Scottish Networks in the British West Indies, c.1763–1807', D.Phil. thesis (University of Aberdeen, 1999).

Hannah, Leslie, *Inventing Retirement: The Development of Occupational Pensions in Britain* (Cambridge, 1986).

Hansen, Karen Tranberg, *Distant Companions: Servants and Employers in Zambia, 1900–1985* (Ithaca, NY, 1989).

Hareven, Tamara K., 'Recent Research on the History of the Family', in Michael Drake (ed.), *Time, Family and Community: Perspectives on Family and Community History* (Oxford, 1994), 13–43.

Harris, Jose, *William Beveridge: A Biography* (Oxford, 1977).

—— *Private Lives, Public Spirit: Britain 1870–1914* (Harmondsworth, 1994).

Harrison, Mark, *Public Health in British India: Anglo-Indian Preventive Medicine, 1859–1914* (Cambridge, 1994).

—— *Climates and Constitutions: Health, Race, Environment and British Imperialism in India, 1600–1850* (New Delhi, 1999).

Hart, Gwen, *A History of Cheltenham* (Gloucester, 1981).

Hartigan, John Jnr, 'Unpopular Culture: The Case of "White Trash"', *Cultural Studies*, 11 (1997), 316–43.

Hawes, Christopher, *Poor Relations: The Making of a Eurasian Community in British India, 1773–1833* (Richmond, Surrey, 1996).

Hay, Elizabeth, *Sambo Sahib: The Story of Little Black Sambo and Helen Bannerman* (Edinburgh, 1981).

Hay, Stephen, 'The Making of a Late-Victorian Hindu: M. K. Gandhi in London, 1888–1891', *Victorian Studies*, 33/1 (1989), 74–98.

Heathcote, T. A., *The Indian Army: The Garrison of British Imperial India, 1822–1922* (Newton Abbot, 1974).

Hembry, Phyllis, *The English Spa, 1560–1815: A Social History* (London, 1990).

—— *British Spas from 1815 to the Present*, ed. by Leonard W. Cowie and Evelyn E. Cowie (London, 1997).

Hendrick, Harry, *Child Welfare: England, 1872–1989* (London, 1994).

Heward, Christine, *Making a Man of Him: Parents and Their Sons' Education at an English Public School, 1929–50* (London, 1988).

Higonnet, Anne, *Pictures of Innocence: The History and Crisis of Ideal Childhood* (London, 1998).

Higson, Andrew, 'Re-presenting the National Past: Nostalgia and Pastiche in the Heritage Film', in Lester Friedman (ed.), *British Cinema and Thatcherism: Fires Were Started* (London, 1993), 109–29.

Hill, John, *British Cinema in the 1980s* (Oxford, 1999).

Hirsch, Julia, *Family Photographs: Content, Meaning and Effects* (New York, 1981).

Hobsbawm, Eric, 'Falklands Fallout', in Stuart Hall and Martin Jacques (eds.), *The Politics of Thatcherism* (London, 1983), 257–70.

—— 'Introduction', in Arlen Mack (ed.), *Home: A Place in the World* (New York, 1993), 61–4.

Hockings, Paul, 'British Society in the Company, Crown, and Congress Eras', in Paul Hockings (ed.), *Blue Mountains: The Ethnography and Biogeography of a South Indian Region* (Delhi, 1989), 334–59.

Hollingsworth, Alan, *Cheltenham* (London, 1983).

Holzman, James M., *Nabobs in England: A Study of the Returned Anglo-Indian, 1760–1785* (New York, 1926).

Honda, Takehiko, 'Indian Civil Servants, 1892–1937: An Age of Transition', D.Phil. thesis (University of Oxford, 1996).

Honey, J. R. de S., *Tom Brown's Universe: The Development of the Victorian Public School* (London, 1977).

Howarth, Patrick, *When the Riviera Was Ours* (London, 1977).

Howe, Stephen, *Ireland and Empire: Colonial Legacies in Irish History and Culture* (Oxford, 2000).

Hunt, Lynn, *The Family Romance of the French Revolution* (Berkeley, CA, 1992).

Hunt, Mary Felicity, 'Secondary Education for the Middle Class Girl: A Study of Ideology and Educational Practice, 1870 to 1940, With Special Reference to the Harpur Trust Girls' Schools, Bedford', Ph.D. thesis (University of Cambridge, 1984).

Hutchins, Francis G., *The Illusion of Permanence: British Imperialism in India* (Princeton, NJ, 1967).

Hyam, Ronald, *Empire and Sexuality: The British Experience* (Manchester, 1990).

Jackson, Alan A., *The Middle Classes, 1900–1950* (Nairn, 1991).

Jackson, Louise A., *Child Sexual Abuse in Victorian England* (London, 2000).

Jacobson, Matthew Frye, *Whiteness of a Different Color: European Immigrants and the Alchemy of Race* (Cambridge, MA, 1998).

Jayawardena, Kumari, *The White Women's Other Burden: Western Women and South Asia During British Rule* (New York, 1995).

Jeffrey, Keith (ed.), *An Irish Empire?: Aspects of Ireland and the British Empire* (Manchester, 1996).

John, Angela (ed.), *Unequal Opportunities: Women's Employment in England, 1800–1918* (Oxford, 1986).

Jordanova, L. J., *Lamarck* (Oxford, 1984).

Julien, Isaac, and Mercer, Kobena, 'De Margin and De Center', in David Morley and Kuan-Hsing Chen (eds.), *Stuart Hall: Critical Dialogues in Cultural Studies* (London, 1996), 450–64.

Kaminsky, Arnold, '"Lombard Street" and India: Currency Problems in the Late Nineteenth Century', *Indian Economic and Social History Review*, 17/3 (1980), 307–27.

Kennedy, Dane, *Islands of White: Settler Society and Culture in Kenya and Southern Rhodesia, 1890–1939* (Durham, NC, 1987).

—— 'The Perils of the Midday Sun: Climatic Anxieties in the Colonial Tropics', in John M. MacKenzie (ed.), *Imperialism and the Natural World* (Manchester, 1990), 118–40.

—— *The Magic Mountains: Hill Stations and the British Raj* (Berkeley, CA, 1996).

King, Anthony D., *Colonial Urban Development: Culture, Social Power and Environment* (London, 1976).

—— *The Bungalow: The Production of a Global Culture* (London, 1984).

Knapman, Claudia, 'The White Child in Colonial Fiji, 1895–1930', *Journal of Pacific History*, 23 (1988), 208–13.

Kuhlick, F. W., 'Chronicles of Bedford Modern', published in 23 parts in the *Eagle*, 1947–55.

Kuhn, Annette, *Family Secrets: Acts of Memory and Imagination*, new edn. (London, 2002).

Lahiri, Shompa, *Indians in Britain: Anglo-Indian Encounters, Race, and Identity, 1880–1930* (London, 2000).

Lawson, Philip and Phillips, Jim, ' "Our Execrable Banditti": Perceptions of Nabobs in Mid-Eighteenth Century Britain', *Albion*, 16/3 (1984), 225–41.

Leinster-Mackay, Donald, *The Rise of the English Prep School* (London, 1984).

Lejeune, Anthony, and Lewis, Malcolm, *The Gentlemen's Clubs of London* (London, 1979).

Lethbridge, John, *Harrow on the Hooghly: The New School in Calcutta and Darjeeling, 1940–1944* (Charlbury, Oxfordshire, 1994).

Levine, Philippa, 'Venereal Disease, Prostitution, and the Politics of Empire: The Case of British India', *Journal of the History of Sexuality*, 4/4 (1994), 579–602.

Lewis, Brian, and Harding, Colin (eds.), *Kept in a Shoe Box: The Popular Experience of Photography* (Bradford, 1992).

Light, Alison, *Forever England: Femininity, Literature, and Conservatism Between the Wars* (London, 1991).

Little, Bryan, *Cheltenham* (London, 1952).

—— 'Calcutta in the Cotswolds', *Bristol and Gloucestershire Archaeological Society Transactions*, 98 (1980), 5–10.

Livingstone, David N., 'Human Acclimatization: Perspectives on a Contested Field of Inquiry in Science, Medicine, and Geography', *History of Science*, 25 (1987), 359–94.

Locher-Scholten, Elspeth, *Women and the Colonial State: Essays on Gender and Modernity in the Netherlands Indies, 1900–1942* (Amsterdam, 2000).

Lycett, Andrew, *Rudyard Kipling* (London, 1999).

McBratney, John, 'The Raj Is All the Rage: Paul Scott's *The Raj Quartet* and Colonial Nostalgia', *North Dakota Quarterly*, 55/3 (1987), 204–9.

McClintock, Anne, *Imperial Leather: Race, Gender and Sexuality in the Colonial Contest* (New York, 1995).

McConnell, James, *English Public Schools* (London, 1985).

Mack, E. C., *Public Schools and British Opinion, 1780–1860* (London, 1938).

Mack, Edward C., *Public Schools and British Opinion Since 1860* (New York, 1941).

MacKenzie, John M. (ed.), *Imperialism and Popular Culture* (Manchester, 1986).

—— *The Empire of Nature: Hunting, Conservation and British Imperialism* (Manchester, 1988).

—— 'Essay and Reflection: On Scotland and the Empire', *International History Review*, 15 (1993), 714–39.

MacMillan, Margaret, *Women of the Raj* (London, 1988).

Macnicol, John, 'The Evacuation of Schoolchildren', in Harold L. Smith (ed.), *War and Social Change: British Society in the Second World War* (Manchester, 1986), 3–31.

Malhotra, D. K., *History and Problems of Indian Currency, 1835–1959: An Introductory Study*, 6th edn. (Simla, 1960).

Mangan, J. A., *Athleticism in the Victorian and Edwardian Public School* (Cambridge, 1981).

—— *The Games Ethic and Imperialism: Aspects of the Diffusion of an Ideal* (Harmondsworth, 1986).

—— (ed.), *'Benefits Bestowed?': Education and British Imperialism* (Manchester, 1988).

Marks, Shula, 'History, the Nation and Empire: Sniping from the Periphery', *History Workshop Journal*, 29 (1990), 111–19.

Marshall, P. J., 'The Whites of British India, 1780–1830: A Failed Colonial Society?', *International History Review*, 12 (1990), 26–44.

—— 'British Immigration into India in the Nineteenth Century', in P. C. Emmer and M. Moerner (eds.), *European Expansion and Migration: Essays on the Intercontinental Migration from Africa, Asia, and Europe* (New York, 1992), 179–96.

—— 'The White Town of Calcutta Under the Rule of the East India Company', *Modern Asian Studies*, 34 (2000), 307–31.

Martin-Fugier, Anne, 'Bourgeois Rituals', in Michelle Perrot (ed.), Arthur Goldhammer (trans.), *A History of Private Life, Vol. IV: From the Fires of Revolution to the Great War* (Cambridge, MA, 1990), 261–337.

Martinez-Alier, Verena, *Marriage, Class and Colour in Nineteenth-Century Cuba: A Study of Racial Attitudes and Sexual Values in a Slave Society* (Ann Arbor, MI, 1989).

Marwick, Arthur, *British Society Since 1945*, 3rd edn. (London, 1996).

Mathur, H. N., 'Education of European and Eurasian Children in India, 1860–1894', *Indian Historical Records Commission: Proceedings*, 31, Part 2 (1935), 113–20.

Mechling, Jay, 'Advice to Historians on Advice to Mothers', *Journal of Social History*, 9/1 (1975), 44–63.

Medick, Hans, and Sabean, David Warren, 'Introduction', in Hans Medick and David Warren Sabean (eds.) *Interest and Emotion: Essays on the Study of Family and Kinship* (Cambridge, 1984).

Metcalf, Thomas R., *Ideologies of the Raj: The New Cambridge History of India, Vol. III, Part 4* (Cambridge, 1995).

Midgley, Clare (ed.), *Gender and Imperialism* (Manchester, 1998).

Mills, Sara, *Discourses of Difference: An Analysis of Women's Travel Writing and Colonialism* (London, 1991).

Misra, Maria, *Business, Race, and Politics in British India, c.1850–1960* (Oxford, 1999).

Mitra, Chandan, *Constant Glory: La Martinière Saga, 1836–1986* (Calcutta, 1987).

Moore, R. J., 'The Abolition of Patronage in the Indian Civil Service and the Closure of Haileybury College', *Historical Journal*, 7/2 (1964), 246–57.

Moore-Gilbert, B. J., *Kipling and 'Orientalism'* (London, 1986).

Morgan, M. C., *Cheltenham College: The First Hundred Years* (Calfont St Giles, Bucks., 1968).

Morris, Mandy S., ' "Tha'lt be like a blush-rose when tha' grows up, my little lass": English Cultural and Gendered Identity in *The Secret Garden*', *Environment and Planning D: Society and Space*, 14 (1996), 59–78.

Morss, John R., *The Biologising of Childhood: Developmental Psychology and the Darwinian Myth* (Hove, East Sussex, 1990).

Mugglestone, Lynda, *'Talking Proper': The Rise of Accent as Social Symbol* (Oxford, 1995).

Mullen, Harryette, 'Optic White: Blackness and the Production of Whiteness', *diacritics*, 24/2–3 (1994), 71–89.

Naidis, Mark, 'British Attitudes Toward the Anglo-Indians', *South Atlantic Quarterly*, 62/3 (1963), 407–22.

Nair, Janaki, 'Uncovering the *Zenana*: Visions of Indian Womanhood in Englishwomen's Writings, 1813–1940', in Catherine Hall (ed.), *Cultures of Empire: A Reader: Colonizers in Britain and the Empire in the Nineteenth and Twentieth Centuries* (Manchester, 2000), 224–45.

Nairn, Tom, 'Britain's Living Legacy', in Stuart Hall and Martin Jacques (eds.), *The Politics of Thatcherism* (London, 1983), 281–8.

Nandy, Ashis, *The Intimate Enemy: Loss and Recovery of Self Under Colonialism* (Delhi, 1983).

Newsome, David, *Godliness and Good Learning: Four Studies on a Victorian Ideal* (London, 1961).

Nicholson, Linda, 'The Myth of the Traditional Family', in Hilde Lindemann Nelson (ed.), *Feminism and Families* (New York, 1997), 27–42.

Olsen, Donald J., *The Growth of Victorian London* (London, 1976).

Osborne, Honor, and Manistry, Peggy, *A History of the Royal School for the Daughters of Officers of the Army, 1864–1965* (London, 1966).

Padfield, Peter, *Beneath the House Flag of the P. & O.* (London, 1981).

Parker, James G., 'Scottish Enterprise in India, 1750–1914', in R. A. Cage (ed.), *The Scots Abroad: Labour, Capital, Enterprise, 1750–1914* (London, 1985), 191–219.

Parry, Benita, *Delusions and Discoveries: Studies on India in the British Imagination, 1880–1930* (Berkeley, CA, 1972).

—— 'The Content and Discontents of Kipling's Imperialism', *New Formations*, 6 (1988), 49–63.

—— *Delusions and Discoveries: India in the British Imagination, 1880–1930*, 2nd edn. (London, 1998).

Passerini, Luisa, 'Mythbiography in Oral History', in Raphael Samuel and Paul Thompson (eds.), *The Myths We Live By* (London, 1990), 49–60.

Paxton, Nancy L., 'Disembodied Subjects: English Women's Autobiography under the Raj', in Sidonie Smith and Julia Watson (eds.), *Delcolonizing the Subject: The Politics of Gender in Women's Autobiography* (Minneapolis, MN, 1992), 387–409.

—— *Writing under the Raj: Gender, Race, and Rape in the British Colonial Imagination, 1830–1947* (New Brunswick, NJ, 1999).

Pearce, Tim, *Then and Now: An Anniversary Celebration of Cheltenham College, 1841–1991* (Cheltenham, 1991).

Pedersen, Joyce Senders, 'Schoolmistresses and Headmistresses: Elites and Education in Nineteenth-Century England', *Journal of British Studies*, 15/1 (1975), 135–62.

Pedersen, Poul, 'Anxious Lives and Letters: Family Separation, Communication Networks and Structures of Everyday Life', *Culture and History*, 8 (1990), 7–19.

Pemble, John, *The Mediterranean Passion: Victorians and Edwardians in the South* (Oxford, 1987).

Perkin, Harold, *The Rise of Professional Society: England since 1880* (London, 1989).

Peterson, M. Jeanne, *Family, Love, and Work in the Lives of Victorian Gentlewomen* (Bloomington, IN, 1989).

Phillips, Caryl, *The Atlantic Sound* (London, 2001).

—— *A New World Order: Selected Essays* (London, 2001).

Pike, Elsie, and Curryer, Constance E., *The Story of Walthamstow Hall: A Century of Girls' Education* (London, 1938).

Plummer, Ken, *Telling Sexual Stories: Power, Change, and Social Worlds* (London, 1995).

Pollock, Griselda, 'Territories of Desire: Reconsiderations of an African Childhood, Dedicated to a Woman whose Name was not really "Julia"', in George Robertson et al. (eds.), *Travellers' Tales: Narratives of Home and Displacement* (London, 1994), 63–89.

Portelli, Alessandro, *The Death of Luigi Trastulli and Other Stories* (Albany, NY, 1991).

Porter, Roy, *London: A Social History* (London, 1994).

Potter, David C., *India's Political Administrators, 1919–1983* (Oxford, 1983).

Prakash, Gyan, 'Writing Post-Orientalist Histories of the Third World: Perspectives from Indian Historiography', *Comparative Studies in Society and History*, 32/2 (1990), 383–408.

Procida, Mary A., *Married to the Empire: Gender, Politics and Imperialism in India, 1883–1947* (Manchester, 2002).

Pugh, Simon, *Garden, Nature, Language (Cultural Politics)* (Manchester, 1988).

'The Question of Home', special issue of *New Formations*, 17 (1992).

Ramusack, Barbara, 'Cultural Missionaries, Maternal Imperialists, Feminist Allies:

British Women Activists in India, 1865–1945', in Nupur Chaudhuri and Margaret Strobel (eds.), *Western Women and Imperialism: Complicity and Resistance* (Bloomington, IN, 1992), 119–36.

Rapp, Rayna, Ross, Ellen, and Bridenthal, Renate, 'Examining Family History', in Judith L. Newton, Mary P. Ryan, and Judith R. Walkowitz (eds.), *Sex and Class in Women's History* (London, 1983), 232–58.

Rappaport, Erika Diane, *Shopping for Pleasure: Women in the Making of London's West End* (Princeton, NJ, 2000).

Raychaudhuri, Tapan, 'British Rule in India: An Assessment', in P. J. Marshall (ed.), *The Cambridge Illustrated History of the British Empire* (Cambridge, 1996), 357–69.

Razzell, P. E., 'Social Origins of Officers in the Indian and British Home Army: 1758–1962', *British Journal of Sociology*, 14/3 (1963), 248–60.

Reader, W. J., *Professional Men: The Rise of the Professional Classes in Nineteenth-Century England* (London, 1966).

Reay, Barry, 'Kinship and Neighborhood in Nineteenth-Century Rural England: The Myth of the Autonomous Nuclear Family', *Journal of Family History*, 21/1 (1996), 87–104.

Reddy, William M., *The Navigation of Feeling: A Framework for the History of Emotions* (Cambridge, 2001).

Reeder, D. A., 'A Theatre of Suburbs: Some Patterns of Development in West London, 1811–1911', in H. J. Dyos (ed.), *The Study of Urban History* (London, 1968), 253–71.

Renford, Raymond K., *The Non-official British in India to 1920* (New Delhi, 1987).

Riley, Denise, *War in the Nursery: Theories of the Child and the Mother* (London, 1983).

Roach, John, *Public Examinations in England, 1850–1900* (Cambridge, 1971).

Robinson, Amy, 'It Takes One to Know One: Passing and Communities of Common Interest', *Critical Inquiry*, 20 (1994), 715–36.

Robinson, Ronald, 'Non-European Foundations of European Imperialism: Sketch for a Theory of Collaboration', in Roger Owen and Bob Sutcliffe (eds.), *Studies in the Theory of Imperialism* (London, 1972), 117–42.

Roediger, David R., *The Wages of Whiteness: Race and the Making of the American Working Class* (London, 1991).

Rosaldo, Renato, 'Imperialist Nostalgia', in *Culture and Truth: The Remaking of Social Analysis* (Boston, MA, 1989), 68–87.

Rose, Sonya O., *Which People's War?: National Identity and Citizenship in Wartime Britain, 1939–1945* (Oxford, 2003).

Rosenwein, Barbara H., 'Review Essay: Worrying About Emotions in History', *American Historical Review*, 107/3 (2002), 821–45.

Ross, Ellen, *Love and Toil: Motherhood in Outcast London, 1870–1918* (Oxford, 1993).

Roychowdhury, Laura, *The Jadu House: Intimate Histories of Anglo-India* (London, 2000).

Rubinstein, W. D., *Men of Property: The Very Wealthy in Britain Since the Industrial Revolution* (London, 1981).

——'Education and the Social Origins of British Elites, 1880–1970', *Past and Present*, 112 (1986), 163–207.

—— *Capitalism, Culture, and Decline in Britain, 1750–1990* (London, 1993).

Said, Edward W., *Culture and Imperialism* (New York, 1993).

St Paul's School, Darjeeling: Commemorative Volume, 1823–1973 (n.p., 1974).

Samuel, Raphael, *Theatres of Memory, Vol. I: Past and Present in Contemporary Culture* (London, 1994).

—— and Thompson, Paul (eds.), *The Myths We Live By* (London, 1990).

Sargeaunt, John, and Hockliffe, Ernest, *A History of Bedford School* (Bedford, 1925).

Schneer, Jonathan, *London 1900: The Imperial Metropolis* (New Haven, CT, 1999).

Schumpeter, Joseph A., *Imperialism and Social Classes* (New York, 1951).

Schwarz, Bill, '"The Only White Man in There": The Re-racialisation of England, 1956–1968', *Race and Class*, 38/1 (1996), 65–78.

Scott, Joan Wallach, 'Experience', in Judith Butler and Joan W. Scott (eds.), *Feminists Theorize the Political* (New York, 1992), 22–40.

Sen, Indrani, 'Between Power and "Purdah": The White Woman in British India, 1858–1900', *Indian Economic and Social History Review*, 34/3 (1997), 355–76.

Sharpe, Jenny, *Allegories of Empire: The Figure of Woman in the Colonial Text* (Minneapolis, MN, 1993).

Sinha, Mrinalini, *Colonial Masculinity: The 'Manly Englishman' and the 'Effeminate Bengali' in the Late Nineteenth Century* (Manchester, 1995).

—— 'Britishness, Clubbability, and the Colonial Public Sphere: The Genealogy of an Imperial Institution in Colonial India', *Journal of British Studies*, 40 (2001), 489–521.

Smith, Andrea L. (ed.), *Europe's Invisible Migrants* (Amsterdam, 2003).

Smith, Anna Marie, *New Right Discourse on Race and Sexuality: Britain 1968–1990* (Cambridge, 1994).

Smith-Rosenberg, Carroll, 'The Female World of Love and Ritual: Relations between Women in Nineteenth-Century America', *Signs: Journal of Women in Culture and Society*, 1/1 (1975), 1–29.

Sollors, Werner, *Neither Black Nor White Yet Both: Thematic Explorations of Interracial Literature* (New York, 1997).

Spangenberg, Bradford, *British Bureaucracy in India: Status, Policy and the I.C.S. in the Late 19th Century* (Columbia, MO, 1976).

Spence, Jo, and Holland, Patricia (eds.), *Family Snaps: The Meaning of Domestic Photography* (London, 1991).

Stack, Carol B., and Burton, Linda M., 'Kinscripts', *Journal of Comparative Family Studies*, 24/2 (1993), 157–70.

Stallybrass, Peter, and White, Allon, *The Politics and Poetics of Transgression* (Ithaca, NY, 1986).

Stanley, Liz, *The Auto/biographical I: The Theory and Practice of Feminist Auto/biography* (Manchester, 1992).

Stasiulis, Daiva, and Yuval-Davis, Nira (eds.), *Unsettling Settler Societies: Articulations of Gender, Race, Ethnicity and Class* (London, 1995).

Steedman, Carolyn, *The Tidy House: Little Girls Writing* (London, 1982).

—— *Childhood, Culture and Class in Britain: Margaret McMillan, 1860–1931* (New Brunswick, NJ, 1990).

—— *Strange Dislocations: Childhood and the Idea of Human Interiority, 1780–1930* (London, 1995).

Stepan, Nancy, *The Idea of Race in Science: Great Britain, 1800–1960* (London, 1982).

—— 'Biological Degeneration: Races and Proper Places', in J. Edward Chamberlin and Sander L. Gilman (eds.), *Degeneration: The Dark Side of Progress* (New York, 1985), 97–120.

Stevens, Lawrence, *A Short History of Eastbourne*, comp. by Marie Lewis and Owen Daish (Eastbourne, 1987).

Stewart, Gordon T., *Jute and Empire: The Calcutta Jute Wallahs and the Landscapes of Empire* (Manchester, 1998).

Stoler, Ann Laura, *Race and the Education of Desire: Foucault's History of Sexuality and the Colonial Order of Things* (Durham, NC, 1995).

—— *Carnal Knowledge and Imperial Power: Race and the Intimate in Colonial Rule* (Berkeley, CA, 2002).

—— and Cooper, Frederick, 'Between Metropole and Colony: Rethinking a Research Agenda', in Ann Laura Stoler and Frederick Cooper (eds.), *Tensions of Empire: Colonial Cultures in a Bourgeois World* (Berkeley, CA, 1997), 1–56.

—— with Karen Strassler, 'Memory-Work in Java: A Cautionary Tale', reprinted in Stoler, *Carnal Knowledge*, 162–203.

Strobel, Margaret, *European Women and the Second British Empire* (Bloomington, IN, 1991).

Sullivan, Zohreh T., *Narratives of Empire: The Fictions of Rudyard Kipling* (Cambridge, 1993).

Symonds, Richard, 'Eurasians Under British Rule', in N. J. Allen *et al.* (eds.), *Oxford University Papers on India*, Vol. 1, Part 2 (Delhi, 1987), 28–42.

Tabili, Laura, *'We Ask for British Justice': Black Workers and the Construction of Racial Difference in Late Imperial Britain* (Ithaca, NY, 1994).

—— 'Women "of a Very Low Type": Crossing Racial Boundaries in Imperial Britain', in Laura L. Frader and Sonya O. Rose (eds.), *Gender and Class in Modern Europe* (Ithaca, NY, 1996), 165–90.

Teo, Hsu-Ming, 'Wandering in the Wake of Empire: British Travel and Tourism in the Post-Imperial World', in Stuart Ward (ed.), *British Culture and the End of Empire* (Manchester, 2001), 163–79.

Thane, Pat, *Old Age in English History: Past Experiences, Present Issues* (Oxford, 2000).

Thom, Deborah, 'Wishes, Anxieties, Play, and Gestures: Child Guidance in Inter-War England', in Roger Cooter (ed.), *In the Name of the Child: Health and Welfare, 1880–1940* (London, 1992), 200–19.

Thomas, Imogen, *Haileybury 1806–1987* (Hertford, 1987).

Thomas, Nicholas, *Colonialism's Culture: Anthropology, Travel and Government* (Princeton, NJ, 1994).

Thompson, Paul, 'Family Myth, Models, and Denials in the Shaping of Individual Life Paths', in Daniel Bertaux and Paul Thompson (eds.), *International Yearbook of Oral History and Life Stories, Vol. II: Between Generations: Family Models, Myths, and Memories* (Oxford, 1993), 13–38.

Thorne, Susan, *Congregational Missions and the Making of an Imperial Culture in Nineteenth Century England* (Stanford, CA, 1999).

Thurber, Cheryl, 'The Development of the Mammy Image and Mythology', in Virginia Bernhard et al. (eds.), *Southern Women: Histories and Identities* (Columbia, MO, 1992), 87–108.

Thwaite, Ann, *Waiting for the Party: The Life of Frances Hodgson Burnett, 1849–1924* (London, 1994).

Tikekar, Aroon, *The Kincaids: Two Generations of a British Family in the Indian Civil Service* (New Delhi, 1992).

Tosh, John, 'From Keighley to St-Denis: Separation and Intimacy in Victorian Bourgeois Marriage', *History Workshop Journal*, 40 (1995), 193–206.

—— 'Imperial Masculinity and the Flight from Domesticity in Britain, 1880–1914', in Timothy P. Foley *et al.* (eds.), *Gender and Colonialism* (Galway, 1995), 72–85.

—— *A Man's Place: Masculinity and the Middle-Class Home in Victorian England* (New Haven, CT, 1999).

Underwood, Andrew, *Bedford Modern School of the Black and Red* (Biggleswade, 1981).

Urwin, Cathy, and Sharland, Elaine, 'From Bodies to Minds in Childcare Literature: Advice to Parents in Inter-war Britain', in Roger Cooter (ed.), *In the Name of the Child: Health and Welfare, 1880–1940* (London, 1992), 174–99.

Vicinus, Martha, *Independent Women: Work and Community for Single Women, 1850–1920* (Chicago, 1985).

Visram, Rozina, *Ayahs, Lascars and Princes: The Story of Indians in Britain, 1700–1947* (London, 1986).

Wald, Gayle, *Crossing the Line: Racial Passing in Twentieth-Century U. S. Literature and Culture* (Durham, NC, 2000).

Walkowitz, Judith R., 'The Indian Woman, the Flower Girl, and the Jew: Photojournalism in Edwardian London', *Victorian Studies*, 42/1 (1998/1999), 3–46.

Walton, John K., *The English Seaside Resort: A Social History, 1750–1914* (Leicester, 1983).

—— 'The Seaside Resorts of Western Europe, 1750–1939', in Stephen Fisher (ed.), *Recreation and the Sea* (Exeter, 1997), 36–56.

—— *The British Seaside: Holidays and Resorts in the Twentieth Century* (Manchester, 2000).

Walvin, James, *Beside the Seaside: A Social History of the Popular Seaside Holiday* (London, 1978).

Ward, Stuart, 'Introduction', in Stuart Ward (ed.), *British Culture and the End of Empire* (Manchester, 2001), 1–20.

Ware, Vron, *Beyond the Pale: White Women, Racism, and History* (London, 1992).

—— 'Moments of Danger: Race, Gender, and Memories of Empire', *History and Theory*, 31/4 (1992), 116–37.

Webster, F. A. M., *Our Great Public Schools: Their Traditions, Customs and Games* (London, 1937).

Webster, Wendy, *Imagining Home: Gender, 'Race' and National Identity, 1945–64* (London, 1998).

Weeks, Jeffrey, 'Pretended Family Relationships', in David Clark (ed.), *Marriage, Domestic Life and Social Change: Writings for Jacqueline Burgoyne, 1944–88* (London, 1991), 214–34.

Westaway, K. M. (ed.), *A History of Bedford High School* (Bedford, 1932).

Williams, Philip M., *Hugh Gaitskell: A Political Biography* (London, 1979).

Winsland, Mrs D. E., 'St Winifred's', *Eastbourne Local Historian*, 92 (summer 1994), 21–3.

Witting, Clifford, *The Glory of the Sons: A History of Eltham College, School for the Sons of Missionaries* (London, 1952).

Wollen, Tara, 'Over Our Shoulders: Nostalgic Screen Fictions for the 1980s', in John Corner and Sylvia Harvey (eds.), *Enterprise and Heritage: Crosscurrents of National Culture* (London, 1991), 178–93.

Woods, Philip, 'The Montagu-Chelmsford Reforms (1919): A Re-assessment', *South Asia*, 17/1 (1994), 25–42.

Woollacott, Angela, *To Try Her Fortune in London: Australian Women, Colonialism, and Modernity* (New York, 2001).

Wright, Patrick, *On Living in an Old Country: The National Past in Contemporary Britain* (London, 1985).

Young, Douglas, *St Andrews: Town and Gown, Royal and Ancient* (London, 1969).

Young, Robert J. C., *Colonial Desire: Hybridity in Theory, Culture and Race* (London, 1995).

INDEX